THE PERSONALITY OF POWER

THOUGHT IN THE ACT

A series edited by Erin Manning and Brian Massumi

BRIAN MASSUMI

The Personality of Power: A Theory of Fascism for Anti-fascist Life

DUKE UNIVERSITY PRESS   DURHAM AND LONDON   2025

Project Editor: Michael Trudeau

Designed by Matthew Tauch

Typeset in Quadraat and Meta by Westchester Publishing Services

Library of Congress Cataloging-in-Publication Data

Names: Massumi, Brian, author.

Title: The personality of power : a theory of fascism for anti-fascist life / Brian Massumi.

Other titles: Thought in the act.

Description: Durham : Duke University Press, 2025. | Series: Thought in the act | Includes bibliographical references and index.

Identifiers: LCCN 2024039429 (print)

LCCN 2024039430 (ebook)

ISBN 9781478031598 (paperback)

ISBN 9781478028352 (hardcover)

ISBN 9781478060543 (ebook)

Subjects: LCSH: Trump, Donald, 1946– | Fascism—Philosophy. | Personality and politics—United States. | Political culture—United States—History—21st century. | Radicalism—United States—History— 21st century. | Right-wing extremists—United States—History— 21st century. | United States—Politics and government—21st century.

Classification: LCC JC481 .M126 2025 (print) | LCC JC481 (ebook) | DDC 306.20973—DC23/ENG/20241216

LC record available at https://lccn.loc.gov/2024039429

LC ebook record available at https://lccn.loc.gov/2024039430

Cover art: Rafael Lozano-Hemmer, *Eye Contact, Shadow Box 1,* 2006, in *Pseudomatismos,* 2015–2016, Museo Universitario Arte Contemporáneo, Mexico City, Mexico. Photo by Oliver Santana, 2015. Courtesy of Rafael Lozano-Hemmer and Oliver Santana.

CONTENTS

PART 1

Trumping the Personality of Power

The "F"-Word

Throughout Trump's time in power, mention of the word "fascist" was routinely met with rolled eyes and admonitions to avoid gratuitous mudslinging, even if said with an interrogative accent or cautiously preceded by "proto-" or "semi-." It doesn't help to bandy about false equivalencies, went the refrain. When the Trump presidency reached its crescendo on January 6, 2021, with the storming of the US Capitol by the advance guard of his most ardent supporters, it became dramatically clear that the warnings had not been exaggerated. Hundreds of self-described "patriots" had attacked the linchpin of representative democracy—the peaceful transition of power—and had done so not in adherence to a coherent ideology but in fealty to Trump's person. Four years of Trump's relentless social media bush-beating had flushed out a congeries of white supremacists, antigovernment conspiracy theorists, and increasingly right-wing conservatives united by such attitudes as white grievance (in reaction to the growing ethnic diversity of American society and the amplification of African American voices by the Black Lives Matter movement), "Western chauvinism" (a self-descriptor of the Proud Boys who were among those who spearheaded the charge), a hatred for the "elites" of urban America (anyone with managerial or scientific expertise and a presumed cosmopolitanism), and anti-feminist, anti-queer, and anti-trans backlash. For many, Donald Trump was a savior figure. For the evangelical crowd, quite literally. "He will protect us" signs graced many a rally. "We're doing this for him," crowds chanted.

"For him": power had repersonalized around Trump—or more precisely his media figure—to an extent unheard-of in recent American history, exceeding in intensity even the personality politics of Ronald Reagan. It was around Reagan that the tendencies now reaching a peak expression had first begun to coalesce again in the late 1970s, after being briefly backgrounded, post-McCarthy, by the rise of the civil rights movement and other social movements of the 1960s.

Most shocking to Americans whose savior is not Donald Trump was perhaps the attribution of the status of "enemy" to the political adversary. In the Capitol crowd, the peppering of Confederate flags visually made the point: This is war. This is civil war. It was spelled it out in no uncertain terms on a popular T-shirt: "MAGA Civil War January 6, 2021." Your very existence, these artifacts were saying, is an existential threat to us. We are armed against it. "You will not replace us!" When a significant minority of the Republican Party itself recoiled in horror and belatedly (and as it turned out, momentarily) distanced itself from the figure on whose coattails the party had ridden for four long years, they too became the enemy. Republicans supporting the peaceful transfer of power, even arch-enablers of Trump such as Senate Majority Leader Mitch McConnell and Vice President Mike Pence, were threatened with death. In the immediate aftermath of the Capitol storming, far-right social media confirmed that a personality-centered movement willing to kill and to die "for him" was nearing a break with its collaborators in the political establishment, threatening to spin off from existing party politics into its own frenetic orbit.

The spin-off of right-wing passions from the established institutions of politics is the turning point. The catalytic point. The conversion point where a brewing proto-fascism heats up to the point that a full-boil fascism can be heard bubbling beneath the lid of politics as usual.

Fascism sparked on Pennsylvania Avenue. It remains to be seen whether it will light a prairie fire, but it is those who would not abide the use of the word during the years of Trumpian agitation on the campaign trail and in the White House—now in retrospect so clearly in continuity with what occurred on January 6—who should be admonished for their political timorousness.[1] The question of how the spark will continue to

---

1 William E. Connolly is one prominent academic theorist who has consistently emphasized the need to think of how the antecedents of fascism are active in the contemporary social and political field. See Connolly, *Aspirational Fascism: The Struggle for Multifaceted Democracy under Trumpism* (Minneapolis: University of Minnesota Press, 2017).

1.1 January 6 Insurrection. Photo by Lev Radin / Shutterstock.

smolder should Trump return to the White House for a second term, or after he recedes from the scene, is as pressing moving forward as it was—and should have been recognized as being—in the lead-up to his 2016 election.

It has sparked. That has to be taken stock of, even if there was more than a hint of the farcical in the event. Marx said that historical events appear first as tragedy, then repeat as farce. It seems to be a characteristic of the "post-truth" age to skip directly to the latter—a situation which is, if anything, all the more tragic.

This Book

To be clear, this book is not an essay in history. Nor is it an empirical account in a cultural studies or sociological vein. It is a philosophical essay, aspiring, as Deleuze says philosophy should, to the creation of new concepts. Trump is taken as an exemplary case in which existing tendencies take on new variations, and emergent tendencies become perceptible. Concepts are distilled from Trumpian speech and gesture, which bear more on their mode of operation than on interpretations of their meaning (of which there is precious little). The concepts undergo extensive philosophical development before being rethreaded back through Trump World to generate more ideas meant to wrap themselves around the singularity of the Trump phenomenon and how it relates to fascism. The ideas also loop around each other in multiplying orbits. The hope is that this results in virtuous circles producing a growing toolbox of distinctions.

The emphasis on mode of operation is in keeping with the process philosophy orientation of this endeavor, which can be summed up briefly as taking constituting activity and events as primary, rather than already-constituted things and subjects. The interest is ultimately through Trump rather than in him: his exemplary case is for diagnostic purposes. The question of what constitutes fascism is refracted through the prism of Trump. The questions begin before the facts, in the stirrings of "fascisizing tendencies": tendencies that prepare the ground for fascism and funnel toward it. The book focuses its lens on the Trump presidency of 2017–2021 and the period following the January 6, 2021, attack on the US Capitol and up to the 2024 presidential election and his second bid for president. A conceptual X-ray examination of a key period such as this is sufficient to diagnose fascisizing tendencies in early stages of metastasis, revealing the direction in which they are moving. Only occasional asides will be made to later episodes, where they add useful detail or accent.

Since Trump's power so evidently revolves around his person, what constitutes personhood will be the main philosophical stake. This is a tricky task, since we all already know what a person is, if only because we are one every day. However, in large part because of that intimacy, which is always already us and ours, our knowledge of personhood is steeped in presuppositions and rife with rationalizations. A certain estrangement is necessary to enable a fresh take. Bringing a constructive estrangement to the presupposed is the most important service philosophy can provide. In the case of personhood, this requires a great deal of effort and some fairly gymnastic mental maneuvering. It is with this in view that the book indulges in long developments of philosophical concepts, woven in and among the discussions of Trump, fascism, and fascisizing tendencies. The two most intensely philosophical sections are parts 2 and 3. Recaps are provided at the end of these parts that should enable readers less invested in the philosophical ins and outs to take a shortcut in order to concentrate on the material more directly pertinent to Trump and fascism in parts 1, 4, and 5. A comprehensive glossary of key terms will be published separately to serve as a reference and a guide.

Ultimately, the book's chimerical format combining in-depth political analysis and fundamental philosophical inquiry in equally intense doses comes from the conviction that not only is the content of conventional thinking about personhood and the political inadequate but so is the very logic we use to understand them. A postscript encapsulates an alternative logic gleaned from the process-oriented thinking deployed throughout the book, following conceptual paths blazed by C. S. Peirce, Gabriel Tarde, Henri Bergson, William James, A. N. Whitehead, Gilbert Simondon, Gilles Deleuze, Félix Guattari, Susanne Langer, and Édouard Glissant, among others.[2] This the logic of "mutual inclusion." It addresses how things dynamically come together in becoming, without abrogating their difference.

The Decline and Rise of the Personality of Power

Fascism itself is a concept that is steeped in presuppositions and rife with rationalizations, in its case because it is so often assumed to be foreign to the world we know. Yes, it is necessary to avoid false equivalencies with past events, as critics of the word grumpily remind us. But it is just as necessary to recognize its uncanny closeness, in every era, as

---

2 The most direct inspiration behind the approach to fascism developed here is Gilles Deleuze and Félix Guattari's *Anti-Oedipus: Capitalism and Schizophrenia*, which exhibits a prescient understanding of fascism that still strikes me as the best place to begin in the analysis of its contemporary forms. Deleuze and Guattari, *Anti-Oedipus*, trans. Robert Hurley, Mark Seem, and Helen R. Lane (Minneapolis: University of Minnesota Press, 1983). On Deleuze/Guattari and fascism, see Brad Evans and Julian Reid, *Deleuze and Fascism: Security, War, Aesthetics* (London: Routledge, 2014); Rick Dolphijn and Rosi Braidotti, eds., *Deleuze and Guattari and Fascism* (Edinburgh: Edinburgh University Press, 2022).

a potential outbreak and passing of a threshold. Our ready-made conceptual tools are not well suited to understanding its current stirrings. An effort must be made to grasp the unique characteristics of fascism's drawing-close-upon-us in the present juncture.

I have argued elsewhere that over the last three decades, beginning in the Reagan years, the traditional model of ideological assent produced through a psychological identification with the charismatic leader became obsolete.[3] Reagan's hold was, and still is, widely interpreted in terms of charismatic personality politics, or what is popularly termed the cult of personality. I argued, however, that something very different from what is conventionally meant by "personality politics" was going on.

Throughout his presidency, Reagan's policies, when polled individually, were consistently opposed by a majority of voters. Ideological adherence was tenuous. His discourse was famously fragmented, presenting very little in the way of a coherent ideational framework. His body image, while playing on media stereotypes of the rugged American male, was beset by an undertow of fragility and evoked dismemberment as often as wholeness and strength (*Where's the Rest of Me?*, wailed the title of his autobiography).[4] I became convinced that the double default, of discourse and body image, was not a defect but, rather, a positive mechanism successfully playing between two registers.

The fitful self-suspension of discursive unity allowed the register of the body to flash through the cracks in crumbling discourse. The flicker between bodily wholeness and dismemberment effected an affective capture foregrounding proprioception—the nonvisual sense of the body's deformations in movement—over visual image integrity and constancy of form.

The model suggested was closer to mime than to identification. The mime stages the body, subtracted from speech, in a segmentation

---

3 Kenneth Dean and Brian Massumi, *First and Last Emperors: The Body of the Despot and the Absolute State* (New York: Autonomedia, 1992), 87–152; Massumi, "The Bleed," in *Parables for the Virtual: Movement, Affect, Sensation*, 20th anniversary ed. (Durham, NC: Duke University Press, 2021), 49–72.

4 Ronald Reagan and Richard B. Hubler, *Where Is the Rest of Me?* (1965; repr., New York: Karz, 1981). For analysis of the autobiography and the trope of dismemberment, see Massumi, "The Bleed," in *Parables for the Virtual*, 49–72.

of its movements. "Mime," José Gil explains, "dismembers the body: we know that the training of mimes takes them through this basic exercise—separation of the limbs in such a way as to completely remove the connections and make the parts they join independent from each other, thus abolishing the rigidities and stereotypes that cultural coding has imprinted on them." This means that every articulation, every gap between segments, holds the potential for any next gesture. This fullness of potential, however, is also a threat. "The audience is held in a continual 'suspense' due to an unconscious anticipation of a 'failing,' in which the performer might suddenly lose the ability to continue his or her discourse. Because of this fear of broken communication, this art walks a tightrope."[5]

It was *because* Reagan walked the tightrope of broken communication that he was the "Great Communicator." The rise of potential in the gap made palpable a full proprioceptive body—a virtual body replete with any-next potential—while the fall of imminent failing simultaneously activated an abstract grasping desperately to hold on (this rise and fall of potential is constitutive of the "full body" as theorized by Deleuze and Guattari, a concept that will feature prominently in what follows). The tension between the rise and fall of bodily potential exerted an infra-linguistic "fascination." The proprioceptive "bodies without an image" of the audience were riveted to it, adjoined to it, forming a transindividual body politic.[6] This is closer to Simondon's transductive "communication of subconsciouses"—which operates at the affective level of bodily capacitation and its dephasing—than it is to a cognitive, subject-centered identification with the eternal wholeness of an ideal visual image.[7] "Reagan" was the proper name of the collective assemblage that actuated and sustained this dynamic through rhythms of image circulation

---

5   José Gil, *Metamorphoses of the Body*, trans. Stephen Muecke (Minneapolis: University of Minnesota Press, 1998), 107–8.

6   Infra-linguistic fascination: Gil, *Metamorphoses of the Body*, 107. Body without an image: Massumi, "The Art of the Relational Body," in *Couplets* (Durham, NC: Duke University Press, 2021), 342–57.

7   Communication of subconsciousnesses: Gilbert Simondon, *Individuation in Light of Notions of Form and Information* (Minneapolis: University of Minnesota Press, 2020), 275.

oscillating between the rise of the full body and its fall toward dismemberment, and between this polarization and the discourse it broke into, suspended, and relaunched in a fitful rhythm.

The "person" of Reagan, politically, was not the man. It was not the actual image of the man, nor was it his "persona" in the sense in which that word is used to designate an inauthentic contrast between the man and his image. Reagan was the being of the media figure produced by the collective assemblage orbiting around his movements—the gestures suspending discourse, triggering the rise/fall of the full body in the breaks, and self-absenting the man through that transindividualizing dynamic. Reagan was "machinic" in Deleuze and Guattari's sense of a processual mode whose operations claim a subjective autonomy of operation—without a separate subject as agent of the action (Raymond Ruyer would say they are "autoconducting," or self-driving).[8]

Following this line of reasoning, Reagan was a media figure whose machinic person(a) represented a personalizing of power in a new mode. The "personality" of this power was an optical (or more accurately, proprioceptive) effect of this machinery: the aura of the full body, at every move haunting the relational field with potential and taunting it with failure. The dynamically animating ghost in the machine. Ronald Reagan ghosted the person.

Once a dynamic of this kind "takes" (attains a consistency), it abides as a self-operating tendency, like a habit of the body politic, poised to return with variations across periods of subsidence. It continued into the George H. W. Bush administration and returned with Bush II, subsiding in the intervening Bill Clinton years and afterward with Barack Obama, in favor of their more traditionally personality-based affective dynamics (in Obama's case, hope as a focal point of subjectivation beaming from his person).

It is of the nature of ghosts to return and haunt. George W. Bush was a faded revenant Reagan. He was even more challenged in the production of conceptually and grammatically coherent speech, and refigured Reagan's "dismemberment" as spasms of stumbling and strange

---

8 Raymond Ruyer, *Neofinalism*, trans. Alyosha Edlebi (Minneapolis: University of Minnesota Press, 2016), 85.

rhythms of whole-body disappearance and reappearance, flickering in a "barely there" of being.[9]

The contemporary complexion of the personality of power in the Reagan lineage takes a significant turn with Trump, as indicated by Trump himself in his ruthless ridiculing of Biden during the 2020 presidential campaign. On the grounds of his age and supposed mental and physical frailty and the intermittence of his campaign appearances, Trump bestowed on him the nickname of "Barely There Biden," taunting that he "doesn't even know he is alive."[10] What Trump was responding to was not in fact a Democratic version of George W. Bush's persona, but a traditional, and arguably obsolete, political figure seen through the lens of the personality of power—the only one Trump understands. What Biden was cultivating was the image of the head of state as a regular guy, in the traditional model of personhood, who just happens to sit at the head of state: a steady manager working tirelessly in the corridors of power in the interests of the nation, immersed in the practical details of governing (what Carl Schmitt calls the "pure normativist," as we will see in a moment).

Trump forged his own relation to the full body, while remaining in many ways in the Reagan frame of personalizing power: not barely there, more like brazenly everywhere. And the furthest thing possible from the steady manager of the conventional levers of power.

Resolving the apparent contradiction of an anomalously personal personality of power will be a major stake in what follows. The resolution

---

9   Massumi, "Barely There: The Power of the Image at the Limit of Life," in *Couplets*, 232–84.

10   For "Barely There Biden," see Richard Wolffe, "Don't Call It a Comeback: Trump's Tulsa Rally Was Just Another Sad Farce," *Guardian*, June 21, 2020, https://www.theguardian.com/commentisfree/2020/jun/20/donald-trump -tulsa-rally-crowd-empty-seats. For "Doesn't even know he is alive," see Philip Rucker and Felicia Sonmez, "Trump Defends Bungled Handling of Coronovirus with Falsehoods and Dubious Claims," *Washington Post*, July 19, 2020, https:// www.washingtonpost.com/politics/trump-defends-bungled-handling-of -coronavirus-with-falsehoods-and-dubious-claims/2020/07/19/1b57cb3e-c9e6 -11ea-91f1-28aca4d833a0_story.html. Trump also nicknamed Biden "Sleepy Joe" and "Hid'n Biden." See Mark Leibovich, "When Joe Biden's in Town, but It's Hard to Know," *New York Times*, September 22, 2020, https://www.nytimes.com /2020/09/22/us/politics/joe-biden-campaign.html.

will be sought in *a reformulation of what it means to be a person to include in its very definition the self-driving of the machinic, in its collective operation*. The person-"effect" of dynamics such as Reagan's ghosting of the machine will be given a positive genealogy in the fundamental operations of perception, their discursive and social media amplifications, an affective regime dominated by reaction, and a discursive regime expressive of it. It will be seen as an emergent effect with its own character, and a reality of its own, after its own manner. In the case of Trump, it will be seen to have a powerful political efficacy in its own right through its ability to performatively index the potentials of the full body and channel them, reactively, into the register of threat. It will be suggested that this power can only be understood by rethinking the operations of the social circulation of signs in ways that take seriously the notions of collective personhood and collective individuation, while remaining sensitive to singularity. The question of what constitutes a media figure will have to be broached, and for that a new take on what figuration is in the first place will be required.

Who Decides?

The political efficacy of the new figure of the personality of power harks back in strange ways to Carl Schmitt's concept of sovereign decision, also widely mistaken for personalist in a sense compatible with traditional definitions of what a person is felt to be: a discrete subject with a well-regulated interiority separate from the social, exercising individual agency authored by an "I" in exclusive ownership of its thoughts, actions, and emotions.

Schmitt's concept of decision is mistaken for personalist because he formulates the question of sovereignty as *"Who decides?"* The impression that Schmitt is delivering decision to a principle of the personality of power in the traditional sense of person is reinforced when he criticizes the normative governmental notion of sovereignty for its substitution of an impersonal self-regulating system of government for the preeminence of the one who decides.

But then he pivots. He announces in no uncertain terms that when he is speaking of the one who decides, he is *not* speaking in psychological terms. He is not speaking of a person who is an individual in the same sense as "the people," private citizens of the nation. He is not speaking of decision "in a private-individualistic sense as a psychological expression of private emotions and tendencies."[11]

The one who decides has an entirely different status, coinciding with what Schmitt calls a *"point of ascription."*[12] What is ascribed is the distinction between friend and enemy that Schmitt takes to be foundational to the political. This distinction, he insists, has no empirical content. It is not sociological, pertaining to empirically already-existing subgroups of society, any more than it is psychological, pertaining to personal feelings of antagonism. It "cannot be derived from other criteria. . . . It is its own ultimate distinction."[13] Lacking in content, the ascription of this ultimate distinction is purely performative.

Sovereign is he who performs the ascription. This is not a matter of personal whim, in a merely individual act. The act of decision is a channeling of a collective feeling of a certain sort. It is enacted when there is a perception of an existential threat to the nation's "way of life," so that the war footing that the friend/enemy ascription sets in place is felt necessary to "preserve one's own form of existence."[14] The sovereign is acting in and on that collective feeling; for and through it. The sovereign's individual person at the moment of ascription is in an exceptional zone of affective indistinction with the collectivity. In his persona, he is the singular conduit of a collective feeling. By performing the ascription, he becomes the sovereign he is: "Sovereign is he who decides on the exception."[15] For the ascription coincides with the performative suspension of the law. Exceptionally, the nation is gearshifted from business-as-usual politics of peace to the actualization of the conditions of war.

---

11   Carl Schmitt, *The Concept of the Political*, expanded ed., trans. George Schwab (Chicago: University of Chicago Press, 2007), 28.

12   Carl Schmitt, *Political Theology: Four Chapters on the Concept of Sovereignty*, ed. George Schwab (Chicago: University of Chicago Press, 2006), 32.

13   For no empirical content, own ultimate distinction, see Schmitt, *Concept of the Political*, 26; for not sociological or psychological, see Schmitt, *Concept of the Political*, 29.

14   Schmitt, *Political Theology*, 27.

15   Schmitt, *Concept of the Political*, 5.

The game of negotiation and persuasion that passes for the political in times of peace is suspended, replaced by "the real possibility of physical killing."[16]

This, for Schmitt, is Politics with a capital "P": the act of sovereignty par excellence; substance of the state. But it is not a substance: it is "movement."[17] Pure, performative movement. Not a psychological feeling, not an empirical finding, not a moral judgment: an ascription through which collective feeling flows, into collective action. In this event of attribution, one and all are moved to affectively coincide, in transformation. The gears of the nation screech like a siren as conditions shift. The boundaries of the state are hardened into place, friend embraced into the fold, enemy cast out. The conditions for war are actualized.

Collective Individuation

The enemy was not an enemy prior to the ascription. No empirically existing group occupies a priori the status of enemy (this is what theoretically distinguishes Schmitt's brand of authoritarianism from Nazism proper). The enemy results from the ascription. At the point of ascription, it is not only the sovereign who coincides with the people, but the nation with the state, in the act. The act's performance effects a collective individuation. Prior to the act, friend/enemy was real, as ultimate distinction or "borderline concept":[18] as a virtual polarity. At the point of ascription, it actualizes. The form of existence fills with a content Politically worthy of it: the existential struggle against an enemy.

Schmittian decision is not impersonal in the usual sense. It is not he, the sovereignist, but rather his civil antagonist, the "pure normativist," Schmitt says, who believes in impersonal decision, vouchsafed by legal regulation, bureaucratic procedure, and institutional rule. Neither is decision personal in any usual sense. It is traditional "decisionists" who apply their faculty of good judgment toward "implement[ing] the

---

16 Schmitt, *Political Theology*, 33.
17 Schmitt, *Political Theology*, 3.
18 Schmitt, *Political Theology*, 3.

good law of the correctly recognized political situation by personal decision."[19] Personal/impersonal is simply not the polarity privileged by Schmittian decision. Its master distinction between friend and enemy is actualized at a point of ascription constituting a zone of indistinction between the sovereign and the people in the transformative act of becoming-effectively-Political in unison.

In the transindividuality of that point, the impersonal and the personal as normally understood *together* contrast with the "movement" of becoming: a collective individuation performatively catalyzed at the point of ascription. That point is a *singular point*, all movement, all transformation, ascribable to no previously existing content, triggering the actual advent of its coming content, just now taking form in the act. It is a tipping point, the widthless point where becoming trips in and takes on the content produced by the actualization of the friend/enemy distinction. The body of the sovereign, in order to be sovereign, must coincide with the tipping point that serves as a fulcrum for it. It acts as transductive channel for that autonomy of self-effecting transformation (for what else is catalysis, if not that?).

The impersonal, in the bureaucratic institutional sense, is general, neutral, and external. The personal to which it is opposed is particular, characterized by intrinsic qualities, and interiorized. The sovereign is not subject to that alternative. He is the *singular figure of collective becoming*. He is neither institutionally regulated nor personally decisive. He is one with an autonomy of decision that is tributary to "no program, no ideal, no norm, no expediency."[20] He is subject only to the distributed *feeling* of existential threat, "taking" at a point of ascription where the distance between the preeminent body, becoming commanding, and the ordinary bodies of the citizenry, becoming soldierly, collapses into a unison of movement. Neither personal nor impersonal in the usual sense, neither neutral nor characterized by intrinsic qualities, the sovereign is transindividual and passional. He is the personification of a collective individuation.

19 Schmitt, *Political Theology*, 3.
20 Schmitt, *Political Theology*, 27; Schmitt, *Concept of the Political*, 47.

Beyond the Interpersonal

The thesis developed in this book is that the personality of power we observe today is, in its own unique, post-Schmittian way, a personification—an impersonation in the literal sense—of transindividual, passional dynamics that are directly political in nature. The personality of power must be resituated in relation to social and cultural processes reconceived outside the personal/impersonal dichotomy as it is normally formulated.[21] The complementarity "collective/individuation"—designating a process of becoming one among many—will replace that dichotomy. What constitutes the personhood of one *and* many, in the movement of their collective individuation, will be the main constructive question.

The main critical point is the political paradox that *today's "personality of power" cannot be understood in interpersonal terms.* That is to say, it cannot be placed in the psychological register, as it is usually understood to refer to the interactions and identifications of bounded subjects sharing the contents of their interiorities through the mediation of language and communicational technology.[22] Its register is directly that of

---

21 Roberto Esposito resolves the tension between impersonal and the personal in favor of the impersonal, conceptually renewed through the notion of the "third person" as "non-person." Roberto Esposito, *Third Person Politics of Life and Philosophy of the Impersonal*, trans. Zakiya Hanafi (Cambridge: Polity, 2012). Here the strategy will be to extend the concept of the person to the "fourth person."

22 Notions of subjective identification as the foundation for secondary "projections" of the interior structure of the individual onto the outside collective are a common default position in discussions of fascism and allied formations, and are often involved in accounts based on the concept of charismatic leadership. Theodor Adorno's contribution to *The Authoritarian Personality* deploys the Freudian topology of id, ego, and superego in a theoretical synthesis of the project's typology of authoritarian personality types. The main criterion used in constructing the typology is the "success" of superego identification with the father figure. Theodor W. Adorno, Else Frenkel-Brunswik, Daniel J. Levinson, and R. Nevitt Sanford, *The Authoritarian Personality* (New York: Norton, 1969), 605–743. Richard Hofstadter, in his analysis of the "paranoid style" in American politics, uses a less technically elaborated notion of "projection" that presupposes the identification model. Richard Hofstadter, *The Paranoid Style in American Politics and Other Essays* (1963; repr., Cambridge, MA: Harvard University Press, 1996), 3–40.

the transindividual, and only secondarily that of the person-to-person. Its mode of operation is less communicational in the traditional sense than it is performative: self-effecting and collectively transforming of *situations*. It is processual: self-bootstrapping, ever-emergent.

If Trump has re-rallied the political around his person, what person is this? What is its modus operandi? What is its mode of existence? When Trump supporters declare personal fealty to him, to what collective process are they adjoining their lives?

Accidents of Persons

The presidency of Reagan, in his own, bad-actor way, was such a singular (media) figure: less than personal in the normal sense, but not exactly impersonal. The ascribed enemy was the "Evil Empire" of the Soviet Union, subsequently reincarnated as George W. Bush's "axis of evil" as the Cold War gave way to the War on Terror. The traditional notion of the personality of power was already obsolete by the time Bush reached the political stage. But then, had it ever really been in operation in the way it was thought to be? Was not the entire idea of charismatic leadership insufficiently Political by Schmitt's standards—precisely by dint of being all-too-personal in too traditional a way?

The nature of war changed over this same period, in a way that entails a reproblematization of what constitutes the personality of power. The singularity of decision rose back into relief in a new figuration.

Already in the mid-1970s Paul Virilio was writing of a blurring of the boundaries between war and peace during the Cold War period.[23] He called this "Total Peace": a palimpsest of civil peace superimposed on total war. The policy of deterrence annexed civil society to a suspended war effort that monopolized resources for weapons development, intelligence, and surveillance. The looming threat of nuclear annihilation cast a pall of war over all of society, even as deterrence held it in suspense through the certainty of "mutually assured destruction" (MAD) should an attack eventuate. There was a preexisting, specific enemy ascribed in advance,

---

23 Paul Virilio, *L'insécurité du territoire* (Paris: Stock, 1975).

in shape of the Soviet Union. Any military action on the part of this enemy using nuclear weaponry was theoretically neutralized by MAD. But there was another enemy. This enemy was paradoxically produced by the very success of deterring attack from the recognized, empirically existing enemy. This was the specter that in the course of the intensifying arms race required to maintain deterrence, due to the growing complexity of the evolving weapons systems, a human error or even a technical glitch might trigger a conflagration. This enemy defined the singular tenor of the age. It was an *unspecified enemy*, of the nature of the accident. The accident, by its nature, is unqualified, in potential. Its content cannot be ascribed in advance of its event. The accident, when it comes, is the self-deciding event par excellence: potential self-detonating, unforeseeably.

This accidental enemy built into the otherwise implacable structure of deterrence loomed over all. It overhung the entire field of life, transforming it into an extended battlefield, held in a state of suspense. It is as if Schmitt's sovereign had forgone embodiment, becoming entirely nonlocalized, not so much transindividual as nonhuman, incorporeal figure of the event.

This opened the way for Reagan. Reagan made of himself the body double of the accident, organizing the autobiography he used to launch his political career around the trope of the body-destroying accident. Reagan, the political actor, was a stand-in for the sovereign accident. He gave body to it. It is no coincidence that Schmitt attached sovereign decision not to the person of the sovereign but (quoting Hobbes) to "*accidents of persons*" that are paradoxically one with decision.[24] Deterrence brought the accidental aspect of sovereign decision into its own expression.

When the Soviet Union fell, this enemy did not disappear. It is still with us, according to the Union of Concerned Scientists, whose "Doomsday Clock" in the 2020s has been inching closer to midnight than ever before.[25] It simply receded behind another figure of threat. As the Cold War

---

24   Schmitt, *Political Theology*, 34.

25   Doomsday Clock: See "2024 Doomsday Clock Announcement," *Bulletin of the Atomic Scientists*, January 24, 2023, https://thebulletin.org/doomsday-clock /current-time. The "hybrid war" in the Ukraine has brought back an aftertaste of nuclear threat for the post–Cold War era, in the form of Putin's frequent threats that the use of tactical nuclear weapons is not off the table.

made way for the War on Terror, the media figure of the terrorist waxed ascendent. The terrorist became the unspecified enemy. The terrorist might strike anywhere, at any time, taking any shape, with all the unpredictability of the accident.[26] This is an "asymmetrical" enemy whose protean powers of surprise cast a pall of threat every bit as time- and space-filling as its nuclear predecessor, but wrapping, each time it eventuates, around a human body. The qualities of the threatening body in any given case—its nationality, race, gender, age, religion—cannot be predicted. The figure of the terrorist is unqualified less for lack of content as for a surfeit of it. An entire spectrum of potential qualifications is held in suspense in the intervals between episodes, bubbling and brinking, in a kind of perpetual turnover, like balls spinning on a wheel of fortune. There are rhythms and refrains that direct attention toward certain spectrums of social content and target fear and repression far more regularly to certain habitual qualifications (brown-skinned, Muslim, non-Western). But the ever-present possibility of an exception or an outlier (like a white Briton with a bomb in the soles of his sneakers, to cite one famous example) keeps the balls spinning. The terrorist as unspecified enemy occupies a band of potential in perpetual turnover. This is still a singular figure, but multiply so: a *singular-multiple*. It is always already tending toward ascription to particular human bodies, within habitual margins of expectation, but carries a charge of uncertainty that prevents it from settling into a definite contour. It is a decision to assign or preassign an identity to this superposition of qualities: a performative ascription that no norm or expediency can fully rationalize.

The uncertainty of the unspecified enemy makes it palpably uncertain that the ascription will effectively coincide with a transduction of existential threat. As a result, as the ascription moves transindividually through the defiles of the media apparatus, it can easily be hijacked by tendencies belonging to spheres other than the state in the specialized sense in which Schmitt understands it as the political entity, spheres such as police, governmental, and nongovernmental institutional apparatuses and the communicational/commercial sphere of

---

26 See Massumi, "The Primacy of Preemption," in *Ontopower: War, Powers, and the State of Perception* (Durham, NC: Duke University Press, 2015), 3–20.

the "people." The unspecified enemy becomes a ubiquitous figure: a universal political operator.

Media Figure, Distributed Event

This quasi-decisional, tendency-stoking singular-multiple is what grounds the mode of existence of the media figure in the contemporary networked environment. This is an image-borne mode where decision becomes distributed, fractalizing across a thousand cuts and cue-ins (likes and links), becoming a surplus-value of circulation that flows centripetally toward a central, preeminent figure—such as George W. Bush in the post-9/11 period—only to eddy and no sooner spin off centrifugally in an indefinite proliferation of currents. The lightning rod of the preeminent body transmitting a unified directional charge toward the central front of fomenting war becomes an omnidirectional receiver and frequency multiplier throwing off sparks in all directions, to fall (or not) on combustible social tinder: more a node than a lightning rod; a modulator more than a main line; a primer and a stoker.

The merging of civil space with the theater of war to form a continuous "threat environment," together with the new figure of the asymmetrical unspecified enemy, reintroduces the exception on which the sovereign decides, in a new variation. The exception becomes immanent to the field of relation, where it too fractalizes and becomes scalable. Outs are incised into the fabric of government and society where an autonomy of sovereign decision is beckoned. The most dramatic, but by no means only, example is Bush's "black sites" for torture. These openings-in out onto extra-legal and extra-normative decision are legitimated by the doctrine of preemption. This is the stance that the only way to deal with the ever-present, proteiform threat of asymmetrical unspecified enemies is to act upstream of their action. The "movement" of decision is preaccelerated,[27] operating *in the present on potential* threats to ward off

---

27 Erin Manning, *Relationscapes: Movement, Art, Philosophy* (Cambridge, MA: MIT Press, 2009), 3–28.

their eventuation or deviate their actualization in more manageable ways. In other words, decision changes its time signature. It is no longer in the synchronous present of Schmittian decision (the coincidence of leader and people in a unison of feeling), nor the suspended present of deterrence (time reduced to the not-yet-as-of-now). It acts preemptively in the present on a spinning wheel of *futurities*. Its tense is the future anterior: the could have, would have, will have been a threat.[28]

The singular-multiplying of the media figure, the sinking of black sites of fractalized decision into the relational fabric, and the logic of preemption form an assemblage which, like deterrence, perseveres as a reactivatable tendency, in an increasingly layered and variegated ecology of powers.

Along Comes Trump

Trump is nothing if not an exception as a person, moved by no program, no ideal, no norm, only expediency, practiced chaotically on the fly, in a headlong movement that surfs its own agitations and disordering effects, sending out waves of disturbance that stir up the sediment of society, activating just the kind of tendencies that Schmitt's pure normativists and traditional decisionists strove to curtail, without ever attaining the lightning majesty of Schmitt's sovereign decision. Trump, the media figure, is a stirrer: a node of quasi-chaotic agitation spinning off vortices of disturbance just begging for an ascription to hang themselves onto, in order to give them a sense of solidity and well-foundedness. Trump: the preeminent accident of person.

President Trump's media figure operates as a modulatory and distributive disturber-in-chief, in a chaotic line of descent from Reagan's already post-truth "government is the problem" approach. As with Reagan, Trump's popularity is decoupled from approval of his governmental policies. In a 2018 poll, 60 percent of Trump supporters approved of him for

28   See the analysis of the "operative logic" of preemption in Massumi, *Ontopower*. On the could have / would have / will have been, see *Ontopower*, chapter 7, 189–205.

his person, and only 20 percent for his policies.[29] A similar disabling of discursive coherence and ideological framing applied to Trump as to Reagan.

> His confusing logic, his tendency to jump quickly from topic to topic and his lack of attributions for so-called facts make his remarks sound like a puzzling jumble, and that creates a headache when translating Trump's speeches for non-English audiences. . . . "Most of the time, when he speaks he seems not to know quite where he's going," [a flummoxed French translator] said. "It's as if he had thematic clouds in his head that he would pick from with no need of a logical thread to link them."[30]

For his 2020 presidential run, Trump simply dispensed with the formality of a policy platform, running less as the head of a political party than

29   Philip Bump, "By a 3-to-1 Margin, Trump Supporters Embrace His Personality over His Policies," *Washington Post*, August 23, 2018, https://www.washingtonpost.com/news/politics/wp/2018/08/23/by-a-3-to-1-margin-trump-supporters-embrace-his-personality-over-his-policies.

30   Samantha Schmidt, "'Make America Big Again'? The Headache of Translating Trump into Foreign Languages," *Washington Post*, January 23, 2017, https://www.washingtonpost.com/news/morning-mix/wp/2017/01/23/make-america-big-again-the-headache-of-translating-trump-into-foreign-languages. Another way to put it, from a Florida politician *endorsing* Trump for president in 2024: "You've got English, you've got Spanish, you've got French and then you have Trump. You have to understand what he means." Meryl Kornfield, "Jewish Florida Lawmaker Breaks from DeSantis and Endorses Trump," *Washington Post*, October 24, 2023, https://www.washingtonpost.com/politics/2023/10/24/randy-fine-desantis-ally-endorses-trump. A federal judge, also in Florida, echoed this assessment of Trump's discourse in a decision angrily dismissing his lawsuit against Hillary Clinton for an alleged malicious conspiracy to spread false information about him as frivolous and vengeful. He described the Trump defense of that claim as "a hodgepodge of disconnected, often immaterial events, followed by an implausible conclusion" that is "categorically absurd." Adela Suliman, "Trump Fined Nearly $1M for 'Revenge' Lawsuit against Hillary Clinton, Others," *Washington Post*, January 20, 2023, https://www.washingtonpost.com/politics/2023/01/20/donald-trump-fine-court-clinton. "Trump is a semiotic salad, an assemblage of incongruous, clashing elements that would normally have been smoothed out and homogenized, but instead slide over and jostle with one another, never quite cohering into a single figure. . . . The absurdities and hyperbole, the insults and inconsistency are all crucial to his appeal." Bruce Bennett, "Trump's Body," *Sociological Review*, November 18, 2016, https://thesociologicalreview.org/collections/2016-us-election/trumps-body.

on his own performance as a celebrity personality.[31] Trump supporters consciously processed the disconnect from sound logic, well-formed discourse, and governmental reason as a positive feature, unfazed by the more than 30,573 lies he told while in office whose untruth he made not the least effort to hide.[32] They mocked anti-Trumpists for "taking him literally" instead of "taking him seriously." Some put a uniquely oracular spin on taking someone seriously: his speech errors and discursive lacunae were religiously analyzed as coded messages.

> "I wait for him to misspell or mispronounce something, and then I wait for my Serial Brain to decode," said [a Trump supporter interviewed at a rally], referring to a YouTube channel that she says analyzes the missing letters in the president's tweets—and the garbled words in the president's mouth—for clues to what's going to happen in the future.[33]

As the nonvisual sense par excellence, the proprioceptive body is without an image. Reagan's body image of strength and rugged masculinity in movement was continually undermined by visible frailty and frequent stumbling, and haunted by the autobiographical specter of dismemberment. The proprioceptive body-without-an-image offered a virtual completion compensating for the self-undermining of Reagan's body image, eroded by the accident. It was the *oscillation* between the supplementing proprioceptive full body-without-an-image and the self-eroding visible image of the body that captivated the nation, more than any straightforward identification with the positive content of any given

---

31 The Republican Party did produce new platform for 2024. Unconventionally brief, it consists in a "semiotic salad" modeled on Trump's speeches and built around his rally slogans and all-caps pronouncements on X, completing the personalization of the Party under Trump. Robert Draper, "A Republican Platform That Could Read Like a Trump Rally," *New York Times*, July 8, 2024, https://www .nytimes.com/2024/07/08/us/politics/trump-republican-platform.html.

32 Glenn Kessler, Salvador Rizzo, and Meg Kelly, "Trump's False or Misleading Claims Total 30,573 over 4 Years," *Washington Post*, January 24, 2021, https://www .washingtonpost.com/politics/2021/01/24/trumps-false-or-misleading-claims -total-30573-over-four-years.

33 Dan Zak, "Fear and Gloating in Cincinnati," *Washington Post*, August 2, 2019, https://www.washingtonpost.com/lifestyle/style/fear-and-gloating-in-cincinnati /2019/08/02/a6055256-b51f-11e9-8949-5f36ff92706e_story.html.

imagery. People's attention and desires were hooked into the *tension* between the poles of the oscillation, the *intensity* of the imaging. The felt vitality of the nation was linked to the vagaries of the preeminent body's image-borne intensities, in transindividual resonation.

Trump's persona induces a very different body-without-an-image. The most unforgettable image of the Reagan presidency was the photograph catching his wince of pain as his would-be assassin's bullet entered his body. Trump, by contrast, evoked the image of *himself* as a shooter as he prepared to run for president, bragging that he could gun someone down on Fifth Avenue and no one would bat an eye. The image of gratuitously gunning down an unsuspecting bystander was less a demonstration of his personal prowess than an assertion of his exceptionality. Physical prowess is not in any case a part of his persona. Rather than staging his moving body in manly exercise, he carts it. Reagan cleared brush and was a pioneer in the celebrity fitness advice industry;[34] George W. Bush jogged obsessively; Trump rides golf carts. He assiduously avoids more strenuous physical activity than the swing of the club on the theory that the body has finite resources that exercise would fatally exhaust.[35] The Reagan and Bush media figures sought to open finite bodily existence onto an affective infinity of transindividually felt capacitation, proprioceptively supplemented. They did so through immanent means: the pulsing of bodily capacitation on its own plane of potential, taking media imagery as its assemblage of expression. Reagan inaugurated this assemblage with a focus on the limbs (or lack thereof—playing the threat of amputation in his autobiography). Trump, in keeping with his nods to the personality of power, plays the face. He puts on a caricature of the strongman face, chin thrust up, eyes looking down from on high, lips purposefully pursed, skin radiating (orange). He alternates between this face and other equally practiced expressions, mostly denoting disdain. This facial showmanship has been widely commented upon, taken seriously if not literally.

34 Ronald Reagan, "How to Stay Fit," *Parade Magazine*, December 4, 1983, 4–6.

35 Rachael Rettner, "Trump Thinks That Exercising Too Much Uses Up the Body's 'Finite' Energy," *Washington Post*, May 14, 2017, https://www.washingtonpost .com/national/health-science/trump-thinks-that-exercising-too-much-uses-up -the-bodys-finite-energy/2017/05/12/bb0b9bda-365d-11e7-b4ee-434b6d506b37 _story.html.

One commentator likened the performance to the exaggerated character play of professional wrestlers mugging in the ring.[36]

Trump deflected from the body to the face, in a personalizing shift. But then he deflected the face into caricature. The caricature rebounds upon the body, overcoding it. The body begins to wear the facial expression in the form of equally exaggerated images of heroism and superhuman power. In popular iconography, Trump's head often features atop the costumed bodies of comic book superheroes and Hollywood he-men. The face overcodes the body, forming a relay of mutual reinforcement that symbolically attributes miraculous powers to the figure of Trump (see part 5, the "Faciality" section). These powers are taken literally, if not seriously, and form the basis of a strenuous affective attachment.

Trump's most high-profile accident of persons providentially reinforced the facialization. Ronald Reagan's would-be assassin shot him in the torso, and the photo of the attack showed him teetering, full-body falling forward, arm raised and flailing. Trump's assassin's bullet grazed his ear, providing him the opportunity to produce a grimace of over-acted determination. The bloodied facial expression dominated the news cycle, just days before his July coronation as 2024 GOP presidential candidate nomination. He had "faced" death. He now had dramatic imagery of an existential threat against himself, complementing the one he uttered against others going into his first campaign. It not only rivaled Reagan's, but went one better, portraying what was widely qualified as a "miraculous" salvation. It showed him not teetering, limbs akimbo, but rising up from near-death, as if resurrected (after having—heroically?—ducked down). His base was stoked like never before.

Miraculation

This is another kind of full body: what Deleuze and Guattari call a "miraculating" body.[37] This is a deific body signaling "quasi-causal" (nonlocal, nonlinear, non-instrumental) powers of transformation. When this

---

36 David Denby, "The Three Faces of Trump," New Yorker, August 12, 2015, https://www.newyorker.com/culture/cultural-comment/the-three-faces-of-trump.

37 Deleuze and Guattari, Anti-Oedipus, 10.

deific body attaches to the head of a leader, it produces a "magic of the state."[38] "Jesus Christ is my savior, Trump is my president," goes the slogan popular among right-wing Christian Trump supporters and widely sold on T-shirts and baseball caps. "I am the chosen one," cried Trump, in case anyone missed the parallel. [39] After his resurrection from a July 13, 2024, assassination attempt, the acronym GEOTUS upped the ante on POTUS in social media chatter: he went from mere "President of the United States" to "God-Emperor of the United States."[40]

Because the powers of the miraculating body are nonlocal and do not follow the pedestrian path of normal instrumental efficacy, this formation is of a paranoid cast by nature. Dramatic standout events with specifiable causes punctually electrify. Radiating around them, threats of a less specified nature recede to the horizon, melting into a surrounding atmosphere crackling with the static electricity of a vague, all-encompassing associational web of floating efficacies liable to micro-shock a body, following an affective rather than instrumental logic. The threats the miraculating body fields are as nonlocal as its powers, which follow the threats to the horizon, as atmospheric and affectively efficacious as they are.

38 Michael Taussig, *The Magic of the State* (London: Routledge, 1997).

39 Tom McCarthy, "'I Am the Chosen One': With Boasts and Insults, Trump Sets New Benchmark for Incoherence," *Guardian*, August 21, 2018, https://www .theguardian.com/us-news/2019/aug/21/trump-press-conference-greenland -jewish-democrats. In the same press session, Trump referred to himself as the "King of Israel." Those around him reinforced that message. See Martin Pengelly, "[Secretary of Energy] Rick Perry Tells Donald Trump: 'You Really Are the Chosen One," *Guardian*, November 25, 2019, https://www.theguardian.com/us -news/2019/nov/25/rick-perry-donald-trump-chosen-one; Sarah Posner, "White Evangelicals Think Trump Is Divinely Ordained. He'll Do Almost Anything to Keep It That Way," *Los Angeles Times*, June 14, 2020, https://www.latimes.com /opinion/story/2020-06-14/donald-trump-st-johns-church-white-evangelicals -campaign-2020-pandemic-protest. Trump's habitual use of the third person to refer to himself is in keeping with this self-aggrandizement.

40 Drew Harwell, Michelle Boorstein, and Josh Dawsey, "Trump's Close Call in Assassination Attempt Fuels Talk He Was 'Chosen' by God," *Washington Post*, July 16, 2024, https://www.washingtonpost.com/nation/2024/07/16/trump -religion-messiah. At the Republican Party convention, Republican delegates wore simulated ear bandages as a sign of Trump's facial stigmata.

1.2 Graphic by FashionHouse/Shutterstock.

"Magical thinking" and conspiracy theorizing become the order of the day. Already-operating tendencies, of racist, heteronormative, and misogynist cast, opportunistically bind to the affective flotation of miraculating powers, condensing the atmosphere of threats so that it precipitates into repetitive figures of the enemy they preferentially specify. These figures retain the singular-multiplicity of the unspecified enemy, but within a restricted bandwidth, cycling through a carousel of stereotypical specifications circling in refrains. Around each specification, there is a floating background-surround where ascriptions communicate, blurring into and out of each other to form serial variations, sometimes forming hybrids or segueing seamlessly into other figures. The progressive, the Democrat, the demon, the child molester, the cannibal, the racialized other as animalized, the non-gender-conforming as corrupting, the urban antifascist as bloodthirsty invader of quiet suburbs and idyllic American small towns, form a pool of potential determinations whose movements into and out of each other constitute the domestic unspecified enemy as singular-multiple spectrum of threat, punctually actualized in specific forms beading into endless series.

All of this harks back to the most archaic of affective formations around the preeminence of individuals as figures of state, of the kind associated with early, absolutist state formations.[41] But nowadays it is so fully ascribed to accidents of persons that the machinery of state can be dispensed with affectively, in libertarian abandon. The figure of the "deep state," personified in shadowy bad actors behind the scenes, becomes a link in the relay of the unspecified enemy. The affective circuit joining Trump to his supporters forms a united front against the deep state. The fact that Trump is afforded such faith *because* he is the head of state is bracketed, as is the conviction that the salvation of the world is felt to hinge on his occupying the office of the president. These points are maintained under erasure. It is as if, miraculously, everything passes

---

41 Dean and Massumi, *First and Last Emperors*. In absolutist state formations, the monarch or emperor embodies the soul of the nation and at the same time transcends it as the representative of divine power on earth, in a direct line of filiation from god or the gods (examples are Louis XIV in France as "Sun King" radiating Christ's order throughout the realm, and the emperors of traditional China serving under the "mandate of heaven"). The people are the body of the state and the organs of the head of state—his executing hands and devoted heart. Hobbes's absolute leader as "leviathan," unforgettably illustrated in the frontispiece of his famous work of the same name showing a monarch of monstrous size whose body is composed of his subjects' bodies, is in this line. In Hobbes's analysis, the head of state "bears" the personhood of his subjects in his own person, magically endowing them with an absolute unity that overcodes their individuality. Thomas Hobbes, *Leviathan*, rev. student ed., ed. Richard Tuck (Cambridge: Cambridge University Press, 1996), pt. 2, chap. 17, p. 120. The result is a collective personhood flush with transcendence and subjected to its normative imperatives. Medieval European kingship included the earthly body / transcendent soul dichotomy in its legitimating doctrine of the "king's two bodies." This refers to the doubling of the king's physical body with the spiritual body of Christ. Ernst H. Kantorowicz, *The King's Two Bodies: A Study in Medieval Political Theory* (Princeton, NJ: Princeton University Press, 2016). See also Dean and Massumi, *First and Last Emperors*, for parallels in ancient China. The present essay will develop a theory of collective personhood and collective individuation in which transcendence, absolute unity, and ideal normativity cede to a processual immanentism more compatible with a Spinozan ethics.

between Trump and each of his supporters, the state aside. The state, become one with the "deep state," is exorcised out of the equation.

The strength of the affective bond is such that Trump's base of support is rock solid. It remained stable around the 40 percent level throughout his presidency, and after, regardless of his gaffes, backtracks, and betrayals, and regardless of the actual performance of his administration (the debacle of his bleach-hawking COVID-19 response, the failure to build the border wall and to make Mexico pay for it, the declining performance of the economy, the failure of his bromance with Kim Jong Un to change relations with North Korea, the myriad court reversals of his executive overreach, to name just a few). In a measure of the fealty accorded to Trump, a consistent 60 percent of his supporters declare that there was nothing he could do or say that would alter their approval.[42] When he started his presidential campaign saying that he could shoot someone on Fifth Avenue and no one would care, it was taken as silly braggadocio. But when he ended his presidency by inciting five deaths on the Capitol Hill end of Pennsylvania Avenue, including one by shooting, before skipping out to Mar-a-Lago, it no longer sounded like a joke.[43]

Are You an Act?

Taking Trump seriously but not literally involves never forgetting that the way to his political career was paved by his years as a reality TV star on The Apprentice, which remade him an icon of success at a low point in

---

42   Ryan Struyk, "6 in 10 People Who Approve of Trump Say They'll Never, Ever, Ever Stop Approving," CNN, August 17, 2017, https://www.cnn.com/2017/08/17/politics/trump-approvers-never-stop-approving-poll/index.html; Owen Daughertym, "Poll: 62 Percent of Trump Fans Say They Support Him No Matter What," Hill, November 11, 2019, https://thehill.com/homenews/administration/469058-poll-62-of-trump-supporters-say-nothing-the-president-could-do-would.

43   Trump's personal approval rating in polls has remained remarkably consistent, dipping only temporarily after the January 2021 siege of the Capitol and the 2022 midterm elections. It has remained in the 70–80 percent range among Republicans and in the 40 percent range overall.

his business fortunes, with three bankruptcies under his belt.[44] It has become a commonplace to say that he adapted his reality TV persona for his role as president, in a twenty-first-century update of Reagan's cinematic political persona. Trump too was an actor. He freely admitted it. "Anthony Scaramucci, who served as Trump's communications director[,] . . . recounts the president's response when he asks him, 'Are you an act?' 'I'm a total act and I don't understand why people don't get it,' Trump replies."[45] He is a total act with real, performative consequences.

Trump's supporters, for their part, did get it. It was the air of unreality in the reality act that made him special. If he were merely real, he would be as ordinary as the next random person. But being a simulacrum of real, that's special. It makes one realer than real.[46] As in: a celebrity (god). A week after he lost reelection in 2020, still acting as if he had won in a landslide, Trump made an appearance by motorcade, driving past his supporters gathered in the nation's capital to cheer on his unfounded allegations of election fraud. An awed supporter who saw him pass by in his limousine was beside herself with joy and trembling. "He looked fake," she enthused, royally impressed. "I'm still shaking."[47]

It's only natural that if you really truly perform a fake persona, it will really look truly fake.[48] Not that the truth or falsehood of Trump's claims is the issue. Presidential counselor Kellyanne Conway warned us the very next day after Trump's inauguration, supporting press secretary Sean

---

44 Patrick Radden Keefe, "How Mark Burnett Resurrected Trump as an Icon of American Success," *New Yorker*, January 7, 2019, https://www.newyorker.com /magazine/2019/01/07/how-mark-burnett-resurrected-donald-trump-as-an-icon -of-american-success.

45 Ashley Parker, "New Book Portrays Trump as Erratic, 'at Times Dangerously Uninformed,'" *Washington Post*, January 15, 2020, https://www.washingtonpost.com /politics/new-book-portrays-trump-as-erratic-at-times-dangerously-uninformed /2020/01/15/4d45bf44-370f-11ea-a0id-b7cc8ec1a85d_story.html.

46 Massumi, "Realer Than Real," in *Couplets*, 16–24.

47 Katelyn Burns, "President Trump Briefly Drove by the 'Million MAGA March' on His Way to the Golf Course," *Vox*, November 14, 2020, https://www.vox.com /policy-and-politics/2020/11/14/21565197/trump-million-maga-march.

48 As Bruce Bennett comments in "Trump's Body," "Trump's excessive assertion of distinctive inauthenticity" functions, counterintuitively, as "a sign of authenticity." "Patent artificiality makes the 70-year old billionaire more authentic. . . . Its obvious artlessness implies that nothing is being concealed." Case in point: hair.

Spicer's insistence that the visibly smaller crowd in attendance was really vastly bigger than Obama's, that we had entered the world of "alternative facts."[49]

That is the issue: Foucault's will-to-truth has morphed into the will-to-alternative-facts. The fake-shaken 40 percent of the electorate feel unshakably that all this *should* be real: Donald Trump *should* have attracted a vastly larger crowd. After losing the election, he *should* have remained president. Democrats *should* under no circumstances get a majority of votes. People of color *should* not have the electoral power to determine the outcome of an election. These claims are not empirical, but *aspirational*.[50]

If the formula for preemption is "would have, could have, will have been," the formula for Trumpism is *"thus should it be—so be it"* (to formulate it using the Yoda syntax favored by QAnon for its motto, "Where we go one, we go all"). As if willing it so, all together now, with feeling, under the auspices of the preeminent person, is miraculously enough to "make it so" (shifting to *Star Trek* phraseology). The present regains its rights, and then some. Now is hardly soon enough for this desire.

But the present is now in the subjunctive rather than the indicative mood. The present is no longer pregnant with futurity and beholden to it, as with preemption. Neither is it in prolonged suspense, as with deterrence. Nor is it the old developmental present, presupposed by the pure normativist and the traditional decisionist, that passes through ordered phases of formation. That present has been disabled by the

---

49   Alexandra Jaffe, "Kellyanne Conway: WH Spokesman Gave 'Alternative Facts' on Inauguration Crowd," NBC News, January 17, 2017, https://www.nbcnews.com/storyline/meet-the-press-70-years/wh-spokesman-gave-alternative-facts-inauguration-crowd-n710466.

50   A local 2020 election official supporting Trump's election denialism makes the aspirational aspect clear: "My vote to remain a no [against certifying the results] isn't based on any evidence, it's not based on any facts, it's only based on my gut feeling and my own intuition, and that's all I need," because what I feel should be, should be. Annie Gowen, "An Ex-Professor Spreads Election Myths across the United States, One Town at a Time," *Washington Post*, September 8, 2022, https://www.washingtonpost.com/elections/2022/09/08/an-ex-professor-spreads-election-myths-across-us-one-town-time. This is a version of what I have elsewhere called the ascription of an "affective fact" (Massumi, "The Future Birth of the Affective Fact," in *Ontopower*, 189–205). Later in this essay, fascism and fascisizing tendencies will be discussed in terms of a causally challenged affective regime.

short-circuiting of evidence, judgment, and negotiation replaced by an immediate *so be it*. The present is now the immediate present of the fiat of desire: a "should" willing itself *already* to be fact. This aspirationally self-effecting decision, no sooner said than already done, is not entirely a stranger to Schmittian decision, which constitutes its own "autonomous moment."[51] Trumpian decision functions, in its own petulant way, as a point of ascription of the friend/enemy distinction. It is "magical thinking," operating as a province of the magic of the (head of) state, rising orangely above the swampy deep.

The Reign of the Self-Knockoff

Specific ascriptions of the enemy in this regime, performed by fiat, stand out in relief against the churning background of preemption's Catherine wheel of specifications as they spin into and spark out of each other. Saying that the figure of the enemy is now "unspecified" does not connote the opposite of specification. It connotes turnover *of* specifications: an ongoing *process of specification* navigating fluid conditions of overdetermination. The media is unspecified by virtue of being overfull of potential ascriptions, reciprocally referring and mutually modulating, oscillating in time with the pulse of the exceptional body at the head of the state, crowned by its radiating face. The media form the singular-multiple solution out of which, with each sovereign performance, a recognizable friend-enemy compound precipitates, now the product of magical thinking effecting an alchemy of performative ascription.

The preeminent figure under whose miraculating auspices this process runs is just as singular-multiple as the ascribed figure of the enemy. That Trump is not an ordinary person is signaled in his nickname "the Donald." He is a category unto himself. The definite article actually designates a spread, just as "the cat" spans a whole spectrum of variation, from the domestic companion animal to the lion in *The Wizard of Oz*. "The" Donald is not a *particular* figure. It is a singular node full of potential ascriptions. And it is not *general*, in the sense of a well-ordered logical

---

51 Schmitt, *Political Theology*, 12.

category that defines the essential characteristics that a particular must display in order to fall obediently under its identifying umbrella. The media figure, The Donald no less than the unspecified enemy, is a *generic* in something close to the sense of a generic medication that spins a particular brand into a multiple, in an indefinite and potentially uncontrolled series of knockoffs. The Donald is the kind of person that is a knockoff of itself, cycling through series of self-ascriptions as fickle as the enemy ascriptions produced as his correlate in a parallel series of specifications. The Donald is his own generic. Trump is changeability in person—within, of course, certain limits of variation. (Later in this essay, the generic will be refigured as the "collective singular."[52])

This applies to various levels. Trump's personal appearance itself drifts. The tint of his hair changes from treatment to treatment, dancing with changes in the color of his sun-lamped skin and the greater or lesser prominence of the raccoon-eye effect of the protector goggles. The press commented on the "whiplash" swings between the persona appearing at his rallies, not infrequently characterizing the performance as "schizophrenic."[53] A senior administration official commenting on Trump's statement about his own failed coronavirus response: "This is not the first time this president has looked schizophrenic, because there's a long history of him vacillating between incompatible messaging and policy directives."[54] In particular, scripted Trump and extemporaneous Trump were like two entirely different people.

52   See the "Collective Singular" and "Class-Naming the Collective Singular" sections of part 2 and the "Real Distinction" section of the postscript.

53   Philip Rucker, "Trump's Whiplash: Three Personas in Three Speeches, but the Same President," *Washington Post*, August 23, 2017, https://www.washingtonpost.com/politics/trumps-whiplash-three-roles-in-three-speeches-but-the-same-president/2017/08/23/bb3c4602-881c-11e7-a94f-3139abce39f5_story.html; Michael Gerson, "Trump's Rhetorical Schizophrenia Is Easy to See Through," *Washington Post*, August 24, 2017, https://www.washingtonpost.com/opinions/trumps-rhetorical-schizophrenia-is-easy-to-see-through/2017/08/24/2163ab42-88f3-11e7-a50f-e0d4e6eco70a_story.html.

54   Philip Rucker and Robert Costa, "Commander of Confusion: Trump Sows Uncertainty and Seeks to Cast Blame in Coronavirus Crisis," *Washington Post*, April 2, 2020, https://www.washingtonpost.com/politics/commander-of-confusion-trump-sows-uncertainty-and-seeks-to-cast-blame-in-coronavirus-crisis/2020/04/02/fc2db084-7431-11ea-85cb-8670579b863d_story.html.

Ornamental Masculinity

Perhaps most suggestively, The Donald oscillated dramatically between cartoonish invincibility and extreme fragility. He put on an image of hypermasculinity that could not be taken literally by serious people. He regularly recruited others to validate it, underlining that the image could not sustain itself and required third-party validation. His occupation of his office was bookended by this bolstering by others.

As he began his campaign, his personal doctor, Harold Bornstein, released a letter preemptively responding to worries about his age and obesity, providing backup for Trump's attempts to deflect such concerns by turning them around and aiming them at Hillary Clinton's stamina, using one of his favorite rhetorical devices, beloved by American school-children: the "I know you are but what am I" defense. The physician's letter declared unequivocally that Trump (unlike Hillary, it was pointedly suggested) would be "the healthiest individual ever elected president."[55] Bornstein's own longevity was not as impressive. He was removed from his position two years later for divulging which anti-baldness drug Trump was taking. Ronny Jackson, his successor as Trump's personal doctor, learned the lesson and went one better, claiming that the president's genes were so superior that he would live to the age of two hundred if he just cut back on Big Macs.[56]

The hyperbole was manifest. Also transparent was its role as a compensating mechanism for swings to the opposite pole, of wound-licking vulnerability. When Trump was at his lowest, when he recoiled into moody isolation and pouting silence in the face of the opprobrium directed toward him after his incitement of the storming of the Capitol, his campaign press secretary stepped up to assure the nation, in

55 Jeremy Diamond, "Trump's Doctor: Trump 'Will Be Healthiest Individual Ever Elected' President," CNN, December 14, 2015, https://www.cnn.com/2015/12/14/politics/donald-trump-medical-bill-health/index.html.

56 Dan Mercia, "Dr. Ronny Jackson's Glowing Bill of Health for Trump," CNN, January 16, 2018, https://www.cnn.com/2018/01/16/politics/dr-ronny-jackson-donald-trump-clean-bill-of-health/index.html.

an entirely gratuitous statement, that Trump was "the most masculine person to ever hold the White House."[57]

This is one of the areas where it is essential to take Trump seriously rather than literally. In the charismatic leadership paradigm, the head of state has to project an effective strongman image and appear to embody the positive ideal of masculinity in order to induce his followers to identify with him through that image and, through that identification, form a mighty body politic. This is patently not the case with Trump. One of his most vocal celebrity supporters, comedian Roseanne Barr, called him the "first woman president of the United States." A columnist riffed on this statement, writing,

> Oddly, he has a lot in common with the basest, most unfair stereotypes of femininity. He is ruled by feelings rather than facts. He is fickle, gossipy and easily grossed out. He uses florid language, like "beautiful" and "perfect," and says he and North Korean dictator Kim Jong Un "fell in love." He deals with adversity like a Mean Girl with a burn book, via insults and freeze-outs.[58]

57 Monica Hesse, "Trumpist Masculinity Reaches Its High Water Mark," *Washington Post*, January 12, 2021, https://www.washingtonpost.com/lifestyle/style/capitol -riot-zip-tie-guy-men-trump-masculinity/2021/01/12/486a516e-5447-11eb-a08b -f1381ef3d207_story.html.

58 Monica Hesse, "The Weird Masculinity of Donald Trump," *Washington Post*, July 16, 2020, https://www.washingtonpost.com/lifestyle/style/the -weird-masculinity-of-donald-trump/2020/07/15/0dfe3854-c43e-11ea-b037 -f9711f89ee46_story.html. Trump on his relationship to Kim Jong Un: "The word chemistry. You meet somebody and you have a good chemistry. You meet a woman. In one second you know whether or not it's all going to happen." Bob Woodward, "The Trump Tapes: Twenty Interviews That Show He Is an Unparalleled Danger," *Washington Post*, October 23, 2022, https://www.washingtonpost .com/opinions/interactive/2022/trump-tapes-bob-woodward-interviews -audiobook. In 2018, Trump asked Disney management to instruct comedian Jimmy Kimmel, host of an eponymous late-night TV show in the United States, to lay off on his jokes about Trump. Kimmel's response was to liken Trump to a popular (and misogynist) meme-figure of the tantrum-prone, entitled white suburban housewife: "In other words, President Karen demanded to speak to my manager." Trish Bendix, "Jimmy Kimmel Responds to Reports He Caused a 'Trumper Tantrum,'" *New York Times*, February 28, 2023, https://www.nytimes

Feminist Susan Faludi wrote of his persona as an "ornamental masculinity" custom-tailored to "our image-based times," likening his performance of it to a "pantomime" (harking back to the Reagan mime-effect discussed earlier, with the difference that the oscillation is between faces, rather than between the frail body and the fullness of its virtual double).

These were not dramatic reveals: they were stating the obvious. Trump's image is not of the traditional strongman, but rather that most contemporary of male figures: the "toxic masculinity" of the spoiled manchild. He oscillates between performances of self-aggrandizing puffery for the adoring audience and self-sorry vulnerability compensated for through cattiness, if not outright aggression, directed toward others. That very oscillation was the operative mechanism. The cartoon-character hypermasculine pantomime and the meanness of the catty man-girl (or the hurt puppy biting the hand that feeds it) marked the outside limits of a spectrum containing a graded multiplicity of masculinities filling the span between. Trump supporters did not identify with the image. If they "identified" with anything, it was the oscillation itself.[59] The spectacle of it

---

.com/2023/02/28/arts/television/jimmy-kimmel-trump.html. In his perceptive article "Trump's Body," Bruce Bennett also notes "a curious mix of masculine and feminine codes, a bricolage of macho bravado, vanity, and emotional sensitivity" revealing "a certain ambiguity of gender that is normally submerged beneath his leering misogyny."

59 Faludi's Trumpian "ornamental masculinity" is a version of what in feminist sociology of contemporary gender is called "hybrid masculinity," as against "hegemonic masculinity" (traditional masculinism) understood as implying, in the words of Debbie Ging, "a fixed character type or an assemblage of toxic traits" (642). Ging analyzes a spectrum of "ostensibly contradictory formulations" (653) of hybrid masculinity populating the anti-feminist "manosphere" (betas, zetas, incels, geeks, and pickup artists, among others). What they have in common is to "confound certain gender formulations" while availing themselves of "greater creativity . . . and strategic performativity" (653), often expressing gender fluidity and not infrequently taking on characteristics coded as feminine. Hybrid masculinities do not oppose the male domination of women, but aim to bolster its power by creating a compensatory proliferation of hybrid categories for male supremacists who keenly recognize that they cannot live up the putative standards of emotional and physical strength and rugged attractiveness required to occupy the "alpha" rung of the masculinist pyramid (the worshipped—and violently envied—"Chad" of incel culture). Hybrid masculinities, according to Ging, "embrace some aspects of hypermasculinity" (642) and repudiate others, while passionately serving its

was mesmerizing. Its performance through continuous streams of tweets commanded the nervous attention of the population, producing a fascination and an anticipation for a next installment in the reality show.

Trump played on the installment form in December 2022. Not a month after announcing his candidacy for the 2024 presidential race, he solemnly ballyhooed a "major announcement" coming the next day. What it turned out to be was the issuance of "digital trading cards" in the form of NFTs (nonfungible tokens). The "cards" featured amateurishly Photoshopped images of Trump as cartoonish popular culture figures caricaturing hypermasculinity. The images oozed with kitsch. A journalist rightly commented that the kitsch was not a defect but an essential part of their functioning.[60] The kitsch, he surmised, operates as a wink among MAGA insiders, signaling their difference from and opposition to the "elites" whose haughty sense of taste would presumably be wounded by such images. No one, obviously, takes these artifacts of ornamental masculinity literally, as suggesting that Trump is an exemplary specimen of masculine strength and fitness. But they do take them seriously, in their performative political functioning as winkingly ascribing the enemy.[61] The NFTS

male supremacist purposes. "Hegemonic masculinity" exploits this "by borrowing aspects of other masculinities that are strategically useful for continued domination" (642), ultimately blurring the boundary between hegemonic and hybrid masculinity. It is this blurring that Trump's oscillations play to, as a way of addressing the full spectrum of contemporary masculinities—that sliding scale running in mutually resonating and overlapping degrees from Alpha Chad to sorry incel—in order potentially to induct them into his orbit. This is the hypermasculine spectrum. Debbie Ging, "Alphas, Betas, and Incels: Theorizing the Masculinities of the Manosphere," *Men and Masculinities* 22, no. 4 (2019): 638–57. See the discussion of hybrid femininity in the section "Man-Standard, Standard Man" below.

60 Philip Kennecott, "Trump NFTs Are Not Art. Unless You Consider Grifting an Art Form. These $99 Trading Cards Are Laughably Bad. That's the Whole Point," *Washington Post*, December 17, 2022, https://www.washingtonpost.com/arts -entertainment/2022/12/17/trump-trading-card-nft-art.

61 Trump himself takes ornamentality seriously. Corey Robin comments on Trump's "attraction to the surface of things," expressing itself as an "obsession with décor" that is "less monumental than ornamental." He quotes Trump tracing this to the influence of his mother, whose "flair for the grand and the dramatic" counterbalanced his sado-patriarchal father's focus on "competence and efficiency." Corey Robin, *The Reactionary Mind: Conservatism from Edmund Burke to Donald Trump*, 2nd ed. (Oxford: Oxford University Press, 2018). A psycho-

1.3 Trump Digital Trading Cards, four-pack.

sold out in one day, netting the Trump brand $4.5 million. The price crashed two weeks later, following a not unusual trajectory for Trump's business initiatives.[62]

An instance of the oscillation in Trump's imaging of maleness occurred following the assassination attempt. Comments about his grit

---

analytic interpretation of a Trump personality structure as a function of this ambivalence between parental figures would not be wrong, but it would be too pat and easy. It would miss the directly social and political dimension of personhood that is the focus of this essay and the main point of Deleuze and Guattari's *Anti-Oedipus*, falling back into the interiorized model of individual identification, projection, and unresolved Oedipal conflict.

62 Josh Taylor, "Donald Trump's Digital Trading Card Collection Sells Out in Less Than a Day," *Guardian*, December 17, 2022, https://www.theguardian.com/us

and manly power proliferated. The image of his facing-down-death-grimace multiplied at rallies and the Republican convention. It was often accompanied by the song "Macho Man" by the Village People—a song enshrined in popular culture as a paean to the camp image of hypermasculinity seriously but not literally performed in the gay community.[63]

Affective Adjunction

Trump's fundamental political strategy is to use whiplash changeability to monopolize attention through a chaotic use of social media that continually agitates the space of communication. The strategy is to *induct* the nervous bodies of the populace, destabilized by the endless media march of the unspecified enemy, into a passional engagement with the *rhythm* of Trump's morphing media figure. People do not identify so much as their lives are *affectively adjoined* to the Trump figural dynamic, with different valencies, positive or negative, MAGA or never-Trump. No one not living in a pre–social media cave is unaffected.

Those who engage positively and approvingly have no need to see themselves reflected in Trump's image. That kind of identificatory mirroring requires a perception of similarity. Trump's life, born to wealth and capitalizing on privilege to inhabit the celebrity stratosphere, bears no similarity whatsoever to the lives of his supporters. Instead of seeing their similarity to Trump as in a mirror, what they see is *their own difference in his oscillation*: their own perceived exceptionalism. Adjoined to the spectrum, they are under no compulsion to embody one of its poles. It is the job of the preeminent person to embody both at once, so that any given individual can participate in his process by embodying a graded degree in between.

-news/2022/dec/17/donald-trumps-digital-trading-card-collection-sells-out-in-less-than-a-day; Nayazunissa, "Prices of Donald Trump's NFT Collection Plummet More Than 70%," *TheNewsCrypto*, December 26, 2022, https://thenewscrypto.com/prices-of-donald-trumps-nft-collection-plummet-more-than-70/.

63 Ethan Meyers, "Trump's Return to Rally Stage Met with Prayers, Excitement and Confusion over JD Vance," *Guardian*, July 20, 2024, https://www.theguardian.com/us-news/article/2024/jul/20/trump-vance-michigan-rally.

License

Trump does not fulfill the traditional role of the leader as *legitimating* an ideology or coherent set of policies. What he does instead is *give license* to his supporters to be themselves, on the Trumpian spectrum, and in so doing arrogate to themselves a degree of his miraculousness. The Trump media figure is a collective individuation machine. "Where goes one (Trump), we (supporters) go all," to our own miraculous degree, on our own slice of the spectrum.

The Trump media figure gives license to his supporters to be themselves—even their worst selves, their most selfish, petty, hateful selves—and then to congratulate themselves on that achievement, as if by acceding to this figure of themselves they were effectively participating in a glorious refounding of the nation. Many militia groups liken themselves to the Founding Fathers. The reference is explicit in the case of the "Three Percenters," whose name refers to the historical myth that only 3 percent of the population had participated in the struggle for independence against the British (illustrating a strange, if not unexpected, strain of elitism in Trumpist "populism"). The calls for civil war are for a rebirth by fire (or at least a lot of breast-beating).

What is felt as liberating was precisely for a leader to give license rather than to legitimate.[64] Legitimation is institutionalizing, and institutions reassert a normative structure. Trump is famous (and loved) for shredding all of the norms of good government, ethical business practice, and morally concerned personal behavior. His giving over of himself to giving license was in the service of a *post-normative personhood*. Trump followers express their feeling of their own exceptionality by mockingly distinguishing themselves from the "normies" who believe in—or at least acquiesce to—the normal functioning of the established governmental institutions, support inclusion in these institutions of

---

64 Herbert Marcuse, in a classic essay, also notes how Nazism created for its supporters a "sphere of acquiescent license" that is experienced as freedom. Herbert Marcuse, "State and Individual under National Socialism," in *Technology, War and Fascism: Collected Papers of Herbert Marcuse*, vol. 1 (New York: Routledge, 1998), 83–84, 86.

marginalized groups, and value civility in politics. Those who are deep in the QAnon conspiracy theory movement go so far as to stake a claim to neurodiversity by labeling themselves "autists," referencing the widely debunked stereotype of autistics as savants obsessed with apparently random details, but also, inevitably, given the toxic atmosphere of the imageboard websites QAnoners frequent, as intractable to social norms and prone to meltdowns of rage.[65] As the analysis of hypermasculinity showed, the "post-normative" is not the simple opposite of normative. It exceeds it, but also carries it. It carries the norms in its oscillation, swinging back and forth between their vigorous reassertion on the one hand, and on the other, exaggerated and distorting expressions that stretch them beyond their pale. "Post-normative" here is less a beyond of normativism than a *normopathy*—normativity swollen with license.

Certain normopathic figures who exaggerate the masculine image to the hyper-extreme have gained high visibility and celebrity status in right-wing circles. Milo Yiannopoulos, who became a lightning rod for progressive demonstrators on university campuses around the time of the 2016 presidential campaign, is perhaps the best-known example. The most toxic, however, is without a doubt Andrew Tate, who explicitly labels himself hypermasculinist and misogynist and spouts racist and homophobic statements. Affectionately called by his many enthusiastic followers "the king of toxic masculinity," Tate, like Trump, rose to political prominence through reality TV, as a controversial participant on *Big Brother* (UK). He

---

65   QAnon developed on the infamously post-normative imageboard websites 4chan, 8chan, and 8kun. An Anti-Defamation League report explains the autism reference: "Followers who analyze Q's posts, known as 'breadcrumbs' or 'Q drops,' call themselves 'autists' (This is a reference to what chan board users call 'weaponized autism,' complementing the ability of QAnon followers to find and make connections between Q's posts and random topics and events, and does not necessarily imply that the users are autistic) or 'bakers.' They decode the 'crumbs' to make 'bread,' threads that weave together Q's posts to create a better understanding of the clues and information they reveal." Anti-Defamation League, "QAnon," September 24, 2020, https://www.adl.org/resources /backgrounder/qanon. For a critique of conventional ideas about autism (including the trope of the autistic savant), as part of a project of an affirmative account of neurodiversity, see Erin Manning, "Not at a Distance: On Touch, Synesthesia, and Other Ways of Knowing," in *For a Pragmatics of the Useless* (Durham, NC: Duke University Press, 2020), 245–79.

parried his name recognition from that show into the role of social media influencer, becoming the most popular influencer among American Gen Zers, in some months exceeding Trump in number of internet searches for his name. Known for celebrating Trump's statement about women, revealed in a video released in 2016, that he could "grab them by the pussy" anytime he wanted, his image is all self-aggrandizing hardness, entitlement, and aggression. At the same time, he styles himself a self-help guru for young men supposedly beaten down by feminism, offering them moral support to overcome their insecurities.[66] Here the ornamental-masculine oscillation—between what are coded as masculine and feminine character traits—that is internal to the Trump-person is distributed between Tate, as polestar of hypermasculinity, and his followers, who are felt to have been feminized by uppity women and minorities and thought to require assistance to live up to their manly birthright. Tate claims for himself and his followers the right to absolute license in the name of freedom. "I'm not a fucking rapist. But I like the idea of being able to just do what I want. I like being free."[67] Among the many things wrong with that statement is the fact that he was arrested for rape and human trafficking in December 2022, is currently awaiting trial in Romania, and is then to be extradited to United Kingdom, where he faces similar charges.[68]

As Tate's statement illustrates, the license to swing past the norms is felt as "freedom": the freedom of men to "grab them by the pussy" and disparage woman and sexual minorities; the freedom to express one's

---

66 "Who Is Andrew Tate, the Misogynist Hero to Millions of Young Men?," *Economist*, December 30, 2022, https://www.economist.com/the-economist-explains/2022/12 /30/who-is-andrew-tate-the-misogynist-hero-to-millions-of-young-men.

67 Lindsay Dodgson, "Andrew Tate's Biggest Legal Challenge Will Be His Own Statements on Rape and Exploitation, Lawyer Says. There Are a Lot," *Business Insider*, January 13, 2023, https://www.businessinsider.com/andrew-tate-how -own-statements-now-huge-legal-problem-2023-1.

68 The fact that Yiannopoulos is gay (or as he now says, "ex-gay," having demoted his husband to "housemate") and Tate is biracial puts a complicated twist on things. For one thing, it indicates the constructedness of the categories composing the Man-Standard (see next section), gainsaying their pretention to reflect essential characteristics of natural groupings. It makes it clear that belonging to a category is an existential posture (analyzed below in terms of an affective regime of reaction).

racism out loud, resuscitate its most virulent symbols like the Confederate flag, and practice micro- and macro-aggressions with impunity; the
freedom during the COVID epidemic to endanger others' lives because
wearing a mask feels emasculating to those on the hypermasculine
spectrum (but then why do superheroes wear masks?); the freedom to
intimidate those who disagree by brandishing weaponry during demonstrations and in capitol buildings; the freedom to spread unfounded allegations and indulge in the satisfactions of conspiracy theorizing drawing
on long-standing anti-Semitic tropes so central to the fascist tradition.
In other words, the freedom to indulge the most regressive tendencies
from a patriarchal and racist past that have suffered a challenge in recent
decades from the "progressive" enemy and its "political correctness."

Man-Standard, Standard Man

It may seem counterintuitive to argue that the construction of the
media figure of hypermasculinity includes a feminine-stereotype pole.
However, this is a pragmatic necessity, on two counts. First, it accommodates female supporters, licensing them to a bandwidth on the spectrum where they overlap with the Trump media-figure dynamic, while
largely remaining in the less-valued, subordinate position traditionally
assigned them in patriarchal culture. Second, it introduces a margin of
maneuver into ornamental masculinity.

The manly man no longer has to be steadfast, self-sacrificing, and
uncomplaining, as older stereotypes would have it. The post-normative
man can play the spectrum in self-gratifying ways. He can whine, wal-
low in self-pity, and nurse feelings of victimization. In fact, the feelings
of victimization are essential for orienting the ascription of the enemy
along the fault lines of resentment fueling the political expressions of
ornamental masculinity. This can tend toward the more or less genteel,
pseudo-intellectual end, exemplified by Jordan Peterson heroically defending himself and his followers from such deadly affronts to masculinity as gender-neutral pronouns while living on a diet exclusively of
beef. Or it can take the more extreme and aggressive form of the self-
described neo-reactionaries of the alt-right, who brandish weapons

filled with the ammunition of white male grievance (as well as actual bullets) in the fight against the "anti-male" bias of "mainstream culture" and the fantasied plot on the part of Jews and people of color to "replace" the white race, not to mention degender Mr [sic] Potato Head.

The inclusion of the feminine in the structure of the masculine is also a feature of the traditional normative figure of masculinity, but in a different configuration. Traditionally, the female was "ex-included": included as the abject other that must be symbolically expelled from the male orbit (but not so fully that women can't continue to prepare his breakfast). The othering can take virulently misogynist forms, such as those analyzed by Klaus Theweleit among the proto-Nazi militias that helped prepare the ground for Hitler's rise.[69] But the othering "normally" goes just far enough to define a contrasting identity against which the male can define himself. Because the male identity requires this foil, the stereotypical counter-identity assigned to woman must be figured as a working part of the male identity. This is clear to see in the prominence of women activists, commentators, and politicians in far-right circles, in the United States, beginning with Anita Bryant and Phyllis Schlafley in the 1970s and 1980s, and now diversified into a large and growing contingent of figures too numerous to list. Women's leadership may be accepted by men as a complementary power for upholding traditional male dominance.

As Kathleen Blee's ethnographic studies of women in the contemporary white supremacy movement and her historical studies of its twentieth-century antecedents show, women have always been accorded a role in organizations like the Ku Klux Klan and neo-Nazi groupings (less so among far-right militias and skinheads).[70] Their roles have been for the most part subordinate. But Blee notes a change in the degree to which women can hold influence within violent extremist movements since the 1990s, presumably due to unacknowledged flow-over from feminism causing the prevailing cultural norms to bend somewhat under pressure. The Trump era has been characterized by a proliferation of high-profile women influencers in right-wing media

---

69   Klaus Theweleit, *Male Fantasies*, vol. 1, *Women Floods Bodies History* (Minneapolis: University of Minnesota Press, 1987).

70   Blee, *Inside Organized Racism*; Blee, *Women of the Klan*.

and of women politicians following in the footsteps of Sarah Palin, but staking out more extreme positions than Palin's, short of violent far-right extremism but in resonance with it (examples are commentators Kellyanne Conway and Laura Ingraham, Congresswoman Marjorie Taylor Greene, and Governor Kristi Noem). These right-wing women leaders embody one of the oscillations discussed here. Their femininity does not preclude a kind of advocacy, leadership, and high-power career building that is stereotypically associated with men. These female leaders actively complement men's power, working beside them in the cause of preserving traditional gender roles and defending whiteness.

Robyn Marasco notes a third figure, beyond the figures of abject counter-identity and powerful but still-subservient complementarity. The high-power professional influencers and politicians just mentioned verge on it to varying degrees. It is best modeled for Marasco in female MAGA and QAnon devotees who consciously go about acting like "one of the guys," sidling male stereotypes in order to "gain access to the pleasure of 'masculine' affect and agency." This third figure is that of the infiltrator. "We shake hands like men." Marasco takes Ashli Babbitt, the militarist Trump supporter killed by police during the January 6 insurrection at the US Capitol, as the prime example. Figures in this mold do not embody traditional feminism, she asserts. "If the 'Ultra-Right' . . . had once promised white women the security and safety of patriarchal domesticity, today it offers something else, something more immediately transgressive, more responsive to destructive impulses and antisocial forces, and more proximate to the equality that it rejects and the freedom it renounces. It offers white women an account of their unhappiness and an affective arena to express their rage." This "'female antifeminism' takes shape in reactionary opposition to the interests of Black women, lesbian women, trans women, poor women" and operates "as a vector of fascisation."[71] Its "fantasy" of "access to homosocial intimacy and its secrets" might be considered a form of "hybrid femininity" that remains in the masculinist orbit while transgressing masculinism's norms in their name, upholding them more muscularly than

---

71 Robyn Marasco, "Reconsidering the Sexual Politics of Fascism," historicalmaterialism.org, June 25, 2021.

women have conventionally been allowed to do (hybrid masculinity is discussed in note 58 above).

Whether women are ex-included as a constitutive counter-identity, subserviently included as a complementary power, or endeavor to infiltrate the brotherhood for the fatherland in the service of reaction, they are working parts of the masculinist machine.

This entails the provocative proposition that, with respect to normative and normopathic configurations of the huMan, *there is only one gender*. The historical use of the masculine personal pronoun for all persons and the standard designator "Man" for all humans is indication enough.[72] "Man," as Deleuze and Guattari argue, is a consolidated compound. In its traditional baseline form, it is a structural hierarchy of positions defined oppositionally, which is to say at least as much in terms of the qualities they must expel from themselves as those they claim. The hierarchy extends past gender, to race, age of minority, and animality. There are transversal connections among the subordinate terms that create avenues for associational slippage. The woman can slip into being infantilized and treated as a minor, the Black denigrated as animalistic.[73] The hierarchy, along this slippery slope, is a graded ladder of deviations from the preeminent term of the Man-Standard, or Standard Man: more or less "affluent white male European speaking a major language."[74] The Man-Standard is whiteness in person: the supposedly neutral default

72   Ursula Le Guin wryly plays on the one gender of Man when she declares herself a man because "women are a very recent invention." "Introducing Myself," in *The Wave in the Mind: Talks and Essays on the Writer, the Reader, and the Imagination* (Boulder, CO: Shambhala, 2004), 3.

73   Zakiyya Iman Jackson notes the appropriative inclusion of denigrated blackness in the figure of Man, even as it slips toward other categories: "I reinterpret Enlightenment thought not as black 'exclusion' or 'denied humanity' but rather as the violent imposition and appropriation—inclusion and recognition—of black(ened) humanity in the interest of plasticizing that very humanity, whereby 'the animal' is one but not the only form blackness is thought to encompass." Jackson, *Becoming Human: Matter and Meaning in an Antiblack World* (New York: New York University Press, 2020), 3.

74   Gilles Deleuze and Félix Guattari, *A Thousand Plateaus*, trans. Brian Massumi (Minneapolis: University of Minnesota Press, 1987), 105–6, 178, 292–93, 554n82. See also Massumi, *A User's Guide to "Capitalism and Schizophrenia": Deviations from Deleuze and Guattari* (Cambridge, MA: MIT Press, 1992). For an allied approach to

position of the human that doesn't have to say its name because it is the assumed universal and contains all human variation as a deviation from its standard. The failure on the part of a man to embody the standard steadfastly enough releases a pull that threatens to drag the preeminent term of man downward through the series, polluting him with an odor of the abjection tainting the subordinate terms. The need for a constant effort to defend the purity and "honor" of the Standard and maintain its supposed neutrality is endemic to its structure. This dynamic remains in play across the oscillations and vicissitudes of the Man-Standard.

Avenues of real resistance, beyond the figure of reactionary infiltration that ultimately only reconfirms the masculinist structure mimetically, are likewise endemic and remain in play. A subordinate term can declare its independence from the hierarchy, in a move to collectively affirm and revalue itself. Here again, there is a tendency toward slippage. There is a self-defensive myopia built into the Man-Standard: an inability to perceive past its own constitutive categories. Each of its subordinate terms is in fact brimming with further differentiations to which the Man-Standard is constitutionally insensible. These differences begin to come out from under, toward the expression of their own difference. A cascade of differencings ensues, fractalizing the structure (with the fractalization denoted, for example, by the "+" in LBGTQ+, which stands as an open invitation for further differentiation, signaled by the addition of other initials, such as "2S" and "I"). The one gender of Man is queered (not hybridized) into a proliferation of genderings— or, more broadly, engenderings, emergent modes of life.[75] An analogous process affects other categories, as what from on high seemed to be an identity reveals itself to be a field of differences. Black, for example, is no longer one thing, but many, proliferating into a multiplicity of lines of intersecting distinctions such as class, gender, sexual orientation, national origin or geopolitical background, descent from an enslaved or unenslaved family, and possibility of passing.

---

whiteness as empty normative standard, working from Fred Moten and Stefano Harney among others, see Manning, *For a Pragmatics of the Useless*, 55–73.

75 Erin Manning, *Politics of Touch: Sense, Movement, Sovereignty* (Minneapolis: University of Minnesota Press, 2007), 84–109.

The "intersectionality" of the transversal connections between positions complicates to the point where the *structure* becomes an indefinite *field* of differentiation, with as many unassignable transitions and nonlocal linkages between terms as positions that can be separately identified. Every identity teems with a multiplicity of potential differences pressuring for expression, clamoring to affirm themselves in their singularity. What was a structure of beings resolves itself into a proliferation of lines of becoming. The downward pull away from the Man-Standard has become a cascade of self-affirming escape routes out of it.[76] The affirmations do not simply accumulate into a larger set. A classical set subsumes a countable population of well-defined elements, divided into sub-identities. Here, a change of nature occurs en route. *Becomings* unsubordinated, refractory to the structure of identity, ensue. No sooner are they felt than a tendency to re-corral them into their own identity categories also ensues, reterritorializing the becoming. This creates a recognized political constituency that can advocate for itself. But it also risks backfiring, in effect expanding the Man-Standard through the addition of sub-categories that may act, in what they perceive to be their own interests, to dam the cascade of differencings, turning against engenderings further down the line in ways that reconverge with the imperatives of the Man-Standard (trans-phobic feminism being a prominent contemporary example).

Becoming-Away from Man

The limit toward which the structure runs away from itself with differencings constitutes not a classical set but a *fuzzy set*: a singularly nondenumerable multiplicity of qualitative variations. This nondenumerable multiplicity of correlative becomings is the non-identitarian figure of

---

76   This is the context for Deleuze and Guattari's apparent designation of a hierarchy of becomings in the "Becoming-Imperceptible" chapter of A *Thousand Plateaus.* "Becoming-woman"—which they understand as escaping the norms of Man *and* woman—"comes first" in the sense that they consider it the most accessible escape hatch simply by virtue of its proximity to the apex of the Man-Standard. There is in fact no a priori order of becomings. A *Thousand Plateaus* is full of examples of escapes that move directly to a becoming-animal, a becoming-mineral, or a becoming-imperceptible, among many others.

the "minor" in Deleuze and Guattari's thinking, suggestively articulable with the "blackness" of Harney and Moten's "undercommons."[77] Any identity, no matter how oppositional to Man, remains within its orbit to the precise extent to which it assents to be an identity. For the normative Man-Standard of whiteness is the metaphysical model and historical genealogy of identity. Identity is the signature invention of Europe, a necessary correlate of its invention of race that underwrote its colonial expansion and the rise of capitalism.[78] The minor, in Édouard Glissant's words taken up by Moten, "consents *not* to be a single being."[79] In so consenting-not, it becomes a field-being; a being fielded, uncountably and unaccountably (beyond the norm, toward a revaluation of values).[80]

Both the normative/normopathic structure of the Man-Standard and the becoming-away from it that is tendentially built in, in resistance to it, are presupposed by the Trumpian media figure of ornamental masculinity.

In ornamental masculinity, the classic hierarchy of values enshrined in the Man-Standard remains in force, functioning as a compass for its default directions. What ornamental masculinity enables is for normative ends also to be achieved by non-normative (normopathic) means, dancing with license around the figure of upright masculinity

77 On the concept of the minor, which for Deleuze and Guattari designates a qualitative difference and not simply a numerical count, see Gilles Deleuze and Félix Guattari, *Kafka: Toward a Minor Literature*, trans. Dana Polan (Minneapolis: University of Minnesota Press, 1986); and Deleuze and Guattari, *Thousand Plateaus*, 105–6, 291–92, 456, 469–73. On the concept of the undercommons, see Stefano Harney and Fred Moten, *The Undercommons: Fugitive Planning and Black Study* (London: Minor Compositions, 2013).

78 Sylvia Wynter analyzes the genealogy of the European "mono-humanism" of "Man" in its intimate relation to the consolidation of capitalism through colonization and the slave trade ("Man2," or *Homo oeconimicus*; related to "human capital" as discussed later in this essay). Sylvia Wynter, *Sylvia Wynter: On Being Human as Praxis*, ed. Katherine McKittrick (Durham, NC: Duke University Press, 2015). See also Denise Ferreira da Silva, "Towards a Black Feminist Poethics," *Black Scholar* 44, no. 2 (2015): 81–97. See also the "Identity" section in the postscript.

79 Manthia Diawara and Édouard Glissant, "Conversation with Édouard Glissant Aboard the Queen Mary II," August 2009, https://www.liverpool.ac.uk/; Fred Moten, *Consent Not to Be a Single Being*, vol. 1, *Black and Blur* (Durham, NC: Duke University Press, 2017).

80 On whiteness, and blackness in its relation to neurodiversity as a creative escape from the norm of whiteness, see Manning, *For a Pragmatics of the Useless*.

traditionally embodying Standard universal Man. It is true that the universality of Standard Man falls on hard times, as particularism takes the upper hand: MAGA (Make America Great Again). But this is only an apparent contradiction, since Great America is a nationalist standard of value that is universally applied with masculine muscularity to all nations, under the ultimatum to buckle down and conform to its interests and example, or be ascribed enemy status. Anything smacking of a universalism that recognizes extra-American diversity is excoriated as an avatar of the anti-American "globalist" agenda. In the face of the Great American oxymoron of nationalist-particularist universalism (which also goes by the name of American exceptionalism), supra-national humanitarian ideals and human rights become a tool subordinate identities use to defend themselves, shield the differences they harbor, and fight for survival. From the MAGA perspective, they are the tool of the enemy.

But something else is also afoot. Ascribe its enemies as it will, domestically and abroad, the Man-Standard cannot change the situation that beyond every specifiable enemy lies a limit, a horizon at which the Man-Standard's single being is effectively, existentially threatened. The figure of the unspecified enemy marks that limit. But in the movement of becomings-minor toward the horizon, the figure of the unspecified enemy flips. It refigures itself as a nondenumerable multiplicity of engenderings, affirming themselves. This multiplicity is everywhere in potential, but it is not universal in any usual sense. Neither it is particularist, but rather everywhere singular (multiply so), in a sense of the "singular" opposed to "single" being which will be developed throughout this treatise.

This is way of formulating in positive terms what Trumpism and allied tendencies experience as a horror and a nightmare, and fear more than death. *The enemy, ultimately, is the revaluation of values toward which becomings-minor move.*

Freedom

The Trumpian desire is to stamp out the becoming, plug the escape routes, silence the expression of proliferating differencings, and strike their self-affirming expression with negativity. It is to do so while ex-

1.4 Photo by Betto Rodrigues / Shutterstock.

tending the white privilege erected and defended by the Man-Standard to include the liberating right to whine one's single being: to act out one's personal grievances as self-indulgently, chaotically, pettily, and petulantly as one normopathically pleases. The structure of the Man-Standard must be reconfigured to allow men to arrogate to themselves some of the qualities formerly othered and expelled from it in the Man-Standard's former incarnation as upright normative figure of masculine virtue (qualities classically ex-included in it as characterizing its subordinate subidentities). The notion of freedom embraced by post-normative man has a childishness as well as a femininity to it. "I *won't* wear my mask" is what the five-year-old's "I *won't* wear my mittens" is when it grows up. One of the most popular caricatures of Trump was the Trump Baby Blimp floated to great effect during his London visit in 2018.[81] It is almost too easy to caricature Trump. His masculinity is already a caricature of itself. A self-knockoff.

81 Associated Press, "Trump Baby Balloon Enters Museum of London Collection," January 18, 2021, https://www.nbcnews.com/news/world/trump-baby-blimp -enters-museum-london-collection-n1254594.

The post-normativity of the nondenumerable field-being of the minor in the Deleuze-Guattarian sense accompanies its adversary, the post-normativity of Trumpian persons. In a way, it springs from the same source: both are enabled by the deregulations and deterritorializations of present-day capitalism. In a sense, they are processual correlates. However, the minor mode is completely different in its processual valence. It moves in entirely different ethical directions. It activates a counter-tendency affirming the transindividuality of qualitative differentiation over the more-of-the-same of purportedly individual identity and its constitutive subordinations. It haunts identity with its unencapsulatable difference, suggesting an alternative figure of freedom.

This is the figure of emergent *free variations* arising in a field of relation as a surplus-value of complexity. Free variations cease to define themselves vis-à-vis existing categories. Deleuze and Guattari mark this difference by calling them "inherent variations."[82] A recent example is the move on the part of autistics, affirming their neurodiversity against the norm of the neurotypical Man-Standard, to also affirm themselves as nongendered: from genderings diversifying the one gender of Man in an intersectional matrix, to the engendering of a new singular figure (which at the same time falls on a spectrum: singular-multiple).[83]

Deciding in the Exception

The license conferred upon Trump supporters is a reciprocal of the license the post-normative leader takes for himself. It dispenses the leader of the need to legitimate his actions as head of state. The range of actions taken on an exceptional basis broadened under Trump's 2017–2021 tenure, extending the reach of rule by decree. Legislative initiative was kept to a minimum, replaced by unilateral executive actions, administrative rule-changes imposed without meaningful public or ex-

82 Deleuze and Guattari, *Thousand Plateaus*, 93.
83 On autism, neurodiversity, and queerness, see Melanie (Remi) Yergeau, *Authoring Autism: On Rhetoric and Neurological Queerness* (Durham, NC: Duke University Press, 2018). For an affirmative account of "autistic perception" see Erin Manning, *The Minor Gesture* (Durham, NC: Duke University Press, 2016), 174–88.

pert consultation, muzzling of scientific expertise, and sidestepping of congressional confirmation of key administrative posts by indefinitely prolonged acting appointments, among many other mechanisms.

"The sovereign is he who decides on the exception."[84] Schmitt's formula still holds, but with revisions. There is no longer a need to decide "on" the exception. The state of exception has become the base state. The law doesn't need to be suspended by the exception. It is already riddled with holes that exception can slip into or ooze out of, not only through the ad hoc practices such as those just alluded to, but through more permanent affordances cut out into the fabric of the law by the post-9/11 security apparatus.[85] Now, sovereign is he who decides "in" the exception. And the person of Trump is all in.

Trump got where he is by systematically making exceptions for himself, and of himself, in true post-normative style. The media figure that is his person is defined by the exception. Translated historically, this is another way of saying extreme "white privilege." The sovereign is he to whom the rules do not apply, because he is a "free" individual (a post-normative embodiment of the Man-Standard or Standard Man that is whiteness). This is nowhere more concisely conveyed than in Trump's incomprehension at facing consequences for his incitement of the storming of the Capitol, and in the surprised outrage of his supporters who were arrested for it. It was clear that it never to occurred to them that attempting to violently overturn an election, threatening legislators with death, and trashing a government building was not their birthright, and might land them in a bit of trouble with the law. Some police officers seemed to agree and effectively gave them free rein, some even opening doors for the rioters, giving them directions inside the building, and taking selfies with them. It seems to have slipped their minds to detain them. Muscled law enforcement and heavy-handed police action is for Black Lives Matters protesters and antifa, not white "patriots" in tactical military gear and caveman pelts. It was only in a second phase, following the outcry the January 6 insurrection raised, that the law stepped in, eventually making over a thousand arrests on a

84 Schmitt, *Political Theology*, 5.

85 Massumi, *Ontopower*, 16, 18–19, 53–54.

variety of charges ranging in seriousness from misdemeanor trespassing to felony sedition.

The kind of exceptional political practices Trump favored while in office have been characterized as "weak" because many are of the kind that can be overturned by the next occupant of the White House (and many were by President Biden).[86] But this misses the Trumpian modus operandi: the wielding of exception from the executive office in tandem with the dissemination of personalized exceptionalism throughout society, with the explicit intent of creating the conditions for an overturning of the democratic apparatus of government. Where this became most explicit during the Trump saga was in December 2022, when he called for the "termination" of the US Constitution as well as "all other rules, regulations, and articles," on the same disproven grounds on which he called on his supporters to besiege the Capitol: that the 2020 election was riddled with "fraud."[87]

Trumpian politics, at its most passionate and aspirational, does not aim for a takeover of the apparatus of government as it currently exists. It militates for its sidelining in favor of a state of unfettered exception

86   In an interview published before the January 6 insurrection, Corey Robin takes the position that fascism does not apply to Trump because of his "ineffectiveness" (his ignorance of and disinterest in the level of detailed governmental control). Robin's definition of fascism emphasizes the effective autocratic control of the strongman leader over the institutions of government in disregard of the constitutional order. His objections raise two important issues that have been at issue in this essay: to what extent our ideas of what constitutes fascism have to be revised in the context of the contemporary social media landscape, in particular the shift it brings in the nature of power, public figures, and persons; and what defining characteristics enable a given formation to be classified as fascist. Both issues are dealt with at length in the present work. The strategy pursued here in relation to the second issue is to question the very nature of classificatory logic, suggesting an alternative logic that eschews traditional typological approaches (see, in particular, the "Adequate Ideas" and "Uses and Abuses of the General" sections in part 5 and the postscript). David Klion and Corey Robin, "Almost the Complete Opposite of Fascism: Interview with Corey Robin," *Jewish Currents*, December 4, 2020, https://jewishcurrents.org/almost-the -complete-opposite-of-fascism.

87   Kristen Holmes, "Trump Calls for the Termination of the Constitution in Truth Social Post," CNN, December 4, 2022, https://www.cnn.com/2022/12/03/politics /trump-constitution-truth-social/index.html.

making the country maximally safe for sovereign decision. But since such a state of exception would be at the mercy of preeminent persons' quasi-chaotic decisional agitations in potentially unsettling ways, a stabilizing settlement with the machinery of government would likely arise. The result might be a coalescence of statist and anti-government tendencies in a compromise formation in which a maximum of sovereign decision inspirits the repressive machinery of a maximalist government through holes of exception (maximalist at least with respect to the state's social-order functions, if not necessarily with respect to the deregulated economy). The Heritage Foundation's infamous blueprint for a second Trump presidency, Project 2025, moves decisively in this direction.[88] The "project" is to institutionalize a permanent expansion of the decisional powers of the presidency, among other ways by abolishing the independence of the Justice Department and placing the regulatory agencies under direct presidential political control, in keeping with the doctrine of the "unitary executive."[89] The plan formalizes the outs into exception already riddling governance, writing them into the structure of the state. The project is to put the state itself in the permanent service of the state of exception. Preparing the ground are two Supreme Court decisions granting the president basically unlimited criminal immunity (the appropriately named *Trump v. United States*, 2024) and severely limiting the purview of the administrative state to formulate regulations, opening the way for the executive branch to exploit powers of exception to shred existing regulations in such areas as the environment, health, education, and housing, in the service of neoliberal capitalism's wet dream of even more far-reaching economic deregulation (*Loper Bright Enterprises v. Raimondo* and *Relentless v. Department of Commerce*, both 2024). Project 2025 would refashion American government as a fascisizing "illiberal democracy," not unlike Orbán's Hungary or Erdoğan's Turkey. It would yield an autocratic state formation an enormous step closer to something resembling the classic

---

88 Paul Dans and Steven Grove, eds., *Mandate for Leadership: The Conservative Promise*, Project 2025, Presidential Transition Project (Washington, DC: Heritage Foundation, 2023), https://static.project2025.org/2025_MandateForLeadership_FULL.pdf.

89 Steven G. Calabresi and Christopher S. Yoo, *The Unitary Executive: Presidential Power from Washington to Bush* (New Haven, CT: Yale University Press, 2008).

twentieth-century fascisms in Italy, Spain, and Germany. Were it to reach that point, the fascisizing tendencies flowing through Trumpism would have issued into a twenty-first-century version of full-fledged fascism (of which there is an open-ended variety of potential versionings; see the "Fascism Proper" and "Ur-Fascism" sections of part 5 for more on this variability and the attendant pitfalls of typology, particularly if it is overly wed to historical precedent).

Fringe Fluidity

The individualism of the Trumpian tendency in politics does not contradict the transindividuality that, it was argued earlier, characterizes Schmittian decision. In the model of charismatic leadership, the identification with the preeminent individual is an irrational cathexis that sows delusional beliefs among the "masses," duped into acting against their own interests. It is tempting to apply this analysis to the present post-truth, post-deliberative situation, and to include among the delusions individuals' belief that they are acting as the self-sovereign individuals they take themselves to be. Charismatic leadership is the most immediately accessible and widespread model to explain the political effectiveness of figures like Trump. In one version or another, it undergirds most critiques, popular and academic.[90]

90 The theory of charismatic leadership was introduced into sociology by Max
    Weber in The Theory of Social and Economic Organization, trans. A. M. Henderson
    and Talcott Parsons, ed. and with an introduction by Talcott Parsons (1920;
    repr., Glencoe, IL: Free Press / Falcon's Wing, 1947), 358–407. It has been widely
    applied to fascism in both scholarly and lay political thinking, to such an extent
    that it has long been the "natural" default position. Hannah Arendt already
    called its usefulness into question for understanding the totalitarian leader
    in The Origins of Totalitarianism (1951; repr., New York: Harcourt Brace, 1973),
    362–63. It is rejected here as a guiding concept both because of the traditional
    concept of personhood it assumes and because of the classical classificatory
    logic it mobilizes (Weber's methodology of "ideal types"). Theodor Adorno
    wrote a foundational essay, published the same year as The Origins of Totalitarianism, exploring the paradigm of charismatic leadership in relation to fascism.
    It is a classic statement of the political doctrine of identification through a
    transference relation to the leader as father figure. In places, it suggestively

But there are problems with transferring a model tailored to early to mid-twentieth-century populism and fascism to the present situation, with its transformed communicational milieu and the concomitant mutations capitalism has undergone in its turn toward neoliberalism. For one thing, the figure of the "masses" no longer exists.

The masses have been replaced with "communicational silos" or "social bubbles": a quasi-chaos of quickly forming, frequently reconfiguring, and occasionally metastasizing micro-milieus lacking centralized control. The social landscape is less a "mass," a formless magma, than a boundless basin of sand dunes rolling in the winds of social media, taking emergent shape. The shapes that serially emerge are analogous to one another, but prove on closer inspection to be unique and ever-shifting—though it is as difficult to catch them in the shape-shifting act as it is to see the clouds changing. The outer reaches of the social media basin exhibits "fringe fluidity."[91] This is a term originating in security studies that has also been applied to media phenomena such as QAnon. But QAnon has become majoritarian among Trump supporters. Where is the "fringe" of a boundless basin? What is a majority fringe? In the social media desert, the fringe is potentially any number, anywhere, and everywhere. What becomes of the bell curve of the "normal" distribution when it can be so quickly displaced in a gust of tweets? The top of the curve and its extremes start to flicker over one another, like an unstable sine wave jumping in place.

complicates this paradigm in ways that contain some tentative openings toward the approach developed here. For example, Adorno speaks of the "performance of identification rather than psychologically constitutive, true identification" and refers to "techniques of personalization." What distinguishes the present account, of course, is the rejection of the idea of "true identification," leaving only performative techniques of personalization. Theodor W. Adorno, "Freudian Theory and the Pattern of Fascist Propaganda," in *Psychoanalysis and the Social Sciences*, ed. Géza Róheim (Madison, CT: International Universities Press, 1951), 3:279–300.

91 Daveed Gartenstein-Ross and Madeleine Blackman, "Fluidity of the Fringes: Prior Extremist Involvement as a Radicalization Pathway," *Studies in Conflict and Terrorism* 45, no. 7 (2018): 555–78. Fringe fluidity and QAnon: Drew Harwell, "QAnon Believers Seek to Adapt Their Extremist Ideology for a New Era: 'Things Have Just Started,'" *Washington Post*, January 21, 2021, https://www .washingtonpost.com/technology/2021/01/21/qanon-faithful-biden-trump.

QAnon followers were drawn from the most "whitebread" American-heartland segments of the population (the soccer mom turned cannibal-demon hunter—second coming of Buffy the Vampire Slayer?). When a traditional norm reasserts itself and imposes standard criteria against which individuals and identities are systematically judged, it is through a fixation of this fluidity that is painstakingly constructed, energetically imposed, and precariously poised. On the right, this reining back in is the mission of the moralistic Christian right (so disparaged by more extreme, avowedly post-normative, right-wing groupings such as the Boogaloo Bois).

This mode, in which normative structuring is extracted from prevailing wind conditions of fluctuation, rather than already pre-operating as a foundational ground which then may shift, has to do with what Foucault referred to as "normalization," as opposed to "normation," in which the norm is pregiven.[92]

The masses are homogeneous; the post-truth body politic is granular. The masses are unifocal and single-minded; the post-truth body politic practices distributed attention, flitting and fickle. The masses are structurally orchestrated; the post-truth body politic is dynamically correlated as an ongoing analogical effect of a shared immersion in the winds of the weather system that is social media and the larger threat environment buffeting it.

It may well be true that Trump supporters in the middle and lower socioeconomic brackets (which comprise a smaller portion of his base than often imagined) are voting against their own economic interests. But if what motivates is no longer the calculation of interest, but rather, an affective appetite or *desire*, then interest is moved more than it is the mover.[93] This means that however estranged from the verifiably true people's thinking may be, however fabulist they have become in their embrace of alterna-

92   Michel Foucault, *Security, Territory, Population: Lectures at the Collège de France, 1977–1978*, ed. Michel Snellart, trans. Graham Burchell (New York: Palgrave Macmillan, 2007).

93   "Interest always follows and appears wherever desire places it . . . in a way that is deeper and more diffuse than one's interest." Gilles Deleuze in Gilles Deleuze and Michel Foucault, "Intellectuals and Power," in *Desert Islands and Other Texts 1953–1974*, ed. David Lapoujade, trans. Michael Teomina (New York: Semiotext(e), 2004), 212.

tive facts, it is not accurate to call them deluded. However far from the truth their desire leads them, they truly desire to go there. *What is more important is not the falsehood of their beliefs, but rather that their actions are the truth of their desire.* "Desire" here is meant in Deleuze and Guattari's "machinic" sense.

Rallying Affect

To get a sense of what "machinic" means here, it is necessary to think through the relation between the evident transindividuality of a media figure's mode of operation and the equally undeniable individualism of many of its expressions. What is the relation between these aspects, if it is not simply the delusional substitution of one for the other? How do they work together? How are they joined in process?

It is clear that Trump the person does not exist separately from his persona. The man needs outside completion. In office as president, he continued to hold rallies in campaign style, ignoring the cardinal rule of traditional politics that the process of attaining power is different from the process of wielding it. He is palpably dependent on the adulation of the crowd to validate him and spur him on, as if feeding vampirically on their affective energies, and they on his. In his everyday life, he surrounds himself with adulators and worshipful aides. Even post-presidency in his Mar-a-Lago retreat, he does not lift a finger for himself, not even to post on social media, being entirely dependent on the ever-ready army of toadying aides surrounding him at every step. Actually, he does lift a finger, but only to royally summon a helper (whose role would better be described as existence-supplements than assistants, so necessary is their completion of his person).[94]

---

94 A *Washington Post* investigative team reported on Trump's post-presidency life-style, based on confidential native-informant interviews with Mar-a-Lago regulars. "By evening, Trump emerges for dinner, surrounded most nights by adoring club members who stand and applaud at his appearance; they stand and applaud again after he finishes his meal and retires for the night. He often orders special meals from the kitchen and spends time curating the music wafting over the crowd, frequently pushing for the volume to be raised or lowered based on his mood. In the Oval Office, Trump had a button he could push to summon an aide

In his public role, Trump is a converter. He absorbs the energy of the crowd and returns it to them in a circuit, amplified. The rally is an affective resonator machine amplifying affective agitation and channeling it toward the ascription of a common enemy, actualized through hate, derision, and alternative facts. The Trump-converter is now the point of ascription through which the virtual polarity of the friend/enemy distinction is given empirical content. Electoral success, for Trump and his acolytes in the Republican Party, is a product of this process. The centrality of the ascription of the enemy qualifies the rally assemblage as the expression of a war machine. That ascription cycles through the stations on the spectrum of the unspecified enemy, orbiting around and systematically returning to the immigrant as "poisoning the blood" of the nation and the African American as race enemy, through unmistakable dog whistles when not through direct expressions. One infamous example was the solace he provided, in the face of vocal condemnation, to participants in the white supremacist / neo-Nazi Unite the Right rally in Charlottesville. Trump assured the nation that "there are very fine people on both sides." Except that in the same statement he actually blamed everything on what he saw as egregious behavior on the part of the anti-racist left—effectively leaving only one side with fine people on it.[95]

This enemy-rallying is the most strenuous and sustained in-person work that Trump undertook as president: working the crowd to help

---

to bring him a Diet Coke or snacks. Now, he just yells out commands to whichever employee is in earshot." His main aide, Natalie Harp, "is rarely absent from his side. She is said to cater attentively to his need for constant praise. . . . She often perches herself right outside his office, two advisers said, and follows Trump around all day, including on the golf course. 'She is indicative of the people around him who just love him,' the adviser said. 'Love him too much.'" In relation to the post-normative, another informant stated that "there are no protocols." Said another: "It's like a Barbie Dream House miniature" (realer than real). Rosalind S. Helderman, Josh Dawsey, Ashley Parker, and Jacqueline Alemany, "How Trump Jettisoned Restraints at Mar-a-Lago and Prompted Legal Peril," *Washington Post*, December 18, 2022, https://www.washingtonpost.com /national-security/2022/12/18/trump-life-after-presidency.

95 Donald J. Trump, "Full Text: Trump's Comments on White Supremacists, 'Alt-Left' in Charlottesville," *Politico*, August 15, 2017, https://www.politico.com/story/2017/08 /15/full-text-trump-comments-white-supremacists-alt-left-transcript-241662.

create conditions under which killing and dying became a "real possibility." Much footwork for this, of course had already been done by decades of Republican intransigence, white supremacist agitating, and right-wing militia organizing. One of the places it came to fruition around Trump was at the Unite the Right rally, which occurred during his first year in office, when a woman was killed by a driver intentionally plowing his vehicle into the crowd of anti-racist counter-protestors. This car attack became a model: dozens of such attacks were perpetrated during the height of the Black Lives Matters demonstrations in 2020. Some Republican states have given the practice license by passing new laws limiting drivers' criminal liability in such cases. The entire Trump period was also punctuated with so-called lone wolf attacks fomented by white supremacist rhetoric, from Dylan Roof's attack on a Black church in Charleston during the 2015–16 presidential campaign to the 2019 El Paso Walmart shooting targeting Mexican Americans in the lead-up to the 2020 campaign. These attacks took place against the continuous background of police shootings of unarmed Black men.

With the storming of Capitol Hill, the compass needle of violence swung around toward the region of the unspecified-enemy spectrum occupied by the "deep state" as personified by government figures. In a turning point, momentarily apostate Trump allies among Republicans (Mitch McConnell and Lindsay Graham), as well as the more usual Democratic suspects (Nancy Pelosi and Alexandria Ocasio-Cortez), were targeted. Trump supporters planned their kidnapping and clamored for their execution for their sin of standing in the way of Trump's ascension to the exceptional position of president for life, a desire later reflected in Trump's comment about terminating the Constitution. This was a tipping point toward the right-wing extreme, helmed by the Proud Boys and Oath Keepers, as it flirted with bifurcating from electoral politics and began consolidating around the trope of civil war. Trump's failure to follow through with his supporters' fantasy of his declaring martial law to stay in power at that time, along with his half-hearted denunciation of the siege (obviously scripted by his dwindling advisers and long since recanted), prompted some diehard supporters to abandon him and move closer toward the limit of fluid micro-fascism—feral fascism unhinged from central channeling, structural stabilizers, and institutional mechanisms of capture.[96] Other segments of the pro-Trump population began contemplating abandoning the Republican Party in favor of a populist breakaway "MAGA Party" or "Patriots Party" rallying around what they hoped would be a resurgent Trump.[97] Trump himself quickly pivoted from this possibility when the serially amnesiac Republican leadership once again forgot their reticence about him and came knocking on the door of his Mar-a-Lago estate to plan for the next legislative elections, for a Republican Party reunited under Trump.

Trump's temporarily declining fortunes after the 2022 midterm election frayed that unity, presenting him with competitors from within his own party for the 2024 presidential nomination that were initially welcomed by a segment of his supporters. His fortunes soon turned around, in no small part in sympathetic reaction against the raft of criminal and civil grand jury investigations and prosecutions against him for sexual abuse, election meddling, financial fraud, and official document mishandling (not exactly the morally upright male role model . . .). It is a sign of the lasting effect of the inflection point Trump effected, and the forces he unleashed, that outright criticism by fellow Republicans of Trump or his "stolen election" refrain continued through all of this, even at his most trying moments, to be considered tantamount to political suicide.

Conditions for War

The moment of institutional unhinging glimpsed in the aftermath of the Capitol storming is the becoming-palpable of a bifurcation point. It was the point at which the conditions for fascist civil war were most fully actualized in the long march of the right-wing wave that began around the election of Ronald Reagan in 1979 and has been building ever since.

96 Sheera Frenkel and Alan Feuer, "'A Total Failure': The Proud Boys Now Mock Trump,'" *New York Times*, January 20, 2021, https://www.nytimes.com/2021/01/20 /technology/proud-boys-trump.html.

97 Jack Dawsey and Michael Scherer, "Trump Jumps into a Divisive Battle over the Republican Party—with a Threat to Start a 'MAGA Party,'" *Washington Post*, January 23, 2021, https://www.washingtonpost.com/politics/trump-republican-split /2021/01/23/d7dc253e-5cbc-11eb-8bcf-3877871c819d_story.html.

Proto-fascist tendencies are now more than just emergent, but are incipiently convergent toward a full-fledged fascist movement. It still may well stall, but there is no question that gears were set in motion. When Obama gained power, he immediately dismantled the grassroots electoral movement that had rallied behind him, folding everything back into the institutional sphere of government, to the chagrin of hopeful progressives. Trump's refusal to differentiate the process of gaining power from the process of wielding it kept his actions as president in the sphere of movement, priming it to continue into the post-presidency, and accompanied by the ever-present real possibility of a veer in the direction of fascism.

"Movement," it should be recalled, is how Schmitt characterized the sphere of decision. When Trumpian movement threatens to accompany him in an escape from the two-party system as it has been institutionalized in American politics, decision is on the cusp of going feral. If it spins off from Trump's orbit to follow its own momentum, it can take the virulently self-disseminating, quasi-chaotically distributed form that Deleuze and Guattari defined as *micro-fascism*.[98] This is fascist movement decoupled from the maximalist state apparatus around which it orbits and into which it always tends to flow in the end, and temporarily discharged from fealty to the preeminence of a central authoritarian head of state apt to recapture its runaway movement and divert it to his own purposes (macro-fascism). (For more on micro-fascism, see the "Micro-fascisms" section of part 5.)

Free Indirect Discourse

The "machinic" nature of the process described here might be easy to dismiss as merely metaphorical, until the machinations of social media are factored in. The most sustained and time-consuming

---

98 Félix Guattari, "The Micro-politics of Fascism," in *Molecular Revolution: Psychiatry and Politics*, trans. Rosemary Sheed (New York: Penguin, 1984); Deleuze and Guattari, *Thousand Plateaus*, 255–58, 343–51; Félix Guattari, "Everybody Wants to Be a Fascist," in *Chaosophy* (New York: Semiotexte, 1995), 245; Gary Genosko, "Black Holes of Politics: Resonances of Microfascism," *La Deleuziana*, no. 5 (2017), http://www.ladeleuziana.org/wp-content/uploads/2017/12/04-en -Genosko-Resonance_MicroFascism.pdf.

off-the-rally-circuit work Trump performed in office was watching cable TV, calling in to Fox News shows, and tweeting up a storm, at the rate of at least a thousand tweets a month. Rallies are punctual. The tweet storm was continuous. It consumed up to eight hours a day of his presidential schedule, showing up on his official agenda as "executive time."[99] Executive time: decision time. Decision diffused into the media, like a bloodstain through porous fabric.

Trump's relationship to TV and social media formed what is often called an "echo chamber." He would routinely repeat in his tweets phrases he had heard on Fox News, often within minutes of their utterance.[100] His 87 million followers were regularly treated to memes culled from right-wing social media, including at times from its white supremacist fringes. In return, Fox News would faithfully parrot his statements, treating his most throwaway comments with the gravitas normally due presidential addresses. The right-wing social media would light up around his words.

The impact of his tweets was boosted by industrial-scale bulk retweeting. His tweets "spread in an odd pattern." One investigation found that "more than half the 3,000 accounts retweeting Trump did so in near-perfect synchronicity, so that the 945th tweet was the same number of seconds apart as the 946th."[101] This automated megaphone effect was capable of creating near-hegemonic results, with literally lethal consequences in the case of COVID-19 disinformation. A Cornell University study found that Trump was "the largest driver of the COVID-19 misinfor-

---

99 Maggie Haberman, Glenn Thrush, and Peter Baker, "Inside Trump's Hour-by-Hour Battle for Self-Preservation," *New York Times*, December 9, 2017, https://www.nytimes.com/2017/12/09/us/politics/donald-trump-president.html; David Smith, "'Executive Time': How, Exactly, Does Trump Spend 60% of His Day?," *Guardian*, February 7, 2019, https://www.theguardian.com/us-news/2019/feb/07/executive-time-donald-trump-white-house.

100 Amber Jamieson, "President Trump Parrots Fox News Again with Attack on Chelsea Manning," *Guardian*, January 26, 2017, https://www.theguardian.com/us-news/2017/jan/26/donald-trump-chelsea-manning-traitor-fox-news.

101 Elisabeth Dwoskin and Craig Timberg, "The Unseen Machine Pushing Trump's Social Media Megaphone into Overdrive," *Washington Post*, October 30, 2020, https://www.washingtonpost.com/technology/2020/10/30/trump-twitter-domestic-disinformation.

mation 'infodemic,'" with 38 percent of disinformation posts explicitly mentioning his name.[102] Trump, of course, was also a "super-spreader" of alternative facts about the 2020 election, so much so that following his banning from Twitter after the attack on the Capitol the number of unsubstantiated claims about the election plummeted 78 percent.

The Trump media circuit formed a self-amplifying, self-reinforcing feedback loop. In a recursive loop of this kind, it is no longer possible to assign an originating subject of the utterance. A statement doesn't so much trace back linearly to a source as loop the loop. Trump began gearing up for his presidential campaign saying not what he truly thought, in keeping with a deeply held ideological position and moral outlook, but what he thought his potential supporters desired to hear. This is closer to ventriloquism than to full speech. He says what he thinks they would say if they held the mike. Then they say it back to him in tweets and rally slogans. Then he returns it to them amplified. Round after round. Trump's speech is fundamentally in the mode of indirect discourse, which is the mode of reported speech: he said they thought, they said he said, and he says it back, so they can shout it in the streets. Reported speech without an assignable originator is *free indirect discourse*.[103] The regime of distributed decision runs on free indirect discourse, technologically turbo-charged by social media.

The Expansive Collapse of the First Person

In this regime of enunciation, the very concept of first-person speech tends to get lost. Responding to criticism of Trump for an official trip to a hurricane disaster area in which he did not actually get close to the disaster area, his press secretary Sarah Huckabee Sanders explained:

102 Aaron Blake, "Study Shows Trump Is a Super-Spreader—of Coronavirus Misinformation," *Washington Post*, October 1, 2020, https://www.washingtonpost .com/politics/2020/10/01/study-shows-trump-is-super-spreader-coronavirus -misinformation.

103 Deleuze and Guattari, *Thousand Plateaus*, 80, 84; Massumi, *Architectures of the Unforeseen: Essays in the Occurrent Art* (Minneapolis: University of Minnesota Press, 2019), 139–45.

He met with a number of state and local officials who are eating, sleeping, breathing the Harvey disaster. He talked extensively with the governor, who certainly is right in the midst of every bit of this, as well as the mayor from several of the local towns that were hit hardest. And detailed briefing information throughout the day yesterday talking to a lot of the people on the ground—that certainly is a first hand account.[104]

Yes, an accumulation of secondhand accounts certainly amounts to a firsthand account! By this logic, why wouldn't third- or fourth-hand accounts also be firsthand accounts? Don't they all funnel through secondhand accounts? The first person smears across an indefinite series of enunciative relays, losing its anchoring to a specifiable speaker. At Trump rallies, his supporters would perform the collapse of the second and third person into the first, shouting what Trump just said to them back to him, still in the first person. "I want nothing! No quid pro quo," he shouts. "I want nothing! No quid pro quo!" they shout back in unison, taking the fullness of his desire—his satisfaction with himself, in need of no favors from others—onto themselves collectively. This produced the odd enunciative formation of a first-person chorus of instantaneously reported speech.[105]

Here, "firsthand" is whatever returns to the preeminent individual who constitutes the central node in the communicational feedback loop, resonates with him in a way that amplifies and reinforces his pattern, and is then retransmitted by him. What doesn't resonate and reinforce falls by that very fact under the rubric of "fake news": false speech. What used to be hearsay is now first-person knowledge, and what once was authenticated knowledge is now worse than hearsay because it conceals malign intent. Speech is not legitimated by the reliability of its source. "Expert" equals elite faker of news serving the globalist agenda. Nor is it legiti-

---

104 Taylor Link, "White House Defends Trump's Claim That He Witnessed the Devastation of Hurricane Harvey 'First Hand,'" *Salon*, August 31, 2017, http://www.salon.com/2017/08/31/white-house-defends-trumps-claim-that-he-witnessed-the-devastation-of-harvey-first-hand.

105 Greg Sargent, "New Revelations Just Wrecked Trump's Last Remaining Defenses," *Washington Post*, November 27, 2019, https://www.washingtonpost.com/opinions/2019/11/27/new-revelations-just-wrecked-trumps-last-remaining-defenses.

mated by the verifiability of its content. "Evidence-based" equals elite mystification aimed at pulling the wool over the eyes of "real" Americans.

But again, speech is not legitimated so much as it is given license. It is given license by flowing through the circuit of recursive speech channeling through the preeminent individual's extended first person. What it is given license to do is to circulate further. It is given currency; license to self-amplify. The amplification is the functional equivalent of confirmation. It makes it believable. To be repeated so resoundingly makes it as good as true, even in the absence of evidence—or especially in the absence of evidence. In the conspiracy-theory universe into which so many Trump supporters have plunged headlong, lack of evidence is routinely, and explicitly, taken for proof—of a deeper conspiracy, whose spectral existence is the ultimate object of belief.

Conspiratorial plotting is apparent *action* in the mode of the free indirect: there is always an unassignable "they" acting behind every malignant sign of the unsavory truth. And what is not a malignant sign in this world of fear? If one "they" is revealed, there is yet another they behind it lurking in the shadows. And another behind that one. They after they. The source of malign activity infinitely recedes into the shadowy background of all that is other and evil. So much to expose! Sign upon sign. So much to decipher! To discuss and pass around. So many notes to compare. So many versions to generate in the attempt to follow the sinews of the plot and chart it to its always concealed source. It never ends. This regime of enunciation is not just repetitive. It is powerfully productive, generating a proliferating tide of speech powering the circuit that runs through, and runs circles around, the preeminent individual. (For more on conspiracy thinking, see the "Signs Behaving Badly," "The Understory: The Belief from Below," and "Conspiracy Brewing" sections of part 5.)

The occult power of the "they" of the unspecified enemy acting behind the scenes can be matched only by the equally proliferative counter-they power of its pro-Trump exposers. "The most commonly used phrase" on right-wing internet groups "is some version of 'I heard,' followed by a theory."[106] The "they" is Janus-faced: the shadowy "they" of unspecified

106 Stuart A. Thompson, "Three Weeks Inside a Pro-Trump QAnon Chat Room," *New York Times*, January 26, 2021, https://www.nytimes.com/interactive/2021/01/26/opinion/trump-qanon-washington-capitol-hill.html.

enemy on the one side, and on the other the patriot league of "fake news" debunkers, doxxers, and conspiracy hounds who wage a verbose war against the first camp. These are two sides of the same post-normative coin. The theys co-function to confirm the centrality of the preeminent individual who, occupying the privileged position of the hinge between them, claims messianically to hold the key to future well-being. "I alone can fix it," roared the anointed candidate at the party convention.[107]

But if he "alone" can fix it, why does he need to recruit his legions of supporters? What is he without them? Who "I" is this that waxes "they"? Second- and third-person speech folds into this first person. In an equal and opposite movement, the boundary blurs between what he says and what "they" say in echoing and amplifying resonation. "I" speaks to the murmur of a sea, that of the background speech of what "they" say. The backwash of they-saying sweeps through me, but does not drag me down. Instead, it buoys me, holding "I" in my preeminence, preternaturally coiffed head bobbing above the surface foam. My "I" bobs like a buoy on the expanse of the anonymous murmur. I speak through they, and they through I. "They" here is not the third person. The third person is assignable to an utterer. Indirect discourse freed from a specifiable subject of the utterance, "I" awash with reported speech, is in what Deleuze and Guattari call the "fourth person singular."[108]

The impossibility of assigning a clearly locatable origination of expression in a specifiable utterer enables the preeminent individual to dodge responsibility for his words and actions. At one point Trump was asked whether he accepted responsibility for the bungled rollout of COVID-19 testing: "'I don't take responsibility at all,' Trump said defiantly, pointing to an unspecified 'set of circumstances' and 'rules,

107 Yoni Appelbaum, "'I Alone Can Fix It,'" *Atlantic*, July 21, 2016, https://www .theatlantic.com/politics/archive/2016/07/trump-rnc-speech-alone-fix-it/492557.

108 Fourth person singular: Gilles Deleuze, *The Logic of Sense*, ed. Constantin V. Boundas, trans. Mark Lester with Charles Stivale (New York: Columbia University Press, 1990), 103, 140, 152. "Direct discourse is a detached fragment of a mass and is born of the dismemberment of the collective assemblage; but the collective assemblage is always like the murmur from which I take my proper name." Deleuze and Guattari, *Thousand Plateaus*, 84.

regulations and specifications from a different time.'"[109] Nothing to see here—quick, over there! It's *their* fault (the deep state). Do you accept some responsibility for the attack on the Capitol? Not in the least. My comments were "totally appropriate."[110] It was *they*, not I. They did it all by themself.

The *they* deflects, coating the president with political Teflon.

The Storm of Unknowing

The reign of the fourth person singular also produces the effect of equating what the preeminent individual knows with all knowledge. Anything he doesn't know—anything that lies outside or is unsuited to amplification in the resonator field whose pivotal node he is—is by definition unknown. Who knew health care was so complicated?[111] Nobody knew. Who knew that Abraham Lincoln was a Republican? Nobody! Who knew that war was expensive? That Iraq has a lot of oil?[112] A thousand times, nobody! What falls outside Trump's knowledge is astoundingly rich and broad. The Trumpian epistemological regime is an overweening know-nothingism. All he knows is what he desires—and desires to amplify as a desire in the others of his legion of I.

---

109 Caitlin Oprysky, "'I Don't Take Responsibility at All': Trump Deflects Blame for Coronavirus Testing Fumble," *Politico*, March 13, 2020, https://www.politico.com/news/2020/03/13/trump-coronavirus-testing-128971.

110 David Jackson, "Donald Trump Defends Speech as 'Totally Appropriate,' Won't Take Responsibility for Deadly Capitol Riot," *USA Today*, January 12, 2021, https://www.usatoday.com/story/news/politics/2021/01/12/donald-trump-refuses-take-responsibility-attack-u-s-capitol/6636699002.

111 Madeline Conway, "Trump: 'Nobody Knew That Health Care Could Be So Complicated,'" *Politico*, February 27, 2017, https://www.politico.com/story/2017/02/trump-nobody-knew-that-health-care-could-be-so-complicated-235436.

112 Dana Milbank, "Lincoln Was a Republican, Slavery Is Bad—and More Discoveries by President Obvious," *Washington Post*, March 22, 2017, https://www.washingtonpost.com/opinions/lincoln-was-a-republican-slavery-is-bad—and-more-discoveries-by-president-obvious/2017/03/22/3360c622-0f2c-11e7-9b0d-d27c98455440_story.html.

The epistemological regime of the George W. Bush years was equally "post-fact" in its disdain for what his administration dismissed as the "reality-based community." But it was post-truth in a very different, if related, mode. It was organized around the "unknown unknown" theorized by his secretary of defense, Donald Rumsfeld.[113] This is the proteiform threat of the unspecified enemy of the war on terror, combatable only through preemption. Preemption's object as a mode of power is the ontologically vague figure of threat "before it has fully emerged."[114] Preemption ingeniously makes this vagueness of threat actionable by acting on the time of threat rather than its content.

Under Trumpian conditions of potentialized civil war, the unknown unknown becomes the "nobody knows." Rather than legitimating a new mode of global warfare, it gives license to an erratic, distributed decisionism that agitates the conspiratorial, wheel-spinning present with ill-advised and quasi-chaotically directed action (without actually dismantling the global drone-war machine, relentless proxy warfare, and worldwide empire of a thousand bases inherited from Bush via Obama). This is part of Trump's persona as "Disturber-in-Chief." His deciding in the exception is flailing, by design. The flailing operates to agitate the body politic, aiming to keep it off balance and craving the confirmation and resolve that can flow through his media figure who "alone" can fix what ails it. Deterrence suspended the present. Trumpian decision puts it in a suspended animation of constant agitation. The more the cure is flailingly promised, the harder the followers of the leader work to ferret out false news and interpret the malignant signs that might enable them to shed light on the enemy and neutralize "them." The agitation intensifies as the apocalyptic future of an all-out war between good and evil, which Trumpians call "The Storm," is already brewing. All the preeminent individual need do is keep stirring the brew with daily doses of disorder.

Of the many challenges facing anyone trying to understand Donald Trump's presidency is the fact that it is maddeningly nonlinear,

---

113   Massumi, "Going Kinetic: What is Decision in a Post-deliberative Age?," in *Couplets*, 209–31.

114   Massumi, "The Primacy of Preemption: The Operative Logic of Threat," in *Ontopower*, 3–19.

lurching several times each day between policy objectives that may be dictated by a Fox News anchor, a friend from Mar-a-Lago, or the prime minister of Norway. . . . One of the unending debates of the Trump presidency is whether Trump intentionally creates this chaos or is somehow helpless against it, against the very disorder he causes daily, if not hourly.[115]

Intentioned or hapless? That is no more the question than "True or false?" Just as the I-They dynamic blurs persons, nonlinear agitation blurs the distinction between the intentional, in the sense of having a plan, and the involuntary, in the sense of not deciding. Trump decides. He does nothing but decide. But effectively plan? Formulate and follow through with a considered intention? Trump does have an overarching *aim*—to remain the adulated preeminent individual at all costs, while accumulating massive wealth. In pursuit of that aim, he hatches quixotic plots against the ever-spinning kaleidoscope of his many enemies. But it would be attributing to him a measure of integrated first-personhood that is outside his Janus-field to say that he forms intentions with method, or follows a method with intention. The mode of his action is to agitate a complex field in the hope of triggering effects that may end up serving his overarching aim. This requires a rapid succession of trial-and-error feints and parries.[116] When success comes of this flailing, it can appear just short of miraculous.

Of course, while Trump flails, the henchmen he installed in government are busy *undoing* things: tearing up environmental regulations, undermining health care and workplace safety, limiting the rights of transgender people, removing restrictions on banks, dismantling the immigration system, to name a few. These undoings, whose intention was the negative one of systematically destroying every possible shred of the liberal Obama legacy, are in line, despite "populist" grandstanding, with the deregulatory march of neoliberal capitalism. The few positive actions his administration took demonstrate this. The tax cut for the

---

115 Alexander Nazaryan, "What If the Chaos Is Strategic?," *Atlantic*, June 18, 2019, https://www.theatlantic.com/ideas/archive/2019/06/chaos-works/591688.

116 This dynamic of serial, trial-and-error feints is also characteristic of military action under the doctrine of preemption. See Massumi, "Going Kinetic," in *Couplets*.

wealthy and the rollback of post-crisis financial regulations, both passed early in his tenure, were among the only notable legislative achievements of Trump's presidency. The neoliberal unleashing of capital creates conditions of "creative" social and economic disorder that destabilize the lives of his base—who then turn agitatedly to Trump for a hit of compensatory confirmation and resolve to steel their frayed and fearful patriot nerves. They upon they, sign after sign, chaos to quasi-chaos.

Trump Machine

The characteristics of Trumpian process chronicled above seem to be simple negatives if judged by the historically prevalent normative standards of government and public behavior. But in light of the account developed here, they appear not as lacks or defects so much as positive features of a working machinery. They co-operate as tendencies that bundle together to form a regime of power constituting its own unique mode.

By "machinery," of course, is not meant a mechanical system requiring outside maintenance and fueling. It refers to a complex set of mutually presupposing operations whose iterations, always under variation, *carry an agential force, but lack an agent separate from the operations.* The agential force consists in orienting tendencies whose movements toward polarized attractor states are the functional equivalent of aims. The tendencies are emergent and the aims self-modulating. They function as affective *lures* inducting bodies into certain orientations of the movements of their daily lives.[117]

A *machine* in Deleuze and Guattari's process-philosophical sense is self-driving, in the way the tendencies composing it are.[118] It is made up

117   The concept of the machinic has a kinship with that of "self-organizing systems" as well as with Whitehead's notion of the "organism." The latter has little to do with the usual meaning of the term "organism" as the opposite of "mechanism." For both Deleuze/Guattari and Whitehead, organism in the usual sense and mechanism fall to the same side, and together are contrasted with what Deleuze and Guattari call the machinic. See Deleuze and Guattari call the, *Thousand Plateaus.*

118   The form of this self-driving is what I have called an "operative logic." Massumi, *Ontopower.* Machinic subjectivity: Maurizio Lazzarato, *Signs and Machines:*

not of pieces or parts, but of confluences of tendencies bound together in tension, mutually reinforcing and interfering by turns. Each ingredient tendency is capable of striking out to go its own way, toward achieving its maximal expression unencumbered, or toward joining symbiotically with another self-forming bundle. There are no constants in a machine understood in this way, only coefficients of variation. There is no structure, except as a more or less precarious plateau of metastability amid the variation. There is no necessary content, just dynamic parameters of content formation. *Form* and *content* co-occur in mutual presupposition (one does not come without the other, but each maintains its distinction from the other, the one as enveloping, the other enveloped; the one as conveying, the other as conveyed). The machine is what generates the co-occurrence. The machine, concerned as it is with form-content generation, is always one of *expression*. In each case where there arises a metastability that we can be forgiven for treating as a structure, a certain mode of tendencies' coming together to more or less regularized effect within certain parameters of expression has crystallized. The operators of the crystallization are self-regulating, and as much as possible self-reproducing.

The mode of operation, which can express itself in different forms bearing disparate contents, is termed an "assemblage" (*agencement* in French: an "agencying"). Each crystallization in a particular form/content complementarity can be called an "apparatus" (akin to Foucault's *dispositif*). Assemblages and apparatuses are collective by nature.[119]

The assemblage in relation to the apparatus is the latter's *real potential for variation* (this is the dynamic order of the full body, on which more is said in part 3). It is the (really abstract) "form" of the apparatus's coefficients

---

Capitalism and the Production of Subjectivity, trans. Joshua David Jordan (New York: Semiotext(e), 2014).

119   The exact vocabulary in Deleuze and Guattari, *Thousand Plateaus*, is "abstract machine" (shortened to "machine" here), "machinic assemblage" (shortened to "assemblage"), and "concrete machinic assemblage" (called "apparatus" here to avoid confusion by a surfeit of "machinics" and "assemblages," following Deleuze's own linkage of the concrete machinic assemblage to Foucault's apparatus). Gilles Deleuze, *Foucault*, trans. Séan Hand (Minneapolis: University of Minnesota Press, 1988), 37–38.

of variation.[120] The machine in relation to the assemblage is the assemblage's (maximally abstract) *pure potential for becoming-other*: its power to push its parameters to the limit where it passes a threshold into a qualitatively different mode, or to perform a kind of leap in place where it throws its ingredient tendencies up into the air so that when they land again it is in a new composition. This is not a "form" in any usual sense (hence the scare quotes). It is a form of changeability: a *matrix* (of form-and-content formation). Since the machinic matrix envelops any number of changes in potential, it is multiple by nature.

Following this processual sense of machinism, a regime of expression—which is by nature a regime of power, in that it orients and actualizes potentials—cannot be diagnosed solely by looking at the form or content of expression. It requires a very different mode of thought from traditional sociological or political thinking. Processually, the really abstract (variation, tendency, potential: that which moves the present and moves through it, but is never simply here and now) is considered to be the *most concrete* reality in play. An understanding of the self-formative movement of that reality cannot be had by resolving it into parts and then putting the parts back together into a whole to see how they work. Tendencies move through parts and wholes, and carry them both, as well as their varying relation to each other. In a word, they are *transversal*. Potentials are not subject to simple location in a part or as a whole. They are *nonlocal*. They are never fully determined, for the moment they arrive they have already moved on. It is of their nature to actualize in unpredictable patterns of recurrence, flitting from actualization to actualization. Once afoot, they are never definitively exhausted. Say "red," and you have said an infinity of potential variations, in eternal recurrence. Say "Trump," and . . . on second thought, don't. It's too depressing to think about.

What has been chronicled here in relation to Trump is a *becoming-machinic of the person*. In this becoming, *person and persona fuse*. The one is

120   This is what Deleuze has called a "diagram." Deleuze, *Foucault*; Deleuze and Guattari, *Thousand Plateaus*, 67, 91, 100, 136, 141–48, 258; Massumi, "The Diagram as Technique of Existence," in *Semblance and Event: Activist Philosophy and the Occurrent Arts* (Cambridge, MA: MIT Press, 2011), 29–39.

no truer than the other. It is their indistinction that conditions the production of truth-effects that are alternative facts. These effects really appear, in their appearing to be real. They are *sign effects*, triggered through the circulation of images and words. Their efficacy is real. Through their ascription of the friend/enemy distinction, they stoke tendencies whose unfolding makes a difference in the world. The emissions of signs catalyzing them have performative force. The performance is a *reality show*, produced under the aegis of the post-normative *media figure*. Behind the reality show is nothing realer. Its process is unhidden, lying bald-faced on the surface of circulation. A mode of appearance has become an effective mode of operation, producing real effects (reality effects).

PART 2

Multiple Persons in Joint Possession

Personhood Revisited

This account began with the thesis that Trump's political machinations recentered the political process on the personality of power. But it did so in a new mode, resistant to analysis in the traditional terms of charismatic leadership. Notions of transindividuality, fourth person singular, machinism, and collective assemblage of expression were recruited to grapple with its novel profile. These notions might be seen to imply impersonality, against the thesis of the return of the personality of power. But that is only if the sole alternative is between the impersonal and the personal as we conventionally think of that opposition. There is another alternative: to reexamine what constitutes a person. It is necessary to rebuild the concept of the person on a new conceptual basis, outside the traditional personal/impersonal dichotomy, in order to arrive at an account that does justice to the mode of personhood that has made its appearance so dramatically with Trump, and in a way that effectively breaks with outworn theories of charismatic leadership and the cult of personality. This requires a lengthy philosophical detour.

There is a little-noted convergence, based on no direct influence, between the conceptions of the person in C. S. Peirce, William James, and A. N. Whitehead. These conceptions are exceedingly strange by contemporary standards. Suggestively for this account, these radically empirical takes on personhood harmonize with the notions of transindividuality and machinism coming out of Simondon and Deleuze and Guattari, as well as with Gabriel Tarde's theories of belief and desire motoring transpersonal movements of "imitation," so applicable to today's social media–borne viral contagions (Tarde's concepts are mobilized in the "The Understory: The Belief from Below" section of part 5).

Peirce, characteristically, does not mince his words. "The selfhood you like to attribute yourself is, for the most part, the vulgarest delusion of vanity." The "barbaric conception of personal identity" in which we vainly indulge "must be broadened." Never again must we say "'I am altogether myself, and not at all you.'"[1] There is an eventness to personhood that extends it into the social milieu. Personality is not a walled-in tap of subjectivity. It's a drenching downpour in which we are all caught without an umbrella. As James puts it in the opening passage of his famous chapter "The Stream of Thought," "If we could say in English 'it thinks,' as we say 'it rains' or 'it blows,' we should be stating the fact most simply and with the minimum of assumption. As we cannot, we must simply say that *thought goes on*."[2]

The downpour of thought-going-on does get "canalized," in Whitehead's words, echoing Bergson. "Every thought," James writes, "tends to be a part of personal consciousness."[3] *Tends to.* Thought *comes to* be consciously owned individually. A "broader" conception of the personal would stretch from the open-air downpour to the dribble of the privatized tap. From "it thinks" to "I think," as two poles of thought's going-on: two poles in the same process of *personification*. Nothing would forbid intermediary forms from populating that process: "It thinks in me"; "I think through it"; "We think as I"; "They think for me." Such forms have just as good a claim to personhood as the "barbaric" selfhood we like to attribute to ourselves.

The Piety of the Personal

What is "barbaric" conceptually about the commonplace notion is that it substantializes the eventness: *the* person usurps Schmitt's "movement" and "accidents of persons." We think of our selves, Bergson complains,

---

1   C. S. Peirce, *The Essential Peirce: Selected Philosophical Writings*, vol. 2 (Bloomington: University of Indiana Press, 1998), 2–3.

2   William James, *The Principles of Psychology*, vol. 1 (Mineola, NY: Dover, 1950), 224–25.

3   Canalized: A. N. Whitehead, *Process and Reality* (New York: Free Press, 1978), 107. James quote: *Principles of Psychology*, 1:225.

as reposing on the bedrock of our private personhood, styled as the unchanging substratum of "who we are." Psychological "states" tread across its surface, thoughts and emotions appearing like actors on the stage of our lives. In passing, they produce variations on our personhood. But we treat them in the end as just as invariable as our bedrock selves.[4] We think of them as things we "have." Through self-reflection, we can name them and convince ourselves we discern their essential natures. In our personal development, we come to see the truth they were acting out. We come to understand how they are "really" extrusions of the bedrock, carrying the precious gems of our essential character to the surface. We have now come back to ourselves, as we've always been, but also somehow personally enriched.

The barbarity is that this substantialization makes personal change a vicious circle that it greedily takes for virtuous. A generation ago, we "found ourselves." Now, in this heyday of identity politics and its neoliberal milieu, we wake up to "owning" ourselves. We want the world to reflect our owning. We feel wronged if we don't recognize ourselves in the media, on screen, in books. The world is but the reflecting pool for our bedrock selves. If we don't see ourselves reflected, we shame and moralize. We gripe and lash out. What is barbarous is this *piety of the personal*. The sign of this piety is "I feel" slapped down as a non-negotiable trump card (excuse the expression): *you* don't know, you're not me,

---

4   "Difficulties and contradictions of every kind to which the theories of personality have led come from our having imagined, on the one hand, a series of distinct psychological states, each one invariable, which would produce the variations of the ego by their very succession, and on the other hand an ego, no less invariable, which would serve as support for them. How could this unity and this multiplicity meet? How, without either of them having duration—the first because change is something superadded, the second because it is made up of elements which do not change—how could they constitute an ego which endures? But the truth is that there is neither a rigid, immovable substratum nor distinct states passing over it like actors on a stage. There is simply the continuous melody of our inner life—a melody which is going on and will go on, indivisible, from the beginning to the end of our conscious existence. Our personality is precisely that." Henri Bergson, *The Creative Mind: An Introduction to Metaphysics*, trans. Maybelle L. Andison (Mineola, NY: Dover, 2007), 159.

you have no right to speak about it, it's *my* experience, and *because* it's mine, only mine, it's the truth, the bedrock truth, because I felt it to be. "Honor" it or begone. End of argument.

The piety of the personal is not something that either the right or the left has a monopoly on. Segments of both practice it, in different ways. It is practiced on the right in a particularly reactive form, out of enraged frustration at having effectively had the world for so long as a reflecting pool for whiteness, the assumed (Man-)Standard of personhood, with a sense of having lost that now that the waters are muddied by others of a browner persuasion who are fantasized, as in a game of mirror-image rivalry, as conspiring to "replace" the white "race." In the final analysis, the true barbarity is this summum of reaction, to which the left's identity politics is an understandable self-defensive response. More on forms of reactivity will come later.

But what if the bedrock is a stream formed by the downpour, as James styles it? The parts of us we "have" and the ourselves we "own" do hold water, to a degree. But, as James says, it's missing something to act as though the river were made of the "pailsful, spoonsful, quartpotsful, barrelsful, and other moulded forms of water" we draw from it. The piety of the personal mistakes the shape of the stream for the form of its canalization.

> Even were the pails and the pots all actually standing in the stream, still between them the free water would continue to flow. . . . Every definite image in the mind is steeped and dyed in the free water that flows round it. With it goes the sense of its relations, near and remote, the dying echo of whence it came to us, the dawning sense of whither it is to lead.[5]

A refiguring of personhood is required to get a "sense of its relations." It is only through its relations that we get an understanding of personhood's accidental (historical, conjunctural, eventful) coursings and their (political) canalizations.

---

5 James, *Principles of Psychology*, 1:255.

An Individual Is a Wave

"An individual [hu]man is a wave."[6]

> A wave is the form assumed by parts of a body which are out of equilibrium, such that as fast as the particles return they are replaced by others moving into neighboring positions of stress, so that the whole disturbance is continually propagated into new parts of the body while preserving more or less perfectly the same shape and other characters.[7]

An individual is a dynamic bodily form that is inseparable from, while remaining irreducible to, the matter moving through it. To fail to distinguish between the movement and the matter would be as absurd as "seizing a spinning top to catch its motion."[8] But to try to think one without the other would be equally absurd. They must be thought together, across their conjoint difference. Their distinction must be respected, but not in a way that pits one against the other, as form versus matter. They come together under far-from-equilibrium conditions, in effective fusion. By that is meant seamlessly co-operating to joint effect, co-composing a single, ongoing dynamic shape.[9] There is a real distinction between the patterning of that dynamic shape and body matter, incumbent in their necessarily coming together. (Real distinction will be further discussed in the postscript.[10])

It is crucial to note that for Peirce, "individual" is not synonymous with "person." This variance between the individual and the person will be fundamental to understanding the important distinction between collective individuation and collective personhood in relation to Trumpism.

---

6 Peirce, *Essential Peirce*, 2:124. Whitehead also uses the model of the wave in his analysis of person. Whitehead, *Process and Reality*, 98.

7 Peirce, *Essential Peirce*, 2:515n12.

8 James, *Principles of Psychology*, 1:224.

9 "The existence of the individual is a totally different thing from the existence of the matter which at any given instant happens to compose [them], and which is incessantly passing in and out." Peirce, *Essential Peirce*, 2:124.

10 On real distinction as it features in Spinoza, see Gilles Deleuze, *Expressionism in Philosophy: Spinoza*, trans. Martin Joughlin (New York: Zone, 1992), 27–40.

The definition of the individual hinges on the body. Peirce's definition of the person, as we will see, is in a different register, but one that
is neither reducible to nor separable from the body, any more than the
body's matter is separable from its motion. The body, for its part, is
not a static block of matter with unvarying form. It is a dynamic locus
of matter and moving-through. No sooner do particles of matter move
in than they move on, refreshed by others. This accords with scientific
view of the body as renewing its substance throughout life, reflected
in Whitehead's view of the body as continually shedding and regain-
ing molecules in a self-refreshing holding "pattern."[11] A moment in time
is a cross-section of that lineage of continuing variation, whereby new
matter inherits, and inhabits, ongoing pattern (another name for
dynamic shape). The body at a moment is an abstraction. That abstraction is more usefully rendered by the image of a standing wave than by
that of a static object. But the wave-form, in fact, is ongoing, ever differing in relation to itself.

All of the above applies to the brain—the central nexus of the "it
thinks"—as a region of the body.

> Whilst we think, our brain changes, and that, like the aurora borea-
> lis, its whole internal equilibrium shifts with every pulse of change.[12]
> The precise nature of the shifting at a given moment is a product of
> many factors. The accidental state of local nutrition or blood-supply
> may be among them. But just as one of them certainly is the influ-
> ence of outward objects on the sense-organs during the moment, so
> is another certainly the very special susceptibility in which the organ
> has been left at that moment by all it has gone through in the past.
> Every brain-state is partly determined by the nature of this entire past
> succession. Alter the latter in any part, and the brain-state must be
> somewhat different. . . . It is out of the question, then, that any total
> brain-state should identically recur. Something like it may recur; but
> to suppose it to recur would be equivalent to the absurd admission
> that all the states that had intervened between its two appearances

---

11   A. N. Whitehead, *Science and the Modern World* (New York: Free Press, 1967), 149.

12   This makes it a "metastability": a provisional, often precarious, equilibrium
     subject to shifts.

had been pure nonentities, and that the organ after their passage was exactly as it was before.[13]

The shifting of thought in the brain is the product of many factors incoming from outside its own dynamic form, including changes in the body (nutrition, blood supply, hormones). The brain is a matter-motion wave pattern, in the same manner as is the body as a whole. Just as the pattern that is thought, raining in the brain, is influenced by impinging factors from the body, the body is influenced by impinging factors of the environment (including the "it rains" of the weather). All three are matter-motion patterns: individual loci of continuing variation nested in one another, each in the moment abstractable as a standing wave. Together they form a complex wave, a nexus of interlocking loci that are neither reducible to nor separable from each other. The senses are the throughlines from the environment across the body to the brain and out again in action: the royal road of outside influence, transfixing the nexus.

The incoming of other factors modulates the characters carried by the body's matter-movement. Their slightest impingement on the on-going pattern brings a qualitative change. The impingement is the germ integrated by the wave-shape into itself as a variation on its continuity, making a difference that requalifies it. Hormones and the weather alter mood, changing the character of the moment's standing wave. An individual's mood patterns over time, from one standing wave to the next, are themselves a dynamic pattern, of wider amplitude. They are influenced by such incoming factors as genes, early experience, habit-formation, trauma, and the incidence of signs.[14] Moods are qualitative shifters contributory to, and expressive of, the affective constitution of the character of the individual as a whole (not an object, but a life; a living nexus). As will be discussed later, when the character of reactivity is dominant in that constitution, the body's tendencies are incipiently proto-fascist.

---

13 James, *Principles of Psychology*, 1:225.

14 "Our dominant inheritance from our immediately past occasion is broken into by innumerable inheritances through other avenues. Sensitive nerves, the functionings of our viscera, disturbances in the composition of our blood, break in upon the dominant line of inheritance. In this way, emotions, hopes, fears, inhibitions, sense-perceptions arise." A. N. Whitehead, *Adventures of Ideas* (New York: Free Press, 1967), 189.

Other influences constantly impinge. They strike at the micro-level, infra- to the whole-individual expressions that may develop from them. They are cues or primes, inducing local eddies in the wave-pattern.[15] Certain of the disturbances propagate throughout the nexus, affecting a qualitative change in the overall composition and each of its components. Whitehead calls this *amplification*. The body as a whole, and the brain in particular, he says, must be conceived of as a "complex amplifier." The qualitative change, moodily rising to a peak and permeating throughout, registers as a "dominant element of feeling." This "presiding" feeling betokens the "*character*" of the life of the body for the moment of a standing wave. *A person is present when the bodily nexus "sustains a character"* from one standing wave to the next, under variation.[16]

> The various actual entities, which compose the body, are so coordinated that the experiences of any part of the body are transmitted to one or more central occasions to be inherited with enhancements accruing upon the way, or finally added by reason of the final integration. The enduring personality is the historic route of living occasions which are severally dominant in the body at successive instants.[17]

Character

Character is the pattern of integration inherited from moment to moment, modulated by incoming influences from the outside peaking into a presiding feeling. The pattern's continuity under variation is what we call our *personality*.

The effects of the presiding character emerge from below, but also feed back down. "Owing to the delicate organization of the body, there is a returned influence, an inheritance of character derived from the presiding occasion and modifying the subsequent occasions through the rest

---

15 On cueing and priming, see Massumi, *Ontopower*, 66–67, 74, 82–83, 107–16, 129–34; and Massumi, *The Power at the End of the Economy* (Durham, NC: Duke University Press, 2015), 24–31, 40–41.

16 Whitehead, *Process and Reality*. Complex amplifier, 119. Dominant element of feeling, 188. Presiding feeling, character, 107. Sustains a character, 35.

17 Whitehead, *Process and Reality*, 119.

of the body."[18] The effect of this recursion is to maintain the wave pattern within certain parameters as it variably continues across the incessant incoming of other influences. Certain coordinations and dominant regularities reemerge, giving each successive standing wave a kinship to the last: the eddying-up and trickle-back-down itself contracts a pattern. The iteration of the pattern, regenerated moment to moment, forms a "historic route" that "canalizes" the life of the body.[19] It is this ongoing canalization that we experience as an individual's character in the everyday sense, taking it to be an enduring nature (rather than a serial patterning).

The person is not the matter or the movement—or even the two together. The two together is the individual. The life of the individual hosts the person. The person is an aspect of it. It is the individual's correlational pattern, its "shape" or dynamic form under serial variation. This is not something that can be separated from the matter-motion of the individual, but it exhibits its own real distinction, "carried and sustained" by a life. It is defined less by each successive standing wave as such—the content of each moment in that life—as by the *rhythm of transitions* between them. As the *form of transition* characterizing a historic route, rather than any given way station or even their sum total, it is more abstract than the individual and its matter-motion, in the processual sense of abstraction as really abstract in a way that is most concrete.

No, you cannot separate the spin from the top. The two togethering is what this occasion is concretely. But say a gust of air from a fan squalls their occasioning, which no sooner encounters an accidental roughness on the surface of the table. The shape of this modulation—the *style* of their doing what they do together—will co-depend on the speed and tilt that this new phase of the occasion inherits from its immediate past, as well as on the change in surface conditions. As the spinning top moves across the impingement of outside influences from one modulation to another, it will exhibit a *manner* of continuing. This manner is perceived *through* the movement, and as if *alongside* the matter. It spins off from the

---

18   Whitehead, *Process and Reality*, 109.
19   Whitehead, *Process and Reality*, 107.

spinning, into its own dynamic distinction. It self-abstracts.[20] It is not just a manner, but a mannerism. The self-abstraction of mannerism is a real abstraction (one that occurs in the world).[21]

The mannerism of character is all the more apparent in more complex individuals whose matter-movement is multiply composed, integrating sub-waves (as described in the description of the body/brain/environment integration). The pattern hosted by the individual regenerates because the incoming of other influences resonates through the sub-waves, rippling across their full breadth and height. The activity of the components of the individual becomes correlated as an effect of the interlinkage. It is the *correlation* that is regenerated at each incoming.

To be correlated is not to do the same thing. It is when each component undergoes a change in sync with the others. Each component responds to a causal influence in its own way, but inflected by a sensitivity to how the others are responding. Another way of saying it is that *the activity of the all is in the activity of the one, as directly as the one is in its own activity*—not unlike a musical ensemble jamming to a changing beat. The correlation that carries over from one beat to the next itself makes a difference. It *conditions* how each impingement plays. It exerts a recursive, whole-to-part causal influence (it is a "*quasi-cause*").[22]

Each punctually arriving other-influence acts as a *genetic element* of the ensemble. It is genetic in the sense that a system-wide modulation derives from its impingement, making a qualitative change in the whole. The correlation that moves down the line, in bringing the successive occasions into kinship, constitutes a "*genetic character*":[23] a quasi-causal formative force.

It is an essential part of Whitehead's definition of the person that a genetic character is inherited along the historic route and that it condi-

---

20 This is what I have termed a "semblance," understood as a manner of appearing, without the connotation of falseness that usually accompanies the word; Massumi, *Semblance and Event*.

21 Massumi, *Semblance and Event*, 42.

22 Quasi-cause is a concept from Deleuze and Guattari. See *Anti-Oedipus*, 10. See also Massumi, *Parables*, 225–28; and Massumi, *Ontopower*, 175, 216–17. This is what I have also called the "feedback of higher forms" in Massumi, *Parables*, 189, 198–99.

23 Whitehead, *Process and Reality*, 109.

tions the integral pattern, across its stations and trickling down to all of the differential components mattering-moving together. The genetic character is a collective style, or group mannerism, that both expresses and influences the shape of the wave. Another name for this styling is "*genetic relatedness*."[24]

To underline the irreducible multiplicity of the sub-components ingredient to the wave—the fact that the components are several and respond severally to provocation, each in its own way, in a way open to inflection by the co-activity of other components—Whitehead terms what is called here an individual a *society*. For a multiplicity to qualify as a society, a "*class-name* has got to apply to each member by reason of genetic derivation from other members of that same society. The members of the society are alike because, by reason of their common character, they impose on other members of the society the conditions which lead to that likeness."[25]

Society All the Way Up (and Down)

It is crucial to note here that a single individual is a "society" for White-head, owing to its multiplicity of bodily components and of sub-characters eddying in the current of the overall wave. A *single individual is a collective individuation*. The relation of the single individual to society in the usual sense is homologous to the relation of the individual to its own sub-components. There is a processual analogy between the levels, each of which exemplies the same mode of formation at different im-bricated scales, with ancillary differences pertinent to scale (although scale itself will have to be rethought; see the "Scale and Dimension" section of part 3). All *individuation is in fact collective*.

This entails that there is such a thing as *collective personhood*. The person-ality of the single individual is the patterning of the presiding feeling of a correlated crowd of constituent elements. The crowd of other individuals

---

24 Whitehead, *Process and Reality*, 34.
25 Whitehead, *Adventures of Ideas*, 203–4 (emphasis added).

with which the single individual keeps company has its own personality. It is only for convenience of expression that we continue to say "person" to designate the genetic relatedness of the historic route attaching to the trajectory through the world of a single body, and "collective person" for the historic routes that body travels with others of its kin. It is equally a shorthand to contrast "individual" and "collective individual."

Common Likeness, Reconsidered

The components' likeness, Whitehead said, is "imposed" by the correlation under which they move, under the aegis of their common genetic character. The quasi-causal influence of the common genetic character dictates that each component display in its own local manner the stylistic mark of the activity of the all. "Common" is a bit of a misnomer. The "likeness" is less a common property possessed by all than a token of involvement in the same group mannerism: a dynamic *signature*.

Each component implicated in a pattern carries that pattern's signature style, in its own, partial, way. The "likeness" is a concertation: a being in sync. It is the mark of genetic relatedness. *It is a dynamic likeness based on moving-together, not a substantial resemblance based on the possession of a static common property*—although that can happen as well. But when it does, it comes as an effect of the concertation, rather than serving as the basis for it. This *produced resemblance* is social and differential. It is not tributary to an identity category whose reason is found in the substantial properties of each particular component.

Why, then, insist that a "class-name has got to apply to each member"? If a class-name applies, doesn't this figure the person as an umbrella category? Doesn't it make the person a general idea in exactly the sense of a category that subsumes particulars based on their possession of a common property?

Yes, it does make the person a general idea. But it changes the meaning of "general idea."

A Person Is a General Idea

"Generalization is nothing but the spreading of ideas,"[26] Peirce writes. This processual definition approaches "generalization" from the angle of what it *does*. Similarly processual is the Peircean notion of the "ideas" involved. Both concern transition.

For Peirce, there is no clear cut-off point between conception and perception, only a "shading off" between them. Perception is not passive reception. It directly involves an act of "perceptual judgment." "There are no conceptions which are not given to us in perceptual judgments, so that we may say that all our ideas are perceptual ideas."[27] A perceptual judgment is a "directly perceived" implication that arrives flush with perception, without an extra act of cognition.

The implication carried in perceptual judgment is what Peirce calls "abduction." Given its rooting in direct experience, he considers abduction to be a logical operation more fundamental than either induction or deduction. The most basic case of an abduction is the perception of a transition. The moment of transition—and what moment is not a transition?—is only experienceable as such because its direct perception includes some form of awareness of where it is moving from and going to. The moved-from has already passed when the transition is underway, so it is now abstract, real but no longer present. The moved-from has already passed, and the going-to has not yet arrived, so it is equally abstract, real but not yet present. These are both modes of "real abstraction," in the sense of something that is not actual yet actively factors into what happens. The continuity between the two, in their respective tenses of immediate past and immediate future, is experienced as what Whitehead would call a "vector" character. This is the character of the transition as such, which carries a sense of orientation and impending outcome. The sense of something coming gives the perception a hypothetical cast. Abduction is a directly perceived hypothesis.[28]

26   C. S. Peirce, *The Essential Peirce: Selected Philosophical Writings*, vol. 1 (Bloomington: Indiana University Press, 1992), 349.

27   Peirce, *Essential Peirce*, 1:223–24.

28   For more on abduction, see Massumi, *The Power at the End of the Economy*, 43–48.

The character of each transition is singular, different in every case, for no two acts are ever entirely alike. However, there is already a certain kind of generality in the perception of a transition, in that the transition holds in implication more than one element. It abstractly *covers* the element of the moved-from and that of the going-to with its own character, which is nothing other than the felt relation of continuity between them. Something that covers a multiplicity of elements as a function of its own character is a general.

Conventionally understood, a general covers particulars from above, as a universal under which they are subsumed, and in which they participate by virtue of the characteristics they display. The relation is hierarchical, and the category itself displays no characteristics. The category "dog" does not have four feet. It is an existentially empty logical umbrella under which a set of particulars is placed, separately from any direct perception in which they may be involved. It is an abstraction in a totally different sense than an abduction or an emergent unity. It is a *mere abstraction* (a merely logical construct) as opposed to a real abstraction. It is a merely, not really, *abstract general idea* (on which, much more to come).

In an abductive hypothesis, the general does not subsume particulars under an empty designator. Rather, it covers a multiplicity of elements co-involved in the plenitude of an act or movement, flush with perception. In so doing, it constitutes a singular—a singular-multiple—whose *character* it is. "The only logical terms which are in perfect strictness singular are the subjects of perceptual judgments."[29] The hierarchy between the particular and the general is replaced by a co-implication of the singular and the multiple, effecting a switch to a different logic. "Particular" is then a misnomer for the elements that are brought together. (The different logic, that of "mutual inclusion," is discussed in detail in the postscript.)

Index and Event

The singular character is the felt quality of the elements' patterned relation: their directly perceived manner. The elements are not merely members of a logical set. They are aspects of an event. Rather than the empty

29 Peirce, *Essential Peirce*, 2:221.

designator of a set, the general that covers them is the dynamic *index* of an event. Its felt quality signposts the components' in-the-act-together, as smoke does fire. The class-name attached to this signposting function is itself an index. It is a second-order index, derivative of the same event, at one remove, but still dynamically connected to it by the umbilicus of the event. "An index always denotes a reacting singular."[30] As we will see, the crucial point for a process-oriented approach is that the index also points, *through* the reacting singular, to its conditions of emergence: the potential it expresses.

Word and Event

The word itself, the class-name that serves as an index, "is perceived . . . in the mode of immediacy."[31] Its perception involves a repetition of the feeling of the event's character, with a loss of vividness proportionate to its experiential remove from the reacting singulars. The repetition of the word envelops the felt quality of the event. This makes the word a vehicle for the event's spread. Through words, the vector character of the transition is extended, taking on the power to wander far beyond its point of departure in the event—without losing its singularity. Its singularity, on the contrary, is further multiplied.

Genetic Element, Abductive Impingement

The line of transmission is a personal historic route. The consecutive stations, or standing waves, composing it share a character, namely the felt quality of the events' patterned belonging to each other along the historic route. This continuing "genetic character" is a derivative of punctual "genetic elements." It self-abstracts from their abductive impingements on a life as it passes through its successive transitions.

An impingement may be word-borne through language, but it could just as well be a *perception* arriving from the body's exterior milieu, or an

---

30 Peirce, *Essential Peirce*, 2:221.
31 Whitehead, *Process and Reality*, 183.

affection rising up from the body's interior milieu (associated with anything from genes to hormones and blood sugar to involuntary memory and daydreaming to gut feeling to interoception and proprioception, to name a few). These are not two separate domains. Every perception involves an affection, and affections may express themselves in a change in perception. Every word hits as a perception, and also involves affection. The derivative genetic character amplifies the power of such "genetic elements" to make a difference, raising it to a higher, coordinate level. Genetic character qualifies as a person by Whitehead's definition, whatever its nature or scale.

Word, perception, affection: these list what Deleuze and Guattari call, from the angle of their signposting of potential, *point-signs* or "machinic indexes."[32] Later it will be necessary to add "image" to this semiotic list.

The word-index becomes a class-name when the spread constitutive of its generality occurs not only following a vector-line of transition but also in breadth. This happens under the action of habit.[33] The contraction of a habit fuses a multiplicity of components in the moment into a transition toward a shared outcome. It embraces their multiplicity in the same hypothesis. Once contracted, the habit spans singulars belonging to different moments. Each triggering of the habit occurs in a situation whose details vary to some extent. The action of the habit extracts a *like hypothesis* from the diversity of the triggerings, bringing them effectively together across their difference. "Like" is meant here in the reconsidered sense of a produced resemblance, the display of a common dynamic character arising from the iteration of a shared genetic element (the form of the habit's triggering). Habit's performative spanning of singulars constitutes a *general in the act*. The "action of habit

---

32 The point-sign is a mysterious concept that comes from Guattari into Deleuze and Guattari. It is rare in its occurrence and is very hard to interpret in their works. The two occurrences of the concept that come closest to the way I have chosen to deploy it are Félix Guattari, *Chaosmosis* (Bloomington: Indiana University Press, 1995a), 49–50; and Félix Guattari, *The Machinic Unconscious: Essays in Schizoanalysis* (New York: Semiotext(e), 2011), 184. I am aware of putting my own spin on the concept. "Point-sign" and "machinic index" occur in Deleuze and Guattari, *Anti-Oedipus*, 111, 260, 314–16, 318, 352. They are equated here, which may do some injustice to Deleuze and Guattari's text.

33 Peirce, *Essential Peirce*, 1:331, 349.

is nothing but generalization, and generalization is nothing but the spreading of feelings."[34]

The habitual spreading of feelings in-forms character, producing an expanding plane or level on which an individual's signature mannerisms vector. This broadens and bolsters the sustaining of character.

Machinic Synthesis

The contraction of habit occurs as a "passive synthesis."[35] A passive synthesis is an effective fusion that is not the result of an action of an agent but, rather, self-effects. It contributes at an infra-active level to the furthering of a person. Habit is outside the usual passive-active dichotomy. The distinction is not between an action that is done by an agent and one that is done to it, but between an action that can be claimed to have been executed independently by an agent and one that self-effects, infra- to agency and personhood. What self-effects is a subjectivity-without-a-subject.

The self-effecting of a subjectivity-without-a-subject is a way of saying "*machinic*" in Deleuze and Guattari's sense: self-contracting; self-spreading; *agencying* (rather than having agency or being an agent). Habit is not passive as opposed to active. It acts, in a certain machinic mode. Its action is an aspect of a body's conatus, or tendency not only to persist but to spread its power to act. In other words, it is bound up with desire, also in Deleuze and Guattari's sense, as associated with the notion of the machinic.

Spanning the General

The broadening of the character of the event under the action of habit attenuates the constituent feelings entering into the passive synthesis. It mutes the self-expression of the component feelings of the character

---

34   Peirce, *Essential Peirce*, 1:349.

35   Gilles Deleuze, *Difference and Repetition*, trans. Paul Patton (New York: Columbia University Press, 1994), 71–114.

it helps sustain. The feeling of the indexed singular-multiples is watered down, but never fades out.[36] The feeling's at least residual persistence is a condition of the persistence of the habit, its continuing generalization, and the personal character whose historic route the habit helps sustain.

The indexical word that has become a kind of class-name thus never ceases to denote a reacting singular(-multiple). In fact, its span widens to take an expanding web of singulars into abductive kinship—many fires indexed to the same quality of smoke. The equivalent, in the case of an image, of the word's becoming a class-name is the image taking on the generality of an *icon*, through an analogous process of passive synthesis. The image assumes an iconic operation without ceasing to serve as an index—emphasizing that what is indexed is a manner of transition and the potential it expresses, not a thing, and that the likeness of the icon is not foundational but is abductively produced as a lived hypothesis. The index "marks the junction between two portions of experience."[37] (Peirce makes it abundantly clear that indices and icons are not two separate types of sign, but reciprocal aspects of every sign.)

Generalization is compounded along two axes. Under the action of habit, singulars enter into solidarity in the dimension of breadth. At the same time, their solidarity extends across a series of genetically related transitions, vectoring down a historic route. Thus,

> instantaneous feelings flow together into a continuum of feeling, which has in a modified degree the peculiar vivacity of feeling and has gained generality. And in reference to such general ideas, or continua of feeling, the *difficulties about resemblance and suggestion and reference to the external, cease to have any force.* . . . These general ideas are not mere words, nor do they consist in this, that certain concrete facts will every time happen under certain descriptions of conditions; but they are just as much, or rather far more, living realities than the feelings themselves out of which they are concreted. . . .

36 "The consciousness of a habit involves a general idea. . . . Every time one of the associated feelings recurs, there is a more or less vague sense that there are others, that it has a general character, and of about what this general character is." Peirce, *Essential Peirce*, 1:349.

37 Peirce, *Essential Peirce*, 2:8.

[This] does not so much as demand that the special ideas shall surrender their peculiar arbitrariness and caprice entirely; for that would be self-destructive. It only requires that they shall *influence and be influenced by one another.*[38]

Such is a person: a general idea as a living reality; a society of singulars, each of whose activity habitually in-forms that of all the others, influences them and is influenced by them, as they travel a historic route together, sustaining a character, and being sustained by its continuance in return.

Levels

The composition of a person has levels. Singular transitions level up together in habit into a higher generality. Then new levels of habits build on previous habits. Conscious awareness may then bend back on habit-upon-habit to form another derivative, of active cogitation. This self-reflection attenuates to another degree the felt quality of the events, but again without erasing it. Conscious ideas entrain each other, transitioning from one to another. Each such "connection between ideas is itself a general idea, and . . . *a general idea is a living feeling.*"[39] However high it has climbed in level, the process of personhood dips back into the transitional intervals between peaks of cogitation, drawing on the singular-multiple richness they hold, to level up another degree. The "stream," as James characterized it, broadens and eddies as it travels onward, ramifying, differentiating, self-complicating. A person is the continuous self-patterning of a multi-level complex wave-system, held together by habit, sprouting, and spouting, ideas.

Action, or decision, on what is considered the executive level of the person's cogitations is a complex systemic effect.[40] Action is ever subtended by the passive

38   Peirce, *Essential Peirce,* 1:330 (emphasis added).
39   Peirce, *Essential Peirce,* 1:331 (emphasis added).
40   On the distinction between *action* as just defined, *act* (the leveling up of correlated sub-feelings from passive synthesis into a peak expression that landmarks it for potential insertion into a line of action), and *act-likes* forming the field of *activity*

syntheses of habit, and decision by the lived hypotheses of abduction. Cognition (limiting the meaning of the word to conscious awareness and reflection) is anything but self-effecting. Its sense of its own independence is an effect of the attenuation of infra-feeling as it levels up from the singular-multiple to the general.

Conscious reflection cleaves to the general level in a way that enables it to neglect its own genesis, attending only to its relating to itself on that general level. It does not notice that the relation is broken at every moment, impinged upon by waves rising up, its own operations dripping down, to renew themselves with singular-multiple momentum. It is only when something irrupts uncontrollably from these intervals of re-relating that consciousness realizes, without ever really taking cognizance of the fact, that it is not actually master in its own domain. The awareness of the irruptions takes the form of *emotion*. Emotion is the sign of the genetic complexity of thought breaching the neglectfully placid surface of reflection. Emotion relates the broken self-relating of conscious thought to its constituent turbulence (that of accidents of persons).

Collective Singular

Summing up with Peirce: "We may express the matter by saying that all these singular percepts were aspects or parts of one *collective singular*."[41] One singular-multiple. One individual with its personhood, covering a multiplicity of elements. "Personality is some kind of coordination or connection of ideas"; "a person is only a particular kind of general idea."[42]

(germinal movements that are the lowest-level elements, conceived as incipient tendencies always already stirring, including habits itching to trigger, together composing the field of what I call bare activity), deployed as the main conceptual axis of a philosophy of process, see Susanne Langer, *Mind: An Essay on Human Feeling*, vol. 1 (Baltimore: Johns Hopkins University Press, 1967), chaps. 7–11.

41 Peirce, *Essential Peirce*, 2:222 (emphasis added).
42 Peirce, *Essential Peirce*, 1:331, 350.

An Idea Is a Little Person

If a person is a general idea, conversely "an idea is a little person": a "living reality." "Every general idea has the unified living feeling of a person."[43] Every transition, abducted to form a general idea indexing a singular-multiplicity of components, is a little person. Every habit covering this transition, and fusing it with others, is a somewhat bulkier little person. As is each habit-upon-habit built on that habit. Not to mention each reflective bending-back-upon reuptaking into cogitation. And each transition between cogitations.

And all of these together.

Class-Naming the Collective Singular

For there is, according to both Peirce and Whitehead, a mode of reality proper to a collective singular: what is normally thought of as a class or category and relegated to a merely logical status. The class-name Peirce refers to indexes a real individual, of collective scope. "The singular collection of all dogs, the race of dogs . . . is just as much one thing as a single dog is one thing. . . . A class is an individual." A class is a "concrete thing . . . just as much a thing as the ocean is a thing."[44]

What manner of thing is an ocean? A complex, wavy thing. It is made of variable depths traversed by ever-shifting current patterns, and of even more variable surfacings scalloped by even-more-shifting wave patterns. The waves break on beaches or against rocks, or meet incoming flows from rivers and steams, or perhaps subside in bays and inlets. Even though the waves break on the ocean's edge, it provides no definite boundary, because geometrically a coastline is a fractal, receding into unmappable complexity of in-between dimension. It is also constantly advancing as sand accumulates, and receding through erosion. An ocean is also made of temperature differentials and variations in salt and min-

---

43   Peirce, *Essential Peirce*: little person, 1:354; unified living feeling, 1:350.
44   Peirce, *Essential Peirce*: singular collection, 2:222; concrete thing, 2:223.

eral concentration. It embraces a spread of scales from the subatomic to the continental. It is a singularly multiple complex wavy thing of indefinite boundedness that never rests in one form. It is not a thing the way a chair is (or appears to be): an enduring form with static properties that can be precisely circumscribed. It is a dynamic thing: more a consistency of process, operating within plastic parameters, than an object.

Thus also is a person. A personal name is a class-name indexing a complex: a singular-multiple comprising little persons, underpersons whose infra-elements' sub-feeling are summed up in the "presiding feeling" of the *"greater person,"* the overperson, that they collectively compose.[45] The greater person is what we consciously experience to be "me," my self, mistaking, chair-like, the singular-multiple for a definite, bounded particular. Our self is in fact the cresting of the waves on the surface of an oceanic complex—when it is not their crashing on the shore.

Corporate Persons

Where this connects back to the question of Trump and Trumpism is that the greater person who is me is a singular transition enveloped in a greater greater-person who is us, with the me enveloping smaller lesser-persons than myself. Both Peirce and Whitehead assert that what Peirce termed "collective singulars" or "corporate persons" have a mode of reality of their own.[46] Whitehead speaks of *"multiple personalities,"* at the levels both of what we think of as the individual and the collective.[47] Trump (he would be gratified to hear) is a greater person exuding waves of presiding feelings. Trump supporters are sub-feeling little persons agitated by the currents, riding the waves, but also fueling the over-Trump through the fold-in and feedback of their stirrings.

But saying this is not enough. It can be easily slotted back into a theory of identification underpinning the model of charismatic leadership,

---

45 Peirce, *Essential Peirce*, 1:350.
46 Peirce, *Essential Peirce*, 1:351.
47 Whitehead, *Process and Reality*, 107. This is a similar concept to Deleuze's "larval subjects." Deleuze, *Difference and Repetition*, 78–79, 97, 118–19.

where bounded, particular individuals are soldered together into a collective by mechanisms of mediation pivoting on the preeminent person, who is similarly a bounded, particular individual. The soldering is purely symbolic. The collectivity, the story goes, is an illusion. It has real repercussions, but does not have a mode of reality of its own, being nothing more than a deceptive effect. The activity is one-way, from the preeminent individual to the masses, reduced to passive reception.

With Trump, we have seen that the activity is reciprocal and recursive, pivoting on the person of Trump but not reducible to his agency. The movement is two-way. Its effects are not mediated, but have the immediacy of an echoing or resonance. They hinge on the immediate impact of words and images, amplified and spread. Most of all, the structural dialectic between the Trump supporter as little person and Trump the greater person, each conceived as bounded particular individuals as in the charismatic model, is undercut by the fact that each little person is a greater person in relation to the component feelings/habits/ideas composing them: fractal, like the ocean. (Later we will return to this fractality of component sub-persons infra to the dynamic constitution of person under the name of the "dividual"; see the "Dividuation" section of part 3.)

It is on this level of sub-personal infra-feelings that everything hinges. It is at this level that Trump supporters' feelings connect with each other, and all with Trump, and Trump with them. To have an effect, any higher-level awareness must filter back down to the lowest infra-level and then percolate back up again to ripple the surface as it may. It is only through this integral recursion that it can have an effect. Little echoing within greater echoing. Micro-reverberation within macro-resonance. The levels co-composing, one's activity in that of the other across scales, in integral processual (as opposed to structural) coupling and spreading differentiation, collectively singular (under the class-name "MAGA supporter").

Yes, "our own self-consciousness is direct awareness of ourselves as persons." But, Whitehead adds, "there are limits to unified control, which indicate dissociation of personality, multiple personalities in successive alternations, and even multiple personalities in joint possession."[48]

48 Whitehead, *Process and Reality*, 107.

Multiple Persons in Joint Possession

> The recognition by one person of another's personality takes place by means to some extent identical with the means by which he is conscious of his own personality.[49]

This assertion is a necessary consequence of the nested, fractal organization of personhood. A person is to its infra-persons as a greater person is to the little persons it integrates. A person draws on its component sub-persons for its presiding feeling as a greater person draws on the multiplicity of the collective singular it indexes. There is an analogical relation between levels. This creates a transversal *analogy of operation* between individuals on the same level, due to the likeness of their active implication in the same greater historic route, their sharing of the greater person's sustained character, and their kinship in the ways they incorporate the effect of genetic elements into their ongoing constitution: chance variations and other outside impingements; Schmitt's "accidents of persons." In social encounter

> the idea of the second personality, which is as much as to say that second personality itself, enters within the field of direct consciousness of the first person, and is as immediately perceived as his ego, though less strongly. At the same time, the opposition between the two persons is perceived, so that the externality of the second is recognised.[50]

There is analogy between levels and between impersoned individuals on the same level, but *no identity* between them. Trump supporters process likewise, in their co-composing a greater person and being co-composed in it, but they are not the same. The other's personality is directly perceived. The other's character enters the field of the first person's consciousness. Reiterated there, it makes ingress into the first person's life, bringing the two into immediate processual overlap. At the same time, the distance between the two persons that opposes

49 Peirce, *Essential Peirce*, 1:332.
50 Peirce, *Essential Peirce*, 1:332.

them to one another is also directly perceived. The ego, *the I, envelops the difference between persons in its self-constitution, as an overlap doubled by a distinction it does not erase.* The overlap enables the I to interiorize the in-between of persons as the kernel of its own formation. It takes up into itself the moving limit between I and You (and the They behind You). "The psyche is neither pure interiority nor pure exteriority, but an ongoing differentiation and integration."[51]

The integration operates by *processual overlap,* or zones of immediate proximity. The differentiation remains, felt in other's constituting a "less strong" component of the I. The zone of proximity is a generalization—an encompassing of singulars over a spread—in much the same way the contraction of a habit is, and like habit effects itself as a passive synthesis. The I is a contracted habit. The constitutive inclusion of the other in the I means that *the other is a genetic element of the I.* The other formatively "impinges" on me, like any other accident of persons.

My Non-I

The awareness of the impinging other and its overlap with I "enters into the field of direct consciousness of the first person." This does not mean that it necessarily registers on the level of reflexive consciousness. All impingements strike at the infra-level of awareness, which is subconscious. The direct awareness of the ego-other is no exception. It is an instance of what Simondon calls the "communication of subconsciouses."[52]

The field of direct consciousness of the first person *peaks* in reflexive consciousness. It crests as the feeling of "mineness" applied to the zone of proximity between I and You (and the They behind You) formed by the event of impingement. That event is already in the immediate past

---

51 Simondon, *Individuation,* 272. The constitutive relation between self and other is allied to what Bracha Ettinger calls the "co-poiesis of I and non-I." Bracha Ettinger, *The Matrixial Borderspace,* ed. and with an afterword by Brian Massumi (Minneapolis: University of Minnesota Press, 2006).

52 Simondon, *Individuation,* 275.

by the time it settles into the first person's reflexions: "Say 'now' and it was even while you say it."[53]

> Our immediate past is constituted by that occasion, or by that group of fused occasions, which enters into experience devoid of any perceptible medium intervening between it and the present immediate fact. Roughly speaking, it is that portion of our past lying between a tenth of a second and half a second ago. It is gone, and yet it is here. It is our indubitable self, the foundation of our present existence. Yet the present occasion while claiming self-identity, while sharing the very nature of the bygone occasion in all its living activities, nevertheless is engaged in modifying it, in adjusting it to other influences, in completing it with other values, in deflecting it to other purposes. The present moment is constituted by the influx of the other into that self-identity which is the continued life of the immediate past within the immediacy of the present.[54]

The present of impingement is gone by the time it is owned. Its lost arrival is unowned, occurring as it does between I and other, in an interstice of experience, straddling the difference between persons with an overlap. The overlap is what Whitehead means by self-identity. This is not self-identity in the sense of the interiority of a subject. It is conceived temporally. It is the dawning of the present moment in the inherited necessity of conforming to the immediate past impinging upon it and making ingress into it. The self-identity is the processual overlap of the present with its immediate past, with which it coincides, no sooner to depart on a vector to the future. This is self-identity as impetus of otherness.

The immediate past overlapping with the dawning present is aboriginally owned only by itself. It is its own thought, occurring on the level of what James terms "pure experience," or Firstness for Peirce (in this case, a Firstness of Secondness, an immediacy of the first and second person entering direct consciousness together). The direct consciousness is not in the ego. It is an ego. It is its own self, forming the transitional

---

53 William James, A Pluralistic Universe (Lincoln: University of Nebraska Press, 1996), 254.

54 Whitehead, Adventures of Ideas, 181.

in-between of the coming event. It is in the world. It no sooner occurs than it is immediately, unmediatedly *appropriated* by the reflexive I, becoming ego in that owning, a me for I. The ongoing constitution of the person envelops this event of the impingement of the other (the opening for which is the fundamental operation of perception). The event resonates in that constitution, tethering the person's becoming to a relational in-between of encounter, even as it catapults it forward into an individual, unshareable historic route all I's own. Along that route, this differentiated I will pulse back into self-identity, moment to moment following the rhythm of impingement from the outside and other.

The reflexive I is an over-self. First-person reflexive experience is in the mode of *possession*—having, not being. "My process of 'being myself' is my origination from my possession of the world."[55]

This opens a constitutive gap between ego and I. Ego, paradoxically, is in the self-identity that is in the world, other-wise incoming. The I surfs the incomings. This withdraws ego and I from the purview of psychology. Psychology turns inside out. The other is now at the center of psychic process. Other is anything impinging: a sound, an image, a word, a rustle in the surrounds. It is other influences, values, purposes—including those of the immediate past in the historic route of the peak person now newly re-expressing as "I." It is of course also the other in the usual sense, an other person, impinging as a singularly general idea whose character makes felt a life-pattern plying a different historic route that just-then, momentarily, collided with I-now, in an accident of persons.

Again: "The recognition by one person of another's personality takes place by means to some extent identical with the means by which he is conscious of his own personality." In both cases, "only later [is] the event divided into a distinction between consciousness and its object," becoming "my" thought.

In the interval, a process of appropriation is carried out; the thought that follows is accomplished by the preceding thought, inheriting it; such is the retrospective act of appropriation of thought, even

55 Whitehead, *Process and Reality*, 81.

as it also tends toward the future. "Each pulse of cognitive consciousness, each Thought, dies away and is replaced by another . . . Each Thought is thus born an owner, and dies owned, transmitting whatever it realized as its Self to its own later proprietor . . ."[56]

Thus the thought-event, the neutral and indefinite "thought goes on" described by psychology, becomes my thought, the thought of my consciousness, through a work of immediate retrospective appropriation that integrates it into prior thoughts—possesses it. It is a process of interpretation. *To be conscious is to interpret the present still impersonal thought to be mine.* No sooner does the act of possession occur than pure experience transforms and disappears as such; *it enters into a perspective.* The datum becomes my datum, constituted from a past in light of a future. Experience has become material for interpretation.[57]

Strange Intruders

All of this adds a new dimension to the person as general idea, and to the idea as a little person. The reflexive I, far from being a bounded, particular identity, is a synthetic form of overlap with the outside—a "conjunctive synthesis" in Deleuze and Guattari's vocabulary—peaking in individual, first-person expression and in the feeling that fills its moment.[58] The "lesser strength" of the other-component in first-person expression is enveloped in the overtaking "I" that comes to own, and thus supersede, it. What we experience as our "internal" stream of consciousness is thought propelled by the incoming of the other. Each new thought is a "strange intruder" from the other-world.[59] Even "internal" to the flow of its personal historic route, I is its own other (its

56 James, *Principles of Psychology*, 1:339.
57 David Lapoujade, *William James: Empiricism and Subjectivity*, trans. and with an afterword by Thomas Lamarre (Durham, NC: Duke University Press, 2020), 18 (emphasis added).
58 Conjunctive synthesis: Deleuze and Guattari, *Anti-Oedipus*, 16–22.
59 C. S. Peirce, *Pragmatism as a Principle and Method of Right Thinking: The 1903 Lectures on Pragmatism* (Albany: State University of New York Press, 1997), 144.

other owned). Strange intruders come in crowds. Behind each, there are
many, forming a series.

> A thought is itself a sign, and should itself have an utterer (namely,
> the ego of a previous moment), to whose consciousness it must have
> been already virtually present, and so back. Likewise, after a sign has
> been interpreted, it will virtually remain in the consciousness of its
> interpreter, where it will be a Sign . . . and, as a sign should, in its
> turn have an interpreter, and so on forward. Now it is undeniably
> conceivable that a beginningless series of successive utterers should
> do all their work in a brief interval of time, and that so should an
> endless series of interpreters. Still, it is not likely to be denied that
> in some cases, neither the series of utterers nor that of interpreters
> forms an infinite collection. When this is the case, there must be a
> sign without an utterer and a sign without an interpreter.[60]

Thought the Thinker

Think of the intersections at every step in each series: series upon series
within series. An ocean of utterance, enveloped in every ego moment
peaking in I expression. A world-filling reticulation of third persons
enveloped in the first person. They. Blanchot's anonymous murmur,
incoming with every successive just-past impingement that no sooner
comes than was.[61] At the limit of this web of utterances, flowing to
infinity, there cannot not be a sign without an utterer and a sign without an interpreter. Ultimately, as James says, "the thought is itself the
thinker."[62] It thinks like it rains, in the fourth person singular.

60   Peirce, *Essential Peirce*, 2:403–4.
61   On the anonymous murmur (of free indirect discourse), see Maurice Blanchot,
     The Space of Literature, trans. Ann Smock (Lincoln: University of Nebraska Press,
     1989), 26, 47, 50; Maurice Blanchot, *The Infinite Conversation*, trans. Susan Hanson
     (Minneapolis: University of Minnesota Press, 1993), 159, 242, 329; Deleuze and
     Guattari, *Thousand Plateaus*, 77, 105.
62   James, *Principles of Psychology*, 1:401.

The "they" is not a derangement of discourse. It is the condition of thought. The question is not to expunge the they from I and mine. It is how otherwise to own it.

All of this is a way of asserting the "machinic" nature of thought. Thought is self-effecting, operative and ongoing, backward and forward across its world-filling web. Thoughts have no definite beginning or end, no source other than their own event. They are creatures of the stream. Their operation is predicated on overlap (with the other in just-past pure experience) and envelopment (of the difference with the other in the overlap, subsisting in trace form in the ego, as owned by I). "Thought, like an onion, is composed of nothing but wrappings."[63] Thought enwraps us.

Accordingly, just as we say that a body is in motion, and not that motion is in a body, we ought to say that we are in thought and not that thoughts are in us.[64]

Commind

Again, the wrappings and overlap, for greater and for lesser, in non-I and I, incoming owned, forbids us to say: "'I am altogether myself, and not at all you.'"

> Your neighbors are, in a measure, yourself, and in far greater measure than . . . you would believe. . . . In the second place, all men [sic] who resemble you and are in analogous circumstances are, in a measure, yourself, though not quite in the same way in which your neighbors are you.[65]

It is worth repeating with Peirce: the definitely bounded, self-sufficient "selfhood" you like to attribute to yourself is, for the most part, the vulgarest delusion of vanity. This "barbaric conception of personal identity must be broadened."[66]

---

63   Peirce, *Essential Peirce*, 2:460.
64   Peirce, *Essential Peirce*, 2:227.
65   Peirce, *Essential Peirce*, 2:2.
66   Peirce, *Essential Peirce*, 2:2, 3.

The broadening begins as soon as it is realized that "all that is necessary . . . to the existence of the person is that the feelings out of which he [sic] is constructed should be in close enough connection to influence one another" and "that if this be the case, there should be something like personal consciousness in bodies of men [sic]." There is "*corporate personality*"—or what was characterized above as a collective singular indexically supporting a class name—by the very same token that there is individual personality pertaining to a single body.[67] By "close enough" read "impinging."

When Peirce makes this comment in the passage just cited he invokes the extreme case of a perfect harmony of "sympathy," like a nationalist esprit de corps animating a military parade, or the fellow-feeling of a Christian revival meeting. These examples lend themselves to the charismatic version of collective movement that Peirce's thought is being mobilized here to deflect. Elsewhere Peirce corrects this impression: "The question is *not* whether *ego* and *non-ego* are manifestations of some incomprehensible substratum which in some incomprehensible sense is the one substance of them both [as opposed to their reticulation in an open field]. The whole question is what the *perceptual facts* are." The perceptual facts are "an *ego* and *non-ego* "directly acting upon each other," in an impingement governing a transition. "Their characters are a fact that involves them both."[68] This makes every thought a double consciousness.[69] The characters of ego and non-ego, I and non-I, share the accidental quality of surprise. Surprise, in Peirce's account, is the key to answering the question of what perceptual facts are.[70]

This is a thoroughly event-based, rather than a substance-based, explanation. It relies on no mystical union, transcendent togetherness, or mind-melding harmony. It is in fact as thoroughly *differential* as it is eventful. Although I and non-I co-compose a unitary fact, their *contrast* remains forever ingredient to it. The I retains an undertone of otherness

---

67   Peirce, *Essential Peirce*, 2:350, 351.

68   Peirce, *Pragmatism as a Principle*, 145.

69   Du Bois's racialized double consciousness is a hardening of this under the oppression of the Man-Standard. W. E. B. Du Bois, *The Souls of Black Folk* (New York: Bantam, 1989), 3.

70   Peirce, *Pragmatism as a Principle*, 144.

as a birthmark, which is why every thought is inherently co-thought ("a double consciousness"). In addition, the perceptual facts bead together to form series, the transitions with which they coincide composing historic routes. Returning to the multiple-level, fractal-wrapping model developed above, each moment in a life as it travels its historic route, each transition along the route constituting a perceptual fact, takes its place against a tangle of historic sub- and over-routes. Each will be embedded in the world's advance in a different way, depending on what preceded and conditioned its surprise, and what modulation of the direction of its route eventuated from it. There is no absolute harmony or togetherness *even internal to a single life*. There is differential co-involvement in the same compound advancing wave, distributed across levels, and self-sectioning into eddies. The same thing can be said (only more so) of a plurality of individuals falling into step to form a marching collective singular on parade.

The model is one of *integration* rather than unification. The difference is that unification erases difference in the transcendent oneness of a substance, whereas event-based integration retains differences. It is made of difference. It is a bundle of differentials forming a complex patterning of contrasts, webbing the world.

The only unity is a *unity of movement*: a dynamic unity. The movement across transitions of the co-involved facts *correlates* rather than homogenizing them. The correlation patterns the character of a greater person. The orientation of that greater person's historic route is a canalization of the collective. The greater person's component members are swept along the same stream, even if each individual eddies with its own mannerism, expressing a sub-personality (and so on ad infinitum).

The question is then, absent a substratum which would be a common substance, what accounts for the power of canalization? If each sub-personality retains its own character and in itself constitutes a differential, how is it inducted into a correlated movement following a shared orientation? The shared orientation is an outcome of the components' falling into correlation. But what conditions their falling-in together? This is the political question.

The answer is to be found, as always, on the level of the "perceptual fact." Each impingement, or accident of persons, takes place against a background activity that conditions its occurrence. The background-ing proto-orients, or "preaccelerates," accidents-of-persons' peaking in surprise.[71] Conditioned *and* unanticipated. Quasi-causal. Not willed, not caused, in any usual sense of these terms. This quasi-causal back-ground is a kind of infra-stream setting the environmental conditions for different currents to form and peak in waves of owned expression. It is best understood in terms of what Peirce calls the *commind*.

> There is a determination of that mind into which the minds of utterer and interpreter have to be [dynamically] fused in order that any com-munication should take place. This mind may be called the commens. *No object can be denoted unless it be put into relation to the object of the commens.*[72]

> Consciousness is really just a net connecting one person with another—only in this capacity did it have to develop; the solitary and predatory person would not have needed it.[73]

Which circles us back to the general idea and the person.

> The consciousness of [or more accurately, the consciousness that *is*] the general idea has a certain "unity of the ego," which is identical *when it passes* from one mind to another. It is, therefore, quite analogous to a person; and indeed a person is only a particular kind of general idea.[74]

Recap

1) From a process-oriented perspective, the base definition of gen-erality can be given as a spanning of a multiplicity of elements, where the spanning has a reality of its own over and above the individuality of the elements,

---

71 Manning, *Relationscapes*, 3–28. How this preaccelerating background condition-ing works in racism is addressed in the "Accidents of Persons Predisposed" section of part 5.

72 Peirce, *Essential Peirce*, 2:478 (emphasis added).

73 Friedrich Nietzsche, *The Gay Science*, ed. Bernard Williams, trans. Josefine Nauck-hoff and Adrian Del Caro (Cambridge: Cambridge University Press, 2001), 212.

74 Peirce, *Essential Peirce*, 1:350 (emphasis added).

2) The general does not suppress the individuality of the elements. It boosts them, collectively, to another level of organization.

3) That reality of the general is a dynamic shape, or pattern. Patterning is the emergent level of organization arising from the coming-together of elements moving-together across a shared trajectory, to joint effect.

4) A pattern is an integration of different elements into a dynamic unity (a "static" object, as will be discussed later in the "Real Distinction" section of the postscript, is a lowest-degree dynamic unity). The integration can be thought of as the fusion of their several effects into one overall effect. Together in the patterning, the elements effectively count as one. Spinoza: "If a number of individuals so concur in one action that together they are all the cause of one effect, I consider them all, to that extent, as one singular thing."[75]

5) A pattern has character: a qualitative manner that expresses its singularity.

6) What has character is a person. Conversely, a person is a character (or figure, on which more later).

7) A character has the effect of one, but is internally differentiated, carrying a many internal to its constitution.

8) What carries is matter in movement, which is what constitutes a body when it counts for one across successive occasions in a historic route.

9) The body is an individual. Or better, because it is matter-in-movement, an individuation.

10) The person—the pattern of the individual's matter-in-movement or "bodying" (see below)—is really distinct from that individual. You can't separate the top from the spin, but it is the spinning that has a character.

11) The name of a character is a class-name. The class-name is not a general that subsumes particulars. It an index of a multiplicity of elements dynamically coming-together to joint effect. The character

75 Baruch Spinoza, *The Ethics*, in *The Complete Works of Spinoza*, vol. 1, ed. and trans. Edwin Curley (Princeton, NJ: Princeton University Press, 1985), E2, D7.

has a singularity. The elements are a multiplicity. The class-name therefore indexes a collective singular (or singular-collective).

12) A collective singular is a "living reality": a real population exhibiting a kinship in character due to common genetic elements entering into the constitution of the individuals composing the population. The class-name indexes a reality. The individuals compose singular variations on the character of their collective. What is indexed is a continuous variation within a spectrum of character in which each participates. The spectrum is fractal, and in principle infinite.

13) Each element entering into the constitution of a character, or person, has its own character: the pattern of its sub-elements coming-together and moving-together. Persons are Russian dolls.

14) In view of this, the words "individual" and "collective" are relative. Every individual is composite, but can count as one on the level of its effective patterning. Every counting for one envelops multiple elements. Even proper names index collective singulars.[76]

15) Consequently, all persons are collective persons, and all individuals are collective individuations. It is a matter of perspective whether, with respect to a given nameable instance, we refer to it as a person or an individual or as a corporate person or collective individuation. It is approaching the same living reality from different angles: the multiplicity of its constitution or the unity of its effectively counting as one due to the integration of that multiplicity into an overall effect.

16) There are thus sub-persons and sub-individuals: little persons and greater persons. This applies to all levels of organization. Every level is further divisible (until you reach the full body and the plane of immanence, which are infra-personal fields; see part 3).

17) The foregoing points are necessary but not sufficient to the definition of a person. A person is nothing without experience. In other words, character is not simply a patterning. It is directly *felt*, as a

76 On the proper name as indexing a multiplicity, see Deleuze and Guattari, *Anti-Oedipus*, 86, 311; and Deleuze and Guattari, *Thousand Plateaus*, 27–28, 37–38, 84, 142, 153, 263–64.

dynamic unity. And it *feels*: it registers its component elements' characters in its own.

18) The feeling is a thinking-feeling. It comes as an immediate perceptual judgment of character, and the perceptual judgment presents directly felt hypotheses, or abductions. The most basic abduction is the expectation of a continuing from a just-before, following an arc. The thinking-feeling of the arc is a synthesis of successive moments. This synthesis self-effects, or is self-conducting: it is a "passive synthesis."

19) Passive syntheses, like all things, have a conatus: a striving. The most basic form of the conatus of a passive synthesis is tendency: a self-proposing arc of activity. Habit is the self-conducting repetition of an arc of activity (acquired tendency). The greater portion of the activity of an individual or person is habitual.

20) The self-proposing of tendency and self-conducting of habit goes unfelt in the constitution of the person. But their feeling (Whitehead would say "prehension") of their own elements continues underneath and through it all. This is an example of unfelt feelings, feeling that are in the constitution of the peak-level person but not felt by it (for more on unfelt feelings see the "Micrologic and Amplification" section of part 3 and the "Optive Matter" and "Perspective" sections of part 4).

21) The fact that the greater portion of the activity of an individual or person is habitual, and habit is a passive synthesis that self-effects, has grave consequences for the concept of agency. It must be replaced by a concept of agencying. In other words, a "machinic" concept.

22) An individual person, such as one belonging to the collective singular class-named "human," is not an interiority. It is constitutively open to the outside. This is because the body that is matter-in-movement is not a container, but a sieve, whose holes are the senses. The body is a port of ingress for "other" influences. These ingresses of the other are constitutive elements in the body's personing.

23) I am made of other. I am how I own those other influences, how I possess them and integrate them into my character. Looked at from a slightly different angle, how I possess them is also how

I am possessed by them (how I am made of their influences).[77] I am possessed of a non-I, and it, possessed, is me. Or, to put it another way, "your neighbors are, in a measure, yourself, and in far greater measure than you would believe."

24) There is a necessary place in the understanding of personhood for the the impersonal, or non-personal, as constitutive—on the level of what will be called here the infra-personal. *The impersonal element is self-identity.* Self-identity as defined by Whitehead as the continued life of the last moment in the onset of the next, is an infra-personal element of process personing.

25) On the level of discourse, the non-I is the impingement of others' sign emissions on my personing.[78] "They" possess me through their sign-strikes, in impingement and overlap. And I possess them in turn through the way in which I integrate their sign-strikes into the life patterning that is my ongoing character. Multiple persons in joint possession.

26) The mutual possession of persons in social discourse machines a collective thinking-feeling: a commind.

Why?

Why go through such conceptual contortions that seem to lead us so far away from Trump and fascism? Because they loop us back to them, equipped with new conceptual tools. They are meant to provide a rigorous basis on which to assert the reality of collective individuations and collective persons, without metaphor or exaggeration. The concept of collective personhood is necessary to remove fascism from the vice-grips of the theory of charismatic leadership, in order to renew its understanding. I cannot "identify" with my non-I—whose very otherness is constitutive of the person I am. I can only integrate it into my ongoing differentiation.

77 For an analysis of other influences as constitutive of self, see Jane Bennett, *Influx and Efflux: Writing Up with Walt Whitman* (Durham, NC: Duke University Press, 2020).

78 For an analysis of the impingement of the other as radical sympathy, see Massumi, *The Power at the End of the Economy,* 57–78.

PART 3

The Full Body and I

The Full Body Retooled

The concept of the full body was mobilized in the first part of this essay in a first approximation of the collective agencying (machinic assembling) of individuation and personhood with respect to the body of the leader. There are any number of kinds of full body, each associated with a different social formation and defining its "socius." Deleuze and Guattari speak of the socius as a system of coding, in tension with decodings. Codings involve territorializations (systemic captures), in tension and processual coupling with deterriorializations involving decodings (escapes). The socius is the field of emergence of social *figures*.

In *Anti-Oedipus*, Deleuze and Guattari speak of the full body of the earth, of the despot, and of capital, correlating respectively to non-state tribal societies ("primitive" societies in the anthropological literature of the twentieth century), extremist state societies ("barbaric" societies), and capitalist society (from its tentative precursors in the "pores" or at the limits of other forms of society to its coming to full expression in what Guattari called "Integrated World Capitalism," which in the time of his writing on it in the 1970s and 1980s was just beginning to consolidate into what we now, in its heyday, refer to more simply as neoliberalism).[1] All full bodies have quasi-causal powers. The Trump full body is a despotic full body with "miraculating" quasi-causal power. Living as it does in a "modern," "democratic" society, it is what Deleuze

---

[1] Félix Guattari and Antonio Negri, *New Lines of Alliance, New Spaces of Liberty,* trans. Michael Ryan, Jared Becker, Araine Bove, and Noel LeBlanc (London: Minor Compositions, 1990); Guattari, *Chaosmosis,* 122.

and Guattari call an "archaism with a contemporary function."[2] As we will see, it essentially overlaps, in the figure of its personhood, with the capitalist full body, or field of operative potential. It is this overlap that gives Trump's archaism its contemporary function.

The full body was discussed above in terms of potential qualifications that may be applied to bodies through ascription, such as friend or enemy, man or woman. This is in fact only one side of the full body: the side on which it faces the merely abstract class-names corresponding to socially coded roles, or collective persons indexed by abstract general ideas. On its other side, through the far side of the collective singular, it faces the infrapersonal turbulence of which these class-names are ultimately limitative derivatives, labels for pailsful, spoonsful, quartpotsful, and barrelsful of process, apportioned. This far side is the realm of "intensities," in Deleuze and Guattari's vocabulary, or, for Whitehead, simply "feeling." At the limit, underyond the reach of consciousness, at the level of thought thinking itself like it rains, intensity recedes into "pure feeling," corresponding to James's "pure experience" of "thought going on."

The full body forms the background activity of thought (integration, differentiation, passive synthesis, generalization) from which individual thoughts formatively peak, and from which they formally stand out. It is the "context" of all conscious reflection and all emotion—of all individualized personal experience.[3]

Part 2 of this essay ended with Peirce's enigmatic statement that "no object can be denoted unless it can be put into relation with the object of the commens," the commind. Take "denoted" loosely, stretching to "qualified," "attributed" (not to mention indexed and iconized). Then consider that *the full body is the object of the commind*. And that "they" is its speaking subject.

This is less a conclusion than a restarting point, toward retooling the concept of the full body for Trump World.

---

2 Deleuze and Guattari, *Anti-Oedipus*, 132, 240, 251, 257–58, 260, 310.
3 Context is understood here in Susanne Langer's sense of a field of immanent constitutive factors. See Langer, *Mind*, vol. 1; Massumi, "From Aesthetic Frights to the Politics of Unspeakable Thought with Susanne Langer," in *The Bloomsbury Handbook of Susanne K. Langer*, ed. Lona Gaikis (London: Bloomsbury, 2023).

Figuring the Full Body

In part 1, the question of what constitutes a media figure was raised and, related to that, "figure" was at times used interchangeably with "person." Figuration is a complex concept, requiring, for a processual take on it, a quadriplex distinction between figural, figurative, figuration, and figure.

The *figurative* is the collective assemblage, or bundled array of jointly varying operations, that enables a discrete figure corresponding to a qualified person, individual or collective, to stand out from the background of the social field of emergence to count as one. *Figure* refers both to the qualification of an individual body to which a class-name applies, and to the class-name itself on which the applied qualification is based (since the figure as class-name is attributed to the body, and the body becomes into it, the figure straddles these levels). The *figural* is the field of potential from which figurative potentials are drawn: the full body considered in its infinite fullness with alternate qualifications. It is the "figure-matrix."[4] *Figuration* is the process of transition from the figural to the figure through the figurative: the transduction of the full spectrum of potential alternative qualifications into a limitative set of actual figures.

It was intimated (not unproblematically) that this process was a structuration. The system of qualifications corresponding to recognized social roles (the Man-Standard in the foregoing analysis) was spoken of as the "structure" of society (the full body as socius, seen from the angle of its coding). In our era, the structure of the socius, it was contended, is as self-destructuring as it is self-structuring, as post-normatively decoding as coding. With respect to its self-destructuring aspect, it was said that it was more accurate to call it a "field" of differentiation than a structure.

It is necessary to specify *self*-structuring and *self*-destructuring because the transition that is figuration occurs without an agent separate from the action. The appearance of a figure is the full body thinking itself into recognizable form, ultimately without an assignable utterer or interpreter

---

4 Deleuze and Guattari, *Anti-Oedipus*, 244.

(but rather an as-good-as-endless seriation of them). This is an agencying: the functional equivalent of agency, but without an actor; a subjectivity without a subject. It is machinic.

Schizzing the Structure of Society

The full body was described as being composed of potentials supporting contrasting qualifications, or performative ascriptions. On the full body, these are held together disjunctively, in and as their difference from each other. As conceived by Deleuze and Guattari in *Anti-Oedipus*, the full body is a *disjunctive synthesis*: a holding of potential ascriptions together in their difference from each other. There are two modes of disjunctive synthesis. Exclusive disjunctive synthesis holds potentials apart-together in such a way that they tend to segregate out into different figures, answering to different class-names applied to bodies to cover their counting for one. An inclusive disjunctive synthesis holds potentials bound together, still in their difference from each other, in such a way that the complex cannot be divided and segregated out without changing in nature. The full body toggles between these modes of disjunctive synthesis. The first plots to the general idea in the guise of the "merely abstract" traditional category. The second pertains to the general idea as really abstract, or as the "living reality" of a collective singular.[5]

The full body is full in the sense that it is fully saturated with distinctions. There is no empty space on the full body. It is a continuum. What are thought of as opposing qualifications, like man-woman or friend-enemy, immediately call upon each other across their difference, filling the hyphen separating them with a resonation that pulls them in together, in processual collusion and mutual inclusion. All exclusive disjunctive syntheses are worked from within, in spite of themselves, by a movement toward mutual inclusion. Exclusive and inclusive syntheses are not exclusive of each other. They co-occur, following simultaneous

---

5 Exclusive disjunctive synthesis: Deleuze and Guattari, *Anti-Oedipus*, 9–16, 39, 75. Inclusive disjunctive synthesis: Deleuze and Guattari, *Anti-Oedipus*, 60, 70, 78, 162, 183, 287.

tendencies toward segregation and mutual inclusion. They double each other, on different levels or in different dimensions of the same level.

The hyphen between contrasting terms is active. The pull of the in-between toward mutual inclusion exerts a gravitational force on the opposing potential qualifications, creating a field of distortion. One side may move toward the other, in a trans-movement. Or the two may enter into an oscillation. The trans-movements and oscillations are creative, producing the potential for new qualifications: new possibilities of ascription or transformations of the existing ascriptions.

The ascription or self-ascription of these qualifications/transformations to an empirically existing individual body or aggregate of bodies helps catalyze the formation of a new *existential territory* added to the social landscape.[6] An existential territory is a complex of mutually referring operations that spans a field composed of degrees of freedom of movement, feeling, and thought. The operations unfold in the field as spatiotemporal dynamisms: to put it simply, modes of life.[7] The territory can be marked as a place, or it can be an abstract space (for example, what is commonly spoken of in terms of an identity, but not limited to that).

In current social theoretical and political parlance, the process of territorialization is referred to in terms of "positionality." This is unfortunate terminology because territories are emergent fields, limited by thresholds rather than boundaries. It is only later, as a secondary operation of structuration, that they discipline their fielding and settle into a fixed form with clear coordinates that agonistically position them vis-à-vis others. The emergence of a new mode of life is dispositional: occurring in the alluring in-between of "positions."

The formation of a new existential territory is connective. For example, a new manner of connecting organs of the human body toward

---

6 Deleuze and Guattari, *Thousand Plateaus*, 310–50.

7 This brings us back to the proprioceptive nature of the full body of the leader, discussed earlier. The spatiotemporal dynamisms, in mutual inclusion as pure potentials on the plane of immanence or as real potentials on the full body (a distinction that will be developed later), from which they unfold to take on specific spatiotemporal shape and the form and content that comes with it, can only be felt proprioceptively (the sense modality dedicated to movement and the variations of the body in movement). See Massumi, *Parables*, 177–207.

a peak of experience gives rise to habits and practices that self-affirm as a new mode of sexualized life. That new mannerism or mode of existence—including the codes that come to govern it and the life trajectories that both form and result from the codes—is the existential territory. Existential territories arise emergently through "*connective synthesis.*" Once formed, they add themselves to the full body's disjunctive system of distinctions, as a potential emergence and a potential ascription. In the vocabulary of *Anti-Oedipus*, they are "recorded," remembered by and in the world's constitution.[8]

The full body is both an archive of existing ascriptions, and a creative field of emergence for new ones, or variations on the old. It is an abstract surface of recording: a non-personal memory—including of the future, if the powers of emergence incumbent in it are taken into consideration.

The full body is more accurately called a field than a structure because of its ordering as a continuum. It is saturated with any number of potential distinctions. As discussed in part 1, these plunge from the cut between any two qualifications into an infinite, proliferative regress. The cuts-between correspond to the formative "interval" between consciously registered thoughts, coinciding with the impingement of "strange intruders" discussed in part 2 (and in part 5 in terms of the "pathic"). The insistence of the cut means that on the full body, $1 + 2$ does not equal 3 (anything but that Oedipal number, which only gets a foothold through the forcing of the full body into the territorial confines of the bourgeois family). $1 + 2 = n$. N, any number: nondenumerable. The full body is a fuzzy set.

The cut-between in the full body's proliferating infinity is what Deleuze and Guattari call the *schiz*. Schizoanalysis is named for it. Any sign that points to it is a *point-sign*. What the point-sign ultimately points to is an angle of insertion into the infinite potential held within the full body. It is like a signpost to potential on a highway to transformation.[9]

---

8 Connective synthesis: Deleuze and Guattari, *Anti-Oedipus*, 1–8, 68–75. Production of recording: Deleuze and Guattari, *Anti-Oedipus*, 10–15, 75–84.

9 Schiz: Deleuze and Guattari, *Anti-Oedipus*, 131–32, 230, 244, 260, 325; Manning, *For a Pragmatics of the Useless*, 146–97. Point-sign: Deleuze and Guattari, *Anti-Oedipus*, 112, 260, 328, 352, 366; Guattari, *Chaosmosis*, 40–50; Guattari, *Machinic Unconscious*, 184.

Point-Sign

The point-sign performs the cut of the schiz. To feel the potential, even over a threshold or on the horizon, is already to fall prey to its gravitational pull, attracted toward trajectories as yet unknown. This is the pull of *desire*. The point-sign—in its functioning as the performative *index* of a potential infinity of qualifications to come, signposting the immanence of the full body—is the fundamental operator of desire.[10] The potentials array themselves in trajectories, potential transitions from one to the next. These present as a tangle, a web of potential seriations, or series formations, receding from the schiz toward as-yet unknown, unarisen territories (for the potential for novel connections accompanies the transitions). At the point-sign, the trajectories and connections—a plethora of potential existential territories—present together, in absolute proximity, in the cut.

In the only glosses of the mysterious concept of the point-sign in Deleuze and Guattari's works, Guattari likens it to quantum tunneling. The series it envelops are abstract (but real), presenting a purely logical order (such as the series receding from the Man-Standard in *A Thousand Plateaus*: becoming-woman, becoming-child, becoming-animal, becoming-mineral, becoming-imperceptible). There is no need to move sequentially along them. "Mutant flows" can jump from one qualification to another, or from one series to another at any distance, in no time flat—just as a subatomic particle can tunnel through space-time.[11]

With this in mind, the "absolute proximity" of potential ascriptions of the full body can be imaged either as a collapse into an infinitely dense point in space—a *"black hole"*—or a diffusion into an infinitely fast set of movements between all possible points in space, co-occurring in the same widthless moment—a diaphanous *"white wall."*[12] To approach a black hole or a white wall is to approach the *"plane of immanence"* of

---

10 "Machinic indices": Deleuze and Guattari, *Anti-Oedipus*, 318, 322, 339, 350.

11 Point-signs, tunneling: Guattari, *Chaosmosis*, 40–50; Guattari, *Machinic Unconscious*, 184. Series of becomings: Deleuze and Guattari, *Thousand Plateaus*, 232–309. Mutant flows: Deleuze and Guattari, *Anti-Oedipus*, 346, 374.

12 Deleuze and Guattari, *Anti-Oedipus*, 167–91.

the full body: its absolute limit, enveloped in its every expression; the virtual whole of it. These are two images we can usefully apply to something that is essentially without an image, by dint of being too full of qualifications to have one itself. Both figure the "whole" of the fuzzy set of the plane of immanence as an infinite *superposition* of dispositions. But it doesn't really have a whole, since what defines its consistency are proliferating cuts in the middle, schizzes. If it is a figure, it is a fractal. But it is not a figure: it is the *figural*—the field of figurative potential, from which ascribable figures emerge.

The "art" of schizoanalysis is to escape capture in normal or normopathic structures of personhood, while navigating the Scylla and Charybdis of falling into a black hole and being annihilated by its life-crushing density, or being torn apart by the equally unlivable velocities stirring alluringly behind the transparency of the white wall. The approach to the white wall is the movement of "deterritorialization" and "decoding" that Deleuze and Guattari call *schizophrenia* (as a collective process, as opposed to a pathology ascribed to an individual).[13] In both of these offices, portal to a black hole or breakthrough of the surface of the white wall, the point-sign indexes the absolute limit of the full body, and thus of society's orderings (the socius). It points through to where the full body falls outside its effective field of differentiations into pure, abstract potential. Nothing can live in pure potential.

Capitalism operationalizes point-signs economically. It is schizophrenic in that sense. But it always pulls back before hitting the absolute limit. In the moment of danger, it reorders the movements indexable to the full body into a limiting, but supple, system of disjunctions, conjunctions, and translations between deterritorialized flows. This is what Deleuze and Guattari call an "axiomatic," in contradistinction to a code.[14] A territory is coded. It is composed of an arrangement of specifiable qualifications and more or less fixed positions (or more accurately, remarkable points) and point-to-point trajectories between them. An axiomatic is a hyper-complex code of the in-between of qualifications

13 Deleuze and Guattari, Anti-Oedipus, 4–6, 281–83.
14 Deleuze and Guattari, Anti-Oedipus, 238, 240–62; Deleuze and Guattari, *Thousand Plateaus*, 434–73.

and positions: a transformational map of the potential translations be-tween them.

Axiomatics are open-ended, in that axioms can always be added or subtracted. But they are also limiting, because they are governed by a privileged operator acting as a master-key, around which all the trans-formations revolve. Any movement approaching the absolute limit of a black hole or white wall is turned back by the pull of that operator. For individual bodies, the pullback is personhood and the key opera-tor is the privative owning of character (I-me-mine). For capitalism, the key operator is the capitalist relation itself: the quadratic distinc-tion worker-capitalist/money as means of payment-investment money. Working together, these distinctions form an assemblage that snares bodies within a limited but infinite field of operations: the capitalist field. They set a *relative limit* defined by how the axiomatic self-reorders (adds or subtracts axioms) in the face of the danger of an absolute de-territorialization that would entail the breakdown of the system.

Not to pull back to the relative limit is what Deleuze and Guattari term revolutionary. Schizoanalysis is the "art" and "ethics" of refusing to snap back into recognized personhood and the vicissitudes of the self-deforming grid of the axiomatic, while at the same time endeavor-ing to avoid a breakdown—moving instead to a "breakthrough," toward brave new worlds of potential: a "new earth."[15] The artfulness of this is knowing how to reterritorialize just enough to survive. But not only survive—to thrive on the newly ascribable potentials of an expanded full body outside the capitalist pale, in touch with the unplumbed potentials of the infra-personal.

Umbral Union

The status of distinctions marking potential ascriptions changes as the full body approaches its absolute limit of the infinite superposition of potentials, or the plane of immanence that is the full body's open virtual

---

15 Breakthrough: Deleuze and Guattari, Anti-Oedipus, 132–36, 278. New earth: Deleuze and Guattari, Anti-Oedipus, 131, 299, 319, 382; and Deleuze and Guattari, Thousand Plateaus, 432, 510.

whole. A threshold is passed to a new logic. The components of the full body at this level

are things that do not exist. That is to say they do not belong to the universe of fundamental hypothesis, being neither B nor M in the dichotomic mathematics.[16] In other mathematics, they have no existence in the universe of quantity. But joined together in sets, they do. They are just like chemical radicles, each having a certain number of unsatisfied wants. When each of these is satisfied by union with another, the completely saturated whole has an existence in the universe of quantity. Surely the word *umbral* utterly fails to suggest all that; while the word *radicle* gives the idea exactly. The mathematics which results from following out this idea of Leibniz which I rediscovered for myself and applied to dichotomic mathematics is, in mathematics taken generally, now most usually called the theory of matrices. But I do not think that the icon of a matrix exhibits the idea quite so well as the idea of a chemical radicle does. The application of this ideas to logic gives the *exact logic of relatives*.[17]

Extrapolating from Peirce's mathematical concept, the plane of immanence of the full body is a matrix, full not of things having quantity, but of "radicles" having only relation. The radicles enter into "union" with each other in a non-mutually-exclusive way (in a matrix). They do not have individuality in the sense of being outside and alongside each other. They are in superposition. Although they do not have individuality, they do have "wants." This gives them a valence (making them values rather than substantial things). A valence of wanting is a desiring. They are seeds or incipiencies of aims, orientations, and tendencies, only as yet without the actual aims, orientations, or tendencies. When a

16 By "dichotomic mathematics" Peirce means a mathematics built on a two-value logic. Rather than saying X and Y as we might tend to today, he says B and M (*bonus* and *malus*), to underline that the terms designate values. For a process philosophical approach, a fundamental twoness is a *contrast*, which is something quite different from an opposition (the contrasting colors of a painting are not in opposition, but in differential concertation). On contrast, see Whitehead, *Adventures of Ideas*, pt. 4, 241–96.

17 Peirce, *Pragmatism as a Principle*, 125.

selection of them joins together in union, aims, orientations, and tendencies spark into motion, and they enter the world of quantity. They are then at the cusp, approaching the on-ramp of the road to individuation, of emergence into qualifiable form that can stand as a definite term in relation with another similarly emergent form. In themselves, they are subject only to an "exact" logic of relation—relation *as such*, absent any actual terms in relation. In themselves, they are pure forms of relation holding potentials for individuation, in the transition toward which their wanting relation produces or acquires its own terms. Their pure forms of relation are forms of potential transition to qualifiable form (forms in the conventional sense, as composed of actual parts joining in actual wholes whose definiteness makes them susceptible of measure). They are valences of pure potential. This is the realm of Schmitt's "borderline concepts," at the limit, encompassing far more, infinitely more, than friend/enemy (see the "Collective Individuation" section of part 1 for Schmitt on borderline concepts; for more on umbral union and its status as a concept, see the "Umbral Union" section of the postscript).

There has been a lot of discussion in the foregoing of the performative, downward causality of ascription. The desiring of potentials in umbral union governs an upward causality, from the plane of immanence, through the field of the full body, toward structure. This upward causality is self-conducting, an agencying without an agent. But it collides with the downward flow of overcoding ascription, hazarding capture in the qualifications of structure and their canalized trajectories. Quasi-causality operates recursively at the intersection of these two causal streams, drawing its own emergent effects from their interferences and resonations. The upward drift of potential does not only lend itself to capture. It also performs escapes from the overcoding of structure and the modulations of established quasi-causalities, in a striving to retain its own self-conducting momentum.

Umbral union takes us to the far philosophical reaches. There are, however, two points that are important to bring back from the thinking of this liminal realm.

The first is that at the limit the full body, although distinctions cease to retain their individuality, they do not lack value or fall into undifferentiation. Instead, they differentially join in an exact *logic of relation*. This is the logic that underpins collective individuations and personings, at the aboriginal level of the integral passive synthesis that composes the spectrum of radicles in its entirety (passive synthesis being another word for umbral union). In the traditional vocabulary of metaphysics, these radicles would be called "primitives." In passing, if we deviate Peirce's "radicle" from its chemistry reference and give it a vegetal turn, referring to germinal roots, it combines well with Deleuze and Guattari's "rhizome," which would refer to the network of potentials the radicles grow into as they emerge toward the full body (thus constituting the "real potential," or most accessible spectrum of potentials, conditioning the full body's individuations).[18]

The second point is that the logic of relation is inseparable from desire, in Deleuze and Guattari's machinic sense: the wanting of relation. This means that while its field is outside the realm of quantity, it is not outside intensity. It is, rather, the degree zero of intensity—already on the continuum, with nowhere to go but up; not yet something, but something already doing. What the full body is full of is umbral union and its multifaceted but non–mutually exclusive wantings.

Body Matter

The account so far has explained what is "full" about the "full body." But what in what sense is the "full body" a "body"? It is a body in the sense that all of what was just described is integrally *felt*: the allure of the point-sign, the relief of the pullback, the expanding and contracting fields of potential associated with each respectively. The full body exists only in the performance of a deterritorialization catalyzed by point-signs, or a reterritorialization pulling it back into coding and axiomatization.

Each movement is an *intensity* of feeling: the registering of a larger or smaller infinity of potential held in the present, and inscribed in mem-

18 In *A Thousand Plateaus*, Deleuze and Guattari call what Peirce calls radicles "particles of becoming." Becoming is intensified when they are "emitted" in a way that gives them maximum capacity to self-conduct into actualization (4, 32–33, 40–41, 54, 56, 70, 249–50, 254, 256). "Pure potential" and "real potential" are terms from Whitehead that will be discussed further below.

ory (which, when it is not the memory of a person, is the memory of the world). The intensities, Deleuze and Guattari say, "fill" the full body, to a degree (along the continuum departing from the zero degree of the plane of immanence). Intensities are the "substance" of the process, in Spinoza's sense of that term—synonymous for Deleuze and Guattari with matter.[19] The full body is not a body in the sense of a discrete lump of living flesh and bone; and it is not matter in the sense of a slab of un-living nonflesh. "A body," Deleuze and Guattari write, "can be defined as that which is capable of actions and passions."[20]

It is worth noting that this definition echoes what Peirce said about general ideas: that they form the spans constituting their generality because they are able to influence and be influenced by each other, to form continua of feeling. Thus ideas, having actions and passions in the sense of influencing each other and registering each other's influ-ences, are bodies. This makes the metaphysics of process-philosophical thinking a radical form of materialist realism (a radical empiricism) that brushes aside the conventional dichotomy between the abstract and the concrete, a gesture summed up in the phrase "real abstraction." The plane of immanence is the immanent limit of the material, where it shades into a zone of indistinction with the ideal (the realm of real things that do not exist, to paraphrase Peirce on umbral union).[21]

The schizzes and reterritorializations of the full body are the actions and passions of a field of potential feeling itself into variations on itself. The umbral union discussed in the last section is the aboriginal, act-like

---

19 Deleuze and Guattari, *Thousand Plateaus*, 153. This definition of matter can be usefully inserted into the earlier discussion in part 2 of matter-motion and the imbrication of levels.

20 Deleuze and Guattari, *Thousand Plateaus*, 80.

21 This is in fact similar to the materialism of modern science, where the ultimate physical components of the universe are particles that are abstract in the sense of having no simple location or definite boundaries, having the reality instead of dynamic loci of intensity within fields, with the capacity to influence each other in immediacy at a distance (through entanglement and quantum tunneling). The plane of immanence is the metaphysical expression of this quantum plane, which is the plane of mutual inclusion of all potential, immanent to the classical physical world. It is one of the ways that Deleuze and Guattari follow Bergson's precept that philosophy must be cognizant of and complementary to the science of its day.

substance of the full body, subtended by the plane of immanence.[22] The intensive variations emergent from its potential are its germinal filiations, sprouting into the world of quantity and qualifiable forms. This is a real dimension of the world—the dimension of emergent variations, rising to meet their ascriptions.

This definition of matter as intensity is in keeping with Bergson's dynamic definition of matter in terms of degrees of contraction and expansion of potentials, spiraling through lines of actualization toward quantifiable form—forms that are countable, and thus separately qualifiable, patient for individual ascription. At the limit, matter or the substance of the world is "pure feeling," in Whitehead's words.[23] And for Deleuze and Guattari, as for Whitehead, the world is literally made of feeling. Whatever is capable of actions and passions is material (bodily, substantial), in the special sense that it receives and conveys movement, and is thus rippled by lines of force that register as a modification (action/passion). Deleuze, commenting on Nietzsche: "Every relation of force constitutes a body—whether it is chemical, biological, social or political"—or even abstract (in potential).[24]

The exact logic of relation is no more a stranger to force than it is to desire. It is, as a matter of intensive fact, their umbral convergence, for powers of emergence. Both force and desire permeate the full body and its filiated products.

Individual and Person

At this point, it is necessary to develop a distinction that has been made use of in the foregoing discussion but not yet explicitly glossed: *individuation*, in contradistinction to personhood.

An individual is a stream of matter that bears a certain consistency, presenting repeated qualifications of itself, under variation. Recall Peirce's statement that "an individual [hu]man is a wave."[25]

22 Act-like: see part 2, n. 40.
23 Whitehead, *Process and Reality*, 113.
24 Gilles Deleuze, *Nietzsche and Philosophy*, trans. Hugh Tomlinson (New York: Columbia University Press, 2006), 40.
25 Peirce, *Essential Peirce*, 2:122.

A wave is the form assumed by parts of a body which are out of equilibrium, such that as fast as the particles return they are replaced by others moving into neighboring positions of stress, so that the whole disturbance is continually propagated into new parts of the body while preserving more or less perfectly the same shape and other characters.[26]

Whitehead adds: "Owing to the delicate organization of the body, there is a returned influence, an inheritance of *character* derived from the presiding occasion and modifying the subsequent occasions through the rest of the body."[27] In other words, certain coordinations and dominant regularities reemerge, giving each successive standing wave a kinship to the last: the eddying-up and trickle-back-down, the return influence of the eddying upon itself, forms a pattern. The iteration of the pattern, regenerated moment to moment, forms a "historic route" that "canalizes" the life of the body.[28] It is this ongoing canalization that we experience as the character of an individual human. Character is the qualification of a personhood by its own ongoing patterning. It is the qualitative expression of the life of the body's consistency with itself, across the movement of its developing variations: what we call in everyday life a *personality*.

This implies a *distinction between the person and the individual*, no less so than there is a distinction between a top and its spin. To fail to distinguish between the top's matter and its movement would be as absurd as "seizing a spinning top to catch its motion";[29] likewise, the individual (matter-movement) and the person (matter-movement's patterning).[30] The police can seize an individual, but not its person. To fail to distinguish these would be absurd. But it would be equally absurd to separate the two sides. This is about two sides of strictly the same thing: aspects. Matter and movement are in mutual presupposition, neither

---

26 Peirce, *Essential Peirce*, 2:515n12.

27 Whitehead, *Process and Reality*, 109 (emphasis added).

28 Whitehead, *Process and Reality*, 107 (emphasis added).

29 James, *Principles of Psychology*, 244.

30 In the postscript, the matter-movement distinction will be differentiated from the individual-person distinction as a "modal" versus "real" distinction, as part of an effort to nuance the logic of mutual inclusion proposed in this book.

equatable with one another nor separable from one another. The same goes for individual-person: aspects, necessarily coming together in their difference.

Call the top—matter or substance as it varies along a historic route exhibiting action and passion and place-holding intensity—an *individuation*. Call the spin—the patterning of that movement across modulations in intensity—a *personing*, or character.

Return now to the full body. Its matter does not spin with one intensity, but many, too many, at the limit an infinity of them, all at once, in superposition. The matter or substance of the full body, its constituent intensities, is a *collective individuation*. The complex, ever-shifting patterning of them is a *collective person*. The full body is the spinning top of bodily potential, personing.

The distinction between collective individuation and collective personhood applies to every level and every degree (although they converge toward umbral union on the degree zero of the plane of immanence, where they infinitely recede into the germinal want of themselves).

Micrologic and Amplification

The schiz was described earlier as the hyphen between the distinctions constituting potential qualifications of individual bodies. In the schiz, the intensities and patternings of the full body recede into absolute proximity with one another. The distinctions are not lost; they enter into superposition. But in the approach to the absolute limit (umbral union), at the borderline of existence, the patterns become imperceptible. Apace with that becoming-imperceptible, the intensities tend to the paradoxical status of unfelt feelings.[31] The absolute limit, as its name implies, is never actually reached, being virtual (the plane of immanence). What happens is that distinctions, patternings, and intensities become *micrological*: answerable only to an exact logic of wanting relation, absent terms in relation.

---

31   Susanne Langer, *Feeling and Form: A Theory of Art* (New York: Charles Scribner's and Sons, 1953), 20. Langer's "unfelt feelings" are close to Whitehead's "negative prehensions." Whitehead, *Process and Reality*, 23–24, 26, 41.

The individual body is a "complex amplifier."[32] It is a pickup mechanism for micrological differences that it bumps up to a perceptible macro level. On the way up, the superposition is undone. The tangle of patternings unspools into a single trajectory or "historic route." The distinctions resolve into alternatives that must be chosen between, characterized by contrasting felt feelings, or actualized intensities (now moving through form-content articulations).

The individual—a bodily individuation spun with character, or personality—is this selective distillation of the full body's potentials. It is a singleton, reductive of the singular-multiplicity of the full body. It is not a particular, in the usual meaning of that word to designate a member of a classical set to which it logically belongs, and which subsumes it under a general category. Instead, it is a *derivative function* of a fuzzy set, plotting its own curve. Here the individual person is genetically, not merely logically, related to the full body (this harks back to the discussion earlier of Whitehead's "genetic elements" operating immanently to individual emergence). The filiation is real, in the intensive dimension of potential.[33]

Individualization

The individual person, as derivative function, is an *image* indexed to the full body, and through it to its limit, the plane of immanence. An image is a processual figure considered from the angle of perceptibil-

---

32 Whitehead, *Process and Reality*, 119.
33 Deleuze and Guattari, Anti-Oedipus, 154–55. It is important to distinguish this concept of intensive filiation from filiation and alliance in anthropology, where filiation is a diachronic line of genetic descent through time (rather than a line of emergence immanent to the moment) and alliance refers to acquired synchronic horizontal relations (for example through marriage). In anthropology, filiation is primary in relation to alliance, whereas for Deleuze and Guattari, alliance is primary in relation to filiation in the anthropological senses of the words (alliance is a form of connective synthesis). Both unfold together from intensive filiation. Deleuze and Guattari, Anti-Oedipus, 147, 155–56; and Deleuze and Guattari, *Thousand Plateaus*, 246–47. Viveiros de Castro takes up this idea of the primacy of alliance in his work on Amazonian metaphysics. Eduardo Viveiros de Castro, *Cannibal Metaphysics*, trans. Peter Skafish (Minneapolis: Univocal / University of Minnesota Press, 2017).

ity. The image points back down the line of its own emergence, indexing a region of intensity which it makes perceptible—or better, whose
perceptibility it *is*. The image is the becoming-perceptible of a region
of relation, imbued by nature with force and desire. It is a subset of
umbral union expressing itself in registrable form-content. The image
does not, however, resemble or directly correspond to the region of the
full body it indexes. This nonresemblance and noncorrespondence is
entailed by its taking a registrable form articulating content. A derivative function does not resemble or directly correspond to its generative
equation. It throws it a curve.

Deleuze and Guattari in fact say that the individual person is a second derivative image, an *image-of-an-image*.

To understand why, it is useful to return to the friend/enemy distinction. The friend is not one thing, but many, potentially infinitely many.
But this infinity is a smaller infinity, because the full body has split into
two opposing camps. These were spoken of earlier as a full body and an
anti-full body, but that was no sooner corrected to say that they are two
regions of the same full body, divided by a *relative limit* falling between
them on the full body.

The two regions of the full body are what Deleuze and Guattari call
"*bodies without organs*." One way of thinking about the body without
organs is as a relatively limited, but still infinite, range of distinctions,
qualifications, and potential historic routes (although in *Anti-Oedipus*,
the terminological difference between the full body and the body without
organs never completely sets and is allowed to drift).[34] It is analogously

---

34 Because of this opening of the body without organs onto the full body, the
terminological distinction between them is not firm. The vacillation between
the two terms is strengthened by the operative analogy between their orders
discussed in the next paragraph. In *A Thousand Plateaus*, the "full body" falls out
of use, replaced by the "body without organs" of various dimensions. Deleuze
and Guattari, *Thousand Plateaus*, 149–66. The terminological vacillation migrates
to the "body without organs" and (or as) the "plane of consistency" ("Does
the plane of consistency constitute the body without organs, or does the body
without organs compose the plane? Are the Body without Organs and the Plane
the same thing?" Deleuze and Guattari, *Thousand Plateaus*, 507). Their immanent
limit is the pure "plane of immanence" of destratified matter. The plane of con-

organized to the full body in every way, other than having a more limited ambit. The relative limit between the two regions and their opposing qualifications does double duty as an immanent limit. When a movement or feeling falls into the crack between, plunging into the schiz, it recedes from its assigned region and opens out onto the full body. There it hazards the Scylla and Charybdis of falling into black hole or breaking through a white wall to the plane of immanence.

The individual person is most proximately a derivative of a body without organs, with the full body nested in its image like a Russian doll—a strangely deformable Russian doll that is not inside without also wrapping around. For the full body is the person's expanded field of potential, or what Simondon would call its "associated milieu."[35] The body without organs is a filter through which potentials of the full body are bidirectionally strained, from the "inside" (the open field) coming up and going out (*affect*, coming to expression) and from the outside (the world's accumulation of already-constituted things) going in and down (*perception*, trickle feeding the personality's development with provocations striking from without). The intersection of affection and perception makes the micrological distinctions of the full body selectively available for pickup and bump-up to the macro level.

The body without organs is itself an image of the full body, a more limited field selectively indexed to it but (again) neither resembling nor corresponding to it. It is the smaller infinity of a more restricted collective person and collective individuation (can spinning tops form Russian dolls?). The individual body is in turn a pickup and a bump-up from the body without organs. It selectively strains its collective personhood—the multitudes it contains in potential—down to a single pattern coordinating a selection of qualifications that integrate into the curve of a personal history. The person's historic route is composed of a certain range of repeated and varied circuits among which preferential

---

sistency, as a level of real potential, would correspond in the vocabulary develop here to the realm of pure potential as it verges onto the plane of immanence.

35 Simondon, *Individuation*, 49–45; Gilbert Simondon, *The Mode of Existence of the Technical Object*, trans. Cécile Malaspina and John Rogove (Minneapolis: Univocal / University of Minnesota Press, 2017), 59–66.

trajectories arise. This preferential range of potential fills with habit-formed, and habit-forming, intensities and propensities, composing a personality. From the bodily perspective, the formation of the person siphons a collective *individuation* into an *individualization*.[36]

Scale and Dimension

There is an operative analogy between how the body without organs derives from the full body, and how the individual person derives from the body without organs. It is this analogy that justifies calling the individual an image-of-an-image (of that which, moving toward the absolute limit, is imageless). The move from image to image-of-the-image is also a move from collective personhood and individuation to singleton personhood and individualization.

Although . . . if you consider that an individual person's character is a coordination of intensities and a round robin of contrasts featuring a crowd of sub-characters contributing to an integral ordering across a multiplicity of trajectories, the singleton is a singular-multiple as well. Formally, there is *collective personhood and collective individuation all the way up*. The individual is a collective in a tighter pattern, self-congruent enough that its character, or personality, is capable of presenting a united front enabling it to count as one (thus participating in the world of quantity, while continuing to live in intensity). The relevant criterion is the scale of the enveloped infinity.

Instead of "scale," it would be more precise to say *dimensionality*, referring to the number of degrees of freedom of feeling and movement obtaining on a given level (dimensionality is defined by the integrated packet of degrees of freedom a field or level offers for movement or transformation). There is in fact an inverse relation between scale and dimensionality: the more macro, the more restricted the range of potential; the more restricted the range of potential, the smaller the number of degrees of freedom.

36 Simondon, *Mode of Existence*, 63–66.

Dividuation

The term *dividual* is a way of reminding ourselves of the fundamentally multiplicitous nature of the person, immanent to its individualization.[37] "Dividual" reminds us that what counts as one is always a complex, not a block.

To return to the top, the two dimensions, of bodily movement and spin pattern, individuation and personification, fuse without becoming confused. They retain a distinction, which allows them each a specific angle of address, in thought and action. The same applies to the sub-personal and sub-individual elements. They too retain a distinction, even in an individualization, as differentiable tendencies with their own presiding characters. What we take to be one can always be divided—but as Deleuze and Guattari repeat in a refrain, it cannot be divided without changing in nature (without being precipitated into a becoming occasioning a change of dimension).[38]

Every point-sign, every machinic index—every strike of a word, image, perception, affection—cuts into the complex from a particular angle, refiguring the distinction between dimensions and elements, re-jigging how the activity of the one is in the other, to concerted effect. Every point-sign is a trigger for their becoming-together. It effects an *analysis in act*, taking "analysis" in the etymological sense of "up loosening" (for retying together). The strike of the point-sign cuts in to shake loose. It descends through the lineaments of distinction, jigging the differences all the way down. They then rejig all the way up, into

---

37   Massumi, *Power at the End of the Economy*, 8–10, 14, 32–36. The term was developed in anthropology by Marilyn Strathern, *The Gender of the Gift: Problems with Women and Problems with Society in Melanesia* (Berkeley: University of California Press, 1988), 12–15, 348–49n. In relation to capitalism, see Gerald Raunig, *Dividuum: Machinic Capitalism and Molecular Revolution*, vol. 1, trans. Aileen Derieg (New York: Semiotext(e), 2016). Jonathan Beller writes of a "fractalization of fascism on the 'subject' side" as "an expression of an overall informationalization of social relations subject to historically imposed computability." Jonathan Beller, *The World Computer: Derivative Conditions of Racial Capitalism* (Durham, NC: Duke University Press, 2021).

38   Deleuze and Guattari, *Thousand Plateaus*, 33, 483.

a next collective step along the historic route, like an interstitial shoe bootstrapping itself into a top hat (which we ceremonially wear as our personhood).

Cut: schiz. This analysis-in-act is the object of what Deleuze and Guattari call schizoanalysis.

Its first lesson: processually speaking, the individual person is not subject to psychology.

Overcoding

Corresponding to the rise in diminishing scale (decrease in degrees of freedom) leading to individualization is a transition from complex field to *structure* (structure does happen—just at a derivative level). Under the action of point-signs, the individual person winks through one eye to the body without organs and through it to the full body of potential and the plane of immanence that is its absolute limit. Through the other eye, it takes in the coded structure of social roles that sediment into the world's accumulations. The code actively neglects the fuzziness of the sets of potential from which the individual emergently derives, in order to insert the individual into a classical set in the role of a particular subsumed by a general. The general category is applied to the body, folding back down on it to canalize its potential further in conformity with its code. It *overcodes*.[39]

This is where the move from level to level ceases to be a differentiation (an image or image-of-an-image, derivative without resemblance or correspondence) and functions instead according to a principle of conformity. The individual person is forced into the channels that social coding selectively designates for it, so that its patternings snap to grid and conform to code. This models the person to the general category, doubling any proper name it may bear with a class-name. In its conformity to that category, and its assumption of (subsumption under) the class-name, the person comes to resemble other particulars in its category more than it differs from them. This is *produced resemblance*.

---

39 Deleuze and Guattari, *Anti-Oedipus*, 196–98, 208–22, 211–13; and Deleuze and Guattari, *Thousand Plateaus*, 219–30, 388–89, 427–28.

From that angle, the person is no longer a singular-multiple, or even a singleton, but a *particular* instance conforming to a general rule. Each particular under the same category stands as an *icon* of it.

The general category is not a collective person or individuation. It is a purely logical structure that is existentially empty in itself: a general idea in the classical sense. It must hijack bodies to give itself a face in which to see its own image. This image is the image-of-an-image that is the person, overlain with an iconic reflection. The general category is a model that mirrors itself upon the body and person, turning it into a wan reflection: a degraded copy of the category's empty order. This *application* of the category channels the body's potential into the reproduction of the code characterizing the general category: its system of distinctions and rules of conformity. The body's energies are usurped: *capture*. The Man-Standard is the modern paragon of categorical capture.

Under the effect of the general category's subsumptive power, the person becomes a pale reflection of an empty order: a simulacrum. At the same time as on its other side, through the eye turned toward the full body as it wraps around to field the body, the person sees itself as an emergence, an emergent self-patterning. Deleuze and Guattari's abandonment of the term "simulacrum" as synonymous with the person as image-of-an-image after *Anti-Oedipus* marks a shift in emphasis from the aspect of the coded capture of bodies to the aspect of their emergent expression of potentials—a shift of perspective, from one side of a person's face to the other.[40] This shift is important in the context of the contemporary condition of personhood, where, as we have seen, overcoding has largely lost its structural integrity.

Figural, Figurative, Figure

To summarize the constituent dimensions: the *figural* (plane of immanence as filtered by the full body); the *figurative* (the spinning Russian tops of the full body within and around the body without organs, channeling

---

40 Simulacra: Deleuze and Guattari, *Anti-Oedipus*, 264–71, 321–22); Deleuze, "Plato and the Simulacrum," in Deleuze and Guattari, *Anti-Oedipus*, 253–66; Massumi, "Realer Than Real."

up, filter upon filter, to the macro scale); the *figure* (the singleton person and its life's individualization, with one eye facing the relational micrologic of its own potential and one eye facing the macrologic of the socially roled usurpation of it); *structure* (the usurping model of conformal personhood and canalized individuation that captures potential by applying upon it a coded general category, for which the figurative provides the field of application).

Or again: imagelessness, image/image of an image, reflective model.

It is the last step in the ladder of becoming that disaggregates with social media and Trump. It largely loses its powers, but remains in place, called into service to pull patternings and intensities back from the brink when the allure of the schiz and the black hole or white wall of potential into which it leads proposes a deterritorialization that moves too far toward the limit of a body without organs or full body. The overcoding clamps back down on bodies, reimposing at least a modicum of structure. The result is a reterritorialization: a confinement of patternings and intensities within certain prescribed boundaries, in a way that opposes them to each other.

The point-sign—the performative strike of an impingement cutting into complexity's ongoing—tunnels through it all. It is bidirectional. In one direction, it points down through the body without organs to the fully body, and through the full body to the plane of immanence. In the other direction, it points up from the body without organs to the individualized person, and through it to the general level of the overcoding structure, where it dead-ends in the emptiness of a general category holding no potential of its own. Or: at which point it dips back down in the cracks between applications of the general model's conformal model into the dimension of umbral union, to feel into matrixial form a subset of otherwise potentials and the alternate trajectories they harbor.

Affect and Intensities

The words and images circulated by social media operate as point-signs: performative analyses-in-action, each strike of which rejigs the complex, micrologically if not noticeably at the macro level. The images do not basically function as representations, nor the words as semantically well-formed statements answerable to standards of truth-value. They operate bi-directionally, along the point-sign axis that transverses the levels, from the full body's recessive threshold onto the plane of immanence to the macro structures of overcoding, such as the Man-Standard.

In the direction facing the full body, the point-sign indexes the spinning top of the individual body and the person to an entryway into the abstract range of potentials conditioning the full body and its coming to expression in collective individuations, collective personings, and individualizations. In the course of the foregoing account, these potentials have been described in terms of potential trajectories (movements, sequencings of movements, historic routes) and intensities (felt qualities produced through the movements, sequencings, and historic routes). Taken together, they can be summed up in one word: "affect." Affects are defined, as always from a Spinozist-Deleuzian-Guattarian perspective, as modes of affecting and being affected. Adapting Spinozist vocabulary, Deleuze and Guattari will say that affects are the modes of the full body's substance as it comes to expression.[41]

The web of potentials is organized as a *disjunctive synthesis*: a distributive mutual inclusion of a multiplicity of contrasts in the same complex, open system (the same field). Every *connection* along a trajectory—every collision, encounter, or aggregation—combusts a number of potentials.

---

41 On affects as modes in Spinoza's sense, see Deleuze and Guattari, *Thousand Plateaus*, 153, where they also say that bodies without organs are "attributes" of substance. Spinoza's *Ethics* considers extension and thought as the only two attributes human knowledge can discern. But Spinoza also states that in principle there is an infinity of attributes. Deleuze and Guattari take him at his word, displacing the "parallelism" between extension and thought into a multiplicity of bodies without organs. The result is to bring the concept of mode closer to that of the attribute, given that a body without organs is an order of affective modes. At that point, it seems to make little difference if we simply dispense with the often confounding concept of the attribute entirely and think of levels of modal order. Deleuze and Guattari seem to retain it vestigially in order to assert a "real distinction" between bodies without organs, on the model of Spinoza's definition of attributes as being really distinct. But it is hard to see what is lost by considering this a "modal distinction" and migrating "real distinction" toward the emergence of fusional unities-of-multiplicity that have their own character (see the postscript below).

This detonation of potential constitutes a processual locus that is "re-corded" as an added contrast in the disjunctive synthesis of the field of potential (full body / body without organs). The combustion of poten-tial leaves a remainder, consisting in the felt intensity of the potentials released through the dynamism of the coming-together, or *conjunctive synthesis*, of the elements entering into connection. Conjunctive synthe-sis is another name for the dynamic fusion of a multiplicity of elements yielding a joint effect that has its own feeling and character: the overall feeling of a pulse of process, culminating.[42]

These intensities are what point-signs most directly index. They are the felt smoke of umbral fires expressing themselves through actual connections taken up into disjunctive and conjunctive synthesis. The overallness of the fusional feeling is what enables the index to point to the pulse of process that produced it as something that can count as one. When subsumed under a category, that oneness is abstracted from its complex conditions of emergence in the co-operation of connective and disjunctive syntheses. This enables it to be indexed by point-signs as if it were a discrete unit. This belittles the intensity by discounting its complexity. But the intensity remains, in neglected excess.

Intensity envelops a qualitative more-than of what records as one. Its counting for one in fact carries a charge of multiplicity. However belittled, the intensity still envelops in its genesis the Russian doll–like ladder of sed-imenting levels or strata discussed above.[43] Its overallness is the basis of an individualized person's ability to count as one despite being composed of a virtual infinity of sub-individuals with their own sub-personalities. The enveloping of complexity by intensity is what holds the process together. It is the glue of the world—fascia of the full body's many-becoming-one.

It might be more precise to say that affect is the glue of the world. Affect is the power of a body to affect and be affected in a connective en-counter that is in processual embrace with disjunctive distributions and conjunctive culminations, with the feeling of the transition incident to every encounter. Intensity is that feeling. It is an aspect of affect, reg-

---

42   An analysis of connective, disjunctive, and conjunctive synthesis opens Anti-Oedipus (1–22, 68–137) and unfolds throughout the book. They are not temporally or spatially distinct. They are three coincident dimensions of process.

43   Deleuze and Guattari, *Thousand Plateaus*, 39–74.

istering the felt quality of transition. It fills existence for that moment of transition, and registers as its subsisting trace. The registering or recording of the trace marks the transition as a locus on a trajectory or historic route. This memorialization renders it indexable as processual locus (a potentially repeatable occurrence, as always with variation). The indexing makes the transition reaccessible. The trace of the transition is at once a past potential achieved, and future potential to come: a once and again, and a this and a more-than.

The intensity of affect is experienced by the body as what fills, over-fills, its personing of the moment with felt quality and future. Spilling, filling, content—the dynamic form of expression of which is the character pattern whose transitioning down a historic route constitutes personality. Intensity is the stuff of life.

Emotion

It is out of this stuff of life that the person forms its *emotions*, understood as a translation of the many dimensions of the affective event, with the intensities, transitions, and strata it envelops, into a peak episode that counts, and counts as one: individualization of affect. Emotion is the translation of intensity into a different kind of content: one that can be reflected on consciously. This interiorizes it as an individualized content whose possession is now privatized, moving from my-non-I to I-me-mine. Interiorized, it is the content of a personal narrative that runs asymptotically to the overall historic route of an individualized body's life travels. The personal narrative follows the historic route, without actually touching on its micrological complexity or the full force of the potentials it brings to interiorized expression. The complexity continues to be felt as life's uncontrolled edge (the nagging sense of not knowing all there is to know about one's own emotions) or overflow (the sense of being "outside of oneself"). The edge and overflow are the insistence of intensity, subsisting in excess, in and through its capture in emotion. Emotion and intensity are processual correlates.

The translation of intensity into emotion, and emotion's extension into narrative, is formatively influenced by the overcode applied to that person. This application is what gives the general category a hold on the particular body, and that body an intimate claim to a social role. Emotion is the ground on which the behavior of the body is rationalized. It is the avenue by which the empty category (such as, once again, the Man-Standard) arrogates content to itself, giving substance to the rationality of its normative rules by hijacking the stuff of life that is intensity. This never comes without the frictions, slippages, and exceptions that always accompany the limitative functioning of rules: *escape*, propelled by the excess of intensity over its normative channeling. From the point of view of the normative rules applied, this excess can only be perceived as the irrational flip side of a body's reflective consciousness of itself. This is where the rational/irrational binary imposes itself. That binary rebrands what from a processual viewpoint is a singular struggle between limitative potential (channeling, overcoding) and the affirmation of emergent potentials (intense reconnection to the full body as field of potential).

Overcoding exercises a downward causality of conformal modeling descending from the general level to the particular, and through it back down to full body and plane of immanence. This forms a recursive feedback loop grafting higher-level operations onto the plane of immanence. Implanted in the field of potential, they remain in reactivatable trace form as limitative or segregative potential, persisting in tendency and habit. These limitative potentials are exclusive disjunctive potentials unfolding as tendencies and habits effecting a self-curtailing of potential. They filter back up to re-express, in a reinforcement of the conformal channeling of the Man-Standard. Like all pulses of process, this return peaks in an overall feeling owing to conjunctive synthesis. The feeling includes a disavowed inkling of incompletion that registers the fact that the pulse of process has given itself short shrift by not metabolizing the potentials it may have otherwise, and has fallen short on its own intensity. The disavowed inkling intimates a needling discomfort with how potential has played out that is enveloped in the overall feeling. It is a symptom of processual indigestion. If it rises to the status of emotion, it informs an existential posture of disgruntledness accompanied by a whining conviction that one has not received one's due in life, often with an attendant ascription of enemies held liable for it. This can feed the kind of grievance culture fueling the MAGA phenomenon.

This is processual *reflux*: a belching of process.[44] World-burp of Standard Man. It is central to the mechanisms of reaction and ressentiment that will be discussed below. In reaction and ressentiment, becoming gives its own potential short shrift. Reaction and ressentiment embody becoming's becoming anti-becoming (becoming self-limiting; limitative becoming).

The recursivity of this reflux is one example of quasi-causality. More broadly, quasi-causality refers to the efficacy of nonlocal factors, as when a higher level recursively in-forms those below, or an overall inflects its under-elements, and vice versa; or when a relation creates or synchronously modulates its terms. Also quasi-causal is the upward potentializing force of tendencies rising from the full body toward the emergence of new connections expressing novel intensities indexing potential deviations in a life's course. This uplift is processual *afflux*: a re-nourishing of the world with potential riding intensity to overflow established channels.

Processual reflux and afflux are not separate phases. They are coincident pulses of every processual step. Every step: a struggle between curtailing capture and creative escape.

There is a kind of double affectivo-emotive inscription: the transition and its accompanying intensity are, at strictly the same time, an affective step in the individuation of a bodily life, and an emotive shift in the pattern of a personhood.[45] The double inscription carries a complex valence: a ratio of reflux and afflux. That ratio determines its processual *coefficient* (coefficient of becoming).

Signed, Affect

The point-sign is a stoker of affect. Its performative strike induces a transition and catalyzes the corresponding intensity and its emotional elaboration. The collusion of the emotion with the hold of general categories on the body accommodates the body to ascription.

---

44 Reflux: Deleuze and Guattari, *Anti-Oedipus*, 269.
45 Affectivo-emotive: Simondon, *Individuation*, 272–77.

The strike of the point-sign can be a literal touch, but it may also be abstract. In any case, it operates as an indexical sign. Its fundamental sign-function is to drop an index that cuts transversally through the strata, like a flash of lightning, ionizing a channel for reflux and afflux to come and go along. What the point-sign is ultimately an index of is potential and its taking up in a coefficient of becoming.

Indexicality can be bound up with any type of sign in the semiotic menagerie. For example, it underlies the iconicity of images and of a person's conformity with its class-name. The only kind of sign it cannot be is a signifying sign (more on which in the "Signs Behaving Badly" and "Faciality" sections in part 5).[46] The very definition of the signifying sign is as a symbol divorced from indexicality and iconicity (Saussure's "arbitrary" sign). The *signifier* is the kind of sign native to the general level of structure and overcoding, a point that *Anti-Oedipus* hammers in time and again.

A sign is a vector. It brings what is distant into the absolute proximity of an affectivo-emotive event. Its gateway is perception. Perception, as Whitehead says, is how forces of the outside cut in through openings in the porous organization of the physical body.[47] The words and images of social media are not representations; they are not mediations. They are direct conveyances of point-signs. They cut to the quick. We are transfixed by them. Their lightning-strike force directly occasions affectivo-emotive events. The rhythm of relay from one to the next constitutes an ongoing modulation of the life of the body and the experience of the person. The modulations cut across the levels, inflecting the full body and its collective individuations and collective personhood at the same time as the individualized body and its singleton personhood, in double articulation (a cleaving together in processual embrace).

"Anything which focuses the attention is an indication. Anything which startles us is an indication, inso far as it marks the junction between two portions of experience. . . . An index stands for its object [ultimately, in every case, the full body] by virtue of a real [eventful] connection with it."[48]

46 Deleuze and Guattari, *Anti-Oedipus*, 244; and Deleuze and Guattari, *Thousand Plateaus*, 4, 9, 68, 186.
47 Whitehead, *Adventures of Ideas*, 189.
48 Peirce, *Essential Peirce*, 2:8.

Resonating Chamber

The social media are resonating chambers, overfull with the affectivo-emotive waves. Multiple strikes and relays bring turbulence, forming ripples on the surface of society. The ripples fringe, cancel, or amplify each other, forming interference patterns in quasi-chaotic abandon. These disturbances are picked up by bodies and amplified into emotions, expressing themselves in half-made thoughts that no sooner rise toward formulation than they subside back into the ever-changing flow of the discourse of the "they." The emotions might well aspire to become well-formed statements carrying truth-value, but the tidal movement of what "they" say continually pulls them back, to soak them with the solvent of free indirect discourse. A certain will-to-truth may form in an attempt to reinstate an image of the truth. This inevitably goes awry, if the conditions for the development of adequate ideas are not in place. Reaction ensures that they are not. This is a main topic of parts 4 and 5 below.

The affectivo-emotive range of the social media is wide and varied. But it continually throws a body off-balance. The digitally connected body is a body on edge—on the paranoid edge. This makes for edgy personalities with a tendency toward intensities of paranoia. That tendency is a constant built into the affective complexion of social media—an unremitting pole around which lives come to oscillate.

Adjunction/Induction

Trump does not utter well-formed statements, carrying truth-value and conveying an ideology. He spews point-signs. He performs media strikes. The strikes are not well-targeted, effectively coordinated attacks. They are hit-and-miss disturbances, designed to continually stir things up. They are a turbulence of reflux and afflux. Their efficacy is in their machine-gun scatter and echoing retort. The scattershot delivery has that one constant: a playing to the paranoid pole. Trump specializes in stirring up fear and wariness. His ad hominem attacks and hateful derision are overwhelmingly directed toward social groups historically assigned to subordinate qualifications in the structure of the Man-Standard (women, sexual and racial minorities, non-Europeans from what he likes to call "shithole" countries). These function as foils for the self-aggrandizement of the preeminent term (however ornamental it may actually be).

This targeting, effected by point-signs, is a *performative ascription*. It catalyzes the friend/enemy distinction by attributing enemy status to certain individuals and groups. This is Trump's most direct, most effective form of political action. The agitated bodies of his MAGA followers pick up his disturbances. Bathed in the flow of what "they" say, they say it again, repeating the point-signs in a chorus. This echoing renews, reinforces, and rebroadcasts the associated ascriptions.

An ascriptive contagion ensues, spilling over from the online performance to the performance of acts of aggression offline. The bodies of his followers fall into the rhythm, applying it to their lives each in their own way. There is no model for them to copy, because the figure of Trump does not have that kind of consistency. It is self-deconstructing, functioning more through the quasi-chaotic variations it jerks across than any toeing to a line. Accordingly, the MAGA nation's falling into the rhythm is not a phenomenon of conformism in any traditional sense. It is not an overcoding per se, although it often segues into one. It is quasi-causal. It is not an adherence to a well-formulated ideology. It's an affectivo-emotive *adjunction*. Adjunction is the replacement concept, in this account, for identification, designating the *induction* of bodies and persons into participation in a certain spin of the full body through pulses of reflux and afflux.

Differential Attunement

The trajectories and intensities of Trumpian lives are adjoined to the flow of point-signs. They are tethered to them, but with enough slack that the way in which each body's pickup of the point-signs' disturbances bumps up to the individual-personal level varies, within the limits set by the paranoid tendency holding polar sway over the entire complex system. It is more like a *differential attunement* than a straightforward identification.

The affected bodies are collectively riveted to the same quasi-chaos, to which they react affectively together, but with differences that express in variable emotional forms and their accompanying personal narratives, but within the same polarization. They do not identify, so much as they attune to and interpret the rhythm (in the sense in which we say a group of improvisational dancers interprets a piece of music). The MAGA uptake furnishes the media agitation with a range of content. But the variability is channeled in a certain general direction, in step with the paranoid tendency. That direction leads toward the actualization of the conditions for civil war.

Media Figure

The bodily contagion and its affective modulations constitute a movement of collective individuation. The complex patterning of the field of potential—its self-modulating spin—is a collective personhood. "Trump" is the master spinner. This is not Trump the orange-haired male hominid organism, overfed on Big Macs. As a mere man, a male biological organism, he would have no such reach. As a mere man, however big, he is derisory. No, this is Trump the *media figure*, realer than real. Trump, as media figure, is literally, effectively, contagiously a collective person operating in the associated milieu of a paranoid full body.[49] The adjunction of bodies to this formation catalyzes their individual personifications. They construct—and deconstruct and modulate—themselves in differential attunement with it.

The Man-Standard Again (and Again)

Trump's performative ascriptions always draw on the hierarchy of complementary qualifications constituting the Man-Standard. This continually reactivates the overcoding of the individual Trumpist with an

49 Thomas Lamarre develops a theory of "personating" in oscillation with "nonpersonating" but individuating modes in his transmedia-ecology study of anime, which is in many ways convergent with the notion of the media figure as "personing" developed here. Thomas Lamarre, *The Anime Ecology: A Genealogy of Television, Animation, and Game Media* (Minneapolis: University of Minnesota Press, 2018), 284–86, 355.

archaic, disciplinary structure that is white and patriarchal to the core. The reflux of this application of the structure functions as a corrective. It works to overlay general categories on bodies and persons, remitting their trajectories and intensities to certain conventional ranges, or territories. This *reterritorialization* blocks emergent escapes and mitigates the deterritorializing drift of the discourse of the they, holding it within limits falling shy of a plunge into a black hole or an unexpected veer toward a breakthrough of the white wall. The social roles, or "positionalities," of the Man-Standard are a processual checks-and-balances system.

The overcoding is never complete. The conditions for that are not in place in this era of ornamental masculinity. A hardening of the disciplinary overlay, however, is always possible, in lassitude at the agitation and in fear of continued quasi-chaos. This hardening represents the turning point from the *micro-fascism* of differential attunement to the paranoid full body, toward macro-fascism, *fascism proper*, with its centralized mania for masculinist conformity and its murderous campaigns of annihilation against ascribed enemies.

The Personification of Capital

There is a contrasting pole of Trump's full body to the hardening of the category lines. It marks the other end of the range of potential in which Trumpian persons oscillate. Toward this pole, Trump as media figure adjoining the bodies of his followers is a personification of the deterritorialized flows of neoliberal capital. The sure sign of the personification of capital is when value as a person and capitalist value in the form of financial worth are conflated.

Trump lives this conflation. He asserts that he *feels* his financial worth, and that his feelings change it: "My net worth fluctuates, and it goes up and down with markets and with attitudes and with feelings, even my own feelings. . . . My own feelings affect my value."[50] "He learned he

---

50   Timothy O'Brien, "How Much Is Trump Worth? Depends on How He Feels," *Newsweek*, October 19, 2015, https://www.newsweek.com/how-much-trump-worth-depends-how-he-feels-384720.

could monetize his political standing. And if there is a pile of cash on a desk, Donald Trump is going to take it. . . . He always wants to be making money and sees everything as a branding exercise."[51]

This is what he "models": felt value fluctuating like an affectivo-emotive-financial market index of branded capitalist-being accumulating surplus-value. The adjunction of bodies to this phase of the oscillation on the full body of Trump shapes his followers as personifications of capital in their own small way: little persons clinging for life like profit-seeking lice on the greatcoat of Trump's collective person, in his expansive reality as media figure.

But then, in this age of human capital, are we not all personifications of capital?[52] Are we all not engaged in extracting surplus-value from self-branding? Are we not all riveted to the circulation of point-signs? Are we not all derivative functions of the process dominated in this era of the world by the full body of capital and its figurations? Undoubtedly.

But the question is not there. The question is how, given these conditions, we oscillate. What pole do our oscillations favor? With what rigidity or suppleness do we reterritorialize when we pull back from the unlivable limit of a black hole or the white wall of the plane of immanence? What collective individuations and persons do we co-compose? These are the questions of the "art" and "ethics" of schizoanalysis.

Recap

This account has tried to add a number of facets to the analytic of fascism:

1) The rethinking of the personality of power informed by a distinction between collective individuation and collective personhood, and between these and their individualized derivatives.

---

51 Unnamed senior Trump adviser cited in Michael Scherer and Josh Dawsey, "Books, Speeches, Hats for Sale: Post-presidency, the Trumps Try to Make Money the Pre-presidency Way," *Washington Post*, January 28, 2022, https://www .washingtonpost.com/politics/trump-money-businesses/2022/01/27.

52 Deleuze and Guattari, *Anti-Oedipus*, 232, 254, 264.

2) The idea of an affectivo-emotive resonance governing a differential attunement rather than an ideological identification.

3) The performativity of ascription, effecting the adjunction of bodies to a quasi-chaotic collective dynamic, and the checking of that dynamic by the reflux application of general categories.

4) The point-sign as tunneling hinge-dimension, a transversal axis on which signs of disturbance strike and schiz. From the site of impact, modulations propagate across the levels to take emergent, correlated forms. These selectively, often limitatively or segregatively, embody the potential relations (umbral unions) composing the plane of immanence at the limit of the full body as they filter up through a pluri-faceted synthesis (connective, disjunctive, and conjunctive, all in one go) of the actual (for a pulse of process).

5) The social media as an associated milieu of free indirect discourse stirring up a quasi-chaotic contagion of ascriptions, adjunctions, and applications that both liberate and channel potential.

6) The status of Trump as media figure, or collective person, as a personification of the deterritorializing flows of neoliberal capital; his adjoined bodies, likewise. Not to mention all bodies dwelling in the capitalist field, adjoined to his or not. Media figures come in many kinds, and each kind envelops other potential variations.

7) The fascisizing tendency toward the paranoid pole, gaining dominance on a fear-ridden planet shaken by uncertainty, but remaining in oscillation with the pole of capitalist deterritorialization of flows systematized by an axiomatic. This contrasting pole is the "schizophrenic" pole as held within the relative limits of capital by various forms of flow-checking and canalizing reterritorialization and overcoding.

Why?

The limitative channeling of bodily and personal potentials under the thrall of the fascisizing paranoid tendency is an exemplary instance of what Deleuze, in his analysis of Nietzsche, calls the *becoming-reactive* of active forces. There is a need for a concerted affective analysis of *reac-*

tion, which must cease to function as a convenient insult and become a key operating concept. Spinoza's account of the formation of inadequate ideas, and Whitehead's account of error, can provide a strong philosophical framework. An elucidation of the affective process of becoming-reactive in our time can renew our understanding of what it means to be anti-fascist, turning the "anti-" into an affirmation: a rebecoming-active countering becoming's becoming anti-becoming.

PART 4

Error Incarnate

The Personification of Capital, Reflux

Before moving closer to the analysis of becoming-reactive involved in fascism and fascisizing tendencies, more on the person as personification of capital is advisable, to emphasize the way in which the person in our epoch operates as a unit of human capital, and to return to the idea of the person as an image, or image-of-an-image, of process.

Trump supporters do not simply react to economic conditions. They *are* integrally economized beings (as are we all). The capitalism they so ardently defend against "communist liberals" and other bugbears is an immanent factor in their existential constitution. They do not represent their economic interests (or fail to do so) so much as they embody the interests *of the capitalist process*, in individualized form.

Deleuze and Guattari's analysis of personhood in *Anti-Oedipus* orbits around Marx's assertion that the capitalist is a personification of capital. The capitalist is a "derivative function" of capitalism—a personification of its flows.[1] The person of the capitalist is a privatization of the capitalist process: a participation in it that appropriates its powers of production, transducing them onto an individual scale, assuming ownership over its functioning from the angle of this individual take on it, which also makes the individual (in the double sense of constituting its subjectivity and giving it the power to "make it" in the competitive capitalist world). The person of the capitalist is an image of the capitalist process: a re-presentation of its operativity transposed onto another level, with the introduction of differences obtaining on that level.

---

1 Deleuze and Guattari, *Anti-Oedipus*, 314.

The transduction of the process from the unbounded collective process to the closure of an individual figuration of it is a topological transformation. The capitalist process is a wide-open nature-culture continuum operating according to an axiomatic of deregulated, or de-territorialized, flows: a kind of deformable, self-amending matrix of dynamic connections, disjunctions, and conjunctions. The capitalist is a home-dwelling, network-surfing organism that captures something of those flows, deducting a share of its processual powers for itself, appropriating it to a private sphere. This operation centers on the family, but also extends to a network of coded social roles that the privatized individual might hold. Deleuze and Guattari analyze it as a reterritorialization of the capitalist process achieved by folding the great outside of the many-dimensioned capitalist field into lower-dimensioned confinements of interiority: that of the family home and of the private persons it produces for society.

This requires quite a torsion. The image that is the capitalist is not the kind that resembles what it is an image of. The person of the capitalist does not resemble the capitalist process. It is a topologically twisted, derivative image of it. Neither do persons reproduce themselves like capitalism reproduces itself.[2] Persons are transforms of process. There is a formative gap between persons and process, into which Deleuze and Guattari dive in order to fashion their alternative to the theory of the deluded masses that features in most accounts of fascism and, more generally, in accounts of the political power of affect.

The capitalist is an image of capital, but since its relationship to the capitalist process is torsional, not one of resemblance or straightforward analogy of functioning in one-to-correspondence, you cannot read directly back from the person to the process. The person does not identify with the process in the sense of projecting its own image onto it, conformally.[3] That conformal labor is the job of the overcoding of general categories that pulls the process back from the limit toward

---

2   Deleuze and Guattari, Anti-Oedipus, 262.

3   "There is no longer any need of a collective investment of organs, as they are sufficiently filled with the floating images constantly produced by capitalism." Deleuze and Guattari, Anti-Oedipus, 251.

which it naturally tends. The application of the categories identifies the person, and the person identifies as a function of this, secondarily. The process projects itself into the person to produce forms of individuation that re-present the process, but without representing it in conformity or correspondence to it.

The one constant in capitalism's mode of production is that whatever else it is, it is always a mode of production of subjectivity. Movements on the level of individual persons take up the subjectivity of the process's agencying, asymptotic to its movements: genetically connected to them, feeding back into and furthering them, but neither mimicking their form nor operating in strict parallelism with them. The process's subjectivity-without-a-subject—its self-conducting, self-relating striving to perpetuate and expand its powers—gains a subject restricted to the level of the individualization of persons.

The inability to read back directly from the individualized person to the process gives the movements on that personified level the status of *objective apparent movements*: movements that are genetically tethered to a point to the process, and thus can index it when signposted, but appear in a different form from it, at a skew.[4] Objective apparent movements are *objective illusions*: torsions built into the reality of a relation between levels that really stand for the relation, but without resemblance or direct correspondence (objective illusion is discussed in detail below). When individuals vest their applicable role-image, they are *figuring* the process—becoming figurations of it. The individual person is a processual figure, a term that is closely allied with "image" in this account. Their figuring the process is their truth and their reality. It is not that they invest their being in the process. Rather, *their being is an investment of the process in them.* They are beings of relation to the process. Their existence is integrally adjoined to it, as they asymptotically appropriate it to themselves, feeding off of an angle onto it, as it feeds into them, and feeds itself through them.

Deleuze and Guattari provocatively hold that just as there is only one gender in the Man-Standard, in capitalism there is only one class.[5] If

4 Deleuze and Guattari, *Anti-Oedipus*, 11, 149.
5 Deleuze and Guattari, *Anti-Oedipus*, 253.

the capitalist is a personification of the flow of capital, the worker is likewise a personification of the flow of capitalized labor. Capitalist and worker are complementary figures belonging to the same formation: what has, in the current epoch of capitalism, matured into Human Capital.[6] Each figure, capitalist and worker, is dependent on its contrast with the other for its own distinction. They are the recto and the verso of the capitalist relation personalized. All of society's coded roles cut across this distinction in one way or another. Taken together, they form a reticulated system of reterritorialization: a disjunctive synthesis of the possibilities for persons, assigned to staked territories bestowing entitlements and privileges, and corresponding to a system of class-names. Just as the system of the Man-Standard is the one gender, the system of the Capitalist understood in this way is the one class.

The territories associated with the roles act as dykes and channels preventing the movements of capital from overflowing to the detriment of its own survival. They hold capitalism within certain self-preservative dynamic limits. Dynamic, because, as Deleuze and Guattari discourse upon at length in *Anti-Oedipus*, capitalism's axiomatic is constantly displacing its operational limits: making its territories themselves flow, taking on new configurations and functions as they are displaced, in a perpetual process of recoding that is consubstantial with capitalist-era social evolution. The capitalist process flows through the objective apparent movements of social evolution, figuring and refiguring itself, in constant self-adjustment and self-checking, reemerging always the greater for it. Between every transition in its trajectory (as is the case with all processual trajectories) there is an interval into which capitalism dips to draw forth a dose of emergent potential from the reserves of the full body and plane of immanence—just enough to refresh it and adapt it to new circumstances, but not enough for its flows to escape its master-key relation.

The critical implication of this account of personhood and capital is that *whatever might qualify as anti-capitalist cannot be personal* (at least not in any already-known figuring of it). This has vast implications for nonfascist life, which must draw upon infra-personal powers to reinvent what personhood can be.

---

6 Massumi, *Power at the End of the Economy*.

If under the reign of the capitalist relation the *person*, in the guise of a character role, is an image of the capitalist process, then the empirically existing impersoned *individual* embodying it is an image-of-an-image, fulfilling one of the complementary roles of capitalist or worker as well as others that intersect with, supplement, and bolster them (mother, father, policeman, teacher, etc.). This is what Deleuze and Guattari call, at the *Anti-Oedipus* stage of their own evolution, a simulacrum. The social role assigned an individual is a general category that vehiculates a generic image of personhood (the capitalist; the generic figure of Human Capital). As a general idea, the role itself qualifies as a person. It is a "manner" of corporate personhood according to Peirce's definition discussed in the "Corporate Persons" section of part 2. The personhood of the empirically existing individual conforming to the generic image is a particular image falling under the generic (this here capitalist; an individualized unit of Human Capital). Ironically (or cynically), the genericness is experienced, through the offices of overcoding that applies the role to the body, as the individual's private identity. Identity is a simulacrum, mistaken for a property of the individual.

As pointed out earlier, this is where resemblance and correspondence come in. The application of the role to the individual body is an operation of identification. Identity is not a given, but the product of a social operation of overcoding. The overcoding imposes a resemblance and correspondence between the two levels, that of the general idea and the particular individual. This produced resemblance makes the relation between the particular unit of human capital and its general-level image iconic. The relation of both levels to the capitalist process remains indexical through it all. The unit of human capital and its iconic image point as with two fingers, one embodied, the other abstract, to an asymptotic point of real insertion into a multi-level process that is more encompassing than they and their staked territories. The line of indexical pointing is jagged, since there is no direct path back from the person to the process. The particular individual that embodies the general image is always inflected by idiosyncrasies that bubble up to deform it, if ever so slightly, as it settles into the neighborhood of a life.

As the general image settles down, it refracts through the idiosyncrasies—emergent tendencies—rising from the body without organs.

This gives a tinge of the singular to the individual's generic identity. The patterning of the refraction constitutes the individual's personality. Tinged with singularity, an individual's personality exceeds the mere embodiment of the general image in a particular instantiation of it, while remaining largely structured by that application. Its uniqueness, although held within more or less strict limits by the overcoding, is what sustains the illusion that the applied identity is one's own. What is one's own is in fact the way in which a body undergoes the process of individualizing identification, with what glimmers of singularity showing through the cracks in overcoding as around the frame of an almost-closed door to the outside.

Every form of process has a conatus—a tendency to further its own tendencies while expanding its powers. The conatus of the capitalist process in the extensive dimension is its historical movements of imperialism and colonialism, which have brought its own limits to the limits of the earth, and are now pushing beyond them into outer space. In the intensive dimension, it is what Paul Virilio named *endocolonization*: the subsumption of more and more intimate dimensions of human bodily, perceptual, and affective life under the capitalist relation, to the point that capital becomes an immanent factor in the ontogenesis of the human—making capitalist power an ontopower.[7] This is a colonization of the field of potential, the very field of becoming of the human, sending its tendrils deeper toward the plane of immanence, in an attempt to adjoin even the wellsprings of an individual's singularity to the capitalist process. A corollary to the notion that the capitalist production involves a production of subjectivity is that this production of subjectivity involves a hominization: an elemental becoming human.[8] Speciation goes hand in hand with individualization.

The production of human capital through endocolonization has intensified under neoliberalism. Trump's self-branding is just the peak example. Participation in social media does not just offer the option of

---

7 Endocolonization: Virilio, *L'insécurité du territoire*, 51–64, 71, 100, 158, 161; Virilio and Sylvère Lotringer, *Pure War* (New York: Semiotext(e), 1983), 95–99. Ontopower: Massumi, *Ontopower*.

8 Massumi, *The Principle of Unrest: Activist Philosophy in the Expanded Field* (London: Open Humanities, 2017), 8–10.

self-image curation. It requires it. As avenues for the monetization of one's presence on social media proliferate, so do the pressures to move from self-curation to self-branding. Transforming oneself into an "influencer" or social media personality becomes a powerful attractor,[9] bending social media posts around itself the way space-time bends around a massive heavenly object. The push and pull of it is felt at the smallest levels, permeating everyday Facebook pages, as mega-figures with stratospheric click rates emerge on rival platforms like TikTok. Right-wing political and social commentators, who glorify the pursuit of profit in their praise for capitalism, unapologetically monetize their social media presence. Their tactics run the gamut from the crassest of merchandising (such as conspiracist Alex Jones of Infowars earning multi-millions peddling fake COVID cures and other questionable alternative health products) to faux highbrow guruism (such as Jordan Peterson, prophet of aggrieved manhood, liberally dosed with ornamental masculinity). Political speech and commercial speech merge into one, leaving no distance between techniques of the self and techniques of making money. Capital personified, personhood capitalized, personality adjoined wholesale to the capitalist process. Surplus-value of personing.

This active self-capitalization practiced by the self-branding enterprise-subject, "entrepreneur of himself," is not the only mode in which human capital functions in the digital environment.[10] The continuous background extraction of data accompanying every click monetizes the consumption of social media, down to the darkest corners of the private home and the most intimate recesses of the privatized individual's desire and patterns of attention. Data collection skims off surplus-value from movement, purely as a function of online naviga-

---

9   Fully 57 percent of "Gen Zers" (those born between 1997 and 2012) list "influencer" as their preferred career choice. Madeline Garfinkle, "Gen Z's Main Career Aspiration Is to Be an Influencer, according to a New Report," *Entrepreneur*, September 20, 2023, https://www.entrepreneur.com/business-news/what-is-gen-zs-no-1-career-choice-social-media-influencer/459387.

10 Human capital, entrepreneur of himself: Michel Foucault, *The Birth of Biopolitics: Lectures at the Collège de France, 1978–1979*, trans. Graham Burchell (New York: Palgrave Macmillan, 2008), 215–38. On the related concept of the enterprise-subject, see Massumi, *Power at the End of the Economy*, 39–40.

tion. This is an example of what Deleuze and Guattari call *surplus-value of flow*: an added value directly spun off of rhythms and cycles of circulation, without a significant input of labor.[11] The human body contributes only the most minimal action, mere clicks, whose patterns are extracted by automated data capture. The human input involved approximates for the digital machine what passive raw material was for the industrial machine. Social media, in their role as an extraction mechanism for surplus-value of flow, constitute a direct force of capitalist production. Their circulations of words and images is in and of itself a capital flow.

Social media's production of surplus-value of flow coincides with another form of surplus-value of which Deleuze and Guattari give an original formulation in *Anti-Oedipus*. This is what they call *machinic surplus-value*: an added value directly spun from the operations of technical systems replacing and/or subsuming human labor, in this case the universe of digital machines.[12] Under neoliberalism, surplus-value of flow and machinic surplus-value are as central to the capitalist process as, if not in some ways more fundamental than, living human labor. It is certainly the case that human labor cannot be understood in isolation from the various forms they take, of which social media is but the loudest. With surplus-value of flow, the value-producing role of the human body becomes machinic (a matter for autonomous systems). With the entrepreneurship of the self that is branding, it becomes communicational (disseminatory of point-signs). In both cases, labor in the thermodynamic sense of work—manipulating resistant matter—is largely bypassed. At least the tendency is toward bypassing it to the maximum extent possible, evacuating it as much as possible from its most advanced sectors and offshoring it or off-loading it to the precariat formed by the capitalism's inherent production of inequality (the present-day incarnation of Marx's reserve labor force). Surplus-value of flow and machinic surplus-value together form a pincer movement that, if not entirely dispensing with productive labor in the old frictional sense,

11   Deleuze and Guattari, *Anti-Oedipus*, 228–37, 249, 372; Massumi, *99 Theses for the Revaluation of Value: A Postcapitalist Manifesto* (Minneapolis: University of Minnesota Press, 2018), 28–36.

12   Deleuze and Guattari, *Anti-Oedipus*, 232–37; Massumi, *99 Theses for the Revaluation of Value*, 29–36.

subordinates it as much as possible to smooth, circulatory forms of value allied with, and constitutive of, human capital.

Contemporary personhood is not extricable from surplus-values of flow and machinic surplus-values. There is a circulatory and machinic factor integral to the constitution of personhood. This is obvious from observing the formative intensity of children's libidinal engagement with social media. Their personing is formatively adjoined to social media—as is, inevitably, adults'. Personing, the production of a particular social figure embodying a structural role in society, is a continuing process accompanying the ongoing individuation of the living body through the stages of its life.

But as we have seen in the discussion of Trump's and Trumpists' manner of personhood, society's structural roles are undergoing a destructuring. The increasing prevalence of the enterprise-subject and its associated surplus-values of flow and machinic surplus-values intensifies this ongoing process, which reaches a new threshold with the increasing plasticity of persons in the age of social media. It is as if the structure had become more like a rubberized surface of deformations, run through with pressure lines undermining its integrity. Roles stretch and deform, pulled loose from their moorings in a stably coded system of contrasts. Stretch marks are left, bringing roles into uncomfortable proximity to one another. Their contrasts may then bleed into each other, or oscillate under pressure of proximity. The structure of personhood slackens, to the point that it takes on a new consistency, more responsive to singularities of desire (in the processual sense discussed in part 3). It undergoes the relative deterritorialization already discussed in relation to the Man-Standard.

It is at this point that the codings that held the deregulating movement of capitalism's long-noted tendency toward "creative destruction" (Schumpeter) more or less within normative bounds begin to flag. Capitalism's axiomatic—defined once again as the hyper-complex transformational map of the potential translations between qualifications—is unbound from the remnants of rigid coding. Capitalist culture held on to these codings longest with respect to persons, in the collective person of the Man-Standard and the related ideology of generic humanism. With the plasticization of the Man-Standard, the capitalist social structure becomes an unbounded field of differentiation, limited only by the reach of the quadripartite relational matrix that is its requisite genetic element (worker vs. capitalist / money as means of payment vs. money as means of investment). The Man-Standard continues to operate as a check on the process, as an archaism with a contemporary function.

When the oscillation between the Man-Standard and the deterritorializing direction of the capitalist becomes aggravated, a turning point is approached. It can lead for example toward "illiberal democracy" on Viktor Orbán's Hungarian model, with its nationalist skepticism toward the globalizing push of neoliberalism, or toward an even harder nationalist and authoritarian state capitalism, as in Xi Jinping's China. A range of alternative trajectories is activated. All are nationalist, and isolationist to varying degrees. Nationalism is in turn always spiked with masculinism. The furthermost alternative is fascism, which is not only spiked with masculinism, but overdoses on it, striving to bring it to an apotheosis.

All this to say that the consolidation of human capital as master figure of the capitalist process, and of the asymptotic, torsional relation of personified capital to the capitalist system, must enter into the analytic of reaction. They are basic elements of the personality of power today.

What is important about human capital is that it makes it self-evident that the economy, as a certain Marxism would have it, is not the "base," determining in the last instance, on which social and culture "superstructures" are built and which they serve. There is simply no distance between base and superstructure, making the terms meaningless. They are in such close processual embrace that they co-penetrate. The main argument of Anti-Oedipus is that desire plugs directly into the figures and movements of the field of relation of the "socius," and is only mediated through the family when the Man-Standard is forcibly telescoped into familial figures that are reductively made to function as metaphorical stand-ins for the full panoply of social roles (my father the boss-man, my mother the nursemaid, and other Oedipal figures).[13] The direct plug-in to the capitalist process and its figures and movements is all the more notable now that capitalist surplus-value production has become fully immanent to the genesis of persons as units of human capital, and

13 Deleuze and Guattari, Anti-Oedipus, 62–63, 67, 88–90.

social and cultural movements have become direct machinic producers of capitalist surplus-value.

The reference to the movements of capital is crucial. It is these movements that the person as unit of human capital more and more directly "invests" (becomes an image of). Deleuze argues that the frictional model of thermodynamic work, with its structural condition of the factory, has been superseded as the dominant by the model of open-water surfing: riding the waves of disturbance and extracting from their quasi-chaos a smooth trajectory, wending through work and leisure, and from one stage of life to the next, generating surplus-value of flow marketably defines one's personhood.[14] The pattern that is personhood is now predicated at least as much on emergent surplus-value of flow as on the application from on high of socially coded figures.

14   Gilles Deleuze, "Postscript on Societies of Control," in *Negotiations*, trans. Martin Joughin (New York: Columbia University Press, 1995), 177–82. Again, this is not to say that capitalism has liberated itself from human labor, despite the aspirational project to replace it with robotics and autonomous systems. The exploitation of human labor remains absolutely essential in what Marx called the "realization" phase of the capitalist cycle. The "base" of infrastructure and logistics has if anything become more important, but with a change of accent: a new emphasis on organizing the fluidification of the flow of products necessary to serve the increasingly rapid turnover of consumer demand and to manage the response of the production process to the volatility endemic to the deregulated neoliberal economy. Under these conditions, gaining a logistical edge is a crucial part of generating relative surplus-value, which here is not just a question of arbitrage (exploiting variances in wages and prices in different markets), but becomes a question of producing a properly logistical surplus-value of flow. The fact remains that the capitalization of the financial sector, centering on derivative instruments that are purely instruments of surplus-value of flow, is now many times greater than that of the so-called productive economy. The tables have turned: the productive economy has become a dependency of the financial sector as leading edge of the economy, in a reversal of the classical arrangement where the financial sector was seen as a parasitic epiphenomenon of the productive economy. The two dimensions of the economy are so fully, if asymmetrically, imbricated that the oppositions between "fictional capital" and the "real economy," and "productive" and "unproductive" sectors, no longer obtain. On the imbrication of the extractive, logistical, and financial dimensions of the economy, see Sandro Mezzadra and Brett Neilson, *The Politics of Operations: Excavating Contemporary Capitalism* (Durham, NC: Duke University Press, 2019).

In more traditional Marxist thought, the relation of persons to the economic base was thought of as mediated by the striations of social and cultural codings. Now, the smoothed relation between the economic and the social/cultural/psychological is *immediated*.[15] The person is no longer confined to being an image-of-an-image of the capitalist process (although this too still occurs, to the extent that the Man-Standard remains operative as a check mechanism). It can now surf it, riding flush with its currents, as a first-order image of it. Trump's direct conflation of the ups and downs of his personal feelings and the ups and downs of his personal pool of capital is the case in point. Personhood takes on capital's defining characteristic: liquidity.

Some persons are more liquid than others. The flexibility and entrée necessary to surf volatility and draw a surplus-value of flow from it in order to entrepreneurially glide one's character to the top of the wave is not equally accessible to all. The differential value judgments of the check mechanism of the Man-Standard see to that. They intersect with the imperatives of human capital to reinforce capitalism's endemic production of inequality along already entrenched lines—most dramatically, along race lines.

Capitalism, in the era of human capital, remains the racial capitalism it has been since it underwrote the growing unequal concentration of capital, or "primitive accumulation," necessary for its early consolidation and transformation into an industrial economy with the transatlantic slave trade and the plantation system. The now not-so-primitive accumulation continues piggybacked on differentials between instantiations of human capital. Personifications of capital are differentially embedded in the social field as a function of the continuing intergenerational effects of slavery, intensified on the systemic level by the racism produced or amplified by the ascriptions of the Man-Standard and the dynamics of reaction fed by the objective illusions that their general-abstract functioning inevitably kindles. Some human capital is more equal than others. Some bodies find the way to fashioning themselves as enterprise-subjects blocked by systemic racism. Human capital thus

15   Erin Manning, Anna Munster, and Bodil Marie Stavning Thomsen, eds., *Immediation*, 2 vols. (London: Open Humanities, 2019).

only reinforces the racial inequalities built into the Man-Standard, which co-evolved with the racialization of capital as its abstract general social vector and cultural operator.[16] The inequalities remain, in just as oppressive a form, but on the human capital front with a fluidity that makes many of its effects harder to pin down, emboldening some, in the honeymoon period of the Obama presidency, to cynically (or objectively illusionarily) declare the advent of a "post-racial" society.

Returning to the torsional relation of capital personified to the capital process, it is important to underline that the "immediation" involved is not synonymous with transparency. There is still a certain kind of opacity, due to the superposition of levels and the jagged-line indexing of the capitalist figure through them to the movements of the capitalist process.[17] What is immediated is the event-based readjustment of the levels to each other and to the process, coincident with a step in the historic route of a person, and incident to the strike of a point-sign. This means that what used to be construed as the "masses," although they are not deluded, are still very much prey to error, in the form of objective illusions, racist and otherwise. *Objective illusion is the immediation of error*: error as a "naturally" occurring event that captures bodies, more fundamentally than it deceives minds. *More corporeology than ideology.* Ethnographer Kathleen Blee on recruitment into white supremacist groupings: "Their stated reasons for enlisting in racist groups appeared to have little to do

---

16   On the historical symbiosis between capitalism and the racist distribution of inequality, descending from the centrality of the transatlantic slave trade for the process of "primitive accumulation" undergirding the rise and subsequent evolution of capitalism, and involving the development and application of what is called the Man-Standard here, see Cedric Robinson, *Black Marxism: The Making of the Black Radical Tradition*, 2nd ed. (Chapel Hill: University of North Carolina Press, 2000); Jodi Melamed, "Racial Capitalism," *Critical Ethnic Studies* 1, no. 1 (Spring 2015): 76–85; Sylvia Wynter, *Sylvia Wynter: On Being Human as Praxis*; Ferreira da Silva, "Towards a Black Feminist Poethics." On the role of racism in the production of inequalities in mid-twentieth-century capitalism, see Ruth Wilson Gilmore, *Abolition Geography: Essays toward Liberation*, eds. Brenna Bandar and Alberto Toscano (London: Verso, 2022), pt. 2, chaps. 5–6. On present-day racial capitalism and digital culture, see Beller, *World Computer*.

17   Opacity: Édouard Glissant, *Poetics of Relation*, trans. Betsy Wing (Ann Arbor: University of Michigan Press, 1997), 111–20.

with racist ideology."[18] It results from embodied primings infra- to the ideological level that rise to meet it.

It is here that the analytic of reaction must begin, with a preamble on the embodied necessity of error.

Error Incarnate

The starting point for the account of error is a paradoxical one: from a process-philosophical perspective, all perception is direct perception, and direct perception is fundamentally without error. As Peirce noted, there is no strict dividing line between perception and thought. They shade into each other, into a zone of immediate overlap that is thinking-feeling. The overlap is in the act of abduction: lived hypothesis as one with the world's ongoing (the felt immediacy of an impending future in the present's charge of momentum from the past, one with the actuation of a gesture). The lived hypothesis envelops an affective bracing for the future—an adjustment of the body's power to affect and be affected—that is translated immediately into action or a poising for action. Thinking-feeling is thinking-feeling-bodying. Both Whitehead and Susanne Langer insist that thinking-feeling-bodying in direct perception is without error. It is exactly as it happens. "A thing is what it seems," writes Langer.[19] The perception's appearance surfaces the reality of the situation. Nevertheless, it carries the seeds of error.

Whitehead uses the example of a mirror.[20] Under certain conditions, you might look in the mirror and take what is reflected behind you for something in front of you, where the surface of the mirror lies. You may even reach out your hand to grasp an object and knock your knuckles on the mirror. Whitehead's point is that this result was built into the structure of the situation, which was objectively illusionary. Or, better, the situation featured in itself an objective figuration of itself. The person,

18 Blee, *Inside Organized Racism*, 27.
19 Langer, *Feeling and Form*, 49.
20 A. N. Whitehead, *Concept of Nature* (Cambridge: Cambridge University Press, 1920), 147, 151–53, and *Process and Reality*, 126–27.

as processual figure, has been presented as a topological mapping of its field of potential. This is also a figuration, one that can be thought of as a projection of the n-dimensions of the plane of immanence onto a surface of lesser dimension. This surface of lesser dimension can be thought of as an abstract affective recording surface on which conjunctive syntheses register pulses of complex feeling enveloped in an overall feeling.[21] In this example, the mirror itself accomplished a projection, delivered of a piece to perception and to its co-occurring affective ripplings. The mirror flattened the three-dimensional span of the situation's extensive organization and mapped it onto a two-dimensional surface display occupying the center of attention. The mirror showed the situation as it truly appeared, as a function of its objective figuration.

The appearance of the objective figuration issued directly, without pause for reflection, into the abductive gesture of reaching. The movement of the hand was a performative hypothesis as to the location of the object reached for and the possibilities for manipulation it afforded, accomplished without an act of cogitation separate from the perceiving and the affecting. This abductive act, operating hypothetically in the element of possibility, testifies to a direct conceptual element in the makeup of experience. This does not mean that it the act was mental as opposed to physical. It was both, inextricably. The performed hypothesis was the mental pole of a physical action.[22] The performed hypothesis was the body, the life of the body, stretching its activity into its immediate future. The conceptual element is the body feeling itself forward, into a beyond of where it stands, in a grasping for possibility. What is possible is still in potential, not yet present; present as yet only in potential. What is present only in potential is abstract. The stretch of the hand extended the activity of the body into the abstract: as thinkingly as feelingly, embodying possibility. Thinking-feeling is an immediate dimension *of* the body, defined earlier as that which is capable of action (grasping) and passion (knuckle pain) as two sides of the same transition. Understood processually as an immediation of experience,

---

21 Abstract surface: Massumi, *Architectures of the Unforeseen*, 44–68.

22 Mental and physical poles as two aspects of every experience: Whitehead, *Process and Reality*, 32–33; and see Massumi, *What Animals Teach Us about Politics* (Durham, NC: Duke University Press, 2014).

the act falls more under corporeology—the lived logic of the life of the body—than it does under cognitive psychology.

Unhappily for the knuckles, the abductive act performed itself under conditions where the seeming of what the thing is was objectively "dissembling."[23] The taking of the object behind for one before was a mistake—a *mis-take*—not in the sense that it did not reflect the situation as it truly appeared, but in the pragmatic sense that it did not land felicitously. It did not complete its tendential arc toward the realization of the possible due to the objective figuration of the situation.

Langer characterizes such mis-takes as "prototypes of error."[24] *Proto-errors* are abductive short-circuitings of action. They are corrected pragmatically, by the unhappy result. Full-fledged errors are adventitious outgrowths of proto-errors. They thrive under conditions in which signifying gestures are sheltered from such immediate pragmatic tests as knuckle-banging. For example, rather than going to grasp the object, you might point to it while describing it as lying before you. The mistake has not been put to the test, and may remain unchallenged. Error occurs in the passage from direct perception to denotation, particularly as it is supplemented, as Langer says it always must be, by demonstrative gestures. This is because, as Whitehead points out, all demonstration is "elliptical" by nature because it depends on the active cooperation and corroboration of the context, or processual "background" of the gesture. In the absence of that, it flounders.[25] The mirror in our example made for an uncorroborative context, ripe for the floundering. Signification, in the Saussurian sense, has an even greater propensity to error. The signifying sign's arbitrary relation to its referent allies it more directly to other signs and their systematicity, on their own level, than to indexicality or demonstration in the service of actionable denotation, both of which appeal to the processual background of other levels of potential. "Error arises only on the higher level of 'intellect' (discursive thinking)."[26]

23 Langer, *Feeling and Form*, 49. On "objective dissimulation," see also Deleuze and Guattari, *Anti-Oedipus*, 373.
24 Susanne Langer, *Philosophy in a New Key: A Study in the Symbolism of Reason, Rite, and Art* (New York: New American Library, 1948), 23.
25 Whitehead, *Concept of Nature*, 6–12.
26 Langer, *Feeling and Form*, 381.

Error consists in mis-taking what Langer calls the "symbolism" of the situation. In Langer's particular take on this loaded term, a symbol is direct expression of *import* in a perceptual event: what the matter is. Langer's "symbol" is what is termed here a direct perception. What direct perceptions present, without its actually appearing, is the composition of contrasting *proto-acts* immanent to the situation (umbral unions and their refigurings of potential moving from pure potential into real potential). Langer calls this virtual-activity complex the situation's "pattern of sentience" or "dynamic matrix of life."[27] The mirror in the example was an integral part of the dynamic matrix of life in the situation. It was entirely true to the dynamic matrix. For one thing, it truly expressed the import of the situation: the manipulability of objects in the surrounds. It also truly conveyed the objective illusion that was effectively built into the constitution of the situation. The problem was that the objective constitution predisposed the body to abductive failure. Import was conveyed, but was misplaced and, as a result, mis-taken. The direct perception literally, truly expressed the dynamic matrix. A corollary to the tenet that things are as they seem is that every direct perception is *literal*, literally true in the processual sense of really expressing the dynamic matrix of life at that moment.[28] That dynamic matrix included the narrowing of the focus of attention to the mirror, bracketed from its relation to its surrounds, that predisposed the body to misplace the import. This was a habitual effect of the body's object-oriented disposition toward everyday action. The word "illusion" "should not be misconstrued to mean that what we *have* directly perceived, we have *not* directly perceived."[29] Error, in the primary sense at issue here, is literally *misplaced import*. That mis-take proceeded from the collusion between the body's (pre)dispositions and the objective figuration of the situation—a collusion that is always itself an integral part of the objective context.

27   Pattern of sentience: Langer, Mind, 1:304. Dynamic matrix: Langer, *Feeling and Form*, 31.

28   "The context itself [the dynamic matrix or processual background] must always be expressed literally, because it has not, in turn, a context to supplement and define its sense." Langer, *Philosophy in a New Key*, 114.

29   Whitehead, *Process and Reality*, 64. Whitehead says "delusive," replaced here with "illusion" to harmonize with the vocabulary being developed.

The Literal

The literal in this processual sense of indexing a processual matrix is different from what we call literal in the everyday sense. The literal in the everyday sense is on a different level. A literal sign or statement is one that conveys what is felt to ground a claim to demonstrative success in such a way that the demonstration may be dispensed with. The literal sign is a substitute for demonstration that makes the gesture of demonstration superfluous. It says, trust me, you won't get your knuckles knocked if you follow where I point, so you don't even have to go that extra stretch. The literal suspends demonstration under its authority.

Literal language at this level is in no way the opposite of figurative language. We literally refer to the "leg" of a chair every day. All literality in the everyday sense is bound with figuration. Its suspension of demonstration depends on the "it goes without saying" of figures we can assume are the object of common knowledge—meaning that they are presupposed to be operative in the background of experience, without the need for that itself to be demonstrated. They are presupposed in their generality—with all the ambiguity that comes with general ideas, due to their loose fit to the singularity of all that occurs. This generalized looseness is the stock in trade of common sense.

Common sense deals in what Langer calls the "practical vision" of "*typical things or such-and-such events.*"[30] The problem is that the typical and the such-and-such exist only on the level of general abstraction. Common sense brackets the singularity of the actually occurring. It substitutes a landscape of presupposed, already-known figures for the context, or background in its processual fullness as dynamic matrix of life. It treats that substitute landscape as the whole of the processual background, when it is in fact only one level among others. It truly expresses this: that generalities are effectively in operation, always already applied. Common sense provides an abstract surface, in the general-category sense of abstract, on which the complexity of the dynamic matrix of life is projected, shedding dimensions in the translation. This

30 Langer, *Philosophy in a New Key*, 216–17.

leaves ample room for mis-takes, of an even more far-reaching nature. *The context itself is misplaced.* When the context, as dynamic matrix, is misplaced, the *import is all but lost.* This is full-fledged error, occurring on the higher level of discursive thinking. Langer defines discursiveness as import delivered to general ideas populating the conventional use of language as a self-indexing structure operating as a combinatory of discrete, preexisting parts of speech.[31]

Literality, in league with common sense, is less an instrument of the plain truth than the handmaid of high-level error. When the general figures presupposed by common sense pertain to persons, they press conformity with the known social roles of the Man-Standard, and subject anything that resists them to uncomprehending caricatures oozing disapproval. Common sense, in league with literality, is the mirror of the Man-Standard. When partisans of Trump warn us that Trump is to be taken seriously, but not literally, they are marking a post-normative twist on the alliance between common sense and literality. The figurative undertow of the literal is acknowledged and even valued. As a result, common sense begins to oscillate: between mirroring the Man-Standard and hypering it; and between the practical vision of typical things and such-and-such events, and colluding in the rationalization of fanciful knockoffs on them. Common sense, in its post-normative twist, helps create the discursive conditions for conspiracy thinking. It is the "elites," not conspiracy thinkers, who are felt to lack common sense.

Arch-Trumpian commentator Tucker Carlson plays professionally on this oscillation. Carlson defamed a Playboy model who claims to have had an affair with Trump, and was sued by her.[32] She lost. Carlson's

31   "Language in the strict sense is essentially discursive; it has permanent units of meaning which are combinable into larger units; it has fixed equivalences that make definition and translation possible; *its connotations are general*, so that it requires non-verbal acts, like pointing, looking, or emphatic voice-inflections, to assign specific denotations to its terms." Langer, *Philosophy in a New Key*, 78 (emphasis added).

32   Eric Wemple, "First Amendment Bails Out Tucker Carlson," *Washington Post*, September 24, 2020, https://www.washingtonpost.com/opinions/2020/09/24/first-amendment-bails-out-tucker-carlson; "Tucker Carlson Knows Exactly What He's Doing," *Washington Post*, February 6, 2023, https://www.washingtonpost.com/opinions/2023/02/06/hunter-biden-tucker-carlson-threat-letter.

winning argument was that his comments were "non-literal." They were greatly exaggerated, Fox News acknowledged, but they were offered in the guise of opinion, and always ended with a rhetorical question rather than a declarative conclusion. The element of "opinion" had less to do with the way the comments were formulated than with the position of Carlson's (now canceled) show in the prime-time opinion slot of Fox's programming schedule. This is Carlson's modus operandi. The formulation of his comments is bombastically declarative, signaling literality, until the closing interrogative flourish. The framing of the show in the Fox schedule and the finale of the rhetorical question frame the literality with non-literality, effectively having it both ways. The gesturing to the literal activates common sense. The result is a

4.1 Literally Schoenberg. Image by Johannes Kreidler.

performative ascription of a general judgment to the body of the litigant that is achieved without hazarding potentially libelous denotation
or declaration: it is only common sense, from the presumed moral perspective of the typical Fox viewer, that the kind of person the litigant
is is the kind who lies, so what Tucker says *should* be true. Mission accomplished. Trump defended, prejudice reinforced. All without legally
endangering Fox News's reliance for its enviable profit margin on post-
truth hucksterism and capitalizing on conspiracy theory. Here the oscillation between the literal and the non-literal (figurative or rhetorical) is
intentionally mined for political effect. Non-literal, but deadly serious.

Before moving on, if anyone doubts the alliance between the literal
and the figurative, consider the ubiquitous contemporary use of "literally" in social media and popular culture at large as an intensifier for a
figurative use of language. As in: "I literally went bananas."

Optive Matter

Bananas aside, could things in the mirror have been different? If there
is a thinking in the perceiving that is one with the act, might the mirror
situation have potentially played out differently, avoiding the unhappy
consequences of the proto-error?

Yes, if for example the body's quality of attention had been different in
the situation. In other words: if the context had been different because of
a variation in that constituent element of it that is the self-positioning,
self-posturing body, and the habits and tendencies it carries in and as
its substance. But it wasn't. The context was what it was. So this is a
counterfactual argument.

The thing is, the context, as it was, included the counterfactuality, in
potential. This is the context in the larger processual sense, of which the
commonsense context is a consensual reduction. *The dynamic matrix in the
literal, processual sense includes counterfactuality*—but not at all in the sense
of "alternative facts." In the sense, rather, of the *fact of potential* carrying import otherwise. Had your quality of attention been different, your
posturing less habitually narrowed, you might have had an increased
sensitivity to the periphery of your perception that might have clued you

in to the location of the object, altering your abductive thinking of the situation. Or subtle variations in light and shadow might have taken on abductive value as cues. A context is complexly primed, full of texturings and backgrounding-foregroundings that are susceptible of making a difference but are not necessarily destined to.[33] These are contributory elements of the situation that include what, looking back at the genesis of any particular act that happened to be performed within it, were seeds of alternative outcomes. These seeds of potential are really, literally in the situation, co-constitutive of the context, co-constructive of any direct perception of it. They are no less there when they fail to bear fruit.

As Langer puts it, "Wherever an actualization occurs there has been an option which the actualization has decided. . . . *Options belong to the very nature of acts.*" "Every act within an individual has to get out of the way of other acts which, nevertheless, are making its situation and perhaps implementing its advance to consummation." If an act misfires, "*its abortive dynamism adds itself to the unanalyzable matrix of the agent.*" "Out of the flood of unfelt options arise the larger ones that resolve themselves in behavioral acts."[34]

Repeat: if an act misfires, its abortive dynamism adds itself to the unanalyzable matrix of the agent. At the limit of feeling are *unfelt feelings* (including umbral feelings) having the status, from the perspective of the agent, of real but abstract existential options (abstract this time in the sense of being singularly virtual). These options are not "choices" in the individualist sense, as in rational choice theory. They are of the substance of the situation. They are potential actions and passions that can be picked up from the submolecular level on which they roil, and amplified into taking actual form. They are what Guattari calls "optive matter," and what Langer calls "*objective feelings.*"[35]

33 Backgrounding-foregrounding: Manning, *For a Pragmatics of the Useless*, 103–14.

34 Langer, Mind: whatever, 1:436; every, 429; abortive dynamic, 377; out of the flood, 436; emphasis added. This, once again, is Whitehead's "negative prehension." Whitehead, *Process and Reality*, 23–24, 26, 41.

35 Optive matter: Félix Guattari, *Schizoanalytic Cartographies*, trans. Andrew Goffey (London: Bloomsbury, 2013), 21, 31–32, 40, 104. The French, *matières à option*, is translated in the English edition as "optional matters." I have chosen "optive" to avoid the connotation of subjective choice. Objective feelings: Langer, *Feeling and Form*, 20.

The reality of alternative trajectories is the flip side of error—and of the generality of discursive truth. Reaction allies itself with common sense to ensure that they remain unfelt options. The anti-fascist life is dedicated to feeling them out into experience.

Perspective

Do not mis-take the implications of the phrase "in the perspective of the agent." The options "resolve *themselves*," Langer says. What she is calling an agent is not an empirical subject, and neither is it a deciding mind. "*An agent is a complex of actions*" reaching its own resolve.[36] An agent is ma-chinic: a self-conducting, self-deciding working-out of options. It is an agencying: a subjectivity without a subject. The complex includes proto-acts that consummate, passing from the unfelt to feeling, and those that do not, remaining in potential and passing unperceived. All belong to the texture of the situation, as real elements in its constitution. It is the tide of unperceived proto-acts at the unfelt heart of the complex that leads Langer to characterize the dynamic matrix as "unanalyzable" in full.

Acts emerge from an umbral "flood" of unfelt options. The way the flood resolves itself into an effectively channeled, individualized flow of action constitutes who (what) the subject will have been at each step of the way, as it surfs the felt passages of a life. "Life," Langer writes, "is the self-expression of impulses," or elemental tendencies, each with its own affective sub-flavor.[37] The behavioral acts composing a life are over-acts. They roil over, and channel out, their outcome selectively resolving an energizing tension among a crowd of "act-like" agitations. These proto-acts do not appear in their individuality, but neither are they erased. They are felt, in effect: in the manner in which feelings felt and unfelt issue in a joint result, summed up in the feeling of a conjunctive synthesis consummating a pulse of process. In the proto-commotion immanent to the act's consummation, the act-like impulses are "internally involved with each other."[38]

---

36 Langer, Mind, 1:314.
37 Langer, Mind, 1:376.
38 Langer, Mind, 1:340.

(This is what in my own work I call "bare activity.") They are in umbral union, mutually included in each other's ferment, like all the shadows of all the world's things rollicking in an infinity of umbral refractions in-acting every possible angle of intersection all at once.

Each intersection is a perspective. But it is not a perspective of a sub-ject on the world (on the world's possibilities). It is a perspective of the world on the person (on the person's potential).[39] Each consummate feeling seals a step in the historic route of a person. The complex of um-bral potential enters into that consummation, including the unfelt feel-ings and the options they harbor, and including any misfires and all that may have entered into the objective illusion conditioning the mis-take. The unfelt feelings are a positive contributor to the outcome, by virtue of having been selected out by the agencying that expressed itself in the objective figuration, through the disposition of the body co-factoring into that figuration. This selecting-out leaves its trace, like an intaglio imperceptibly etched on the abstract surface of experience.

Whitehead calls this "negative prehension" ("prehension" is White-head's term for "feeling" in the broadest processual sense, as a grasping of potentials). Negative prehensions forever enter into the constitution of the person's patterning, in its trajectory through life. The same goes for the misfires. *Unfelt feelings and mis-takes are constitutive factors of person-hood.* A perspective of the world in-forms the person's becoming, for that pulse of process. It in-forms, or infra-agencies, what the person will have been, forever after, given that effective step. The differences that step makes enters into the constitution of the world. The world's coef-ficients of potential rejig around them. *The person's becoming in the world indexes a becoming of the world.*[40] It indexes a modulation of the process of worlding. The person peaks as a torsional image of that process: an individualized expression of what surpasses individuality—namely, the potential from which the individual came, and the potential it produces for the world by producing a variation on the expression of potential in

39 This is what Whitehead calls a "perspective of the universe." A. N. Whitehead, *Modes of Thought* (New York: Free Press, 1968). See Erin Manning and Brian Massumi, *Thought in the Act: Passages in the Ecology of Experience* (Minneapolis: University of Minnesota Press, 2014), 23–30.

40 On "world-process," see Whitehead, *Modes of Thought*, 93–94.

the world.[41] That variation becomes a potential source of influx of otherness for other persons drawing their powers of becoming from the world's field of potential.

This is what, process-philosophically speaking, is meant by perspective: not a point of view on things, but an angle of insertion into the process of their becoming, in becoming. Here, *perspective is objective*, in the sense of being an integral part of the world's makeup.[42] It is as a perspective of the world that a person appropriates the world's potential for its own continued emergence, from an angle. It owns it, selectively, from that angle of emergence. Personification is a drop of worlding. Inversely, the world reenvelops the person, engulfing it in its own subsequent trajectory.[43] It reowns the potential enveloped in the person toward the ongoing of its own process, this time additively rather than selectively. The expressed potential returns, in a reflux running back

41 "The full solemnity of the world arises from the sense of positive achievement [the consummation of a pulse of process] within the finite, combined with the sense of modes of infinitude stretching beyond each finite fact. This infinitude is required by each fact to express its necessary relevance beyond its own limitations. It expresses a perspective of the universe. Importance ["import" in Langer's vocabulary adopted here] arises from this fusion of the finite and the infinite." Whitehead, *Modes of Thought*, 78–79. "There are . . . three factors within immediate existence—namely, past, present, and future. Immediacy of finite existence refuses to be deprived of that infinitude of extension which is its perspective" (83).

42 Langer's notion of objective feeling and Whitehead's notion of feeling (prehension) are convergent with Nietzsche's perspectivism: "Basic question: whether the *perspectival* is of the *essence* of the matter? Rather than it merely being a form of viewing that which is essential, a mere relation between distinct entities? Might the various forces relate to one another in a way that the relation itself is bound up in the optics of perception? This would be the case *if all being were essentially something perceiving*." Which brings us back by another route to the commind of part 2. Friedrich Nietzsche, *Writings from the Late Notebooks*, ed. Rudiger Bittner, trans. Kate Sturge (Cambridge: Cambridge University Press, 2003), 107. Cited in Halbe Kuipers, "Perspectives and Event: A Study on Modes of Existence and the More-Than-Human; Perspectivism and Process Philosophy" (PhD diss., University of Amsterdam, 2022), 2 (translation modified by Kuipers).

43 "The world is included within the occasion in one sense, and the occasion is included in the world in another sense. For example, I am in the room, and the room is an item in my present experience. But my present experience is what I now am." Whitehead, *Modes of Thought*, 163.

down the zigzag path that the flood of proto-acts channeled up through, to rejoin a now edited plane of immanence in-forming the world's potential. It recedes into the field of umbral union renewed by the effective addition of a variation on the relational potential it diagrams.

Recap

1) Mistakes are not just something persons make. More fundamentally, mis-takes make them.
2) Every person's makeup comprises error incarnate. This is an unavoidable aspect of the torsions of personing, as difficult to separate out as the spin from the top.
3) The "delusion" of the putative masses is ontological, not ideological. It is an objective illusion pertaining more directly to a corporeologic of perspective than to discursive thought and its (general) truths and (higher-order) falsehoods.
4) The perspective at issue is an effective angle on the reality of process. It is an objective perspective, bodily performed in thinking-feeling abductively acting itself out. It is a dynamic existential posture that is a take on the world, in which the world takes to the person. It may peak in subjective illusion, but that is only the tip of the processual iceberg: an effect, not a cause.
5) The angling onto the reality of process selectively lifts some potential feelings into the act, and remits others to unfeeling. Both are constitutive. It is the patterning of what is felt and what is unfelt that is formative and enters into the constitution of the person.
6) The perspective on process that the person embodies includes an angle on the capitalist process. This makes the person a truly twisted image of capital, personified (human capital).
7) The analysis of reaction is not an unveiling of a hidden truth by the privileged few who have the rare and requisite cognitive skills. It is a diagnostic study of the patterning of felt and unfelt feelings. It takes expressions literally, in the processual sense defined above: as truly belonging to an objective figuration of the world (torsions included).

8) Anticipating part 5, the diagnostic study undertaken in this book
revolves around attributions of causality and the ascriptions, in
the Schmittian sense, that they foster, with special attention to the
performative role played by circulation of point-signs. Given the
status of persons as human capital, the ascriptions tend inevitably to be linked to attributions of economic causality, in ways that
lead to what could be called an economization of hate (see the
section by that name in part 5).

Why?

The genealogy of error, understood in terms of objective illusion, in
turn understood as rooted in an objective perspective, is coextensive
with the spectrum of fascism and fascisizing tendencies. A consideration of error in these terms is necessary for understanding the species
of belief into which error unfolds as it courses through social discourse
and metastasizes into a form of intellectuality with a genetic disposition toward conspiracy theory.

PART 5

The Regime of Reaction

Passion and Reaction

In the Ethics, Spinoza develops an account of the genealogy of error that dovetails with the one just given, working from Whitehead and Langer. The present account will move into the analysis of reaction by extending this account with a certain take on Spinoza, oriented by Nietzsche and Deleuze's notions of reactive forces.[1]

In place of the mirror, Spinoza invokes the sun. When we look at the sun, he says, we imagine it to be a mere two hundred feet away, within assisted human reach.[2] This is how the sun truly appears. It appears that way because the perception is not capable of effectively "enveloping" its cause.[3] It registers the sun "only so far as the Body is affected by it."[4] It only envelops the state of the body, as affected by the light emitted by the sun. But this reaction of the receptive body is not the whole situation. The situation also involves the sun, as affecting. It involves the activity of the sun, from its objective perspective: its distance from the earth, the optical influence of the earth's atmosphere, and the sundry adventures of photons on their journey to their illuminating extinguishment in our retinas. The situation includes a far-reaching composition of elements in complex relation, necessarily including but in no way limited to our body. This composition is the effective cause of the perception. More

---

1 Spinoza, Ethics; Deleuze, Expressionism in Philosophy; Deleuze, Spinoza: Practical Philosophy (San Francisco: City Lights, 1988); Deleuze, Nietzsche and Philosophy. Citations from Spinoza's Ethics will be given in the traditional abbreviated citation format.

2 Spinoza, E2, P35, S; E4, P1, S.

3 Envelop: involvere in the original Latin. Spinoza, E2, P48, S. Curley translates it as '"involve."

4 Spinoza, E4, P1, S.

precisely, the effective cause of the perception is the *relationality* of this composition as it plays out in the event. When we "imagine" the sun—think-feel it in that objectively illusionary way as lying two hundred feet from our eyes—we have bracketed that complexity. All we have retained is the optical effect on our body, and the abduction of reachability that came with it, divorced from a perception of the situation in its compositional relationality.[5]

It is as if everything has happened between the sun and our eyes, in a direct causal line involving only a dual connection. The neutralizing of the situation's composition reduces the sun to a discrete impinging *object*, as opposed to a remarkable point in the nexus of relational activity, which is what it is in the fullness of the situation's composition. If our eyes are dazzled by it, it is *its* fault, all its fault: bad object. It hurts our eyes, and we turn away. The active reaching we were primed for inverts into an aversion, crowned in a grunt of complaint.

Now the complexity of our own activity is also bracketed, absorbed in a passive reaction. The mis-take retained a certain positivity of action, in the form of the proto-act of potential reach. That has now been suppressed. We're in no mood to reach. *Reaction is the absorption of the active share of direct perception in a feeling filling an interval of impotence.* That active share is the "thinking" that comes with the feeling: the proto-act of the hypothetical potentiation for action that constituted the abduction. Reaction separates the thinking from the feeling, and focuses on the feeling, as if all the world were filled with it, and only it. In so doing, it separates the body, for a pulse, from what it could hypothetically do.

This is an example of what Spinoza would call a sad "passion," which is when in an encounter the body's power to act passes to a lower degree.[6] Here the absorption of the active share of perception in feeling,

---

5 Imagination: Spinoza, E2, P48, S: "The imaginations of the Mind, considered in themselves, involve no error"; E4, A1, S: "An imagination is an idea which indicates the present constitution of the body"; E4, P9, D: "An imagination is an idea by which the Mind considers a thing as present, which nevertheless indicates the constitution of the human Body more than the nature of the external thing. An affect, therefore, . . . is an imagination."

6 Spinoza, E3, P11, S.

separating the body from what it can do, voiding it of its positive powers for a beat of existence, will be termed the *pathic*—the ground zero of sad passions.[7] (For more on the pathic, see "The Pathic Is the Pivot" section in this part.)

"Voided" is too strong: "short-circuited" is better. Every direct perception is a thinking-feeling involving an abduction. Every abduction activates tendencies. And every tendency is a striving to follow through with itself—a *proto-will* already stirring below the level of reflective consciousness, constituting the enactive thinking of the feeling: the feeling pressing to actively think itself out (the elemental impetus of what Deleuze and Guattari call desire). It is this striving (conatus) that is short-circuited, leaving the feeling nowhere to go but circle in on itself, intensifying the feeling tone of the moment. Any action that breaks out of the circle will be a *reaction*, a self-defensive gesture or a lashing out at the object that has been ascribed all of the blameworthy causal efficiency of the situation. For a more elaborated reaction, a *response* that regains a measure of the short-circuited activity potential, a detour is necessary. If that detour runs through discursive thought and the general ideas it traffics, it elaborates the punctual reaction into an affective regime of reaction, erecting on the objective illusion an edifice of higher-order error. Paradoxically, it does this by converting the abductive proto-will of the encounter with the object into a cogitative *will-to-truth* that attempts to reconstitute the lost causal fullness, while lacking the conditions to succeed in that quest.

Before looking at this process, and how it leads toward conspiracy thinking and feeds reactionary politics and its fascisizing tendencies, it is helpful to look at what the alternative is, or how what Spinoza terms "adequate ideas" arise.

---

7 A joyful passion is when the body's powers of existence pass to a higher degree. To anticipate what is coming later, the trick of combating reaction is to contract habits of thinking-feeling that immediately orient experience toward augmentations of its powers of existence as it returns from the pathic infra-moment of suspension—or what is called a "micro-shock" later in this essay—so that it is the sad affect that is short-circuited.

Adequate Ideas

The first level of adequate ideas are "common notions."[8] This term is widely misunderstood to refer to notions that are common to many brains, like the general categories of the Man-Standard or commonsense ideas. What it actually refers to is what is common to two or more *bodies in encounter*.

In our two examples of objective illusion, the mirror and the sun encounters, one of the things all of the elements involved have in common is spatiality. Each element embodies an objective perspective. The objective perspectives are disjunctive, in the sense that no two can be superimposed upon each other without remainder, even though they necessarily overlap. Their overlap weaves their disjunctiveness into a continuous but patchy field. This is not homogeneous Cartesian space (at least in the present interpretation, if not for Spinoza himself). It is a space of inclusive disjunction composing a variegated field.

Another thing all of the elements have in common is that each makes a difference in the composition of the field, and in what can transpire in the space. They *condition* the encounter. To make a difference is an efficacy: a *power*. Ultimately, what all of the elements have in common is their *participation* in the same encounter, from the efficacious angle of their objective perspective and the powers to which it gives a foothold.

The power of a participating element is not static or self-contained. It plays off the powers of other elements, which fortify, curtail, or inflect the capacities a given element can effectively enact in the situation. The participation is relational. Each element is a relational component. What occurs, occurs *between*, in the overlap of perspectives and the play of powers. Given the relationality of what happens, it is artificial to isolate any given element as a discrete cause. The sun dazzles because its rays participate in the activity of our eyes, which participate in the disjunction between our body's objective perspective and the sun's, with all of the contributory elements, from atmospheric conditions to habits of perception, that effectively intervene in that distance. The "cause" is a *relational cause*. It is not a linear. It is irreducible to a simple point-to-point causation. It is, rather, a catalysis drawing a joint effect from

8 Spinoza, E2, P38–39; Deleuze, *Spinoza: Practical Philosophy*, 54–58.

multiple contributions. The sun does not just impinge. It impinges in just this way, as a function of this situation's composition and the powers each of the participating elements brings to its conditioning.

The objective illusion of the sun's proximity and the graspability of the object in the mirror cannot be undone. The situation was as it seemed. It truly appeared that way in direct perception, and that appearing cannot be revoked. It is possible, however, to "*double*" the impingement with an experience and understanding of the relational causality in play.[9] In the case of the mirror, we do this by attending to the composition of the situation. Our objective perspective makes a kind of leap in place, enlarging to encompass the perceptual impingement of the mirror in the awareness of a relational array. With that enlargement comes a renewed capacitation for grasping that expresses itself in a new set of abductions, activating tendential arcs that effectively compose with the situation but were previously backgrounded.

By "composing" with the situation is meant expressing an accord between, on the one hand, the lived hypotheses that comes flush with the abductions and, on the other, the felicitous terminations of possible actions that the hypothetical proto-activity sketches out. Our powers to act are maximized for that situation, and with them our powers to think further and feel more within it, following our actions. The new set of abductions doubles the original objective illusion. Doubles and supplants: it replaces it on the advancing crest of forming experience. Now it is the objective illusion that is relegated to the background. It is still there, still a true aspect of the conditions of emergence enabling the renewed perception. It is just that it has been relegated to the status of an unfelt feeling. It has been revised into a negative prehension, enduring in trace form, enveloped in the process of its own supplanting. The trace is never obliterated, but it can be relegated to the background and supplemented.

This changes our understanding of error. Everyone is prey to objective illusions. No perception is untinged by them (if only in the form of what we may retrospectively dismiss as "subjective" anomalies). They cannot be expunged. No one can leave them behind or become immune from contracting them. But what we can do is to double them

9 Deleuze, Spinoza: Practical Philosophy, 80, 129.

and dislodge them from the forefront of experience, so that they retain the status of supplanted proto-errors, rather than maturing into full-fledged errors that mislead discursive thinking.

The doubling and dislodging must be as embodied and enactive as the original perception. It cannot be cognitive in that sense of a mere cogitation. Thinking may take the lead, discursive thinking may well be involved, and cogitation can assist. But they must be mobilized pragmatically. They must recur to thinking-feeling. They must lead back to the participatory relationality of the situation, so that new habits are contracted, informing subsequent abductions that are more in accord. In a word, they must be *immediated*. They must settle into the immediacy of direct perception's thinking-feeling.

The sun example is one where discursive thought is likely to enter into the formation of an adequate idea of our encounter with it. We are likely to mobilize scientific and geometrical knowledge, gleaned communicationally from others, in our recomposing of the situation. The key point, however, is that for this knowledge to make a difference it has to take effect. It has to be put into practice, and when this is done, the discursive knowledge involved becomes direct perception. *Practice becomes perception* through the contracting of habit (the becoming self-conducting of thinking-feeling issuing in activity). Once we contract new habits, and the abductions they convey graft themselves into our bodily activity, we will forever after directly and immediately see the sun at an unreachable distance, even though all the conditions for the original objective illusion of its graspable proximity are still in place. The sun-seeing situation has been counteractualized.

A crucial consequence of all this is that *imagination*—in Spinoza's sense of the effect of an impingement on the body of a perception or thought experienced in isolation from its conditioning relational field—is *a necessary constitutive factor in adequate knowledge*.[10] The significance of this is that it forbids any appeal to the traditional rational/

10　This is a different sense of imagination than is often used in my work, where it is tied to the ability to "surpass the given" by "improvising on the percept" in a speculatively pragmatic manner; see Massumi, *What Animals Teach Us about Politics*, 17. This definition ties it to creative powers of emergence. This is close to the way it is used in various aspects of Deleuze's work, often with respect to the notion of fabulation.

irrational dichotomy that is so readily trotted out in explanations of the affective aspect of politics and the affective derangements accompanying reactive thinking-feeling. Rational/irrational, illusionary/true, even true/false, are off the mark. All knowledge, even adequate knowledge, keeps company with objective illusion. Objective illusion is what it seems—and its replacement perceptions are likewise what they seem. It is less that a falsehood is replaced by a truth, and more that a seeming is doubled by another seeming. The objective illusion's discordant seeming is replaced by one more in accord with felicitous playings-out that effectively express the relational composition of the situation.

You could say that the metaphysical question of truth, understood as a formal correspondence between words and things vouchsafed by epistemological principles, cedes to a pragmatic definition as in the work of William James, specified here as a practical accord between the proto-activity of thinking-feeling and the felicity of its future playing out. Alternatively, you could say, similarly to Nietzsche, that the question is not truth at all but, rather, the *power of the false*.[11] The movement is not from falsehood to truth, but from seeming to seeming again. More precisely, it is from the powers incumbent in one mode of seeming to the expanded powers incumbent in another mode. This way of putting it construes the training of habit and the habit's entraining of perception into new abductive tendencies in oxymoronic terms, as a *construction of immediacies of experience*. This refers to the process whereby corrective or exploratory practice becomes direct perception. The process then falls under the rubric of fiction: effective fiction, as real as it can seem. To emphasize its immediately constructed nature, this can be called fabulation.[12] By this reckoning, fabulation becomes the reality principle.

Whichever way we choose to go on this, what is clear is that error is not merely cognitive. It is lived, full-bodily. It is corporeological, ontological. It is ontogenetic: involving a becoming. The deflection of objective illusion from developing into full-fledged error must likewise be corporeological, ontological, ontogenetic. It must bear on modes of

11 Gilles Deleuze, *Cinema 2: The Time-Image*, trans. Hugh Tomlinson and Robert Galeta (Minneapolis: University of Minnesota Press, 1989), 126–55; and Deleuze, *Negotiations*, 95–96.

12 Deleuze, *Negotiations*, 125–26.

life and recur to the immediacy of thinking-feeling. As argued earlier, (proto-)error is a constitutive factor in the formation of the person. It does nothing to intellectually correct or debunk mis-takes and erroneous beliefs. It does nothing to argue and deride. These approaches do nothing to re-form the patterning of thinking-feeling that is the person, because the trace of objective illusion is still felt, meaning that its error-prone proto-will is still exerting a power of priming action and inflecting thought and its enaction. Modes of counter-living that support its doubling and replacement must be proposed, in situation, and rendered at least as compelling as reaction. They must be proposed for the desiring.

From the Singular to the Singular-Universal

The common notion, as first-level adequate idea, bears on the singularity of a situation of encounter. It expresses as an enactive understanding of the powers of the elements involved, from the relational angle of their joint participation in the situation. There are actually three levels of adequate ideas according to Spinoza. The third and highest level moves from the singularity of encounter to what can be termed the *singular-universal* of "essence." Essence in Spinoza is very different from the scarecrow version dominant in many traditional metaphysics that has raised the hair on the back of the necks of theorists since the onset of poststructuralism. Essence in Spinoza is another word for the *nexus of powers* immanent to the life of a body. A body's essence is its potential.[13]

In the common notion, the body is grasped *in* a nexus with others in fortuitous—that is to say, eventful—encounter. On the third level, the body is grasped *as* a nexus. With the common notion, the body is already thought-felt as harboring potentials that are real but unactualized: expressible but not expressed. These potentials are limited to those which, to use a Whiteheadian term now, have "made ingress" into the situation: which are addressable in the situation, given the conditions

---

13   "The essences are neither logical possibilities nor geometric structures; they are parts of power, that is, degrees of physical intensity." Deleuze, *Spinoza: Practical Philosophy*, 65. See Spinoza, E4, preface; and E4, P4.

of the situation, if not yet actually addressed. This is what Whitehead calls "real potential." Spinoza's "essence" pertains to what Whitehead terms "pure potential."[14] Pure potential refers to all the powers a given body might express in *any* situation.

"Any" is a tricky word. It is very different from "all." If pure potential were an "all," it would be a totality, with a static structure. As an "any," it is an openness. Real potential is all the powers a body could express in any situation—and the world's situations are not pre-formed, so you can't just add them up like beans in a jar. Each is fortuitous. Each is nothing until it hazards an appearance in the world. A body's essence is its power to vary the powers it expresses through the vicissitudes of situations' hazardings. You can imagine it by thinking of the body in every possible configuration, as its powers augment and diminish according to the conditions holding sway in each situation.

Except that you can't imagine it. Imagination, in Spinoza's definition, is anchored in the singularity of a situation, and it constitutionally misses the relationality of which the essence is the apotheosis. Neither can you think it fully in reflective thinking. Reflective thinking can abstract from the singularity of a situation, but not enough. It is stunted by the general categories it must mobilize to do this. What essence asks for is not a general idea, but a singular idea expressing an any. In other words, what it asks for is a thinking of a body as it is outside *a* given situation *and*, potentially, in *any* situation. A-and-any. This is a singular way of thinking the universal, in contradistinction to the general. The universal is not abstract in the way a general idea is. It is *superabstract*. So abstract that it is beyond imagining and reflective cogitation. It is only accessible through intuition.[15]

Intuition is not thought made intimate and personal. Quite the contrary, it is the thinking-feeling of the highest abstraction, beyond the ken of the person. It is thought embodied, to the limit of the body's powers of variation. Its "object" (which is not one) is the full body, or even, at the limit, the plane of immanence. Through intuition, the life

14 Real potential versus pure potential (also called general potential): Whitehead, *Process and Reality*, 23, 65.
15 Spinoza, E2, P40, S2, III; and E5, P36, S.

of the body and its personhood plugs into dimensions of becoming beyond its own. Bergson expressed this as experiencing a connection into durations above and below the human scale.[16] Intuition is the non-personal of persons' capacity to think-feel the *other* influences and values that Whitehead says in-come to imbue situations with real potential.

One reason the body's universal-singular powers of existence cannot be imagined or reflectively thought is that "any" is labile. It includes emergences. In the interplay of powers, new powers may arise. An adequate idea embraces this. Its intuition is a thinking-feeling of change: a direct perception of change. Intuition is a grasping of import, as defined above, at its widest extent.

That is the point to hold onto: *thinking-feeling change*. Articulating it in terms of intuition might sound uncomfortably mystical to some. But it is actually entirely pragmatic. The point is that it is impractical to expect to make change an object of the imagination or of reflective thought. Imagination, as it develops from immediate reaction, can harness general ideas to form composites, like the famous example of the winged horse beloved of philosophers. But this is just compositing existing properties to yield a purely fictional being (as opposed to fiction as fabulation, a process expressing a true power of the false, a power to actualize a real counterfactual). Reflective thinking, for its part, cannot embrace indefinite sets of singulars without confecting the general categories that imagination hijacks for its fictioneering. Intuition, as Bergson says, is a method: a *practice*. It is a practice that becomes perception. It is direct perception *enveloping* a relational causality of singular-universal scope in thinking-feeling. It expresses that envelopment, even though it cannot make explicit all that it embraces.

Imagination and reflective thought miss the essence of things precisely by purporting to make their object explicit. It may seem odd to say, but imagination, like reflective thought, is just too literal (in the everyday sense of the word discussed earlier). Intuition is literal in the contrasting processual sense, of pointing not to a thing but to the dynamic matrix of life. In other words, intuition is *figural thinking*. Figural thinking

---

16 Henri Bergson, *Creative Evolution*, trans. Arthur Miller (Mineola, NY: Dover, 1998), 177.

is nonrational. Nonrational, not irrational. Nonrational and pragmatic. How else can change be thought, given that it is by definition what lies beyond the order in force, rationally analyzed as given? The analysis of fascism and reaction has no choice but to work with nonrational powers of thought. To be a thinking-toward the potential of a nonfascist life, it must surpass the given. It must send out tensors to the future. The only way it can do that is to find them, not in the present, but immanent to it, in "essence."

Is it too much to argue that figural thinking can be made politically operative? To claim otherwise would be tantamount to abandoning change, despite all rationalist protestations to the contrary.

Uses and Abuses of the General

We jumped from the first level of adequate ideas to the third. We skipped over the second for a moment because it requires some backtracking. The second kind of adequate ideas are what Spinoza calls universal ideas.[17] These are the general ideas studied in part 2. They are sandwiched in between the other two kinds of adequate idea. Spinoza bitterly critiques them when they are malformed, in which case they become merely abstract general ideas.[18] However, if well formed (as Peirce's collective singulars), they can adequately assist in passing from the first kind of knowledge (common notions) to the third (intuition).[19]

---

17 Spinoza, E2, P40, Schol. 2, III.

18 Spinoza, E2, P40, Schol. 1.

19 Universal ideas are malformed if they flub this transitional role by forgetting that their coverage of a spread of instances cloaks unique details, thus missing the singularity of common notions and returning to the common sense impression of them as being general in the sense of being common to and alike in different brains. This places them at the mercy of the objective illusions of the imagination. They also misfire if they are produced by leaping from a single encounter to the immediate attribution of essentially defining properties, so that the next encounter with the same thing, or another judged to be of its kind, can only reconfirm the judgment, with no possibility of new observation or nuancing conceptual development. Spinoza calls this "random knowledge." The "Accidents of Persons Predisposed" section gives a startling example of this in relation to racism (also making

In the terms mobilized in this account, the adequate use of general ideas is linked to the notion that general ideas index collective persons, and constitute in their own right a mode of personhood. To review, general ideas can function as "collective singulars," and there is an abductive use of them associated with this status. In their usage as collective singulars, the general does not *subsume* particulars under an empty designator as is the case for the abstract general idea, but, rather, *covers* a multiplicity of elements. "Coverage" is taken here in a sense not entirely unlike what reporters used to do in the pre-social-media world: be ready to swoop down and bring to expression a co-involvement of factors. In the case of the general idea, that co-involvement constitutes the character—the patterning—of a population. The patterning enables the population to count as one in subsequent processing in thought and language, without losing the singularity of the patterning *or* the multiplicity of the population. Another way of putting it is that the general category functions as an index of a peopling of the world: a process of patterning, under variation across a multiplicity. This is a step toward the singular-universal, which covers a multiplicity of elements belonging to different collective singulars, as their members may potentially enter into any singular situation and contribute to its patterning.

The fundamental action associated with general ideas, whether abstract general or collective singular, is to be *applied*. When a collective singular idea, for its part, is applied, it does not offer a solution. It locates a problem. Because of the multiplicity of the population and the activity associated with its patterning, what the general idea applies to is not fully definable in advance. Its application poses the question: What else? What else might have this character? What other emergence might demand coverage by it, while at the same time making it vary? In other words, the general idea as a collective singular is an attunement aid to the perception of change, and its uptake into further processing in thought and language. It is a kind of indexical placeholder for intuition to take over and move that processing into practice, become perception. In this use of the general idea, it is not merely abstract. It is a lever for the su-

the point that this kind of "random" leap is always background-conditioned by already circulating abstract general ideas of spurious common notion variety).

perabstract. The merely abstract general idea does not pose a problem, but rather obscures the problematic nature of its application. It misses singularity by presuming to know already what it covers, and to hold the key to its own application in its self-reflective, formal definition. This makes it insensible to singularity and the variational "what else?" it harbors in potential. Superabstraction levers the singular-collective up to the singular-universal. The collective singular remains useful and necessary for its powers of indexation.

The path from the singular to the singular-universal can be traveled in the reverse direction: back from the singular-universal of intuition to the singularities involved in situations of encounter, as articulable in common notions. The general in this usage is a kind of gearshift mechanism between the first and third kinds of adequate ideas. The passage of thought through to the third and back down to the first, in simultaneous mounting and descent, allows reflective thought to sandwich itself in between them in a way that serves their purposes, without arrogating all thought to itself, as happens all too often in philosophy as in common sense. It gives reflective thought, and the abstract generality it trucks in, a foothold in the process of thinking-feeling, in spite of its inability to explicitly express either singularity or the singular-universal. It makes it a go-between for them, of value precisely to the degree that it enables transits across itself rather than staking a proprietary claim to own and hold thought. It can help bump the singular up to the singular-universal, and index the singular-universal to the singularity of a given encounter. When this movement occurs in both directions at once, it motors intuition, guaranteeing that its universality does not lift off from singularity just to sideline itself in the merely abstract. It also dynamizes reflective thinking, making it approach its own limit of the direct perception of relationality. By linking reflective thought to the transit to the singular-universal, it gives the person, as operator of reflective thought, an avenue of connection to the superabstract, in spite of its remaining as such beyond its ken, and as out of reach as the sun.

As an aside, habit, as was said earlier, is already a general in this way, in that it registers the character of a bundling of proto-active tendencies into one exercise, and indexes their coming-together toward an issue in a way that enacts their reaccess, reactivates them, without holding them to mere repetition. A habit that cannot bend to cover new details or extend itself to new situations is dysfunctional. It must embrace variation, within bounds of repetition (or embrace repetition stretching its bounds through variation).[20] This is why habit qualifies as thought in the act, and not mere reflex (reaction). It gearshifts in its own self-contracting way between multiple singulars and their actively counting for one. Habit's coverage of variation in its repetitions give it a hint of universality. General ideas, put into practice, can share in this functioning of habit as *reactivating*—rather than reactive or reflective.

The countervailing usage of general ideas knows nothing of the superabstract. It is merely abstract. Where general ideas have been critiqued in this essay, merely abstract ideas have been the target. General ideas of this kind lack character. They are of purely logical confection. They are made of an assemblage of discretely conceived properties linked together, not by abduction, but by deduction or induction. They are empty categorical boxes in which things logically fit (or not) when the general idea is applied to them. The application operates a triage. It determines which things belong together by logical right, and which are out. It lays down a boundary, in what amounts to a policing operation.

The policing applies even to what is taken in. A preeminent term thought to exemplify the category most fully is consecrated. This consecrated term is erected as a model or standard against which others in the fold are measured. A hierarchy of greater or lesser perfection in relation to this standard is instituted, ascribing differential value to the things it subsumes. The triage tests the conformity of a thing to the model, and if it passes the test, assigns it a place in the hierarchy. The test is the concrete presence in a thing of the abstract logical properties with which the category is constructed. For example, if "man" is defined as a rational animal that walks on two legs and has an opposing thumb, to be fully a man one must embody all three properties as predicates. A two-legged creature with an opposing thumb that is socially judged not to be rational will fall into a sub-category of "man," such as "woman" or "child." The

---

20 Ravaisson includes change in the very definition of habit and defines it as a general in much the same sense as Peirce. Félix Ravaisson, *Of Habit*, trans. Clare Carlisle and Mark Sinclair (London: Continuum, 2008), 25.

set of two-legged creatures with an opposing thumb who make the grade will form a community of ranked particulars instantiating the general model. Add to that white skin, European descendance, speaking a major language, and embodying human capital (the predicate list could go on), and we know exactly where we are. We are back at the Man-Standard.

Merely abstract categories are weaponized general ideas. Alone, separated from the singular-collective and singular-universal, they have very little use other than as weapons, their veneer of logical neutrality little more than a cover for a power operation. Logically, they are of questionable use. If relied on exclusively, they are counterproductive. They relegate to the status of the negligible any aspect of a thing's character that does not correspond to the limited set of defining properties enshrined in the modeling. They do not allow for emergent properties, taking character to be essential in the traditional sense and unchanging. They reduce potential to the exercise of the standardized functions built into the static structure of the defining properties.

The application of abstract general ideas is the quintessential act of overcoding. They fold down their own structure over the complex of the relational field, filtering it into their own simplicity, exhorting things to conform to them. They forget that their own genesis depends on the origination of generality in habit, and that habit is emergent from the relational field. They fold back down following the reverse trajectory of their own genealogy. They also forget that singular tendencies and proto-wills, striving to express themselves, enter into the constitution of habit, and that habit-formation in no way exhausts their variety and multiplicity. They recognize none of this. They only recognize themselves as done deals, and endeavor to impose that limiting recognition onto things. They form a circle of self-reflection. They apply themselves in order to recognize themselves in things, to shore up their own authority for another round. They make out as if thought is already a foregone conclusion, and all that remains is to apply it, formulaically. This is in fact a reflective stunting of thought. It is a clouding of thought by the supposed transparency of logic under the thrall of the general-particular.

That supposed transparency is political through and through. The general idea's shrink-wrapping of logic into a circle of self-reflection makes it a motor of the rational cognitive subject, whose capacity for self-reflection is its defining characteristic and highest achievement. This is the supposedly sovereign subject assumed by the Man-Standard. The normative triage functions of the abstract general idea serve the Man-Standard. This is not logical transparency. It is whiteness.

General ideas in the singular-collective sense serve thought by recognizing that the relational field has a certain opacity. The opacity is not due so much to elements being hidden as it is to the micrological status of the aboriginal stirrings of the relational field, which makes them imperceptible from higher-level perspectives, until they ascend the levels to reach a threshold of appearance, compounding with others as they go, perhaps composing emergent properties en route. Until they reach that threshold of perceptibility, they have the status that Michel Foucault attributed to "statements": not visible, but unhidden.[21] General ideas, in this intuition-oriented usage, index that unseen complexity. They are avenues of approach to it on which intuition can travel. They hinge into the complexity of singular encounters expressed by common notions, enabling an exploratory groping of their texture, and the texture of their connections, actual and potential, to other situations of encounter. This inserts thought into the realm of import—potential manners of mattering—in its widest extent, as it approaches the plane of immanence. General ideas in this usage can be tools in a pedagogy of the singular, and in the transit to the singular-universal. They can work in this way if they are used as antennas for probing the world's constituent differences, sensitive to its process of differing (its tendency toward the emergence of new distinctions).

Abstract general ideas misplace import. Rather than foster attention to what Spinoza calls the "internal constitution" of things, they obsess over their own internal structure, and thus only assert their own importance. Rather than adventuring into the opacity of what is not visible yet unhidden, they content themselves with the transparency of their own reflection, bouncing off of the world as from the surface of an artificially stilled pool, back into their own closed orbit of foregone definition. Rather than helping to reactivate, they encourage reaction—against

---

21 Michel Foucault, *The Archaeology of Knowledge*, trans. A. M. Sheridan Smith (London: Routledge, 1989), 122.

anything that troubles the placid surface of their reflective pool. They separate thinking from what it can do.

The Sting of the Normal

Speaking of "usage" and likening ideas to "tools," while a serviceable shorthand, implies that they are merely utensils in the abstract hands of persons, separate from their being. But if, as argued earlier, an idea is a little person, then abstract general ideas, like all persons, are a dynamic pattern more than they are a thing. Like all dynamisms plying the relational field, they harbor a conatus: a tendential striving with its own characteristic arc, tantamount to a will. Resituated in the goings-on in the field, restored to their own distributed, relational causality and collective genealogy, they can be seen as self-conducting. It is less that persons falling under the human category take hold of ideas as utensils and merely use them as a means toward their ends, than that abstract general ideas take hold of persons. They recruit them into the dynamic of their own striving and reproduction.

This of course can only be done once a body has been ascribed human status—precisely through the application of the category as Man-Standard. It is that application which corroborates the body's possession of the property of being "rational," the sine qua non of the "human" as generally-abstractly defined. To be ascribed that status is to be socially possessed by that definition. It is to be overcoded by it, becoming it by application. The overcoding defines the recognized nature of the body. In other words, it is ascribed not just to the surface of the body, but to its internal constitution (its life). The ascription is performative, achieving what it says, in the very saying of it. The human body and its personal life can then deploy the abstract general idea as a part of its own dynamic. But this does not undo the fact that it is deployed by it. The body is used by the tool as much as the tool is used by it.

The relation of the hominized body and the life of its person to the abstract general idea is the same as the wasp to the orchid. The body is socially adjoined to the dynamism of the idea to serve as its reproduction organ, while the idea reciprocates by serving a function for it. That function, fundamentally, is imposing and policing normativity: conformity to the standard. That conformity ensures that the idea will find further application, disseminating its powers of clouding thought. In short, the general idea gives the hominized body the sting of the normal, with all the policing and boundary-keeping, but also forms of security that come with it. The dynamic of the countervailing usage of the idea, as an adjutant to intuition, is *supernormal*: surpassing the structure of the given and its foregone definitions, toward relational emergence, with no pre-assigned end, unsubsumed to identity.[22]

The Politics of Logic

However nitpicking they may seem, it is essential to attend to the logical distinctions developed above, between the singular, collective singular, singular-universal, general-particular; between the micrological, abstract, and superabstract. Because logic is anything but neutral and transparent. It is political through and through.

The practice of political critique and its popular practice of debunking does not take this seriously enough. It proposes a reform of the *contents* of thought, in the pursuit of which it typically brandishes exactly the same categorical logic of the general-particular, complete with the triaging, boundary policing, and hierarchy of value that goes with it. It rarely if ever pauses to problematize *modes* of thought, least of all its own.

The merely abstract general has a predicate-subject structure: its application is a predication, or attribution, of defining properties to a body.[23] It is at the heart of normative structures such as the Man-Standard. Plas-

---

22 Supernormal: Massumi, *What Animals Teach Us about Politics*; Massumi, "The Supernormal Animal," in *Couplets*, 119–32.

23 For critiques of the Aristotelian predicate-subject logic, see Whitehead, *Process and Reality*, 30, 49, 51, 54, 56, 5, 137–38, 145, 157; Whitehead, *Adventures of Ideas*, 276; and Simondon, *Individuation*, 476–77. Peirce argues that the abstract general ideas that take this form are "hypostatic abstractions" that are by nature vague. Peirce, *Essential Peirce*, 2:394–95. Tarde says that propositions expressed in terms of them are actually "disguised conclusions": "judgment[s] congealed in a notion." Gabriel Tarde, "La croyance et le désir" (1880), in *Essais et mélanges sociologiques* (Paris: A. Maloine, 1895), 189, http://classiques.uqac.ca/classiques /tarde_gabriel/essais_melanges_sociologiques/essais_melanges.html. Deleuze

ticized, it also flows through the deviations of post-normativity (as we will presently see as the analysis of reaction and fascisizing tendencies advances). And it also grounds what has come to be known as cancel culture, a particularly fierce counter-weaponization of the normative logic of the abstract idea and its triage function. If this traditional logic is not sufficiently problematized in relation to gender, it stunts queer thought and politics, bouncing its will to affirm singularity and differencing back into the identity structure of category-based thinking. The categories may fracture and multiply as they chase after the effervescence of the emergence of variation in the relational field, but if they do not throw off the yoke of the general-particular in favor of a logic of the singular, collective singular, and singular-universal, all they achieve in the end is a multiplication of identity categories. This merely pads the field of the general with more particulars. As a result, the problem of the hierarchy of values inherent in the operations of the general is not resolved (again, witness the conflict between a certain feminism and the trans movement).

Identity is nothing other than conformity to an overcode. It is by nature normative. It captures differencing, subordinating it to a logic of resemblance. No amount of counter-mobilizing its generalizing powers in the name of resistance can countermand that.

This is not even entering into the discussion of the fact that identity, as underwritten by the abstract general idea, is the signature invention of European modernity, a historical correlate to and derivative of its nineteenth-century invention of the nation-state (itself a correlate to and culmination of the centuries-long project of colonization so central to the maturation of capitalism).

The takeaway: *It is indispensable for politics also to be staged on the battleground of logic. The struggle over modes of thought is a political struggle.*[24]

---

speaks of the "artificial blockage" native to the logic of resemblance of what is called here the abstract general idea. Deleuze, *Difference and Repetition*, 12, 32.

24 The formal logic that lends itself most powerfully to process-oriented thinking is category theory (in a completely different sense of "category" than the abstract general idea critiqued here). Category theory is a logic of transformational relation that is topological through and through, and is unsubordinated to the logic of the general and the particular; see Rocco Gangle, *Diagrammatic Immanence: Category Theory and Philosophy* (Edinburgh: Edinburgh University Press, 2016).

The status of the general idea as a person, and the role of the abstract general idea in the constitution of human persons, gives a new twist to the dictum "The personal is the political."

The Logico-Politics of Resemblance

A general idea, in its functioning as a sign, points to a *property* (or, in logical terms, a predicate). The property is either sensuous (for example, the color of a body's skin), or abstract (like a life being conducted rationally). In the case of the abstract property, its presence or absence is concluded by induction based on the observation of the sensuous properties of bodies. The presence of the property in a body is the hallmark of its membership in the category of which the property is a defining quality. The qualification has a double meaning. On the one hand, it puts the seal of approval on the body's logical belonging to the category, certifying it as fit to type. On the other hand, it has a political force, in that it admits the body into the system of prerogatives vouchsafed by the category.

The fundamental operation here is *resemblance*. To be fit to type, the body must display a likeness to the properties composing the general idea. This is an abstract likeness, a merely logical construct, given that the idea as such is nonsensuous and itself has no observable properties. The body and the idea belong to different dimensions, the particular and the general. The particular and the general logically require each other, since neither would have meaning alone. But in actuality, they are mutually exclusive, since they are logically what they are in opposition to each other. They occupy incompatible registers, one sensuous and the other nonsensuous. The only observable aspects of ideas as such are the linguistic point-signs that index their logical construction.

The abstract likeness of the body to the general idea marks it as possessing a nature in common with others subsumed under the same category. The meaning of common here is completely different to its meaning in Spinoza's term, common notion, where it connoted a shared participation in a singular encounter. Here, it refers to a logical participation in an abstract nature that is by definition general. The application of the category to the body performs its participation in that abstract nature. It ascribes the associated qualities to the body, adjoining its particularity to the dynamic life of the general idea.

The body becomes its idea's fleshly vessel. This process is closer to incarnation—the imbuing of a transcendent nature in a particular instantiation—than it is to embodiment in the process-philosophical sense of the immanently emergent taking-form of the dynamic patterning of a continuing locus of influence in the world (a bodying; a mattering; a spinning top of being in becoming).

The fundamental operation with respect to the general idea is resemblance—or, more precisely, the logico-political *production* of resemblance. But the production of resemblance is at the same time the production of a certain notion of difference. Difference by this notion is defined as falling outside a given common nature and into another category of sameness. This subordinates difference to resemblance. Difference is allowed no positive determination. This, perversely, *makes the same the principle of difference*. This holds even within a category whose elements share a common nature. Each thing falling within the purview of that category exhibits the same defining properties, but to varying degrees. That means that there are greater or lesser degrees of belonging to the category, in descending a ladder of deviation from the preeminent term, with each step corresponding to a lower value. In both cases, difference is defined negatively, as a defect of resemblance. It falls under the reign of the same: the abstract general idea revolves around the *same difference*. The practice of triage and exclusion inherent to this notion of difference is the logico-political invention of negation. *Negation* is a political practice of excluding and devaluing, complementary to the logical production of resemblance.[25]

The abstract general idea produces resemblance to make the world safe for negation. The adequate idea, by contrast, affirms difference. What it indexes, in its functioning as a sign, is a relational field, not a property. Relation is also nonsensuous, but not in a merely abstract way. Quite the contrary, it is nonsensuous in a way that in process

---

25 Difference subordinated to the production of resemblance: Deleuze, *Difference and Repetition*, 28–69.

philosophy is the very definition of the concrete.[26] Relation, and the events that play it out, is the basic element of the world's real constitution. Although nonsensual in the sense that no particular set of sensory inputs corresponds to a relation as such, relation is the fundamental unit of the real according to William James's radical empiricism.[27] The adequate idea points to that constitution. Its principle is not likeness, but differing. Integral to that constitution is the potential for new emergences: the potential for change. This is what is logically brushed aside by the abstract general idea's practice of negation.

The general idea only positively retains concordances based on resemblance. The adequate idea, at its highest level as concrete singular-universal, also embraces the *discordances* in the world. Conative tendencies, as self-conducting proto-wills willing nothing so much as their own furtherance, are as apt to collide and compete as to conjoin for a joint result that fuses their multiplicity into a collaborative counting for one. Tendencies are *positively* different from each other. They have valence. They are willfully distinct in their wanting, in their defining impetus, even if an accord may arise that makes them bundleable. The abstract general idea revolves around the same difference. The adequate idea, for its part, revolves around the *"differingly different."*[28] Its thinking of potential has to be sensitive to the positive differences concretely (effectively) composing the world. It has to embrace, as James said of his radical empirical version of process thinking, the disjunctions as well

---

26 "The most concrete fact capable of separate discrimination is the event" (Whitehead, *Concept of Nature*, 189), and events in Whitehead are forms of relational transition.

27 "The relations that connect experience must themselves be experienced relations, and any kind of relation experienced must be accounted as 'real' as anything else in the system." William James, *Essays in Radical Empiricism* (Lincoln: University of Nebraska Press, 1996), 42.

28 "The truth is that difference is differing [la *différence va différant*], that change is changing [le *changement va changeant*], and that they accordingly take themselves for their own end; change and difference attest to their necessity and absolute character." Gabriel Tarde, "Monadologie et sociologie" (1893), in *Essais et mélanges sociologiques* (Paris: A. Maloine, 1895), 267, http://classiques.uqac.ca /classiques/tarde_gabriel/essais_melanges_sociologiques/essais_melanges.html (my translation).

as the conjunctions. It has to logically *affirm* them—posit them as real and operational—before doing anything else thoughtful with respect to them. It must radically affirm before judging critically. The meaning of "critical" changes accordingly, to connote the diagnosis of tendencies, in an evaluation of their manner of mixity in different situations.

The abstract general idea does the inverse: it judges critically, in the usual sense of the term, in order to affirm narrowly (only what remains after its normative triage by the production of resemblance). Then it disciplines, in order to curtail potential, to limit it to the confines of its applied definition. The concrete general idea, on the other hand, fosters potential, in all its complexity, not least of all because its own powers of comprehension grows apace with it (and it too has a conatus).

Signs Behaving Badly

The activity of adequate general ideas further an intuitive plumbing of the relational field, connecting common notions (apprehensions of the real potential incumbent in singular situations of encounter) with the singular-universal (the field of relation as it encompasses a potential infinity of situations of shifting demeanor, asymptotically approaching the plane of immanence of thinking-feeling) through the gearshift mechanism of the general idea (as indexing a collective singular). This augments the relational powers of thought, in immersive participation in the world, and in effective connection with the complexity of its texturing. This augmentation expands outward from the impinging effect of an other on the body, to embrace the other from the point of view of its readiness for relation and the potential consequences of its entrance into a variety of situations of relation. In other words, it works toward an intuitive embrace of the powers of others to be and to do. Their powers are synonymous with their "essences," or their real internal constitution from the point of view of their potential for activity. This is the processual direction in which the adequate idea points when it functions as a point-sign. More broadly, as a sign, an adequate idea "envelops" (Spinoza's term) the relational essence of things (remembering that all signs combine different modes, not only indexicality, and that the assertion that all thoughts are signs is fundamental to Peirce's semiotics),

The contrast with the abstract general idea, as normative category, cannot be starker. What does it point to as a point-sign? A mis-taking of causality, through a missing of relation. What does it envelop as a sign? A misplacing of import. It cultivates the up-cycling of proto-errors of the objective illusion native to all perception and thinking-feeling into full-fledged errors of discursive thinking, whose practice then becomes perception, to normatively disciplining and negating effect.

The cycling into error occurs through a hypertrophy of the faculty of *association*. Composing with the powers of others to affect and be affected is necessary to maximize one's own capacities for thinking-feeling in the act, and toward action. This is part of the conatus, or the striving of a body to remain in existence and to augment its powers of existence: the impetus animating its every pulse of process, and giving proto-acts and the explicitly expressed actions issuing from them an overall quality of willfulness. When the path toward an adequate comprehension of the complex conditioning of situations and the relational causality it catalyzes is short-circuited by reaction, this impetus is thrown back to and absorbed in the realm of abstract general ideas, where it enters into the conventions of discursive thinking. No longer having an effective outlet, it circles there as around a black hole of thought.

Trump's enemy-ascribing emissions of point-signs are empowered by its detouring of thinking-feeling, which bounces it from the point-sign into the regime of the signifying sign. This is the regime of endless referral from one sign to the next on their own level, untethered from indexicality's pragmatic insertion of thinking-feeling back into the texture of the relational field. The signifying sign purports to guide indexicality by means of its function of reference. Yet the foundational doctrine of Saussurian linguistics is the arbitrariness of the relation of the signifying sign to its referent. Poststructuralism was obsessed with this, worrying over the ineluctable tendency of the regime of signification to veer off into an anxious, endless, aimless relay from sign to sign, in restless orbit around the black hole of the arbitrariness of its relation to its referents. Indexicality goes on the skids. The point-sign's ability to empower thinking-feeling to dive into the relational potential of the full body and the plane of immanence deviates into an aquaplaning over it, on a slick of signification.

For the point-sign, practice becomes perception. For the signifying sign, *reference becomes referral*. Searching for a purchase in the world when its own dynamic obviates that impetus, the signifying sign throws thought into a whirl of frenzied paralysis. The exemplary expression of this is the conspiracy thinking that has always been a feature of the reactionary right, but has made a particularly dramatic splash since Trump's 2016 run for the presidency.

Association is the modus operandi of this circling of thought in the merry-go-round ineptitude of the abstract general idea, which separates thinking-feeling from what it can do and delivers it to a sphere of belief inflated by association. For this leg of the journey, the conceptual resources developed by Gabriel Tarde, the too-long-forgotten founder of micro-sociology, are essential.

The Understory: The Belief from Below

Association doubles and replaces reaction, but not, as the adequate idea does, with a thinking-feeling of relational complexity. Quite to the contrary. It doubles and replaces it with a reductive play of resemblances that makes a farce of belief.

Belief in a certain sense is constitutive at the micrological level. This is the level of proto-activity, or "minimal activity" in Tarde's conception: the just stirrings of experience below the threshold of conscious awareness (in what I call "bare activity").[29] Belief is a synthetic activity, constituting a lowest-level general. It is the primitive force that bundles multiplicities of elements into a count-for-one. This conjunctive synthesis is predicated on the connective synthesis of the multiplicities falling into effective proximity with each other, converging toward a unified effect. It registers in an overall felt quality enveloping the multiplicity of the elements.

---

29 Minimal activity: Didier Debaise, "Une métaphysique des possessions: Puissances et sociétés chez G. Tarde," *Revue de métaphysique et de morale* 4 (2008): 454. Bare activity: Massumi, *Semblance and Event*, 1–3, 10–11, 22, 23, 27; Massumi, *Ontopower*, 44–48, 74–75; and Massumi, *Power at the End of the Economy*, 20–21.

Each of the elements participates in the production of that quality, but retains a certain under-autonomy: a capacity to vary in its own right, and thus to make its own difference. In other words, it carries its own tendencies as a dividual. Take any object as an example. From the point of view of reflective thought, it is composed of different properties such as color or hardness. Each of these may change with the circumstances over time, while the object continues to count individually as the one it was. What these "properties" are in fact are nexuses of relational activity (for example, for color, between light and surface and eye and brain) expressing a certain pattern exhibiting a sub-character. For the object to appear as an object, the characters must fuse into the overall quality, to give the object its own character on its own level, with its own capacities to make a difference. For this to happen, the relational activities of each of the component regions of activity must interlink, and the effects of their activity overlap.

The coverage of an overlap was Peirce's baseline definition of generality, with generality being the hallmark of the person by his definition. The object—or any other outcome of a micrological conjunctive synthesis—is a "little person." Tarde calls it a tiny "soul."[30] Its appearing as one is the product of a fusion binding its constituents to each other to joint effect. In Tarde's definition, *belief is this binding force*.[31]

It is a primordial force of habit. What the binding does is deliver the object as if fully formed to subsequent perceptions. Its counting for one, with its now familiar character, then goes without saying. It becomes a habit of perception, presupposed by perception's every exercise. Belief is not a cognitive attitude toward an object of perception. At its most basic, it is the *passive synthesis of the object of perception*. "Passive," once again, is not the opposite of active. It is mode of activity that is not within the conscious purview of a subject: one that self-conducts, or contracts itself, or is self-agencying, like an underlying habit. Belief, as the binding force of this passive conjunctive synthesis, creates the basic building blocks of conscious perceptual awareness and delivers them to it.

---

30   Tarde, "Monadologie et sociologie," 246; Debaise, "Une métaphysique des possessions," 455. See also Deleuze, *Difference and Repetition*, 74.

31   Debaise, "Une métaphysique des possessions," 455.

The under-autonomous genesis of the "raw" (but actually already elaborated) material of perception is not "primitively felt as effort" by the thinking-feeling person who receives it. It must "begin by *surprising* the being from which it emanates and who doesn't at first know that it emanates from it."[32] This is for the very good reason that it only emanates from an apparent interior retroactively, after the being to whose internal constitution it will contribute to takes possession of it, or appropriates itself to "me." At the threshold of this recursive owning by a greater person, the perceptual belief strikes as *other*: my non-I. It begins as a surprise: a *micro-shock*.[33] At the instant of its strike, the greater person affected by it *recognizes* itself in it. This leads Tarde to the odd formulation that the habit, as product of belief at the level of minimal activity, is "an *unconscious imitation of oneself by oneself.*"[34] By this he means that the recursive-owning-in-the-instant of the product of passive synthesis refigures the other as a self-possession, producing the strange phenomenon of a *self-recognition of the new* (for each appearance of the object is a veritable event repeating the synthesis anew, with variation). This recognition is the passing of the passive synthesis from unconscious micro-activity to conscious awareness; from infra-activity to the possibility of reflective thought and what the person will experience as voluntary action—neglecting the constitutive under-autonomy of the tiny dividual souls that primes and conditions that thought and action, inflecting and modulating it in advance of its owning, and giving it an indelibly machinic cast.[35]

32   Gabriel Tarde, *Maine de Biran et l'évolutionnisme* (Paris: Les empêcheurs de penser en rond, 2000), 110.

33   Massumi, *Semblance and Event*, 67, and *Parables*, xxxvi–xxxvii. Micro-shock is integral to Peirce's definition of the index: "Anything which startles us is an indication." Peirce, *Essential Peirce*, 2:8.

34   Gabriel Tarde, *Les lois de l'imitation*, 2nd ed. (Paris: Kimé, 1993), 98 (emphasis added), http://classiques.uqac.ca/classiques/tarde_gabriel/lois_imitation/lois _imitation.html.

35   William E. Connolly is among the few who integrate into the theory of fascism the conceptual lineaments of this micrological level of the constitution of experience, emphasizing its bodily nature and recognizing the "strivings" (conatus) of the multiplicity of "micro-agents" constituent to every action and perception expressing at the macro level. William E. Connolly, "Bodily Stresses, Cultural Drives, Fascist Contagions," *Theory and Event* 25, no. 3 (2022): 693.

This throws the traditional theory of charismatic leadership and the affective politics of fascism quite a loop by *placing imitation in the genesis of persons*. Imitation is not the mediated relation of a fully formed subject seeing its own reflection in the preeminent greater person with which it identifies. It is not a "projection" of the self. It begins with the ingression of the other, and is part of what *constitutes the person* in the immediacy of thinking-feeling. It is only as a derivative of this that imitation in the projective-reflective sense can operate (when it does—which is only under the thrall of Oedipal mechanisms, which Deleuze and Guattari argue are not invariant or foundational, but are produced historically).[36] What the person experiences as its *identity* is the habitual performance of that self-imitation, in a repeated refinding of oneself overcoded by the social categories that are applied to it. The application, or ascription, extends the self-recognition into a recognition by others of its own level. Identity is at the crossroads of the relational causality of synthetic emergence cresting in the belief that conditions perception and the quasi-causality of ascription swooping down on it and sweeping it up into social circuits. It is only after identity is manufactured at this causal crossroads that *identification* between identified persons can intervene.

The owning of the striking other as a recognition of oneself marks the crossing of the threshold of minimal infra-activity into macro awareness. The infra-activity remains as a trace, still agitating as a genealogical force from within the production of the self, remnant and reactivatable. Its story goes untold. There is complex genesis that is lost to the narratives of discursive thought that produce and fortify conscious belief: an *understory*.

The understory is a story of difference and synthesis. The overstory— the discursive narrations whose constituent elements the understory delivers—is a story of the Same. It starts with self-imitation bootstrapping the person into its own recognition, producing its felt resemblance to itself, as if that were really the beginning of the story. As Tarde observes, what becomes "explicit and verbal" on this level through the proposition, with its abstract general logic, is "always, at bottom, a more or less disguised conclusion." The terms obtaining on that level— "attribute" (property) or "subject"—are not primitives. They are "judg-

36   Deleuze and Guattari, *Anti-Oedipus*, 51–56.

ments congealed into a notion."[37] They are perceptual judgments, occurring in the immediacy of thinking-feeling, of a kind that present themselves as foregone conclusions rather than abductive openings. As a contemporary scholar of conspiracy thinking puts it, "The conclusion comes to the evidence, arriving at the instant of interpretation."[38] That is to say, arriving at the moment of ascription.

Conspiracy Brewing

We can already see the basic elements of conspiracy thinking in their incipiency:

—a proposition for investigation that is actually disguised conclusion whose veracity is immediately felt, such that it goes without saying

—the recognition that there is a "hidden" narrative, or understory, that has left traces that nag at the disguised conclusion, so that even though the conclusion goes without saying it has to be painstakingly reconstituted by reflective thought and endlessly re-narrated, to prevent it from being re-engulfed by the dark "swamp" (in MAGA-speak) of imperceptibility that it purportedly illuminated, but whose import it actually missed

—a focusing of cogitation on recognition and resemblance as the fundamental operations of thought; perpetual vigilance in the face of an onslaught of micro-shocks that might present a challenge to the narrative in some eyes, but in the trained (habit-formed) eyes of the cognoscenti immediately feed them with renewed belief

—the diversion of this perpetual vigilance into a tireless will-to-truth, with the exhortation heard so often today in right-wing circles to "do your research"

---

37 Tarde, "La croyance et le désir," 189.
38 Mark Fenster, *Conspiracy Theories: Secrecy and Power in American Culture*, 2nd ed. (Minneapolis: University of Minnesota Press, 2008), 102.

—the ultimate inability of this will-to-truth to conclude, for the simple reason that the conclusion already came first in the immediacy of perceptual judgment

—the sense that the "swamp" of infra-activity is populated not by little synthetic souls with emergent character forming the building blocks of experience, but with vague, menacing presences

This is where projection comes in: when *the structure of greater persons is back-projected onto the infra-personal field of emergence* priming and conditioning them. This injects the general abstract ideas of the social categories those persons embody into the generative activity of the relational field, with the effect of overwriting the relational causality of the differingly-different in congress with the linear causality of the person-to-person in collusion—that same old, timeworn story.

Desire

Belief was defined earlier as the binding force creating fusional compounds that count for one, and which by virtue of that are capable of passing the threshold to perceptibility. Desire, as also defined by Tarde, is the *force of transition*. Whitehead calls it "appetition."[39] Desire is what moves experience from one belief, or consolidated synthetic perception, to the next. It is Tarde's version of conatus. It constitutes a proto-willing operating below the threshold of conscious awareness. This definition of desire is largely consonant with Deleuze and Guattari's, in that it is by nature unconscious and is self-conducting: in other words, it is machinic.

The binding of elements into a belief, or what Tarde calls their "linkage" (*liaison*), is as real as the elements themselves. It is the reality of their relation: their mode of fusing together as one. Tarde argues that desire can seize on the link as such, and *move the link across transitions*. This "conserves the belief-relation" as it moves from one perception to another.[40] The linked elements of the object of these perceptions may

39 Whitehead, *Process and Reality*, 32.
40 Tarde, "La croyance et le désir," 189n84.

differ, even as the belief-relation stays the same. This enables belief to spread across experience and the social field. As it spreads, the vehiculated belief-relation may bump up or down in scale, moving into larger or smaller compounding of ingredient elements as the appetite moving it focuses itself more broadly or narrowly. Desire now spreads tentacles in two co-occurring dimensions: a serial dimension along which one belief transitions into another related belief that replaces it along a historic route (a diachronic exclusive disjunction); and the accumulative dimension of compounds added to the world's store of available or potential objects of belief (a synchronic inclusive disjunctive). Desire produces the conditions for distributive contagions and differential compoundings of belief: what in common parlance are called "mindsets" or "ideologies." But these are not in the mind of an individual. They are in the movements of desire in the world.

The patterning of desire's inclusive and exclusive disjunctions is what Deleuze and Guattari call the "socius." When bodies are ascribed categories, based on the distributive contagions and differential compoundings of belief, the structure of the categories is injected into the socius through overcoding. The socius includes the resistances to, leakages out of, and escape runs from this overcoding. These "deterritorializations" move to the limit of the socius, where it rejoins the "body without organs" or the "plane of immanence." This, too, is desire. This is desire par excellence, doing what only it can do: move beyond the beliefs it moves across.

Generalization upon Generalization, Belief upon Belief

As discussed earlier, the abstract general idea knows only how to index properties, giving priority to the sensuous properties of bodies, which it uses as identifying marks of their membership in a given category. This predisposes it to a mis-taking of causality, taking the most proximate body to an impingement (basically, any form of encounter with an other) for the sufficient linear cause of the impingement's effect. A socially salient property—say skin color—assumes the role of identifying marker of first and last resort. This maker operates as a perceptual rule of thumb point-signing the attribution of causality: a blame marker. This is what was analyzed above in terms of a tendency to objective illusion as a tendency native to perception. The ascription of blame uses one property as a proxy for all of the body's properties, sensuous and nonsensuous. The feeling associated with the salient property is thought-felt in all immediacy to be an indicator of the overall character of the person. This performs a generalization about the body, flush with perceptual judgment.

The generalization spreads from there, because the salient property also serves as a token of the person's belonging to its attributed social category. It doubles as a collective identifying marker. This makes it a hinge between the character of the individual body and the group character: an abstract general bridge across which attributions of character can move in both directions, from the individual to the group, and from the group to the individual. This produces a Doppler effect, blurring generalized individual properties and generalized group properties together like the spokes of a wheel in perpetual motion. This dynamic two-way fade between individual and group character judgments is what vehiculates racism and other prejudices. Both levels of generalization involved (the summing up of individual properties under a general marker and the assimilation of individual character to group character) are examples of the conservation of a belief-relation (the binding of a spread of elements into a synthesis). The movement from one of these generalizations to another and back again is an instance of the transitional movement that is a power of desire. Since the perceptual judgments involved occur flush with experience in the everyday, the foregone conclusions they usher pass for common sense.

Vague Presences

The "commonsense" spread of the belief-relation goes even further. If a character quality that is a defining property of the social category, even one other than the salient property serving as the general marker, is also shared by a different category, then the second category is set up to Doppler into the first. The perceptual judgment effecting the belief-relation blurs across categories. The members of both categories blur together, creating a feeling of equivalency between them. Resemblance bleeds across into a collective-body blur, as bodies bleed into categories, and categories bleed into each other. Not only does an oscillation set in between the individual and collective levels, but categories brush into and across each other. The blurring of bodies results in the composition of a master category into and out of which bodies oscillate: *enemy*.

Why enemy? Because there is a generic sense of the efficacy of a proto-will in every impingement of an other—and even just seeing another body, or an image of a body, marked as individually-collectively blameworthy can be experienced as an impingement. This feeling of efficacy is a mis-taken registering of conatus (of the tendential arcing, or understory striving, of any and every element that enters into a situation of encounter). It is the operation of objective illusion, under the thrall of the abstract general idea dominant in common sense, to make the efficacy appear to be localized in the proximate causal body. That body is then taken to be the willful author of the painful effect. It is taken, in classic reactive fashion, to be a malevolent *agent*, whose *fault* the pain is. Bergson noted this natural tendency to attribute agency even to objects, and the way in which it imbues everyday life with a sense of animacy.[41] When we stub our toe, we curse the table leg, as if it purposely threw itself into our toe's path, and we viscerally wish destruction upon all tables. We are all animists, not from some exotic adherence, but as a

---

41 The sense of animacy is less than the identification of the table with a complete person in the way we conventionally think of ourselves being self-enclosed subjects, but more than the perception of the table as an inanimate object. This in-between of the inanimate and (the myth of) complete personhood is the realm of the infra-. The sense is of the "willfulness" of the conatus of all existential tendencies, as the animacy of the world. Bergson, commenting on the example of a child hitting its head on a table: "The truth is that between the identification of the table with a person and the perception of the table as an inanimate object, there lies an intermediate representation which is neither that of a thing nor of a person; it is the image of the act accomplished by the table in striking, or, better still, the image of the act of striking, bringing with it like luggage borne on its back the table which stands behind. The act of striking is an element of personality, but not yet a complete personality." Henri Bergson, *The Two Sources of Religion and Morality*, trans. R. Ashley Audra, Cloudsley Brereton, and W. Horsefall Carter (London: Macmillan, 1935), 104.

natural product of common sense and the abstract general logic of its objective illusions.

This feeling of animacy is carried across the blurring of the individual and the collective. The effects of impingements that produce pain or discomfort, or that are simply jarring, smear across the levels and lodge in the master category. At that most general level, the effects amplify into macro-fears of indistinct origin. They coagulate into a state of nervous vigilance, in taut anticipation of pain from unidentified sources. The body becomes habitually postured for pain, in a generalized manner. The anticipation becomes the encompassing atmosphere of terror discussed in part 1, accompanied by a pervading sense of loss of control.[42]

In the atmosphere of fear and terror, Whitehead explains, the effect on the body is so foregrounded that the attention to sensuous properties, which play so central a role in the genesis of reaction, gets inhibited. All that is left is a vivid nonsensuous "apprehension of the relevance of the immediate past to the present, and the present to the future": causal efficacy reduced to the bare-bones schema of the dependency of the present on the past and of the future on the present. The "inhibition of familiar sense-data provokes the terrifying sense of vague presences, effective for good or evil over our fate."[43] The general atmosphere teems with these vague presences, rolling into and over each other to form a churning sea of threat. The felt ubiquity of the vague presences suffuses this atmosphere of fear and terror with a note of uncanniness.[44]

This is reaction reaching its full amplitude, in a generalized atmosphere of *reactivity* embodied in individual bodies as a self-defensive posture of generalized suspicion. Reaction swings between two poles. In one direction, the oscillation turns toward the sensuous, in a search

42 Atmosphere: Massumi, "Dim, Massive, and Important," in *Couplets*, 188–207. Atmosphere of fear: Massumi, *Ontopower*, 181, 199–200.

43 A. N. Whitehead, *Symbolism: Its Meaning and Effect* (New York: Fordham University Press, 1985), 42–43.

44 On the atmosphere of uncanniness in conspiracy thinking, see Susan Lepselter, "The License: Poetics, Power, and the Uncanny," in *E.T. Culture*, ed. Debbora Battaglia (Durham, NC: Duke University Press, 2005); and Susan Lepselter, *The Resonance of Unseen Things: Poetics, Power, Captivity, and UFOs in the American Uncanny* (Ann Arbor: University of Michigan Press, 2016), 20–45.

for telltale markers to aid in steeling oneself against a threat. The other direction is toward the nonsensuous pole of generalized apprehension teeming with vague presences.

The feeling of the malevolence of those presences becomes unshakably ingrained. It becomes habitual: a general attitude, or mode of existence. In other words, it becomes a lived article of faith. Belief swings between the same poles, following the movement of reaction. Belief is hypertrophied in the swing toward general dread, where it is swollen with abstract vague presences that are general to the utmost in their uncertainty, but are no less immediately thought-felt for that. What is certain, for belief, is the uncertainty of their ever-presence. At the other pole, belief flips into the inverse pole of over-confidence in its ascription of individual bodies, based on the detection of category markers, as paradigmatic causes of the sorrow. Hypertrophied belief can translate the uncanny atmosphere into paranoia. Over-confident belief primes the body for the acting out of aggression. How not to attack the enemy and annihilate it when it is flushed out into the open? Thinking-feeling swings quasi-chaotically between performatively specifying the individual enemy with confidence (ascription) and the uncertainty of a generalized dread of the atmospherically unspecified enemy.

Association Unbound

A system of multiple inscription results from the generalization of generalization moving between individual and group levels. Bodies on the individual level are ascribed general characters through their identification with a given category on the basis of certain markers, like skin color. If one property indicative of a certain category is felt to adhere in an individual body, then all the other properties associated with it in logical solidarity in the category's construction come flooding in, making an omelet of the body's character. Conversely, individual characteristics of the body come to be perceived as characteristics of the population intended by the general category. This double inscription and two-way transfer of properties between levels sets the pendulum in motion toward the third form of simultaneous inscription. The margin of indistinction between the general and the particular creates an atmosphere of uncertainty, where the categories' boundaries shiver. When this affects multiple categories, there forms a margin of indistinction among them, so that they may leak into one another, with increasing abandon over time. This inscription takes the form of an overall atmosphere of distrust. Desire's take-up of the form of belief—interlinkage; fusional relation—plays into this. Thought is redirected from the relational causality addressed by the adequate idea into the search for *connections*, in the everyday sense of the term, based on resemblances playing across the levels.

The will-to-truth then becomes the bloodhounding of resemblances as they flitter across the social field, in objective apparent movement: the ceaseless activity of conspiracies brewing and hatching. The apparent movement is a product of the oscillation between the detection of individual cases and their apparently clarifying ascription, and the continuity of the atmosphere in its threatening ubiquity. The detection and ascription phase is expressed in that exhortation, so often heard in QAnon circles, to "do your research." But the research rebounds, because any one detection is just the tip of the iceberg, so the "research" must continue endlessly, in a kind of ground-level mapping of the atmosphere— which only thickens as more clues are "found." "Conspiracy theory has no interpretive limits." Following the clues, there is always be more to learn, but "nothing more to *know*," given the foregoneness of the conclusions.[45] The conclusion comes in the act of ascription, in the form of a direct perceptual judgment flush with thinking-feeling.

The production of *narratives* is the only way to introduce any glimmer of a feeling of control. The machinery of reaction enters the byways of discursive thinking. This carries the perceptual dynamic of resemblance-slippage into language, where it is exacerbated by the signifier's tendency to lift out of the orbit of reference into infinite referral from sign to sign. An "excessively integrative interpretive practice that goes beyond the norms of inference" takes over.[46] Association is unbound. The sought-after connections are more and more easily made by association. The process takes on the machinic aspect of a "hyperac-

45 Fenster, *Conspiracy Theories*, 94.
46 Fenster, *Conspiracy Theories*, 95.

tive semiosis."[47] It self-effects, leading the thinker, who is had, rather than following the thinker having thoughts: thought-the-thinker, delivered to reaction. This machining of association is abetted by social media, where collectively elaborated narratives circulate freely, fusing and dividing with amoebic abandon. The variation is assisted by the fortuitous juxtapositions between posts and between text and images. Reactive desire is always at the ready to supply a connection by transiting a belief-relation and superimposing it on the causal gap between juxtapositions of words and images. Association becomes contagious. Belief hypertrophies. The mode of existence of vigilance and self-defensiveness becomes a reflex to believe. The will-to-truth becomes one and the same as a will-to-believe.

Susan Lepselter captures it well:

> And so resemblance becomes not historical but poetic [dealing with figurations; associational]. A structure is felt to lurk below the surface of such resemblances, and, just barely visible, its glimmer becomes uncanny. The parallelism between signs becomes yet another sign [the belief-relation transited by desire], pointing to a referent too large and pervasive to fully grasp [atmosphere; causal disconnect developing from objective illusion]. . . .
>
> The events or images themselves are meaningless. It is when they are suddenly revealed as related to each other that their connection grows charged with the intimation of hidden significance, a "secret meaning" . . . something more, a hidden meaning [giving rise to a will-to-truth]. . . .
>
> What is the referent? Where do you locate the real? Perhaps the places to look are in the trails of resemblance these stories produce [produced resemblance]—the repetition with variation that becomes a sign in itself [thought as sign]. . . .
>
> Dense with partly recognizable tropes, half-articulated memories, and condensed, intensified, and rearranged particles of other social . . . elements [impinging others; the they] from various imaginings blend, intensifying all their effects.

---

47 Fenster, *Conspiracy Theories*, 94–95.

They foreground the naturalized patterns that normally go without saying [beliefs in the Tardean sense, become habits of thought and perception playing on conventional categories]. It is in one sense an endless bricolage, but rather than building something concrete from the "odds and ends" at hand, here the product is never finished; you select the part for the rush of its echo to another part [resonance]. Here each found or revealed sign leads on to other resemblances, other openings. . . . Here those connections are based on resemblance and repetition. This effect entails mimesis [transmitted self-imitation], but the resemblance is partial and fluid. It is felt.

What resonated was the very *fact of* power—its vastness, its hidden sources, and its just visible clues.

A sense of vague but pressing danger . . .[48]

Like stubbing your toe in the dark at every turn on the animate furniture of vague presences of indistinctly menacing power.

Now, not only just seeing a marked body, but just thinking about it—and not only thinking about, but half-thinking about it, or under-thinking it—is enough to trigger a reaction.

Note on the Imagination

The logic of association animating the will-to-believe bumps imagination up to a higher level. Imagination was defined by Spinoza as the tendency of habitual perception to isolate the effect on the body of an impinging other from the relational causality of the situational nexus. The effect can be isolated because it conjunctively counts for one. This, it was argued, occurs as a function of belief.

When belief takes the compounds it produces at this level and re-combines them with other ready-mades, it climbs a level, achieving another degree of separation from the ground-level operations of perception. At this altitude, it can assume a creative aspect. It can produce new objects of thinking-feeling that have never been, and can never

---

48 Cited passages in order presented, all by Lepselter: "License," 33, 43, 44, 46; *Resonance of Unseen Things*, 3; "License," 140, 147.

be, encountered perceptually. These are conjured out of the thin air at that altitude by the binding of ready-made compounds into larger compounds, like wings attaching themselves to horses. A Pegasus is something new, but it is not beyond the principle of resemblance. It is a bricolage of resemblances: wings like a bird, mane and hooves like a horse. The bricolage can take up things that have already been cobbled together not in perception but already in fiction: eyes like bugs + skin like reptile [alien] + craft that can hover like a helicopter and spin like a top [UFO] + something a lot like child kidnapping = alien abduction.

The mobilization of the imagination at this altitude frees the imagination from the more pedestrian pursuit of combining already known objects and situations. It bolsters conspiracy theorizing with invented objects, fantastically combined to create situations no one could have had a glimmer of before their production by belief. Conspiracy thinking

5.1 A nonalien product of the imagination: Blue raccoon on banana. Tourist trinket from Nogales, Mexico, 1980s. Photo by the author.

can now take off from the pedestrian workaday life and fly. And fly it does. Invented objects and situations, and the narratives that endlessly "explain" them, proliferate.

This is the power of the false finding a way to express itself *through* the will-to-truth that purports to be its opposite. The power of the false, thus hijacked by the will-to-truth, makes itself felt in the strange phenomenon that once this process takes off, naturally occurring objects and their pedestrian situations seem *less convincing* than the invented objects and their fantastic situations (a dynamic also seen in the fakeness of Trump's exaggerated person perceived as a token of authenticity discussed in the "Are You an Act" and "The Reign of the Self-Knock-Off" sections of part 1). The power of the false carries belief to a higher power, where the fantastic has more credibility than the ordinary. Why would anyone believe that pedestrian convergences between political power blocs together with the realpolitik of personal ambition against the background of the boring grinding on of the bureaucratic state and the flutter of the media is enough to explain the rise of Hillary Clinton to her perennial status throughout the early 2000s of presumed next-president—when instead you can believe that a cabal of Democrat demons are eating children instead of pizza and wearing their murdered faces like Halloween masks? That narrative is ever so much more affectively engaging—not to mention more in keeping with, and intensifying of, the atmosphere of fear.

Belief Trumps Intent

From the outside, all of this looks a lot like stupidity, or at best gullibility. But it has nothing to do with a lack of intellectuality or intelligence. In fact, it is a hyper-intellectuality—only in the register of the abstract general ideas, replete with the mis-takes of objective illusion amplified into a rollicking system of full-fledged discursive error, raised to the power of invention. Import is misplaced, and the sense of causal efficacy spins its wheels in the mud of the social swamp, failing to find effective purchase for lack of comprehension of the relational field and the tendencies composing it. An example of the misplacing of causality is the astonishing fact that even after the pattern of police killings that the Black Lives Matter movement was responding to, the significant up-turn in anti-Black racist violence in reaction to the movement, and the well-documented evidence of the continued intergenerational effects of slavery, nearly 84 percent of Trump voters feel that racism against *white people*, not anti-Black racism, is the real problem.[49]

It is not a question of lack. Stupidity has a positivity. It has a posi-tive, systemic functioning. Epistemologically, it is the science of the untrained. It arises as a "natural" outgrowth of the inadequacy of thinking-feeling's propensity for objective illusion, fermented into a perception of objective apparent movements of generalization upon generalization. Even as taken up into discourse, it remains an issue of perception: the connections that are taken up into the narratives are im-mediately thought-felt into being. The established narratives then be-come abductively embedded in the perceptions as, once again, practice becomes perception, and perception primes for action.

The abductions (the Peircean kind, not the alien kind) and priming for action make this reactionary dynamic easily channelable toward political ends. Trump's performative ascriptions through his social media dis-semination of point-signs assigns enemy status, for example, to African Americans on the basis of the identifying marker of skin color. Falling on alt-right soil, the ascription channels the priming for action toward racist aggression. High-altitude imaginings, like Pizzagate, are fodder in their own way for other enemy ascriptions, in this case partisan enemies.

It is irrelevant whether or not racism is Trump's direct intent, or whether he personally believes in Pizzagate or that he won the 2020 elec-tion. He most likely does not believe such things in the normal sense of coherent adherence. Nor is it likely that fostering racism is his direct intent. His only steady goals appear to be his own self-aggrandizement and enrichment. However, the machinery of reaction and its associa-tive connection-hounding constitutes what is tantamount to a collective intent that is not reducible to any one individual or group, but follows its own tendency, acting out its own conatus on the level of collective

49   Maureen Breslin, "84% of Trump Voters Are Worried about Discrimination against Whites: Poll," Hill, August 10, 2021, https://thehill.com/homenews/news/575899-84-percent-of-trump-voters-are-worried-about-discrimination-against-whites-poll.

personhood. It can be tweaked and tweeted into serving personal goals, but these are only one element in the machining, and not the most far-reaching. They are not its effectively organizing principle. The regime of reaction is its own agency, with its own operative logic and mode of desire as its organizing principles.[50] Even Trump is subordinate to that regime, because it is only through it that he can wield power. That power is the performative power of Schmittian decision, which as discussed in part I is immediately enactive of a collective individuation and personing.

Modes of Capture

Sometimes an individual intent expresses itself to yoke this automaticity of reactionary desire and capture it for the stated aims of a particular ideology. Ideology is not a cause but a capture of the reactionary dynamic. An example is given in comments made by Andrew Anglin, the editor of the neo-Nazi newsletter the *Daily Stormer*, as reported in the *Washington Post*:

> In a leaked style guide, Anglin once explained that his goal is recruiting new neo-Nazis, and that blaming Jews was the best way to do that. "As Hitler said, people will become confused and disheartened if they feel there are multiple enemies," Anglin wrote in the guide. "As such, all enemies should be combined into one enemy, which is the Jews."[51]

The endless referral from enemy to enemy can be stopped, and confidence in action restored and captured for central ideological direction, by condensing the enemy into one specified master category. This folds the unspecified enemy back down into a single super-category, with a single master narrative associated with it. This reduction creates the illusion that attacks directed at members of that category can be causally effective in generally rooting out the full panoply of threats society is felt

50 Operative logic: Massumi, *Ontopower*, viii–ix, 5.
51 Joseph Menn, "Surging Twitter Antisemitism Unites Fringe, Encourages Violence, Officials Say," *Washington Post*, December 3, 2022, https://www.washingtonpost .com/technology/2022/12/03/twitter-antisemitism-violence-jan-6.

to face. Jews are the ready-made category for this, having been the object of conspiracy theories for centuries, with an abundant nineteenth- and twentieth-century literature that, however contrived and archaic, never seems to get dated (judging by the perennial popularity of *The Protocols of the Elders of Zion*, which is still to this day a core text for the racist right).

It is almost a foregone conclusion that when a reactionary dynamic sets in, it will turn at a certain point in this anti-Semitic direction. This turning point in the reactionary wave licensed by Donald Trump's presidency and post-presidency came in the fall of 2022. A sharp uprise in anti-Semitic aggressions gave rise to widespread concerns in the press about the "naturalization" of anti-Semitism. Elon Musk's deregulation of hate speech on his newly acquired Twitter platform quickly became an enabler, as did Trump himself when he hosted Ye, fresh from an outburst of anti-Semitic remarks, and Nick Fuentes, neo-Nazi social media influencer, for dinner at Mar-a-Lago.[52]

Again, whether Trump is personally anti-Semitic is almost beside the point. It misidentifies the problem. To say that he is personally anti-Semitic is to treat him in the traditional mold of a person, possessing the coherence of an interiorized character with ideological adherences. Trump's character, however, is externalized, requiring the associated milieu of the communicational media to complete its patterning. It is machinic, and post-ideological. As earlier argued, he is in himself (which is to say, in his social media supplementarity) a collective person. His narcissism is boundless. His ego expands to the far corners of the social field. And his "self-interest" is directly political. The politicality of his person is invested in the non-optional fact of his future second presidency. Trump's inability to move beyond the conspiracy theory of his "stolen" 2020 reelection is easily explained: not being president (or at least a presidential candidate) is tantamount to not being himself. It would separate his politicality from his person. It would throw him back to the status of a normal private person, subject like everyone else to the day-to-day laws of the land—as opposed to the exceptionality of his

52   Eugene Scott and Josh Dawsey, "Trump Criticized for Dining with Far-Right Activist Nick Fuentes and Rapper Ye," *Washington Post*, November 25, 2022, https://www.washingtonpost.com/politics/2022/11/25/trump-fuentes-ye.

preeminent role of lightning rod for collective Schmittian decision, sustained by the post-normative approach of rule-by-tweet that he brought to the presidency. Not conceding the 2020 loss is a way of clinging to his status as a collective person of directly political valence.

The collective dynamic of reaction creates a much more dangerous situation than one person being in power who is anti-Semitic, anti-Black racist, anti-LGBTQ, misogynist, trans-phobic, xenophobic, or all of the above, no matter how much power they have. It helps unleash nothing less than a *historic* current with the potential to mature into the world-changing "storm" so dear to the narratives of the extreme right. The onset of the storm would be the transition to a full-fledged fascism.

How far it has gone is indicated by the percentage of people believing conspiracy theories. As of the fall of 2020, 80 percent of Republicans believed at least one QAnon conspiracy.[53] Regardless of how many times it was debunked, the QAnon phenomenon only strengthened over the following two years leading into the 2022 midterm elections, as Trump more and more explicitly egged it on. The number of believers jumped 33 percent, growing to comprise fully one-fifth of the US population. But, then, 40 percent of Americans profess a belief in UFOs. A majority of Republicans and 43 percent of all Americans believe in the existence of demons. An earlier study found that 70 percent of Americans buy into at least one conspiracy theory.[54] Clearly, the sway of scientific evi-

53   Mike Rothschild, *The Storm Is upon Us: How QAnon Became a Movement, Cult, and Conspiracy Theory of Everything* (New York: Melville House, 2021), 132.

54   QAnon believers: Mark Lamoureux and David Gilbert, "QAnon Is Dead. Long Live QAnon," *Vice*, November 15, 2022, https://www.vice.com/en/article /wxnkzq/qanon-q-drop-midterms; and Joseph Gedeon, "'Trump Is a Messianic Figure in the QAnon Calls': Trump's Embrace of the Conspiracy Theory Is Growing Stronger," *Politico*, September 23, 2022, https://www.politico.com /news/magazine/2022/09/23/trump-is-a-messianic-figure-in-the-qanon-calls -00058671. UFOs: Lydia Saad, "Do Americans Believe in UFOs?," Gallup News, August 20, 2002, https://news.gallup.com/poll/350096/americans-believe-ufos .aspx. Demons: Gabriel Miranda, "2 in 5 Americans Believe Ghosts Are Real and 1 in 5 Say They've Seen One, Survey Says," *USA Today*, October 28, 2021, https:// www.usatoday.com/story/news/nation/2021/10/28/do-ghosts-exist-41-percent -americans-say-yes/8580577002. At least one theory: Russell Muirhead and Nancy L. Rosenblum, *A Lot of People Are Saying: The New Conspiracism and the Assault on Democracy* (Princeton, NJ: Princeton University Press, 2019), 48.

dence and rationalist argumentation is sorely challenged, making it all the more evident that an affective dynamic is at work that is not simply the lack of a logic on the part of "deficient" individuals, but is its own, and very compelling, systemic logic.

That affective dynamic is the regime of reaction. The logic is the reign of the abstract general idea sliding away from the referent into the endless referral of association unbound, driven by an unquenchable will-to-truth whose ability to bring itself to a conclusion is stymied by the same principle that fuels it: the play of resemblance that turns away from the complexity of the relational field in favor of the objective apparent movement of conspiracy, brewing and hatching.

Accidents of Persons Predisposed

"Amanda is a twenty-three-year-old racist skinhead on death row for murder and robbery in a southern state." So begins Kathleen Blee's ethnographic report of the "conversion event" that catalyzed this young woman's veer from the everyday racism she grew up with in her family into the virulent racist activism that earned her the electric chair.[55] It all hinged on an accident. A car accident, to be precise. She found herself in the hospital after waking up from a coma. There is no indication that she remembered anything about the accident. But she did remember waking up to a feeling of utter "loss of control," like an afterimage of the feeling of the accident as it happened, prolonging its pathic intensity into what was now her everyday condition. Except now, the feeling was attached not to the fortuitousness of the accident, but to intentional actions—the care she was being given: "IVs in my arms, tubes in my nose," her body being "probed and invaded." By African American nurses. "Don't touch me, don't get near me, leave me alone," she wailed. The outburst translated on the spot into a "new racial commitment." Where once she was a garden-variety racist, sensitive to the generalized threat environment's pervasive racializations but tolerant enough to welcome her cousin's African American husband into the family, now she could not abide the presence of a

55 Blee, *Inside Organized Racism*, 39–40.

Black person. "That was it." She never spoke to her cousin again, and upon leaving the hospital joined a racist gang. The enemy had been specified.

It? What "it" was that? "It" was the strange intruder: the accident, the IV, the tubing, the probing and invasions, all "blurred together with the African American nurses surrounding her bedside." The marker of their skin color bled across this linkage, becoming the marker of the pathic prolonged: the unbearable effect of her accidental car encounter seeping into every corner of her being to become the atmosphere of her life. The cause of the accident was unknown to her. The "proximate body" of whoever or whatever might be held responsible for it in linear causal reckoning was lost to memory, blanked out by the coma. The belief-relation which, in the genesis of objective illusion, binds the proximate body to the simplified causal nexus, and figures it as the linear agent of effect, transfers to the African American nurses. Their skin color becomes the point-sign indexing loss of control.

This is a vivid example of the way in which the individual genealogy of reactionary error, discussed in the mirror example, interfaces with the collective processes of generalization analyzed in the preceding sections. The movement of generalization producing a two-way movement of prejudicial perceptual judgment between the individual and group levels has always already taken place. It has already set in place an atmosphere of fear teeming with vague presences agitated by point-signs and jostling for ascription. Racist ideologies are always already in the air. All of this primes a body for racism. A body is predisposed. All that is necessary for the racism to turn virulent is an accident of persons bleeding the pathic, and the reaction coming out of it, into everyday life. And it is an accident of persons, not just a car accident: Blee emphasizes how incidents of this kind "give you an identity." Or, in the vocabulary of this book, makes you the character you become. Becoming "racially committed" is a personing. The individual "identity" coincides with the body taking on and being overcoded by the "official personality of the group."[56] Personing, individual and collective, in the same stroke.

This example is not unique. Blee follows this report with the story of a hit-and-run victim who did not see the author of her misfortune. "Of

56 Blee, *Inside Organized Racism*, 34, 35.

course," Judy says, echoing Amanda, "that was it." "After I got hit by a car . . . I started getting into politics."[57] By which she means neo-Nazi politics. She just knew the perpetrator was African American, based on no evidence whatsoever. "Of course." Foregone conclusion.

In Blee's studies, this kind of conversion story, associated with bodily trauma, is not exceptional. On the contrary, it is quite common among racist women. "*Their stated reasons appeared to have little to do with ideology.*"[58] Ideology is a part of the priming. It is in the air. But its active role comes after. It works to systematize the conversion and reinforce it by creating a community around it. It is not, in itself, the determinant. Blee does find that men center their conversion narratives on bodily trauma much less frequently. Typically, they do cast it as an ideological conversion.[59] But did it really happen in so cerebral way? Or is it because racist men's Man-Standard modeling makes it difficult for them to admit vulnerability? It is not more likely that strange intruderly impingements are lurking en masse in the hollows of their pasts, and that their present lives are thoroughly haunted by vague presences all around? That the traces of those encounters are still active, if forgotten, always already priming for reaction, prodding its maturation into systematic racism?

The impingements do not have to be traumatic. Through the generalization processes described above, the effects of small impingements accumulate, on the back of point-signs keeping the traces alive. They weave into and out of each other, linking and agglomerating, inflating a joint effect. It is not necessary that there be a dramatic incident. It is not even necessary for the racist-in-the-making to have experienced a harmful or anxiety-producing encounter with members of the category marked blameworthy in order for reactionary hatred to develop. As is so often the case in white supremacist circles, Blee's study subjects' anti-Black racism is coupled with extreme anti-Semitism, even though "none had a bad encounter with Jews."[60] It is likely that many had never even met a Jew.

---

57 Blee, *Inside Organized Racism*, 39.
58 Blee, *Inside Organized Racism*, 27.
59 Blee, *Inside Organized Racism*, 52.
60 Blee, *Inside Organized Racism*, 78.

The analysis here is of reaction in terms of objective illusionary error and the abstract general idea's lending itself to generalization-upon-generalization, implanting predispositions in primed lives that accumulate into atmospheres sustaining them. This is a process-oriented alternative to ideological theories of the genesis of fascism, and reactionary politics in general. The process-oriented account replaces the "ideo-" with the "corporeo-": for a corporeology of fascism. But it also explains how the body is involved when it isn't (explicitly, that is, in an actually impinging encounter with another body). It provides an alternative account of the *general causality* of racism (one that is not "structural" in the way theories of ideology are, but rather processual and machinic, conveyed by the general circulation of point-signs).

In all the causal variations, saliently traumatic or not, the pathic is the pivot.

The Pathic Is the Pivot

Edmund Burke, the standard-bearing man known as the first counter-revolutionary and inventor of modern reactionary politics, is also the first to index these processes to the pathic. His theory of the sublime, published at the curtain call of modern aesthetics in 1764, set in place the pathic underpinnings for his post–French Revolution reaction. His "sublime" is nothing other than an exalted experience of the pathic (introduced above in the section "Passion and Reaction").

The sublime, he writes, is a state of "astonishment" of the "soul," in which "all its motions are suspended." The life of the body (Burke says "mind") "is so entirely filled with its object, that it cannot entertain any other, nor by consequence reason on that object which employs it. Hence arises the great power of the sublime, that, far from being produced by them, it anticipates our reasonings, and hurries us on by an irresistible force."[61]

---

61 Edmund Burke, *"On Taste," "On the Sublime and Beautiful," "Reflections on the French Revolution," "Letter to a Noble Lord,"* Harvard Classics, ed. Charles W. Eliot (New York: P. F. Collier and Son, 1909), 51. Corey Robin discusses Burke's theory of the

In the Spinozist terms favored here, it would be more accurate to say that this moment in the life of the body is so radically filled with the effect of the encounter with the object that all its motions are suspended for an immeasurable caesura, for an offbeat of experience. Thinking has retracted into absolute proximity with feeling, so that no reasoning is possible. The life of the body is "evacuated." "Everything that gave us a sense of internal being and vitality ceases to exist."[62] But this evacuation of vitality and disappearance of thought into feeling is at the very same time an "anticipation"—a preacceleration—of the feeling finding its footing again in thinking, vitally impelled by an "irresistible force."[63] The irresistible force is the abductions that, no sooner than thought is suspended, rush in to fill the void with a forward-flowing current. The suspension of thought coincides with a perceptual judgment through which the abductions make ingress. This zero-degree thinking is flush with the feeling that is operated by no added act of a subject, which has been evacuated, and is recessive in relation to reasoning, or reflective thought. It jump-starts abduction, segueing the experience into bare activity and hurrying through it into a reactivation of the body's life tendencies, in a resuscitation of its capacities, including, by and by—most likely following a thinking-feeling knitting of the brows, an action-readying tensing of the muscles, and preparatory throwing back of the head—its capacity for reflective thought.

The analysis of this suspending-reactivating pathic interval is introduced by Burke in relation to overwhelming feelings before the majesty of nature. But on the same page, under the section heading "Terror," he goes on to state that "no passion so effectually robs the mind of all its powers of acting and reasoning as *fear*." It then stands to reason (or to thinking-feeling) that no passion so effectively hurries life, by an irresistible force, back into a poising for reactionary action than fear. Add to this Burke's observation that since fear is an "apprehension of pain

---

sublime in relation to his reactionary politics citing these same passages, which are taken up here following from his comments. Robin, *Reactionary Mind*, 65–67.

62 Robin, *Reactionary Mind*, 65–67.

63 Guattari defines the pathic as "an absorbant subjectivity given immediately in all its complexity," prior to the subject-object relation (making ingress as a "strange intruder"). Guattari, *Chaosmosis*, 25–26.

or death, it operates in a manner that resembles actual pain,"[64] and we have the beginnings not only of an account of how pathic reaction generalizes beyond actual encounters with impinging bodies, but also of its role in disseminating the feeling of existential threat that Schmitt sees as a necessary condition of the ascription by decision of the friend/enemy distinction. We are on our way to generalized racism, amid the gathering clouds of potential civil war.

Here we see the birth throes of modern reactionary movements, not in ideology, but in passion and reaction. Not in ideology, but in a zone of indistinction between the political and the aesthetic—more fit for a critique of pure feeling than ideology critique.

When the body is re-poised for thinking-feeling re-unfolding, "we may spill out of ourselves" in a "sort of swelling."[65] In reaction to re-action, on the way back into action, we feel our capacities expand to fill the world—from self-evacuation to the powers that the body attributes to itself being "heightened, aggrandized, magnified." This self-aggrandizing is characteristic of the bluster-form of man popularly called toxic masculinity that is so MAGA. But its pathic conditions of emergence do not disappear. There settles into the body a tendency toward a "wild" "oscillation" between the two extremes of fearful suspension in the void of pathic effect, and a magnified feeling of one's capacities.[66] Only the swing of the pendulum to the pathic is likely to be relegated to the status of an unfelt feeling by the Man-Standard training into the body habits of masculine pride. The explanation for the bluster will then skip right to the reflective reasoning that is in processual point of fact its secondary derivative (after the rush of perceptual judgment, abduction, and bare activation). The derivative is back-projected and mis-taken for the cause of the reactionary capacitation, bracketing the passional interval, covered over by a veneer of retrospective rationality. It is because the man is so strongly committed to his racist ideology that he is capable of taking action heroically following its (to him) rational precepts. When this rationalization is not possible, for whatever reason, the oscillation expresses itself in the ornamental masculinity

64 Burke, *On the Sublime and Beautiful*, 51.
65 Spill out: Robin, *Reactionary Mind*, 66. Swelling: Burke, *On the Sublime and Beautiful*, 46.
66 Robin, *Reactionary Mind*, 66.

described in the section of part 1 of that title. In this case, the man acts out both a radical vulnerability and exaggerated hateful bluster, in a back-and-forth rhythm or a strange cartoonish amalgam.

The general causality of racism must factor in not only passion and reaction and their singular playing out under the auspices of objective illusion, but also gender differentiation as a function of the Man-Standard. All of this is part of the affective regime that is reaction.

Faciality

It was argued in part 1 that Trump swung the pendulum of the social dynamics surrounding the preeminent figure of the head of state back toward the face in a new way, after a period in which they tended to be invested in the proprioceptive pulsation between the whole body and its dismemberment, or between disappearance and reappearance. In *A Thousand Plateaus*, Deleuze and Guattari develop a machinic theory of "faciality" that is a necessary complement to alternative theories of fascism beyond the humanistic frame of "charismatic leadership," with its conventional notions of personhood.

"Faces," they write, "are not basically individual; they define zones of frequency or probability, delimit a field that neutralizes in advance any expressions or connections unamenable to the appropriate significations."[67] Faces are apparatuses of capture into normative modes of expression in conformity with "appropriate" significations. Note that Deleuze and Guattari say "significations" and not "sign productions." The face is an assemblage that specifically pertains to the signifying regime of signs. "Appropriate" here means in consonance with the Man-Standard as model for ascriptions in the mode of the abstract general idea, or in resonance with the signifying slippages of its generalizations-upon-generalization fluttering from belief to belief, heaping one upon the other, in endless referral in the service of the production of resemblance.

Animals, by Man-Standard reckoning, have no face. They have muzzles. The muzzle is a part of the head, which is a body part.[68] The human

---

67 Deleuze and Guattari, *Thousand Plateaus*, 168.
68 Deleuze and Guattari, *Thousand Plateaus*, 170.

face surfaces from the head and the body. It is a surface of meaning for human expression serving as an interface between bodies. Its element is the face-to-face: the realm of human communication glossing (over) the body, screening it, overcoding it with discourse. This surface of signification is transpierced by the eyes, those soulful holes providing a "window" into the supposed interiority of the person, in whose depths others are taught to seek their common humanity. The face is the differentiator between the animal and the human. The "huMan," to spell it out in Man-Standard terms. Man-Standard, Standard Man: this is whiteness. The face of "common" humanity, the supposed universality of the human, is the white-Man face. It is not the face of a white man, "it is White Man himself, with his broad white cheeks and the black hole of his eyes": whiteness in person.[69] Whiteness as a mode of general personhood arrogating to itself the status of a universal. This is whiteness as an assemblage, girded by a general abstract structure. The structure includes deviations from its preeminent term in a graded hierarchy of differential valuations, breaking off at the animal (but then reintegrating it, as ex-included otherness, into its subordinate terms as the marker of their devaluation, as in tropes of the bestiality of the Black body or of women's affinity to "instinct" over reason). The face of the reactionary leader, preeminent figuration of the preeminent term, is a central operator of whiteness.

The human expressiveness of the face screens the body into the psychological face-to-face. It glancingly deflects the body into the referrals of the signifier, while at the same time imploding human meaning into the affective black hole of the eyes. The eyes may well be the window onto the "soul," so that in eye contact souls connect. But there is an uneasiness in the fellow feeling. The soul bottoms out in pathic depths where no Man goes, and this too is felt. Human communication posits human commonality, but also makes its limits felt. It is a commonplace that no one knows what ultimately lurks in the pathic recesses of another's soul. Affect, at bottom, is unshareable.

There is something doubly inhuman about the face. There is the inhumanity of the depths: the pathic suspension of personhood at the heart

69   Deleuze and Guattari, *Thousand Plateaus*, 176.

of every affective pulse of life. But there is also a surface inhumanity: the self-conducting of the signifying regime, as it generalizes, and generalizes upon generalization, running away with itself in the "fourth person" impossibility of assigning a specifiable utterer to the meaning effects that propagate through its proliferating byways. The machinism of the face—faciality—is the articulation of these two dimensions of inhumanity, which are entirely bound up with and bracket its humanness, or Standard huManity, as figured in capitalist modernity, while at the same time drawing its limits.

Yes, we can project into another's feelings through the porthole of the eyes (up to a point). We can feel, or feel we feel, the commonality that the category of the human teaches us is what defines "us." We can empathize and, based on that, identify. But this psychologizing of our existence and our relations to the other is squeezed between the limits. On the one hand, it bottoms out in an unshakable sense that the other, in its pathic unshareable singularity, is an alien, strangely intruding, even menacing in its difference. All but an enemy (ascription will change the "all but" to "all"). On the other hand, it spreads itself so thin across the surface of discursive referral that it detaches from any specifiable utterer and outruns its depth. The psychological is sandwiched between the recesses of its own communicative impossibility and the excess of its communicational out-streaming. It operates only by their leave, within the limits they set for it, and for as long as they abide it. Both of these dimensions can only be described as machinic. This means that they are amenable only to a processual description that claims priority over the psychological realm whose operative limits they define.

In psychological mode, the "white wall" is the surface of the face, the broad plane of the cheeks, chin, and forehead that double verbal expression with facial gesture, forming a transition zone between the Man-Standardized individual body and language. Processually, it is something entirely different. It is the surface of the full body. The white wall was glossed earlier (in part 3) as the passage to infinity of the potential of the full body, receding to the absolute limit of the plane of immanence. It is not a solid wall of the kind that would nick your knuckle. It is diaphanous, vaporous, a cloudy wrapping of potential in the total field of its own unlimitedness.[70] Of indeterminate dimensionality, it presents as a wall from the distant perspective of the levels of organization whose limit it constitutes, in its unbounded way. It is the matter of pure potential. When the referential function of signifying signs slips into referral, it skirts across the white wall. The hyperactive movements of discourse weave a film, or apply a veneer, across which signifiers glimmer, backlit by the potential of the white wall but no longer effectively indexed to its many nested levels. It is as if a reflective abstract surface has been thrown over the diaphanousness of the white wall. Signs bounce off of the full body and skim along its surface. They no longer plug into it and transverse it through the point-sign function immanent to all signs. The potential of the full body still glimmers. The abstract surface is backlit by it, giving it its shine. The surface transposes the matter of the white wall into a slippery substance of signification, or what Deleuze and Guattari call "signifiance."[71] Signifiance endows the movement of signs with a backlit feeling of import, even as they now systematically misplace it into referral across the surface. Point-signs no longer rejoin potential. They no longer tether thinking-feeling to the total field of its potential, angling it into its infinity from a precise angle of attack. They are instead refracted. They bounce back into the endless relay of referral, skipping across its surface like pebbles on a pond and the ripples they cause. This cuts the tethering of discourse to the relational causality whose potential the white wall is, at the receding and re-arising, self-refreshing, limit of process. It sidetracks the infinity of the world's potential from pulsing into effective expression in drops of thinking-feeling, moving it into the bad infinity of the ceaseless chatter of signs following upon signs in endless lines of emission.

The white wall is riddled with black holes. In psychological mode, these are the eyes as windows on the soul. Processually, they are unconscious attractor points of passion, collecting traces of the pathic as by gravitational force. They are uncannily alluring, in spite of whispering the menace of vague presences, in their otherness and glossed-over intensity (or perhaps because of this). The residual trace activity of pathic

70 On the total field of experience, see Massumi, "Chaos in the 'Total Field' of Vision," in Parables, 157–76.

71 Deleuze and Guattari, Thousand Plateaus, 79, 112–19.

encounters swirls in the black hole. This exerts a fatal attraction to conscious reflection while remaining refractory to it. Discursive thinking is unable to angle into the potential the traces index, leaving it reeling on the horizon of the black hole. Point-signs whirl in circles around the black hole, even as they fall into it, like water in a toilet that won't stop flushing. Signs orbit around the center, activated by its attractive force but unable to reference it, in obsessive search of a lost problem. Instead of enacting a thinking-feeling of the problem, the circular relay of sign to sign is prone to lubricate narratives that likewise swirl around the surface and refuse to flush themselves, offering solutions in the mode of foregone conclusions native to conspiracy theories that never quite go away. For example, whatever body-to-body or sign encounters may have led to a nagging fear of child abuse settles into the surprisingly resilient narrative of capital city pizza parlors. In the play of resemblance motoring signifying discourse, a jump might occur to another narrative, with entirely different content, but orbiting the same black hole. Another circle then forms around the same gravitational center of attraction. Or, instead of this metaphorical substitution, an analogical jump might be made to another trace entirely. Another circle then forms around a second center. Metaphorical and analogical jumps proliferate, forming a swelling body of narratives. The narratives distribute the black holes as much as they orbit around them. The relay from one narrative to another displaces discourse from the orbit of one black hole, one pathic sinkhole, to another. The black holes *resonate* together in the substance of signifiance that conditions the signifying regime that is their discursive field.

Bathed in signifiance, solicited by narratives, pulsating with potential relays, the black holes serve a selective function. A black hole "acts as a central computer, Christ, the third eye that moves across the wall or the white screen serving as a general surface of reference" become referral.[72] What its displacement "computes" are the abstract general categories underwriting the logic of reaction. The narratives orbiting each black hole ascribe properties to bodies felt to be involved, according the exclusive in-or-out logic of the general and the particular. The triage function of the abstract general idea is carried to an extreme, as binary

72 Deleuze and Guattari, *Thousand Plateaus*, 177.

5.2 Preeminent eyes of power: Trump Digital Trading Card sold as NFT, December 2022.

judgments manically proliferate. The judgments are distributed across the narratives orbiting a black hole. The resonation between black holes creates a proto-connectivity among narratives that provides a medium for the judgments to disseminate across the field of discourse.

Superimpose the eye of Trump on the black hole as central computer, and you have understood his collective machinic character. All of the centers of attraction superimpose on his eye, as master black hole from which energy is nevertheless emitted. All MAGA narratives resonate in it, and through it, with each other. The point-signs emitted in Trump's own social media discourse index not relational potential but circles of signifiance swirling off ascriptions. Trump's power comes from this reactive dynamic, more than any direct intent. His salvific "third eye," abstract vertex of his human/more-than-human (machinic) visage, personifies the dynamic in a preeminent greater person whose miraculating powers are comparable to Christ's (or to a cartoon superhero's).

Ressentiment

Little Trumpy persons' characters are socially patterned through the narrative referrals just described, as a function of the reactions to the affective impingement of the signs they disseminate, and of the friend/enemy ascriptions the signs' performance primes for. The powers of analogy and metaphor that skip through the discourse can also jump into the physical surrounds, carrying the ascriptive mania of abstract general judgment with it. Perceptions are primed by discourse to give rise to the same reactions the signs register, and to repeat the ascriptions they explicitly or implicitly perform, most dramatically when catalyzed by accidents of persons (as described in the "Accidents of Persons Predisposed" section above). In this way, the everyday life of the little person is adjoined to the narratives. The perceptual judgments they prime for are then at the habitual ready, replete with abductive protoactivity ripe for the acting out. People begin to move in imitation—not so much of Trump as an individual person, but of the dynamic of which he has become the processual kingpin, and to which their persons have become adjoined. It is more that they *mime* the dynamic in their own personing than that they imitate an individual. This is not a person-to-person relation of identification. It is a process-to-personification relation producing emergent variations on a theme. Little persons rhyme with the greater person more than they identify with it. In any case, the dynamic becomes immanent to the constitution of a life, so that the person, in miming it, is imitating itself, simultaneously fortified by the collective will-to-believe entraining the inadequate idea, and sickened by the "interpretosis" (hyperactive semiosis) it triggers in the individual rhymer.[73] The dynamic's immanence to their lives is the tracing out of the "full body" whose nested levels condition their real potential.

73 Interpretosis: Deleuze and Guattari, *Thousand Plateaus*, 114, 117.

How, asks Benjamin, do you imitate a storm?[74] Trump trooper Alex Jones and his followers will tell you.

The traces forming the attractors that become centers of discursive orbit continue to be enveloped in the circulating signs. They continue to agitate thinking-feeling, remotely, from the depths of the black hole. They are felt, in effect. From this point of view, the circles of discursive referral amount to a displaced memory of the problem of the trace (which is by nature problematic because the shock it originates with, and the pain or at least disquiet that it can amplify into, poses the quandary of how to respond). The narratives in their entirety are a reaction-formation to the problem of the trace. They carry the memory of the trace, not as a signified content, but as their own slippery form, as refracted into the movements of referral the narratives order. This is not the sort of memory that can surface in a content. But neither is it of the kind that can be forgotten. It is the mode of memory that Spinoza is alluding to when he says, in Deleuze's formulation, that the inadequate idea is born of reaction and expresses nothing so much as "our incapacity to rid ourselves of a trace."[75]

This, according to Nietzsche, feeds ressentiment, which is the mode of reactive being in which "you do not know how to get rid of anything, you do not know how to get over anything, you do not know how to push anything back—everything hurts. People and things become obtrusive, events cut too deep, memory is a festering wound."[76] This perfectly captures the affective atmosphere of reaction. It also perfectly captures the preeminent character of Donald "Stolen Election" Trump.

Ressentiment is the affective tonality of reaction suffusing the atmosphere of fear. It can be paralyzing, when it descends into nihilism or inflates into paranoia. It can also feed hatred. When it does, the reactiv-

---

74 Massumi, *Semblance and Event*, 105–28.

75 Deleuze, *Spinoza: Practical Philosophy*, 74.

76 Friedrich Nietzsche, *Nietzsche: "The Anti-Christ," "Ecce Homo," "Twilight of the Idols," and Other Writings*, ed. Aaron Ridley, trans. Judith Norman (Cambridge: Cambridge University Press, 2005), 80–81. For a comprehensive study of ressentiment in Nietzsche's thought, see Sjoerd Van Tuinen, *The Dialectics of Ressentiment: Pedagogy of a Concept* (London: Routledge, 2024).

ity is apt to rebound in acts of lashing out against negatively ascribed "enemy" bodies. Within Nietzsche's logic of reaction, this acting-out is not a true becoming-active. A true becoming-active can occur only through the sympathetic (relational) composition of adequate ideas doubling the trace (see the "Adequate Ideas" section above). This, by contrast, is a "hardening of consciousness" around the felt-effect of reactive traces which transforms point-signs indexing them into machinic triggers for acts of aggression.[77] It is dangerously disingenuous of right-wing commentators to sneer at the connection between the ressentiment cultivated by Trump and Trumpist discourse and violent attacks against Blacks, LGBTQ people, and other ascribed enemies.

Trump's emissions of point-signs fuels an uncontrollable collective contagion of ascription, born of reaction, drenched in a rain of ressentiment, enveloped in an atmosphere of fear, punctuated by squalls of hate-filled aggression. Trump's person is not separable from this. It is nothing other than the collectivization of this reactionary character pattern. "Reactionary" is not an insult. It is a diagnosis—of a process of personification that is one with a personification of power.

Two questions:

First, what happens if, following a point-sign to a black hole of signifying discourse and reactive passion, a thinking-feeling does not refract in referral across the white wall of signification? It sinks into the black hole. Madness and delirium may ensue, as the referral swirls more and more quickly, and the trace's pathic gravitational pull increases in strength apace with the density of the resonating web of association. The specter of this *breakdown* haunts the regime of signification and personhood, and may in some cases be a factor in racist and other reactionary attacks. Given the collectivity of the signifying regime and the directly political nature of personhood, it is also disingenuous to blame reactionary acts of violence on individual "mental health," as if any mentality were independent of the warp and weft of the social field and immune from the impingements it incessantly delivers. No act is merely individual, let alone one of this resonance.

77 Deleuze, *Nietzsche and Philosophy*, 114.

Second, is there any other possible outcome? Yes: the point-sign might break through the wall of signification and begin to rejoin relational potential again. This enacts an "active forgetting" (doubling) of the trace that Nietzsche says is necessary for a reactive dynamic to re-become active.[78] The trace is no sooner indexed than it is left behind, to take its place in the landscape of relational causality, carried like flotsam in the pragmatic stream of intuitive exploration of the real constitution of the nexus of situations and the powers to think-feel-act that they prime bodies to express. This *breakthrough* is the path toward an anti-fascist life.[79] In his preface to the English edition of Deleuze and Guattari's *Anti-Oedipus*, which has been so central to this essay, Michel Foucault called the book "an introduction to the non-fascist life." The present essay was written on the premise that, given the conjuncture at which we find ourselves in the age of Trumpism, we cannot afford to be content with an introduction. Collectively, we need to actively spin it out into something closer to an epic.

To thread this back into some of other vocabulary developed in this account, the dynamic of the signifying regime is the "figurative" associated with the reactionary full body. The bodies, ascribed and ascribing through its machinations, are its "figures" (or "images"). The breakthrough back to the plane of immanence is a return to the "figural" conditioning the other two levels. The breakthrough constitutes a deterritorialization of the full body. The faciality of the preeminent figure is a territorialization of potentials for thinking-feeling-acting. "The famous personalization of power is like a territoriality that accompanies the deterritorialization of the machine, as its other side."[80] The capture or recapture of bodies and movements into the orbit of the signifying regime is a reterritorialization. Reterritorialization is typically achieved through an application onto bodies of an abstract general idea serving as a social category setting a normative standard, with the concomitant exclusions and differential valuations of degrees of inclusion, enforced by policing.

---

78 Deleuze, *Nietzsche and Philosophy*, 113–14.
79 Breakthrough: Deleuze and Guattari, *Anti-Oedipus*, 131–36.
80 Deleuze and Guattari, *Anti-Oedipus*, 258.

Fascisizing Tendencies

The Trump machine is a relay station for differing tendencies, held in oscillating tension. The oscillations are held together in a superposition of orders.

One tendency is normative and policing, tending to the extreme. The performance of point-signs through social media circulations distribute ascriptions throughout the social field. The circuits of the signifying regime form sluice gates through which point-signs flow, trickling down to the lowest-lying terrain of the social landscape. The associated ascriptions apply the normative categories of the Man-Standard, with accents of reaction and ressentiment. Misplaced causality pools around hatred of minorities and their "elite" defenders. Society cleaves into friend and enemy camps, priming it for civil war.

At the same time, the license taken and granted to others by the preeminent person gives impetus to post-normative distortions of personhood (see the "License" and "Man-Standard, Standard Man" sections of part i). The greater person claims exceptionality. Little persons adjoined to his personhood through their induction into the machine of faciality follow suit. The structural integrity of normal personhood wobbles. The rules of conventional civility are stretched to the breaking point. Venting replaces sharing of opinions, and bullying becomes ubiquitous. Swings between extreme aggressiveness, exaggerated vulnerability, and whining complaint make the figure of Standard Man tremble. Masculinism is violently reasserted, and at the same time becomes "ornamentalized." Or, as in the case of incels, masculinism marginalizes itself, producing the oxymoron of the marginal dominant figure. Coherence of character and steadiness of behavior are struck by a strange plasticity.

The normative and post-normative aspects do not mutually exclude each other. They define poles between which expressions of character oscillate, with a large region of confusing overlap in the middle, superimposed on the top of the bell curve of normality. This fluidity makes the situation ripe for recaptures. The recaptures themselves fall toward one pole of the oscillation or the other, giving a firmer foothold to the respective tendencies, in the form of a dedicated social territory with a specialized reproductive apparatus for the operations couched in it.

Recaptures of the ideological variety are doctrinal. They center on an authoritarian figure who defends the purity of the doctrine and oversees proselytizing for the doctrine's reproductive spread. The organizational form is like a centralized party apparatus or rigid bureaucratic pyramid, sometimes on the model of the military. Longer-established neo-Nazi groups, reflecting earlier waves of the reactionary movements, often fall into this category. They embody an extreme normopathy: a rigidification of the masculinist structure of the "normal" personhood associated with the Man-Standard, weaponized by an acute case of reaction and strongly dosed with ressentiment.

The centralization around an authoritarian figure produces a centripetal movement in orbit around that figure as effective power center. The tendency is to expand that orbit, taking an increasing array of territories under the sway of the ideology and the organizational forms that embody it. The ultimate attractor for it is the takeover of the democratic state and its replacement by an authoritarian one. The more successful this tendency becomes, the more *faceless* it tends to get. The equilibrium state toward which it moves, without any real possibility of reaching it given the inevitable escapes and resistances riddling the social field, is that of a totalitarian machine of state whose corporate personhood is embodied in a bureaucracy. This tendency can take nominally left-wing as well as right-wing forms, depending on which enemies are ascribed and how abstract general ideas are extracted from the endlessness of referral and fixed into an ideology. An ascription of class enemies, when taken over by reaction and systematically hijacked by a preeminent person, can lead from a revolutionary left movement to its ossification in a reactionary state, as occurred with the Soviet Union and other examples of twentieth-century "actually existing socialism" (the model for which was in fact a form of state industrial-capitalism). As the bureaucracy sets in, the preeminence of the peak person at the helm of state loses its burnish, like a once-impressive factory machine left over from the previous century. It normalizes within the stolid terms of the bureaucratic reactionary order, transitioning for example from a Lenin to a Brezhnev. This tendency toward facelessness distinguishes most authoritarian and totalitarian regimes from fascism proper, each in its own way. In China, the counterrevolutionary transition from the faciality of the Mao era coincided with the opening to capitalism, and was characterized not by a Brezhnevian entropy but by the strategic de-facing carried out through Deng Xiaoping's reformism, with its national campaigns against the Maoist cult of personality.

Fascisizing tendencies run through all reactionary state formations. They sometimes, but not always, become *"encasted"* in an authoritarian state: subordinated to the operations of the state as means to the state's ends, rather than as ends in themselves.[81]

There is a form of confluence between fascism and the state that requires a distinction to be made between authoritarian and totalitarian regimes (although the difference is hardly cut and dried). The prime example is classic Italian fascism under Mussolini, in which, as Alberto Toscano reminds us, an authoritarian control over the repressive apparatus of the state coexisted with a radically liberal capitalism prefiguring neoliberalism's deregulatory economics dynamizing a highly reactive context.[82] This accommodation between extreme state centralization and unleashing of capitalist flows suffused by reaction provides a dynamic associated milieu supplying energy for the machinations of the fascist state, helping it to stave off the faceless sclerosis of the totalitarian state. This constitutes another tendential direction in which fascism can develop, merging with the machinery of state so that its ends coincide entirely with its own. In this case, it is difficult to tell whether the state that has captured and encasted fascism, or whether fascism's encastment has captured the state. The result is what Deleuze and Guattari call a "war machine" with the state as its vector, for reasons that will become clear in the "Fascism Proper" section below.[83]

This is an option that is perhaps naturally seductive, in one emergent version or another and to varying degrees, for fascisizing tendencies in neoliberal democratic societies such as the United States under Trumpism and Brazil under Bolsonarism that are at the same time committed to neoliberalism and mired in a reactionary regime of faciality with nationalist overtones. The nationalist element creates a tension between neoliberalism and an isolationism whose protectionist instincts run

81 Deleuze and Guattari, *Thousand Plateaus*, 427.

82 Alberto Toscano, "The Nightwatchman's Bludgeon," *New Left Review*, October 29, 2022, https://newleftreview.org/sidecar/posts/the-nightwatchmans-bludgeon.

83 Deleuze and Guattari, *Thousand Plateaus*, 419.

counter to the geopolitical tenets associated with neoliberalism's rise. The isolationism pressures the war machine to turn inward, toward the self-recolonizing effort of civil war, eschewing foreign engagement and outward expansionism. The self-recolonization effort entails a war of self-purification against non-white immigrants "poisoning the blood-line,"[84] as Trump put it in terms reminiscent of his bedside-table book of Hitler's speeches,[85] as well as against the usual lineup of ascribed internal enemies, or as Trump calls them "vermin" that have to be "rooted out"[86] for the health of the country (with transgender people currently becoming a special focus, in a revenge of the Man-Standard). Through the Trump years and into the 2024 presidential campaign, the US Republican Party has fallen increasingly under the thrall of this tendency.

Tendencies never die. They lurk, and can retrigger: once a potential, always a potential. There is no linear progression. Facialized regimes can become faceless, and regimes that have become faceless can return to faciality. Attesting to this is the reconversion of the faceless regimes of twentieth-century actually existing socialism after they crumbled under their own weight and the pressures of worldwide capitalism and were forced to accommodate themselves to the rise of neoliberalism. In both Putin's Russia and Xi's China, a spectacular refacialization and repersonalization of politics occurred, leading to a new expansionist nationalist variation on the authoritarian state built on a renovation of the older authoritarian machinery. The renovation of the old machinery is supplemented by the digital surveillance tools and cyberwar weaponry of the twenty-first-century security state, which reinforce the encastment of fascizing tendencies through new technological

84   Trip Gabriel, "Trump Escalates Anti-immigrant Rhetoric with 'Poisoning the Blood' Comment," *New York Times*, October 5, 2023, https://www.nytimes.com/2023/10/05/us/politics/trump-immigration-rhetoric.html.

85   Joe Sommerlad, "Ivana Claims Trump Keeps Hitler Quotes by Bed in Resurfaced Interview," *Independent*, December 19, 2023, https://www.independent.co.uk/news/world/americas/us-politics/trump-hitler-speeches-ivana-poisoning-blood-b2466500.html.

86   Marianne LeVine, "Trump Calls Political Enemies 'Vermin,' Echoing Dictators Hitler, Mussolini," *Washington Post*, November 13, 2023, https://www.washingtonpost.com/politics/2023/11/12/trump-rally-vermin-political-opponents.

means. The accommodations between capitalism and the ex-"socialist" machinery creates distortions, such as the cronyism rampant in Russia and the lasting state-capitalism aftereffects of the strange spectacle of China's People's Liberation Army, the right arm of the Communist Party, becoming one of the world's greatest corporate conglomerates in the 1980s and 1990s (until it was suddenly stripped of its profit-making privileges in 1998).[87]

Fascisizing movements also occur in feral forms that resist both capture by and encastment in a state apparatus, and desist from capturing it.

Micro-fascisms

Feral fascistic forms resisting thoroughgoing capture in the larger apparatus of faciality of the head of state are what Deleuze and Guattari term "micro-fascisms."[88] They occur when a black hole refuses the overlay of the "central computer" of the eye of the leader. The black hole declares its autonomy, forming a center of reactionary orbit embodying all of the same dynamics of faciality and reaction, but on a smaller scale, disjunct from the macro-center. The orbiting organizes around a littler greater person who asserts a local autonomy for its own faciality, disciplinary organization of bodies, and policing.

The local militia movement that rose to prominence in the 1980s and has undergone a resurgence in the 2020s is an example of this. Militias will network together, but resist effective centralization. In its ideological expression in the United States, this tendency is often expressed in the doctrine of "county sovereignty," or the belief that the largest unit of political organization allowed by the Constitution is the county level (the Posse Comitatus, founded in the 1960s, is the best-known defender of this doctrine).

The tendency toward far-flung mini-centers proposing themselves as peripheral attractors produces a centripetal movement away from the

---

87 Swaran Singh, "Rise and Fall of the PLA's Business Empire: Implications for China's Civil-Military Relations," *Strategic Analysis* 23, no. 2 (1999): 227–39.

88 Guattari, "Micro-politics of Fascism"; Deleuze and Guattari, *Thousand Plateaus*, 255–58, 343–51.

preeminent person of the head of state. The mini-centers will still resonate with the faciality of the preeminent person and share in the narratives swirling around it, but will participate in the regime of reaction in
their own name. In other words, they resonate with the macro-center,
but refuse total subsumption to it.

Local militias and county sovereignty groupings of this kind shade
into paramilitary groups of national reach. These can provide a conduit
for movements to trickle up from the local level back toward the state
level. The Proud Boys and Oath Keepers, which played a pivotal role in
the January 6 Capitol insurrection to reinstate Trump, are the prime examples. They form their own networks orbiting their own central figure
as black hole, but are eager to jump into the service of the preeminent
person (in the lead-up to the events of January 6, they heeded Trump's
call to "stand by").[89] These groupings are prime candidates for encastment into a fascist machinery, as happened in Germany with the Frei
Corps prominent in the fascist movements of the twentieth-century
inter-war period.[90] They are proto–storm troopers.

The centrifugal tendency of the reactionary movements can go even
further than county sovereignty. One of the unique characteristics of
the present-day situation is the rise of the "sovereign citizen" movement since the turn of the millennium. This is an extreme expression of
libertarianism, which has grown in influence and virulence in tandem
with the maturation of social media. The sovereign citizen movement
holds that individual freedom of choice is absolute, and that no promul-
gated law, emanating from any level of government, is legitimate. It only
recognizes its own, conspiracy-theory-laden, version of common law.
This tendency takes many concrete expressions, including survivalism,
refusal to pay tax or carry a driver's license, opposition to the Federal
Reserve, issuance of personal financial instruments, blockchain boost-
erism, and attempts to declare the independence of personal fiefdoms
or take over public land (as happened in 2016 at the Malheur National

89 Kathleen Ronayne and Michael Kunzelman, "Trump to Far-Right Extremists:
    'Stand Back and Stand By,'" AP News, September 30, 2020, https://apnews.com
    /article/election-2020-joe-biden-race-and-ethnicity-donald-trump-chris-wallace
    -ob32339da25fbc9e8b7c7c7066a1dbof.
90 Theweleit, *Male Fantasies*.

Wildlife Refuge in Oregon). There is often a militarist aspect revolving around the "right" to own and carry firearms. In its ideological expressions, the sovereign citizen movement may be allied with tendencies running the gamut from radical libertarian capitalism to a rigid micro-fascism of last resort. At the limit of this tendency (whether or not they consciously embrace it) are so-called lone wolf attackers who take the law into their own hands and lash out violently at ascribed enemies in the name of the Man-Standard and in the service of the racism, misogyny, and other general-abstract reactionary hatreds that the Man-Standard's valuations and judgments foster.

There results from these overlapping but non-substitutable tendencies a multi-factor tension. There are tensions between the centrifugal forces of the preeminent greater person and the centripetal forces of the mini-greater-persons forming their own orbit, and potentially between these and sovereign citizens and other radical libertarians. The tensions energize another set of the oscillations in the complex tug-of-war internal to the constitution of the regime of reaction.

The results of the tug-of-war between centripetal and centrifugal forces are unforeseeable. As in all quasi-chaotic systems, stochastic elements can play a significant role. Chance occurrences may be amplified, assisted by the resonation saturating the signifying regime. The narrative lines and metaphorical/analogical relays of the signifying regime stretch like fascia throughout its substance,[91] tracing the outline of the full body of the reactionary regime in a web of signifying signs. Thanks to social media, point-signs can be conducted from any one point to any other, or to virtually all at once. Peripheral innervations can spread like a contagion, enabling small perturbations to amplify. Ascriptions fly in all directions. Enemies abound. The social field threatens to break apart, in the push and pull between centralization and decentralization, into a splatter pattern of micro-centers. It is possible for the perturba-

---

91 The fascia forms the largest organ of the body. It is composed of innervated connective tissues interlinking all other kinds of tissue, and is active in pain perception and interoception. The word "fascia," of course, shares an etymological root with "fascism" (although the fascist emblem is a bundle of rods for beating on enemies, with an axe for the final coup de grâce thrown in for good measure).

tion to build into a storm and pass a turning point, where the social field trips into another phase state.

If the turning point favors the centripetal pull, the preeminent person, or a usurper, may be able to recapture the centrifugal movements and rein them in or encast them. The exacerbation caused by the tensions may goad the centripetal tendency into exerting a radicalized force of centralization, toward a full-fledged fascism. Alternatively, a compromise might set in where a head of state, invigorated by the centralist potentials, steers the liberal democratic state in illiberal directions of more or less authoritarian mintage, but shy of full-fledged fascism. Also possible is that the storming may dissipate into a drizzle, leading to a recapture of fascisizing tendencies by the "normal" state of things (the more or less controlled antagonism of the more or less dysfunctional liberal state).

It is important to note that the right does not have a monopoly on micro-fascism any more than it has a monopoly on reaction. Deleuze and Guattari's theory of micro-fascism grew from Guattari's experiences with the far-left micro-fascism of revolutionary, in particular Maoist, splinter groups in the 1960s. This does not minimize the fact that it is the extreme right that is the principal crucible for it today.

> Fascism, like desire, is scattered everywhere, in separate bits and pieces, within the whole social realm; it crystallizes in one place or another, depending on the relationships of force.[92]

A Turning Point?

It may happen that the preeminent person loses its "magic." This opens a space for the normal state of affairs to reassert itself. But it also creates a situation where the system can enter a state of quasi-chaos as peripheral attractors vie for adherents, and new pretenders to the role of preeminent person step in. The preeminent person, faced with the existential threat of the decay of his collective personhood, may be pushed to even more exceptional behavior, to unpredictable effect.

---

92 Guattari, "Everybody Wants to Be a Fascist," 245.

Trump himself seemed to be losing his magic after the 2022 midterm elections. The Republican Party felt it was poised for a landslide victory that would give it full control of both houses of Congress. Instead, the Democratic Party mustered an unusually strong showing for a midterm and held on to the Senate, while the Republicans captured a weak majority in the House. This was blamed on a backlash on the part of moderates against the unhinged MAGA radicalism, conspiracy theory hawking, and erratic behavior of many of the Republican candidates Trump championed. A general fatigue at his inability to move past his ressentiment at losing the presidency in 2020 also seemed to be causing attrition. In response, Trump radicalized his own erratic behavior, cozying up more explicitly to far-right figures and pandering to their racism and anti-Semitism. Certain Republican public figures began to distance themselves from him for the first time, including Rupert Murdoch, who toned down the Trumpist cheerleading of Fox News and his daily papers.

The response to his announcement that he would run for president in 2024 was muted. In reaction to the tepid response, Trump just turned the exceptionalism his behavior expressed up another notch. In fact, it went to the highest setting: he called for nothing less than the "termination" of the US Constitution, as well as "all other rules, regulations, and articles," using the "fraud" of the 2020 election as a rationale.[93] This was prefiguratively indexing the turning point to a full-fledged fascism that would create a total state of exception with him at the helm, ushering in exclusive rule by Schmittian decision. Trump was clearly floating the attractor of a Trumpian fascist dictatorship to see how it would fly. It was a good temporary distraction from his mounting legal problems. The response in the moment was not what he had hoped for. He was soon backtracking, brazenly denying ever having sent the post. He subsequently backtracked on his backtracking. In the fall of 2023, with his 2024 campaign for a second term beginning to heat up, he turned to some of the most fascist-sounding vocabulary he has used (such as the comment about blood-poisoning and vermin cited in the last section) and began floating proposals for a takeover of the administrative state

93   Trump: "A Massive Fraud of this type and magnitude allows for the termination of all rules, regulations, and articles, even those found in the Constitution." Holmes, "Trump Calls for the Termination of the Constitution."

and its law enforcement and security agencies using the doctrine of the "unitary executive" to justify, among other strategies, replacing career bureaucrats with loyal henchmen serving at the president's pleasure.[94] Prominent conservative think tanks led by the Heritage Foundation had already worked out a detailed blueprint for expanding presidential powers in historically unprecedented ways ("Project 2025," discussed in the "Deciding in the Exception" section of part 1).[95] It was only under these extreme conditions that the informal "never-say-fascism" gag rule began to weaken a bit, with the "f"-word tentatively finding its way sideways into the public discourse of the odd mainstream commentator.[96] Shortly before the 2024 election, it was revealed that some had been more forthcoming earlier in private. No less than General Mark A. Milley, chairman of the Joint Chiefs of Staff during the Trump presidency, confided to a reporter upon resigning from his post in disgust that he considered Trump "fascist to the core."[97]

Trump's momentary travails prior to this emboldened a man who was briefly to be a pretender to replace him at the MAGA helm and as Republican presidential candidate: Governor Ron DeSantis of Florida. DeSantis represented the option of an encastment of fascisizing movement in an authoritarian turn of the liberal state. He has organized his interventions around a reactionary "war on woke" featuring, among other things, the curtailment of rights not explicitly enumerated in the Constitution such

94   Calabresi and Yoo, *Unitary Executive*.

95   Dans and Grove, *Mandate for Leadership*. For a quick overview, see Jonathan Swan, Charlie Savage, and Maggie Haberman, "Trump and Allies Forge Plans to Increase Presidential Power in 2025," *New York Times*, July 17, 2023, https://www .nytimes.com/2023/07/17/us/politics/trump-plans-2025.html.

96   For example, see Jonathan Swan and Maggie Haberman, "Why a Second Trump Presidency May Be More Radical Than His First," *New York Times*, December 4, 2023, https://www.nytimes.com/2023/12/04/us/politics/trump-2025-overview .html. Commentator Robert Kagan says everything but the "f"-word in "A Trump Dictatorship Is Increasingly Inevitable. We Should Stop Pretending," *Washington Post*, November 30, 2023, https://www.washingtonpost.com/opinions /2023/11/30/trump-dictator-2024-election-robert-kagan.

97   Ruth Cramer, "Trump Is 'Fascist to the Core,' Milley Says in Woodward Book," *Washington Post*, October 12, 2024, https://www.washingtonpost.com/ nation/2024/10/12/mark-milley-donald-trump-fascist.

as trans people's right to inclusion; voter suppression and gerrymandering to dilute Black voting power; breaches of academic freedom through bans on accurately teaching the history of slavery and race in schools; a ban on gender studies in universities; censorship of libraries; and a clampdown on corporate free speech when it defends inclusion—among other heavy-handed measures. DeSantis represents the "faceless" option of the rule of the state bureaucracy by reaction, in partnership with the neoliberal economy. He is known for his bullying style of leadership and his stolidity and blandness. He was by declared by one of his own close aides to have the "personality of a piece of paper."[98] At a moment when Trump seemed to be falling on his face, it was not out of the question that DeSantis's facelessness might work to his advantage. Faceless leaders, often derided as robotic, bring out and personify the machinic aspect of faciality as such. When the appetite for faciality wanes, this can be a power. As it turned out, faciality was not finished, only discomfited by a Trumpian hiccup, and the DeSantis alternative quickly dispersed.

Fascism Proper

A distinction has been made throughout this account between "fascizing tendencies" and "full-fledged fascism" or fascism proper. The approach deployed here considers "fascism" not as one thing but as a complex field composed of tendencies in tension which vie for dominance, mutually reinforce each other, or fuse to form new alloys. What defines their participation in the same field—their processual coming-together—is their character of reaction, with its resemblance-based logic of the abstract general category serving and served by the Man-Standard. Their processual kinship orients them toward the same attractor state, representing the limit of what they can do as forces of reaction.

The tendencies in a complex field stretch between two poles. At one end, there is a pole of deterritorialization where the tendencies fragment

98 Gabriel Sherman, "Ron DeSantis: The Making and Remaking (and Remaking) of a MAGA Heir," *Vanity Fair*, September 27, 2022, https://www.vanityfair.com /news/2022/09/ron-desantis-the-making-and-remaking-of-a-maga-heir.

or dissipate toward the state of unfelt feelings. In the field of fascisizing tendencies, this is the tendency toward an atomization in a splatter pattern of micro-centers which, if unattenuated by networking and a certain re-energizing pull back toward the center, would spin to exhaustion in their own orbits and sink into inertia, separated from what they can do.

At the opposite end lies the attractor state of the extreme limit of what forces of reaction can do. This attractor state exerts a inward pull on all reactive tendencies all the time, even summoning those moving toward the opposite, dissipative pole. That dissipative pole is never reached by the entire field of reactionary tendency due to the counter-pull of the extreme limit at the opposite pole, which operates as a universal intensifier. It pulls tendencies toward maximal centralization in the tightest of orbits around the preeminence whose person is at the core of the field, operating as a central-computing "third eye" or black hole of faciality" emanating from the head of state. This pole is also never actually reached—both poles are virtual limit-states. It is never reached because the extreme of centralization is also the extreme of rigidification. The self-defensive reflex of reaction, taken to the limit, attempts to control all flows by translating them into ordered, laminar flows following pre-established channels (think of the Nazi rallies portrayed in Leni Riefenstahl's film *Triumph of the Will*). Ultimately, everything must be disciplined into these channels. This inevitably involves great cruelty, because the social field has to be forcibly "purified" of insubordinate elements potentially governed by counter-tendencies and tending toward resistance, escape, or chaotic flow. Entire classes of ascribed enemies may be targeted for eradication, as happened under the Third Reich. The purification can never be complete. There is always the threat of another insubordinate body hiding in the cracks in the social fabric or camouflaged behind a bush. Extreme vigilance is necessary, so much so that the regime falls into a state of constant war with itself that easily flies off its hinges into collective paranoia.

The conundrum of the regime of reaction is that this constant state of emergency inside the territorial borders of the state in which fascisizing tendencies have become encasted is doubled by the perceived existential threats potentially arriving from outside the borders. There is also an ever-present threat of infiltration or incursion, the only solution for which is for there to be no outside. Even absent any threat of incursion, the space outside the borders of the state can be seen as a refuge for hated categories native to other countries, or fleeing the regime. Outside the borders of their continued presence nettles the fascist state, their existence an insult to it. Under the sway of the most extreme fascist tendencies, the state is obligated, as a function of its own reactionary tendencies, to expand outward to occupy and purify all available "living space," as the Nazis put it. Wars of conquest and colonization ensue. What economic liberalism may have accommodated itself to the fascist state is co-opted and, like all movements in the social field, channeled toward the war effort.

This double dynamic is a characteristic of full-fledged fascism, or the regime of reaction in a passage to the limit of what it can tendentially do. The enormous energy of attack required to sustain this situation requires that the virulence of micro-fascist movements be co-opted on a continuing basis and encasted into a centrally directed war machine. This is a fraught enterprise, because the encastment must not tamp down the movements' intensity with the wrong kind of regimentation. Every fascist regime needs its equivalent of storm troopers. But as just discussed, micro-fascist movements have their orbits and tendencies which are sometimes dissociative. They may even turn against the central preeminence and attempt to depose or usurp it. The regime must be ever on the watch against its own most energetic supporters, upon whom it may find itself in the situation of lavishing the same cruelty it directs toward its enemies.

Approaching the limit, pulled unsustainably in different directions at the same time, the full-fledged fascist regime enters a frenzy. The centripetal forces intensify in strength, and as they do, they throw out centrifugal movements with equal ferocity. The obsession with wholeness in reaction to potentially dismembering threats becomes self-dismembering. The state turns as suicidal as it is enthusiastically murderous. "Long live death!" This fascist Spanish Civil War slogan perfectly captures the conundrum in a chilling oxymoron.

Nearing this point, the reactionary regime must pull back into a more stable bureaucratic totalitarianism. It must embrace the faceless, or face its own death. Mussolini and Hitler chose the latter. Hitler prosecuted his war of conquest to the limit of intensity, then at the point of no return disappeared into the black hole of his bunker in the heart of a ruined Berlin near the Reich Chancellery and issued his infamous "Nero Decree" ordering his troops to destroy Germany rather than surrender. The faciality of the regime imploded into that pathic hole at the center of the state, its "third eye" extinguished. The fascist state is at the limit a suicide state. If outward expansionism is stymied by nationalist isolationism, the explosive centrifugal half of the dynamic folds back into implosive centripetal energies, fueling what can be a just-as-suicidal situation of civil war: a self-bisecting fascism.

In *First and Last Emperors: The Body of the Despot and the Absolute State* (1992), Kenneth Dean and I analyzed the centrifugal-centripetal dynamic tension under the rubric of the "absolute State" (Deleuze and Guattari's "Urstaat"[99]), charting its vicissitudes from the First Emperor of China, through later "oriental despotisms" (as they used to be called) and the European absolute monarchies, to its modern-day pantomime of them in the wholeness/dismemberment drama of Ronald Reagan alluded to in "The Decline and Rise of the Personality of Power" section of part 1. The contention was that this dynamic is a *transhistorical tendency* describing one pole of process—a passage to the limit of reaction—that haunts all state societies. More than that, it is of the essence of the state to be sensitive to the attractive pole governing that tendency (in the sense of essence used earlier, defined as the powers immanent in a body or formation). The contrasting pole to this paranoid pole is what Deleuze and Guattari call in *Anti-Oedipus* the "schizophrenic" pole of the becoming-revolutionary of active forces, moving with the logic of the singular-universal rather than the abstract general.[100]

Processually, the reactionary pole maximizes reterritorialization and capture by the machinations of resemblance backed by the standardizing violence of the abstract ideal of sameness. The schizophrenic pole tends toward a maximization of deterritorialization and concrete exploration of the world's potential by the differingly-different. Reactionary movements trace a full body webbed by fascia of cruelty and discipline. Revolutionary movements in Deleuze and Guattari's sense counter that

99   Urstaat: Deleuze and Guattari, *Anti-Oedipus*, 217–21; and Deleuze and Guattari, *Thousand Plateaus*, 424–73.

100   Deleuze and Guattari, *Anti-Oedipus*, 3–5, 35, 102, 136–37, 246.

tendency in a movement of creative escape to the immanent limit of the full body, where it opens out onto the plane of immanence.

Neither of these poles is ever actually reached—there is in actuality no "fascism proper." The poles are virtual attractors, polarizing a field of relation and energizing it with tendential movements. They mark absolute limits that nothing concrete can attain, but that every concrete movement or body necessarily feels. They are attractors in something like the way centers of gravity or magnetic poles are: they have no substance or being, but are no less real for that, in that they effectively govern movements in a polarized relational field whose dynamism they delimit. They are ideal efficacities whose action is as much in the parts (bodies, movements) as in the whole (the integrality of the field). In the vocabulary introduced in part 1, they are quasi-causes. Quasi-causes, though ideal, are real working parts of machines in Deleuze and Guattari's sense. It is their governing of tendencies that is one of the main factors qualifying the machines as "desiring" (the other factor being the emergent tendencies of a part or element that arise as a self-governing consequence of its essence, or immanent power constitution).

The transhistorical character of the movements complexly governed by these attractors makes any general moniker for them somewhat arbitrary. The nomenclature may vary depending on the historical scope intended. The "absolute state," used in *First and Last Emperors*, is one way of encompassing the broadest scope, from ancient to modern. "Fascism" is the most attuned to the problematics associated with the maturation and now senescence of the nation-state as it developed in Europe and colonized the world. "Fascisizing tendencies" is a useful shorthand for tendencies governed by reaction and subject to attraction to one or the other of the two poles limiting the reactionary social field (or, most likely, both at the same time, to varying degrees).

Diagnosing

The variability of the way in which reactionary dynamics play out in the tendential complexity of any field of relation in their orbit makes it impossible to apply a classically empirical descriptive framework that does justice to them. The problem of fascism is less what it is than its *propensity to recur.*

A conventionally empirical historical description of an actually existing formation cannot directly apprehend the powers of repetition-under-variation *across* history. To grasp this movement through history, it is essential to think potential.[101] Since potential is not a discrete thing, and is not in itself observable, approaches influenced by classical empiricism have difficulty factoring it in. The movement of potential expresses most directly in tendency, which is nonlocal by nature, as are the quasi-causal attractors governing them, whose effects are integral and distributive—also not characteristics that factor easily into the conventional empirical causal framework. Without attention to these, a formation is severed from its conditions, which are always transhistorical (moving across the gaps between periods as much as potentializing each from within as it passes through). An indicator of the depth of the problem of potential for historiography is the scandalized reactions that Whitehead's formula for the necessity of potential for history arouses in some quarters: that what *could have been* is as important to the understanding of history as what was.[102] Historiography is fit to some purposes. But it is not adapted to the necessarily conceptual analysis of transhistorical dynamics, of which fascism is a prime example.

What is needed is a radically empirical approach, in William James's sense of an approach that recognizes the reality of relation. This includes recognizing the primacy of relations over the terms in relation (which emerge and become what they will have been in relation). In classical empiricism, relations have no sui generis reality. They are simply descriptions of the playing out of extrinsic interactions between discrete things whose nature is conserved across their encounters. The radical empirical convictions of the present account express themselves in the presupposition that what is being analyzed is a relational field, and that relational fields are immanently conditioned by entangled proto-activities stirring on the micrological level, shading off into the

---

101   Massumi, *Ontopower*, 153–67.
102   Whitehead, *Adventures of Ideas*, 276, 286; Whitehead, *Modes of Thought*, 89–90; Whitehead, *Process and Reality*, 73.

unfelt potential that nevertheless leaves its trace (if only in "negative prehension," as analyzed in the "Perspective" section of part 4). That unfelt potential at the immanent limit of what happens was itself understood in relational terms through the concept of umbral union. The discussions of contrasting logics were used to convey the possibilities for forms of precision proper to relational thought (for more on this, see the postscript).

A radical empirical approach, deemed here to be synonymous with a processual approach, does not describe. It diagnoses. Its transhistorical object are tendencies. Tendencies do not present all at once. They selectively crest in the present as they phase through. They are also not held to observing the logic of mutual exclusion. Unlike physical objects, they can occupy the same space. In fact, they always present in mixture. They may vie to subordinate each other, or resonate in mutually reinforcing ways. They can also fuse into a new tendency of emergent character. Or they may simply mix, living in uneasy cohabitation in relative negligence of each other. In all cases, they are modulated by history's accumulated sedimentation of forms and formations, and modulate them in turn. They move through formations, but also beneath and around them. They are problematic: given any particular conjuncture, their operations cannot be assumed, not least because they are always changing. It is for this reason that diagnosis is necessary.

Diagnosis bears on the kind, orientation, and relative strength of the tendencies at play at a given conjuncture. To distinguish the tendencies from each other, it is necessary to sense which polar limit attractor, and which more proximate attractors, are luring them. The proximate attractors, or what Whitehead calls lures for feeling, delineate relative limits providing the movement toward the absolute limit of reterritorialization or deterritorialization with rest stops or pit stops en route.[103] They may be propositions of various kinds, including organizational models for channeling the movement, master narratives for motivating it, ideological expressions codifying it, sub-facialities orbiting around littler greater persons, tonalities of ressentiment against prime enemies, and strategies of attack against them. The question is never just which at-

103 Lure for feeling: Whitehead, *Process and Reality*, 25, 86–87.

tractor. The real issue is, in which way? In what exact mode, with what territorialities, affected by what coefficients of deterritorialization and reterritorialization, and harboring what manner of operations? The answers to these questions vary according to the angle of approach. They are irreducibly perspectival. They always entail what Foucault called the history of the present (the curve of history as grasped from the angle of the present, as a function of contemporary problematics).[104]

The present account attempted to carry out a diagnosis of fascisizing tendencies from the angle of the Trump machine of desire, with special emphasis on the problem of the personality of power in its present post-normative incarnation. To identify proximate attractors, that analysis had to attend at times to the mundane details of Trumpian expressions for a symptomatic reading of tendential orientations. To situate the tendential movements processually, in their transhistorical reach, it was also necessary to climb the heights of philosophical abstraction. Numerous concepts were suggested for diagnostic service. They revolved most especially around making operable for the problem of fascism a thinking of potential.

The conceptual toolbox was intended not to frame the problem of fascism once and for all, but rather to provide a toolbox for others' diagnoses, for take-up from their own angles of approach, from the conjunctures that concern them. It is meant not to have the last word, but to provision rebeginnings. Rebeginning is non-optional, for the simple reason that the tendential arc of history will continue to do what it has always done: pull surprises out of the magic hat of its complexity.

Ur-Fascism and the Question of Typology

Given the variability and changeability just described, how do we recognize fascism and fascisizing tendencies? Is there a symptomology that can help with the diagnosis?

The problem is that the variability makes it impossible to create a simple checklist of properties to use as criteria for diagnostic purposes. It would be

---

104   Michel Foucault, *Discipline and Punish: The Birth of the Prison*, trans. Alan Sheridan (New York: Vintage, 1979), 31.

easy to compile one, working from historical examples. But it is guaranteed that at least one of the test properties would be missing from every example, and each would display key characteristics not on the list. If examples were excluded based on a missing criterion, there would be nothing left on the list. If, on the other hand, the list were expanded to include all of the properties that seem important to each individual case, it would become uselessly broad. This is not an anomaly: it is a constitutive weakness of the logic of the general abstract idea that schemes of typological categorization traditionally mobilize. What is needed is a processual typology that does not effect a triage operation based on necessary identifying properties or constants, and instead works entirely with variables. A processual logic of fascism understands it in terms of a shifting nexus of variables.

Umberto Eco's essay "Ur-Fascism" suggests a way.[105] He does make a list of characteristics, but precedes them with a warning. Briefly, his fourteen characteristics are

1) A cult of tradition. "There can be no advancement of learning. The truth has already been announced once and for all, and all we can do is continue interpreting its obscure message."

2) Rejection of modernism (but not necessarily a rejection of technology).

3) The cult of action for action's sake. Thinking regarded as a form of emasculation. "Culture is suspect insofar as it is identified with critical attitudes" toward traditional norms. Distrust of intellectuals.

4) Intolerance of criticism. "The critical spirit makes distinctions, and distinguishing is a sign of modernity." Dissent is experienced as betrayal.

5) An ingrained fear of difference. A call against intruders. Racist by definition.

6) Reaction springing from individual or social frustration. "Disquieted by some economic crisis or political humiliation, and frightened by social pressure from below."

7) "The only ones who can provide the nation with an identity are the enemy." Reciprocal construction of identities as part of the

---

105   Umberto Eco, "Ur-Fascism" (1995), in *How to Spot a Fascist* (New York: Vintage, 2020), ebook.

same complex (called here the Man-Standard). Obsession with threats and conspiracies. Feeling of being under siege.

8) Feeling "humiliated by the enemy's vaunted wealth and power."

9) "Life is a permanent war." In contradiction with the anticipation of a golden age of peace after the enemy has been defeated.

10) Fundamentally elitist, in spite of populist rhetoric. Nationalist or group exceptionalism ("we are the best"). Hierarchy allows every level to look at the level below as inferior, enabling elitism and populism to coexist.

11) Everyone is goaded to be a hero.

12) Cult of death (long live death!).

13) Machismo. Will-to-power expressed through sexuality and gender. Contempt for women and intolerance toward nonconforming sexualities. Power figured phallically.

14) "The 'people' is conceived of as a monolithic entity that expresses the 'common will'" and "claims to be its only interpreter." A "qualitative populism" where a certain media discourse, orbiting around the leader and echoing his words, is accepted as the authentic voice of the people, as opposed to the swampiness of elected government.

15) Newspeak. "Poor vocabulary and elementary syntax, the aim being to limit the instruments available to complex and critical reasoning."

The problems with this list are immediately apparent. Some of the criteria overlap, such as 5, 7, and 8 (fear of difference, intruders, and enemies) and 3, 11, 12, and 13 (cult of action, heroism, machismo, and celebration of death). Some do not apply to given contexts. For example, to the extent to which ornamental masculinity injects an element of sniveling hypersensitivity and wound-licking victimhood into today's fascisizing field, the overlap of numbers 3, 11, 12, and 13 cannot be said to characterize the field as a whole. Some are overly broad: for example, number 1's cult of tradition doesn't cover contemporary post-normative variants, including right-wing accelerationism. The inevitability of weaknesses of this kind in any such list are why Eco precedes the list with a warning.

The warning is that fascism is not "a monolithic ideology" and contains "no quintessence, not even a single essence."

It is possible to eliminate one or more aspects from a Fascist regime and it will always be recognisably Fascist. Remove the imperialist dimension from Fascism, and you get Franco or Salazar; remove the colonialist dimension, and you get Balkan Fascism. . . . These characteristics cannot be regimented into a system; many are mutually exclusive and are typical of other forms of despotism or fanaticism. But all you need is one of them to be present, and a Fascist nebula will begin to coagulate.

Fascism is a nebula—like an emergent solar system. All you need is one characteristic on the list, and its orbiting planets start to take form around what will be their central star. This makes it clear that the list is meant as an entryway into the analysis of fascism at the formative level. In other words, it is meant to encourage a processual take on it. The "characteristics" are not properties of a type that can be pre-defined and reapplied as is. They are processual *operators*. They are point-signs. They each point to a problem area where a tension is playing out, for example between populism and elitism, or between modernism (or more broadly progressivism) and tradition. The tension is such that something has to give. Tendencies toward an attempted resolution of the tension are already stirring in it. But what gives is not pre-played. The form and content of the resolution can vary significantly, because the shape the "coagulation" will take is contingent upon the conditioning context, unforeseen historical conjunctures, and the cumulative effects of fortuitous accidents of persons perturbing and inflecting the tendencies. It is certain that each case will be of its own kind.

What holds the operators together as part of the same fascist field is not a belonging to an abstract general type. Rather, it is the lure of an attractor quasi-causally governing their tendential unfoldings (as discussed in the previous two sections). The attractor addresses all of them at the same time, across their differences, in the singularity of each. Its drawing them to itself draws them into each other's orbits. Mutually sensitized to the tendential direction and the processual terminus-point prospectively strung before them, they sensitize to each other. They may then bind to each other's trajectories, working out their differences as they begin to move together. Things will shake down as contingencies intervene. Some tendencies may fall out. Pairs or sets of them may change in dominance, or exchange in taking the piloting role. Emergent characteristics are likely to result from alloys and alliances. It is even possible that the emergences en route sensitize the tendencies' working-out to the lure of a different attractor, leading to a directional veer (for example, from Italian-style fascism to totalitarianism).

The list of characteristics is not descriptive of any given formation. It is neither descriptive nor predictive. It is heuristic. It is a list of operators for a machine whose exact nature, in its next iteration, is not known, but whose field of potential can already be felt, in the form of unresolved problematic tensions already striving to work themselves out. The list is useful as a heuristic aid for scanning a social field with an eye to sussing out points of tension, feeling out their tendential directions and possible affinities for each other. This diagnosis can only be done through a detailed engagement with the singularities of the context, factoring in not only what territorializing presuppositions and structurings are in place, but also what escapes and deterritorializations are potentially brewing. Also necessary is an abductive hypothesizing about the potential effects of contingent encounters of various kinds. This can only be carried out with the aid of intuition (as discussed in the "From the "Singular to the Singular-Universal" and "Uses and Abuses of the General" sections above and the "Modal Metaphysics" section of the postscript). Since the list of criteria is neither descriptive nor predictive in itself, it is a work in progress. It can be heuristically updated as inquiries continue—and history continues to mete out surprises.

None of this is a science. There are no general guidelines or preset norms guaranteeing success. But it is experimental, if not scientific. What can be hoped for is the identification of sensitive points where an intervention might make a difference. Observing the effects of the intervention enables a trial-and-error approach. The analysis continues by phases. Each phase is opened by a heuristic groping and prodding of the landscape of potential, and is closed by an abduction-led analysis-in-act: a speculative pragmatism. The logical model starts from the presupposition of a mutual inclusion of tendencies, and proceeds by following the vagaries of their dynamic relation's self-selective working out. Some of the formations that might recur in new variations were discussed in the preceding sections, where different relations to centralization, the state, and war or civil war were repertoried.

Eco states that only one of the criteria must be in place for a tendency to set to work in a fascisizing direction. Looking at the list, it is clear that different operators are likely to have different magnetizing abilities to sensitize the others to themselves. Their rallying power varies. And they do not necessarily need each other. All are basically self-conducting. Any one of them can go solo or tunnel through the field of potential to re-irrupt in a different problematic field. They are opportunistic co-attractees and potential allies, not Lego-like building blocks or structural elements that are a priori bound to each other.

That said, there is a good argument for elevating certain of the criteria to a special status. The status is not that of a constant, since these characteristics vary as much as any other. But they have a special place as operators.

The first might be called a *master-key operator*. Actually, it is less one criterion than the relation between two of them: the reaction against intruders (5) and the rousing ascription of the enemy (7). These were the two key moments in the analysis of reaction proposed above. The master key is the jagged line of reaction strung between these two moments. This axis of reaction can be taken as master-key operator because it possesses immense power to rally other reaction-ready tendencies to each other. It acts as a live wire catalyzing the "coagulation" of tendencies, as in a processual crucible alchemizing fascism. It has no content in itself, since enemies are performatively ascribed and take many forms (related to race, gender, class, religion, national origin, and so on). Still, it can be treated as the common genetic element in the emergence of any fascism. The presence of a common genetic element qualifies fascism as a collective singular, as opposed to a garden-variety category or abstract general idea. The recurring catalysis along this axis of reaction can be called Ur-fascism. It is not a constant because reaction runs its processual line differently each time. It never strikes twice in exactly the same place. It is an axis of re-origination (what Simondon calls an "absolute origin,"[106] or what has been called a matrix in this essay). It is the Ur-operator of fascism in this sense.

---

106   Simondon, *Individuation*, 44, 60.

There is one glaring absence in Eco's list: there is no criterion bearing on the relation to the capitalist economy. This is where the second special operator comes in. From a certain point of view, Eco's omission is actually a strong point. Capitalism is its own process, with its own operators, master-key relation, and attractor: the endless accumulation of monetary surplus-value. Capitalism is the only effectively universal social process in the current epoch of the world. Having colonized all of space on earth, it has now turned toward completing its endocolonization of personing (as described in the "Personification of Capital, Reflux" section in part 4) as it prepares to launch into the final colonial frontier of outer space. Fascism, or any political formation for that matter, cannot but come to some accommodation with it.

Fascism, however, pre-accommodates itself to it. As Marcuse discusses at length, fascist movements, in common with many authoritarian states encasting fascisizing tendencies, "never attack the economic functions of the bourgeois in the capitalist production process."[107] They retain the principle of private property, and share liberalism's constitutive strategy of the economization of life (the next section discusses the economization of life through the angle of human capital). They may powerfully co-opt productive forces toward state ends, as the Nazi regime did with Germany's industrial giants. They may siphon off capital into the coffers of state actors, through endemic corruption (as does just about every authoritarian state as it encasts fascism). But they remain strongly coupled to the capitalist process. The alliance between capital and the fascist state may even offer the capitalist economy a way across barriers to its expansion that it was incapable of negotiating on its own, "providing a new space for the initiative of the entrepreneur" building on a "pre-existing

---

107 Herbert Marcuse, "The Struggle against Liberalism in the Totalitarian View of the State," in *Negations: Essays in Critical Theory* (London: Mayfly, 2009), 7. In this work, Marcuse does not concern himself with the fraught task of distinguishing between authoritarianism and totalitarianism, using instead an amalgamated term, the "total-authoritarian" state. Elsewhere, he makes a distinction between the state being totalitarian and society begin authoritarian (Marcuse, "State and Individual under National Socialism," 70). This doesn't work for the present project because the collective personing it discusses cuts across the repartition between state and society, immediating the relation.

harmony between the interests of industry, the party and the army."[108] This is the reason for Western liberal democracies' appeasement of Nazi Germany in the 1930s, most notoriously in the form of the Munich Agreement, and the strong support for Nazism among the American capitalist class during the inter-war period. It is also the reason that powers like the United States have historically allied themselves with authoritarian regimes in Latin America and elsewhere that are otherwise anathema to their stated principles. Erosion of the principles of private property and capitalist enterprise moves toward a processual threshold, over which the regime undertaking the state encastment of fascizing tendencies will be ascribed the status of sworn enemy by liberal democracies from day one, and will likely be anathemized with the epithet "totalitarian." Whereas the reaction-against-intruders / ascription-of-enemies axis was a master-key operator of fascism, private property is its *processual coupler* with the capitalist process (its bridge into a different process having its own consistency and master-key operator, making the two processual fellow-travelers: operative accompaniments of each other).

The ways fascism and capitalism alloy or ally are variable. Their entering into processual accompaniment with another is on a different level than the way the operators of fascism bind and collectively work out a course. Both capitalism and fascism are fiercely self-conducting transhistorical tendencies, each with its own dedicated attractor. Thinking them together requires thinking processual mixity. The coming-together of the operators of fascism was already a processual mixity. Each is self-conducting and can be seen as governed by a quasi-causal attractor of its own. Understanding what the lure and prospective terminus is—where a tendency ends up when it expresses itself to the limit—must be part of the analysis. But if fascism is a nebula coagulating into a solar system, there are systems of lower dimensionality that are part of its field which, taken singly, answer to a more limited gravitational pull (as planets in the fascist galaxy). Their axes of formation don't merit the prefix "Ur-." Ur-fascism (the reactionary axis) and Ur-capitalism (whose processual axis is the systemic headlong movement propelled by its master-key relation and expressed in Marx's C'—M—C'' formula

---

108 Marcuse, "State and Individual under National Socialism," 74, 76.

of surplus-value production) are like mega-cloud-fields of problematic potential, birthing.

When galaxies collide . . .

The Economization of Hate

In the age of human capital, the operations of capital have become immanent to personhood to a degree not earlier seen. This endocolonization makes attention to the modus operandi of capitalism in its current phase an absolute necessity for the account of fascism and fascisizing tendencies, which also hijack personing in their own reactive way. Certain concepts addressing capitalism's current modus operandi were put in motion in the course of this essay, such as surplus-value of flow, machinic surplus-value, and human capital as a personification of the flows of capital. However, the task of developing an account of present-day capitalism in its relation to fascism, remembering the principle of processual mixity from the previous section, is a highly complex one. It is particularly complex on the side of capitalism in view of the need to assess the rise and role of the financial sector, with its brain-numbingly abstract derivative instruments. Such an account is beyond the scope of the present essay.[109] A few stray comments on the confluences between capitalism and fascism will have to suffice here.

One thing that can be said is that the concept of economic self-interest is not adequate to the task of articulating fascism and capitalism. The question is often posed as to why supporters of reactionary politics vote in ways contrary to their own economic interests. This assumes a certain class profile among that population. The answer to the question usually involves some version of the deluded masses paradigm. The idea of the deluded masses was critiqued earlier, and replaced with a genealogy of error grounded in the tendencies native to perception in all human bodies, regardless of social standing.

109   On present-day financial capitalism and political potential, see Massumi, 99 *Theses*. For an anthology gathering together different perspectives, see Benjamin Lee and Randy Martin, eds., *Derivatives and the Wealth of Societies* (Chicago: University of Chicago Press, 2016).

In addition, the class profile of Trump supporters is more complicated than is often acknowledged. It is not limited to the working class,
or those who feel financially precarious in the face of the changes that
came with globalization and who worry about falling out of the middle
class. The majority of Trump voters are in fact solidly middle class or affluent, and are motivated more by fear of losing social status than by economic hardship.[110] Most prominent Trump cheerleaders actually come
from the "coastal elites" or have joined them by earning credentials at
iconic elite universities, and many have earned their fortunes in some of
the most advanced sectors of the financialized capitalist economy. Sena-
tor Ted Cruz, for example, has degrees from Princeton and Harvard Law.
"Hillbilly" elegist JD Vance earned a law degree from Yale and worked in
libertarian billionaire Peter Thiel's venture capital firm before entering
politics and quickly rising to the status of Trump's "populist" vice presidential choice. Oath Keepers founder and convicted January 6 conspirator
Stewart Rhodes is also an alumnus of Yale Law. There is a strong element
of racial grievance aggravated by tropes of the "Great Replacement" and
myths of anti-white racism that appeals to some who are solidly ensconced
in the middle or upper classes. Gender panic also plays an important role,
as does evangelical Christianity, a strong majority of whose adherents support Trump unquestioningly, but whose class profile is diverse.

This is not to say that there is nothing to the notion that economic
precarity and working-class background are determinants. One of the
strongest indicators of Trump support and MAGA patriotism are indeed
being rural (and white male) and not having completed a college degree. The point is that the class composition is varied enough that it is
not possible to draw a straight causal line between Trumpism and eco-

---

110   Melinda Cooper analyzes class realignments in voters under neoliberalism,
      arguing that the prevailing image of the US blue-collar worker is an anachro-
      nism. *Counterrevolution* (New York: Zone, 2024). See also Nicholas Carnes and
      Noam Lupu, "It's Time to Bust the Myth: Most Trump Voters Were Not Working
      Class," *Washington Post*, June 5, 2017, https://www.washingtonpost.com/news
      /monkey-cage/wp/2017/06/05/its-time-to-bust-the-myth-most-trump-voters-were
      -not-working-class; Niraj Choski, "Trump Voters Driven by Fear of Losing Status,
      Not Economic Anxiety, Study Finds," *New York Times*, April 24, 2018, https://www
      .nytimes.com/2018/04/24/us/politics/trump-economic-anxiety.html.

nomic interest, clearly or deludedly perceived. It is absolutely necessary to take account of economic factors, but interest is the wrong way to do it. Economic interest is a determinant, but it is not determining in the last instance.

If anything approaches the status of determining in the last instance, it is regime of reaction and its affective genealogy of error. The regime of reaction has a processual autonomy as a self-conducting tendency, which does not prevent it mixing, mating, and imbricating with other tendencies. In our era, it is necessarily imbricated in the workings of capitalism. But it cannot be reduced to that complicity. As asserted earlier, the regime of reaction is simply not organized around interest, but rather constitutes a desire.[111] It constitutes a machinic desire that operates transindividually, on the infra-personal level of conatus more than that of interest.

The imbrication of the regime of reaction with capitalism, although not an adequate causal explanation, is a constitutive factor in the expression of fascisizing tendencies that is everywhere evident. The status of the person as human capital means that economic anxieties are taken personally, in a way far more integral to existence than that phrase usually denotes. Economic impingements may be directly felt as personal derangements, and derangements of the person as economic worry. The most general expression of this are the endless refrains about the "health" of the economy in the media, and the first-place priority given to it in voters' ranking of the issues. In the United States, climate change, objectively the most pressing challenge to the species, barely makes the list, if at all. The *London Telegraph* recently reflected this in an editorial comment that averred that "saving the planet is a laudable aim, but the costs of doing so have to be set against other essential priorities" like consumer purchasing power and the national debt.[112] This is an astoundingly absurd statement (all but requiring a "Stupidity" section; see below). It is fairly clear that consumer purchasing power won't go very far on a dead planet. The statement, however, reflects the commonsense consensus, ostensibly based on pragmatic self-interest. But if you let it sink in, it has the unmistakable ring of pataphysics. It is a

111   Deleuze and Guattari, *Anti-Oedipus*, 257–58.

112   *Telegraph*, "We've Been Too Slow to Fix This Gas Crisis," August 30, 2022, https://www.telegraph.co.uk/opinion/2022/08/30/slow-fix-gas-crisis.

self-caricature of thought. It demonstrates the extent to which the connection of common sense to interest is trumped by desire. It only makes
sense to prefer the health of the economy to the survival of the planet if
one's identification is not with a set of interests, class-based or otherwise,
but with the machinery of capitalism itself, consciously or unconsciously
attributed godly quasi-causal powers superior to the limits of the earth.

The person, it was argued, personifies capitalism. Statements such
as the *Telegraph*'s betray a reactive personification clinging to the phase
of capitalism dominated by fossil fuels that is now ending. This is less
an expression of interest than an expression of bodies' desiring adjunction to the capitalist system as units of human capital. The ferocity of
right-wing animus in the United States toward energy conservation and
any and all post-fossil energy sources and technology, which so evidently runs counter to any long-term rational calculus of interest, can
only be explained in this way. It might be said that climate change de-
niers or minimizers are cynically representing the interests of fossil fuel
companies, and that is true as far as it goes. But the animus expresses
more than support. It expresses nothing less than an existential posture so enracinated that abandoning it would be felt to be tantamount
to the abandonment of the person one is. LED light bulbs, seen from
this posture, pose an existential threat (the phaseout of incandescent
bulbs has been an object of extreme MAGA ire, entering prominently
into some state-level politics, even though it saves consumers money in
the long run). The light bulb menace is a casebook example of reaction-
formation around point-signs indexing unforgettable, unfelt traces on
the full reactive body, and resonating with the causally mis-taken narratives as they slip and swirl around them.

If a light bulb can be perceived as an existential enemy, how much
more so a Jew! Economized reaction easily spirals back into the ever-
ready narrative of the supposed Jewish conspiracy to control the world
economy. This master anti-Semitic narrative is an extreme expression
of the imbrication of economism and reaction. That imbrication is so
ubiquitous, and takes so many forms, that it needs to be constantly
factored back into the analysis of fascism and fascisizing tendencies,
with serious attention to developments in capitalism carrying it across
thresholds to new phases, such as financialization.

In spite of this, something similar to what was said in the last section about fascism also applies to the articulation between fascism and capitalism: there is no pre-set causal link that can be presupposed and appealed to on principle. There are at bottom no constants, only variables (including two special operators). A certain linkage kicks in when the self-conducting processes of fascism and capitalism become sensitized to each other and resonate. One calls to the other; they echo in each other. Their tendential trajectories become magnetized to one another and they bind, without imploding into an identity.

The call can come from either side. In anti-Semitism, a regime of reaction appeals to imaginings about the economy for an assist in its objectively illusionary drive to ascribe enemies. What the capitalist economy offers is the opportunity to sum up all enemy ascriptions in a single figure. The capitalist economy does carry a tendency toward monopoly that concentrates a great deal of power in certain groups, such as the "captains of industry" of the previous phase of capital, updated as today's "oligarchs" and "tech moguls." It is a small reactionary leap of the imagination to conflate these accumulations of power into a monolith, and ascribe it to a particular racialized figure of enemy. With economic precarity, it is the capitalist process that appeals to a regime of reaction. What it gains is a decoy: a mis-taken displacement of enemy ascriptions, away from the boosters and defenders of capitalism that have abetted the production of inequality integral to its process, onto minorities, including those, like migrants and the domestic underclass, who suffer most from it.

These are more than intentional appeals and ideological snares. They are symbioses that develop adventitiously, as each process, following its own line, abducts en route a potential for itself that can be had by piggybacking on the other. The operators are liable to co-operate, and others can add themselves. There is always a certain stereotypy, given the generalizing mania built into the regime of reaction's overuse of the abstract general idea, and the common genetic element of pathic reaction to the "strange intruder," axis of Ur-fascism. The stereotypical figures of anti-Semitism deployed by the racist movements display a remarkable resemblance across time. The processual point is that these are produced resemblances (see the "Common Likeness," "Reconsidered," and "Overcoding" sections in part 2). There are always differences in the field conditions leading to each historical expression of them. The figures' process of reemergence is always singular, even if the final form of their expression is funneled into a figurative resemblance. It is crucial to take the singularities of the field conditions into account to form an adequate idea of the dominant processes plying a given period, and the always unique and changing chemistry of their mixity. An adequate idea is one that includes the process's potential to surprise, so that we are not caught flat-footed when fascisizing tendencies take on unexpected characteristics and unforeseen turns that illustrate yet again that typology is not enough.

Stupidity

The pataphysical tendency of the regime of reaction to express itself in a self-caricature of thought inevitably brings us back to the question of stupidity. It would be inaccurate, not to mention arrogant, to attribute that deviation of the will-to-truth into a will-to-believe that ends in separating thought from what it can do to gullibility or a lack of intelligence on the part of deficient individuals. This is manifestly not the case. Conspiracy thinking is driven by a feisty skepticism, not simple gullibility, and constitutes a highly elaborated mode of intellectuality.

At the same time, it is also manifestly the case that in the regime of reaction expressions of stupidity abound. It is not that people are personally stupid. It's that the full body to which they are adjoined and whose process they personify has enveloped in its constitution a malady of thought. The stupidity produced by the regime of reaction is *systemic*, in the same sense in which we speak of systemic racism (and, of course, is not unrelated to it).

To summarize where thought goes wrong and bounds down the path to pataphysics and systemic stupidity, it is necessary to return to the genealogy of error in reaction. The base definition of reaction was the separation of the effect of an impingement from the relational field of its occurrence. This is a native tendency in perception. Perceptual judgment tends to deduce the cause of an impingement, starting from the effect. It draws a straight line back from the effect to a discrete body that stands out from the background and is implicated in the encounter in what appears to be the most direct and forceful way. Certain of the body's sensuous qualities stand out. Thought, in its susceptibility to the allure of the abstract general idea that animates common sense, flags these as identifying markers. Often, a single easily isolatable quality stands out even more, and is immediately taken to stand in for all the others.

This marker is perceptually judged to place the body in a pre-established category: it becomes a defining property, slotting the particular body into a general category. Under the auspices of the general category, it becomes the marker of an essential nature belonging to the body, and all others in that category, in *like* manner. The causality then blurs. Yes, *that* body did it. But it did it because it is that *type* of body. The linear causality tracing the impingement back to that body now becomes structural, as a perceived group character refracts into the particular body and, in a return movement, attributions of causality slip seamlessly from that individual to the group. The group is guilty as a whole, as a type, because that part of it did this. Conversely, everything impinging that the particular body does is the fault of its type. The principle of likeness placing the individual in the group allows a two-way automatic relay of causal attribution between the individual and group levels. The particular is *overcoded* by the general, and the general is *represented* by the particular body, by virtue of the resemblance between its perceivable properties and the abstract defining properties of the general category.

This smudging of causal attribution across the particular-general, based on the overlay of a general logic of resemblance on particular cases, is the takeoff point of the regime of reaction. If thinking-feeling does not make a U-turn and go back to explore the complex relational causality of the situation, it is already on the road to the endless referral of the signifying regime. From there, it is just a small step into conspiracy.

You only have to think of skin color as a marker, and recall the conversion stories recounted earlier, to see how the logic of the general-particular joins forces with objective illusion to feed racism and other category-based hatreds. The hatred follows because causal attribution, as it happens, is immediately a moral judgment. It is an attribution of *guilt*, not just cause, because of the affective tenor of reaction (ressentiment).

Reaction coincides with the shock of the impingement. In that infra-moment, the life of the body is consumed in the effect of the impingement, its capacity to act suspended for an immeasurable interval filled with feeling (in Peircean terms, a Firstness).[113] Reaction is less passive than pathic: a feeling of being-done-to filling the entirety of existence.

In pathic reaction, the thinking is entirely absorbed in the feeling, for a pulse of existence. In a next pulse, proto-activity will kick in again, and thinking-feeling will begin its abductive arcing toward action. But the restart will be tinged by the feeling, which binds to the objective illusion at the root of the simplistic linear attribution of causality and remains attached to it in trace form. If the pathic feeling is held on to, every new encounter will resonate with it. Each new encounter will rebound on and reinforce the feeling of the ones before. Each subsequent encounter will carry their traces forward in a snowballing accumulation of the feelings, now in solidarity with each other. There forms a pathic web. Across the web, as the snowballing continues, feelings fuse into a single complex character gathering them into itself without erasing their individual traces, which remain reactivatable for the purposes of ascribing particular enemies. The interfusing movement of referral compounds the feelings into a rolling conjunctive synthesis that is constantly renewed, spinning off a disjunctive distribution of ascriptions as it goes, like clods of mud off spinning wheels. If this wheel-spinning compounding of the pathic is nurtured, it flourishes into full-fledged ressentiment, an endless licking of wounds accompanied by a sense of constantly being wronged by the world in general as well as by the ascribed enemies, whose legions blur at the horizon into the unspecified enemy. The causality perceived to be at the basis of the feeling is felt to be everywhere and always in operation: vague presences populating an atmosphere of threat, apt to pop up unexpectedly in some enemy form at any moment. If the ressentiment is allowed to fester, it inflames into hatred.

The ressentiment circulates freely through the orbits of the signifying regime and its dissemination of point-signs, unattached to actual

---

113 Peirce describes Firstness as an absorption of being in feeling so extreme that "the rest of your consciousness, memory, thought, everything except this feeling . . . is utterly wiped out." *Essential Peirce*, 1:259. Imagine it as a "dead infinite ache" or "a piercing endless whistle." Peirce, *Pragmatism as a Principle*, 140. Firstness in its purity is by nature an infra-experience, only approached liminally by consciousness. It coincides with the pathic infra-moment of suspension.

encounter. Hatred may then be inculcated in bodies who have no corresponding encounters, but have developed a reactive constitution through other encounters, pathically compounded into a existential posture that makes them fertile ground for reaction-stoking point-signs. An example, once again, is someone who has developed rabid anti-Semitism without ever having met a Jew. When it reaches this threshold of free-floating general-particular causal attribution, the regime of reaction is in full swing.

A pathic contagion ensues, in which feeling-effects circulate on the back of signifying signs, disseminating objective illusion, misplaced import, and snap moral judgment through the movement of endless referral. Point-signs now point back, not to a particular encounter rooted in the singularity of a situation, but most directly to *encounters with other signs* as carriers of pathic feeling through the byways of referral. The effect is a *referred feeling*—in the same sense in which we speak of referred pain. In fact, they are the same phenomenon. The referred feeling—this animus, this pathos—is the referred pain of a collective person to whose constitution reaction and the pursuit of inadequate ideas has become integral. The pain is referred generally throughout the web of ressentiment, and lands performatively in the lives of particular individuals, who ground it in something close to the electrical sense. The "Accidents of Persons Predisposed" section discussed, through particular examples, how fortuitous encounters occurring against this general background condition can electrify a life into a dramatic conversion to active racism. But under these general background conditions (as described in the "Association Unbound" section), a conversion can also occur in the absence of that kind of traumatic etiology, revolving around life-shattering accidents or other radically destabilizing actual encounters.

This movement of referral is the movement of a certain mode of desire, transitioning from belief to belief, following the lost highways of a will-to-truth motored by a misplacing of import and the mis-taking of causality, as it segues into a will-to-believe that makes every encounter the sign of a foregone conclusion whose inadequacy passes for common sense.

This is systemic stupidity. It corresponds not to an intellectual deficit, but to an acquired existential posture expressing the individual's objective perspective—its angle onto the full body that is the individual's real potential under the given conditions of its life's situations, as they emerge at this conjuncture, in this era. The existential posture is the individual's constitutive participation in the collective personhood that is the full body's patterning. Again, this is not a perspective *on* the world (see the "Perspective" section in part 4). It is a *worlding*. The regime of reaction is a world. Participation in it is ontological. It is a shared mode of existence.

Flash Agents

Certain individuals act as agents of systemic stupidity. They are the specialized organs of reactive contagion.

Édouard Glissant calls them "flash agents" (*agents d'éclat*).[114] The French term combines the connotations of "flashy" or "dazzling," and "explosive." Flash agents emit signs that strike: that hit with impact and produce a shock. They are point-sign bombers. They scatter-bomb the media, hoping for a large impact, but most often settling for an accumulation of micro-shocks. The current moniker for them is "social media influencers." They vie for attention as if it were a rare natural resource, and extract surplus-value from it.[115]

To attract attention, they have to continually stir things up. That is what dedicates them to reaction: they pander after referred feeling-effects. The flash of the signs they emit fills experience for an interval, absorbing attention in their flash, separating it by their dazzle from whatever relational import the feeling-effects might have potentially indexed as point-signs.

Glissant calls them "agents of commotion."[116] His account touches on many of the same concerns developed here:

114 Glissant, *Poetics of Relation*, 165–67, 175.
115 On attention and contemporary digital media, see Yves Citton, *The Ecology of Attention* (London: Polity, 2017). Recall the centrality of attention-grabbing and (micro-)shock or startle to Peirce's definition of the index as point-sign: "Anything which focuses the attention is an indication. Anything which startles us is an indication, inso far as it marks the junction between two portions of experience." Peirce, *Essential Peirce*, 2:8.
116 Glissant, *Poetics of Relation*, 165.

Contemporary violence is the response societies make to the immediacy of contacts [impingement of others] and is exacerbated by the brutality of the flash agents of Communication. . . .

Flash agents . . . are in tune with the implicit violence of contacts between cultures and the lightning speed of techniques of relation. They send consciousness hurtling into the sudden certainty that it is in possession of the obvious keys of interaction or, usually, into the assurance that it does not need such keys [objective illusion]. . . .

The immediacy (pure pressure) of their communication techniques [makes their action] sufficient unto itself [it is performative; decisional]. . . .

There is no stated ideology of communication. The ones in control of it in the world do not even have to justify this control. They plainly sanction it just by the fact that communication is continuously in flux [surplus-value of flow]: that is, its "freedom" [license], made legitimate by its topicality, that is, its transience. . . .

This speeding up of relationships has repercussions on how the full-sense of identity is understood. The latter is no longer linked, except in an occasionally anachronistic or more often lethal manner [neo-archaisms], to the sacred mystery of the root. It depends on how a society participates in global relation [complex relational field of potential], registers its speed, and controls its conveyance or doesn't [dissemination of point-signs]. Identity is no longer just permanence; it is a capacity for variation, yes, a variable—either under control or wildly fluctuating [oscillation between normative and post-normative personhood]. The old idea of identity as root, whenever it proves hard to define or impossible to maintain, leads inexorably to the refuges of generalization provided by the universal as value [the abstract general idea and its underwriting of the Man-Standard]. . . .

The commonplace scatters the intent preserved in structure throughout [desiring machine; collective personhood].[117]

117 Cited passages in order presented: Glissant, *Poetics of Relation*, 141, 166, 166, 166, 141–42, 167.

Relay Agents

The question for anti-fascist life is how to imbue communication with a different desire moved by counter-attractors of relational engagement, thought-felt with a more complex sense of causal efficacies and an intuition of the internal constitution, or powers of existence, of the lives of the others that impinge. Social media is dominated by flash agents, but it is not a homogeneous field. It has many subdomains and micro-climates. For these to be leveraged for another figure of the collective embodying a counter-desire, the role of flash agents will have to be supplanted in those circuits by what Glissant calls "relay agents" who eschew the flashiness.

Relay agents have always functioned in the contact between cultures as operators of an "active relay" staging an interaction between the differing tendencies that make themselves felt in the encounter. But it is "not just the interaction of [the cultures'] tendencies . . . but the workings of their inner structures that become modified." The encounters play out in such a way that the real internal constitution of the cultures mutually modify. Their respective powers resonate in each other, reciprocally inflecting. Relay agents, Glissant says, "are échos-monde [world echoes] working the matter of Relation."[118]

Under their action, "the network of similarity or osmosis, or rejection of renaturing, that formed, manifested itself, cancel[s] itself out."[119] Relay agents counteract the regime of reaction as a network of osmotic resemblance.

To function in this way, to "really work," they need "relative obscurity, like a latency period, in relation to their perception of the results of their action." "The relay agent is active because, first of all, he went unnoticed."[120]

Glissant is calling for the creation of what Deleuze calls "vacuoles of noncommunication."[121] This entails contriving a delay between sign-strike and the feeling effect, a "latency period" that suspends the reflex of reaction to assign a linear cause and judge fault. Doing this gives a

118 Glissant, *Poetics of Relation*: active relay, 178; not just an interaction, 166; *échos-monde*, 178.
119 Glissant, *Poetics of Relation*, 166.
120 Glissant, *Poetics of Relation*, 166.
121 Deleuze, *Negotiations*, 176.

breathing space for thought-feeling to become sensitive to the capillaries of capacity webbing the full body. This amounts to widening the pathic interval of micro-shock so that the body does not exit from it in reactive mode. It becomes capacious, an infra-spread filled with a priming of powers to do and to be, so that it is this activation that a body carries back into effective thinking-feeling.

This counter-reactionary route out of the pathic interval must be built into the mode of expression's character. The field of expression must be conditioned to make it conducive to relay-agencying. Conditioning techniques must be deployed. The necessary techniques are techniques of relation. They add up to a practice of *care for the event*: a tending to the tendencies activated in encounter. Tendencies must be diagnosed and selectively inflected, immanent to their just-beginning-to-unfold.[122]

This shifts the character of political action from the ideological and programmatic to the immanently relational and relationally pragmatic. Programmatic ideological politics remains under the thrall of the abstract general idea, prey to the reactive tendencies it carries to a higher logical power. The movement toward anti-fascist life must enact the contrasting logic of the singular-collective, toward the formation of an affective counter-regime to the regime of reaction, tributary to an alter-power of logic, and an alter-logic of power.

This requires operating on the affective soil of thought-feeling's repeated and varied emergence—reaching all the way down to its substratum of pathic Firstness. Instead of rebounding from the pathic in a way that carries its unforgotten and unforgiven traces into the orbit of the signifying regime, the pathic feeling must refract in a different way, as through a prism through which a spectrum of powers of thinking-feeling shine. It must lose its individual trace in the newborn innocence of the simultaneous contrasts of the glow of potentials fanning. The feeling is spectrally affirmed, for its individual forgetting. The point-signs indexing the feeling no longer dazzle. They scintillate across a suffusion of felt potentials, priming the transformative powers of existence into which they may, if tended, amplify and bloom.

---

122 Manning and Massumi, *Thought in the Act*, 108; Manning, *Minor Gesture*, 193; Manning, *For a Pragmatics of the Useless*, 94.

Belief in the Event

The existential posture that embodies this mode of thinking-feeling may be called belief in the event. Systemic stupidity is the active igno-rance of the event. It is a turning-away from the singularity of the event, transposed onto the general register memorializing the mis-taking of its efficacy and the misplacing of its import.

Belief in the event is entirely different from the will-to-believe ani-mating conspiracy thinking or associated with religion. It is neither a compulsion to confirm foregone conclusions, nor a general striving to maintain a doctrinal faith. It is not a form, and it has no content. It is a manner of action, a quality of acting.

It is close to belief in William James's sense: an enacted faith that when the next step falls, the world will rise up to meet it, replete with potential, brimming with tendencies, teeming with others, and always with a tinge of surprise. It is the existential posture of leaning into the world's powers of self-renewal, first abandoning oneself to them, then walking with them step by step as their relay agent. The quality of be-lief in the event is openness to the other, alloyed with a curiosity for the worlding and a generosity of embrace. These are not the personal qualities of a discrete individual. They are event-qualities in which an individual can participate. They are the character of the event, to which individuals can adjoin as sub-characters. The event-character's pattern-ing is a collective alter-personing.

It might be possible, if not necessarily advisable, to say that the will-to-believe is the province of the right and belief in the world the prov-ince of the left. It is not necessarily advisable to say so because although the first part of the assertion about the right seems incontrovertible, it is not certain that the left has earned the honor of the second. May it become equal to itself, by becoming adequate to the event.

Distinctions of Distinction

For a Logic of Mutual Inclusion

Identity

A large part of this essay has been concerned with modes of thought: different species of ideas and the logics informing them. It was asserted that logic itself was a political issue, and the problem of fascism (it could have been said, any problem) cannot be adequately approached without serious attention to how different logics operate. The most relevant line of demarcation discussed was between the logic of the general and a logic capable of addressing the singular, as what falls outside the general-particular couplet and the logic of mutual exclusion built into that conventional categorical thinking.

Normative personhood was seen to be structured by the perceptual emergence of the general abstract idea in the life of the individual (piggybacking on objective illusion), and the inverse but complementary movement of its collective application to the individual in the service of disciplining behavior and policing boundaries (overcoding). Today's post-normative personhood does not escape from this overcoding. Under the sway of fascisizing tendencies, it plasticizes or "fringe fluidifies" it. This often occurs in ways that license aggressively erratic behavior that actually exacerbates the disciplining and policing. The cry is for "freedom," understood as a state of exception absolving the "sovereign" individual of relational engagement with the complexity and diversity of the social field. This absolution from relationality, equating to a turning away from belief in the event, allows reactive tendencies to take over.

The form of personhood molded by the abstract general idea is summed up in one word: "identity." Personal identity is the signature

achievement of European modernity. It is a derivative of the formation of the European nation-state and the way it incorporated inheritances from the absolute monarchies of the seventeenth and eighteenth
centuries.

The nascent nineteenth-century nation-state operated a double translation of the sovereignty of the monarch. On the one hand, it deposed
it from its throne in order to distribute its power horizontally (or pur-
port to). The abstract general idea of the "people," or of the "citizen,"
was notionally invested with self-sovereignty. The idea of the sovereign
people was used as a synonym for "democracy." The sovereignty was
largely fictional, given that the defining act of the citizen is to vote: in
other words, to abdicate that very sovereignty to a representative class
and the state bureaucracy mediating between it and the "people." The
ethno-racist tenor and boundary-setting/triaging operations of the
nation-state idea need no commentary. The Man-Standard was integral
to its constitution, as eloquently attested to in US history by the founding limitations of the right to vote to property-owning white men—the
ancestors of what would become human capital.

On the other hand, sovereignty was miniaturized to fit the contours
of the individual body. The individual was figured as sovereign in its
own body, fit to exercise the rights of citizenship as long as that body's
affects and deterritorializing tendencies were kept in check by "reason."
Of course, the body was housed in a home, and the home was male-
dominated. The Man-Standard is as integral to the constitution of the
citizen-individual as it is to the nation-state. This individual is, in fact,
the overarching, general idea of the nation-state telescoped down to
the mundane level of the particular, with a compensatory residue of
royalty: Man as lord of his own castle. Updated for the maturing capitalist economy, this yields Man as property owner of his own socially useful, profit-making or wage-earning body: a kind of landlord-of-himself
earning ground rent from his body's life energies. This conventional
notion of the individual has gone through many avatars and shifts in
mode, including hard-core destructurings such as the post-normative
"sovereign individual" of today's extreme-right libertarian movement,
and the more labile fluidifications of human capital. As well as, it must
be said, the identity politics of the left.

There are three points to retain:

1) Identity is a *political construct*. Specifically, it is the expression on the level of the individual body of the organizational modes of the European nation-state. It is complicit in the colonialism that is inseparable from the rise of the nation-states of Europe, and that financed the development of their capitalist economy. It contributes to the construction of both metropolitan and colonial formations of power through the instantiations of the Man-Standard. It is a derivative of these histories. It is a distillation of them.

2) This makes it a fraught enterprise to embrace the notion of identity for politics of resistance against colonialism, male domination, and class exploitation. This leads to an extreme case of "using the master's tool to dismantle the master's house"—something Audre Lorde correctly warned will never happen.[1] It is most especially the case that it cannot happen when the owner's house is one's body, and one's identity is the form of ownership. The equation made in identity politics between the general identity of the group and the particular identity of the person authorizes the general-particular play of resemblances and relay across levels that constitutionally misses singularity. It subordinates differences to similarity, in all of the ways that were earlier rehearsed in the discussion of the abstract general idea as inadequate idea. It carries into oppositional politics the (potentially fascisizing) tendencies toward boundary-setting and disciplinary policing that come with the structure of the abstract general idea. It makes for a self-contradictory oppositional politics that flirts with microfascism, as it attempts to recruit the most widespread historical derivative of colonialism against it and to dethrone the centrality of European modernity by doubling down on its signature product. Dismantling the master's house means dismantling this no-

---

1   It "is an old and primary tool of all oppressors to keep the oppressed occupied with the master's concerns." Audre Lorde, "The Master's Tools Will Never Dismantle the Master's House" (1984), in *Sister Outsider: Essays and Speeches* (Berkeley, CA: Crossing, 2007), 110–14. Lorde herself did not apply this to the concept of identity, as I suggest here that it should be.

tion of identity. It means recognizing that the first identity politics was the identity politics of white colonial European Man, and that this derivation has left its structural mark on all subsequent versions, even of the left. It means finding another logic of resistance.

3) The politics of logic must be seriously attended to. The hard work of decolonizing political thought from the logic of the abstract general idea is necessary for the empowerment of alternative futures. For this endeavor to succeed, an affirmative idea of what an alternative logic might look like is requisite. It is not enough to critique the normative powers associated with the conventional logic, invoking its alternative only negatively, as what the old logic is not (not binary, not exclusive, not hierarchical, not norm-binding, etc.). A positive notion of a different logic must be constructed.

Distinctions of Distinction

Logic is the art of making distinctions. There are different modes of distinction practiced by different logics. Four modes of distinction are of special interest in the context of this account: modal distinction, real distinction, umbral union, and formal distinction. The first three are essential to the counter-logic to that of the general abstract idea, and were touched on above. The fourth, formal distinction, is native to the general abstract idea.

Holding on to the distinctions between these distinctions is a necessary aid to a politics of resistance, if it is to have a hope of avoiding reproducing the habits of the conventional logic, with the attendant risk of falling in with fascisizing tendencies to one degree or another, despite one's best efforts. Equally necessary is a self-apprenticeship in diagnosing their use within a given mode of thought, including an evaluation of the mixtures and relays between them, with attention to their relative strengths as tendencies in any given exercise.

The following sections present the four modes of distinction, as reformulated from the process-philosophical orientation guiding this account (and not necessarily reflecting how they are used more generally in philosophy).

Modal Distinction

Returning to the example of the spinning top: the top, like all bodies, combines matter and motion. Matter was defined, following Deleuze, as that which is capable of action and passion, or to put it another way, carries powers to affect and be affected. Movement expresses a body's power to affect and be affected, which is one with its potential. It can thus be seen to index the body's potential.

Movement itself has two poles: *motion and rest*. Relations of motion and rest are what define a body according to Spinoza.[2] This is not as straightforward a notion as it seems. Relations of motion and rest are variable, and not just in terms of differences of speed. If the top is spinning in one place, we might say that the top is at rest in that position, meaning that it is moving in place. We consider the spin to be the motion. If the top is traveling across a surface, it is being displaced across positions, carrying the spin with it. Now we will tend to say that the displacement is the movement. The movement in place can be called *intensive* (in a first approximation of that term), and the displacement *extensive*. A body's internal constitution combines intensive and extensive movements at all levels, from the physiological through the molecular to the submolecular: coefficients of motion and rest all the way down, taking its own two dimensions of intensity and extensity with it.

A body cannot be conceived without thinking motion and rest together, factoring in the distinction between intensive and extensive movement. The distinctions are *reciprocals*, adapting the mathematical definition: "(of an expression or function) so related to another that their product is a unity."[3] The body counts for one, but its every state necessarily presents a variation on how motion and rest, intensity and extensity, are so related as to express their coming-together in that unity. In their reciprocity, one of these factors cannot vary without the other also varying. They are co-variants. In every instance, they vary to-

2 Spinoza, E2, P13, L1; Deleuze, *Spinoza: Practical Philosophy*, 122–13.

3 *Oxford English Dictionary*, s.v. "reciprocal," sense II.7.a, last modified 2009, https://www.oed.com/dictionary/reciprocal_adj?tab=meaning_and_use.

gether, and at every variation they reform their unity, with a variation on it as well.

With each variation, the body's potentialization will also vary. Its powers to affect and be affected will change in their ratio, in ways that may make new potentials more easily accessible at some times, and at other times may withdraw potentials. The body's power to affect and be affected will vary accordingly, notching up or down, to a higher or lower degree of capacitation. This is intensive movement in a deeper sense, as qualitative change.[4] A rise or fall in degree of capacitation is a change in degree of intensity. The reciprocity between motion and rest unfolds not only as extensive displacement, but as a variation in *degree of intensity*.[5] Qualitative change and the associated change in degree of intensity is nonlocal. It is distributed across a unity of reciprocity, equally in the parts and in the whole.[6] It also occurs "in place," if by that is meant a pulse of process (a processual locus) rather than a position in extensive space.

Modal distinction pertains to *reciprocals whose intimacy of relation makes their dynamic product a variable unity whose movements correspond to nonlocal changes in degree of intensity implicating qualitative changes that are equally in the parts and the whole*. The reciprocals cannot be separated from each other in actuality. But at the same time the processual complexity of the body they co-compose cannot be adequately analyzed without distinguishing between them. This is because they come-together always differently, and the differences in their coming-together correspond to qualitative changes the body undergoes. A body's capacity for change—the powers to affect and be affected that compose its potentials or powers

---

4 Movement in place, exemplified by the top spinning in one spot, is a lowest-degree expression of intensive movement. At a higher degree, intensive movement is a *transformation in place*: a change in nature. Deleuze and Guattari sometimes call intensive movement "speed," reserving the word "movement" for extensive movement. Deleuze and Guattari, *Thousand Plateaus*, 381.

5 The qualitative change accompanying differences in degree of intensity is minimal in the case of an object like a top, compared to living things or subatomic creatures. In the top it is limited to such changes as variations in its moment of inertia and in its sensitivity to gravity associated with angular velocity.

6 Elsewhere, I have called this co-modulation of parts in relation and the variational whole they compose "intricacy." Massumi, *Architectures of the Unforeseen*, 56–64.

of existence—is more fundamental to its processual definition than any given state. The very "essence" of a body, its nature, is nothing other than the spectrum of variation of powers of existence it can potentially express. Spinoza also calls this its "internal constitution." *Modal distinctions parse constitutive differences in the internal constitution of a thing* (in the widest sense of "thing," as anything in process).

If the modally distinct factors or dimensions that are in reciprocity in the constitution of a thing are separated in actuality, the thing is no longer itself. It decomposes. It is denatured. Thought cannot embrace the nature of things without addressing modal distinction. This task is most fully accomplished by attending not only to the naturing composition of reciprocals across its spectrum of variation, but also to the denaturings that come of their separation: the life and the death.

Modal distinction pertains to *co-variant factors or dimensions that necessarily come together in actuality, but that are just as necessarily separated in thought.* The fact that they are necessarily separated in thought does not mean that they are merely "distinctions of reason."[7] They must be taken up in thought *because* they are in the constitution of things.

To take them up, it is not sufficient for thought to denote or represent them. It must repeat them, analogically, in its own abstract matter, in the form of modulations in its own capacity for action and passion. It must make of itself an iteration of them.[8] It does this by indexing

---

7 For Hume, a distinction of reason "implies neither a difference nor separation." For example, the whiteness of a white globe and its spherical shape "are the same and indistinguishable; yet [we] still view them in different aspects, according to the resemblances, of which they are susceptible." David Hume, *A Treatise on Human Nature*, vol. 1, *Text*, eds. David Fate Norton and Mary J. Norton, Clarendon Hume ed. (Oxford: Oxford University Press, 2011), 21–22. The difference between modal distinction as defined here and Hume's distinction of reason is, first, that the object in its unity is not considered to be the same, but rather to be internally differentiated in such a way that its multiplicity counts for one. Second, the thinking of modal distinction is irreducible to a play of resemblances, and the differences subordinate to them, in our viewpoint on the object. The invocation of resemblance and subjective perspective ally Hume's distinction of reason to the abstract general idea as understood here.

8 This is what Simondon calls "allagmatics," or the "double becoming of being and thought." Muriel Combes, *Gilbert Simondon and the Philosophy of the Transindividual* (Cambridge, MA: MIT Press, 2012), 14–16.

thought-signs, as point-signs, to the potentials in things, tethering itself to the full body through their movements—remembering, with Peirce, that all thoughts are signs.[9]

Thought making itself an iteration of modal distinctions is effective abstraction: abstraction that is enacted in thought. An effective abstraction is a lived abstraction. This is in opposition to the merely abstract status of general ideas, which thought reflects rather than effects; reflectively applies externally, rather than mimetically iterating in itself.

Modal distinction not only pertains to bodies and their movements. Tendencies, which have been so central to the analysis of fascism as developed here, are also modally distinct wherever they co-occur (which is everywhere in bare activity, and more often than not in its unfoldings). Modal distinction also pertains to situations, to the extent that they envelop tendencies. The potentials of the full body as they enter bare activity, which is composed of germinal tendencies, must also be understood in terms of modal distinction. The modal distinctions pertaining to the full body at this level parse what Whitehead calls the real potential of the bodies individuating on its basis and the persons adjoined to it. Pure potential, into which the full body verges on its underside, concerns umbral union, or the composition of the plane of immanence that lies at the immanent limit of the full body (see below).

Modal distinctions do not have set form or content. They are defined by the reciprocity of their relations as it plays out processually, precisely through variations in form and content. Their playing-out exhibits a *manner*. The manner is how the movement carries a spectrum of potential for qualitative change through the degrees of intensity with which the actual expression of the potential varies.[10] Modal distinctions are recognized not by any resemblance of form or content, but by the manner in which their comings-together carry potential to make a difference. It is precisely here that they hinge into the second species of distinction.

---

9 Peirce, *Essential Peirce*, 2:403.
10 On "carrying" in this processual sense, see Manning, "Carrying the Feeling," in *Minor Gesture*, 132–64.

Real Distinction

The manner of movement moving across qualitative changes is the *pattern* that was discussed earlier as constituting character (which, sustained by a historic route of occasions, such as the series of experiences attaching to the life of a body, defines a person).[11]

The pattern of the movement has a peculiarity: unlike the reciprocals answerable to modal distinction, it is in a sense separable from the singular occasion of the reciprocals' playing out. It occurs with them, as their integral effect (through their conjunctive synthesis), and they are its necessary condition. But it has its own emergent qualities: a play of contrasts, or a rhythm, all its own. These define its character. The same character, the same pattern, can also be found in other occasions, conditioned by different bodies. It can also be found across sense modalities. The same dance movement can be performed by different bodies. You can tap your foot to the same rhythm you sing to. A schema of visual contrasts in a painting can be reiterated in sound contrasts in a musical piece. An oboe can play the same musical phrase as a tuba. Of course, as the last example makes obvious, there are always differences. No two iterations are alike, in the sense of presenting exactly the same qualities. There is always at least a difference in undertone or overtone.

What is peculiar about a pattern is that it is *amodal*: indifferent to the particular qualities that give it its content, without which it nevertheless would not be.[12] The pattern asserts its own difference as a character in its separability from its contents. It must touch down in content, but it carries its own form from one touchdown to the next. The word "form" should not mislead. This is not a shape or a container. It is a *dynamic form*, composed of the differential relations between qualitative elements, like the notes of a melodic line as they vary continuously over the span of the piece.

11 On movement-moving, or the self-modulation of movement forwarding itself, see Manning, *Minor Gesture*, 127, 153–54.

12 On the amodal, also called "vitality affect," see Daniel Stern, *The Interpersonal World of the Infant* (New York: Basic Books, 1985), 53–61; Massumi, *Parables*, 184, 186; Massumi, *Semblance and Event*, 17–18, 74, 109–11, 125–26.

Each instance in which the pattern occurs is singular. But the pattern itself is singular in its own way. The way of patterns is to repeat and vary across occasions, jumping from one to the next across discontinuities in time and place. Ultimately, the pattern is more in the across-ness of its iterations than it is in any given instance it characterizes.

The reciprocals answerable to modal distinction were said to *vary with* each other. A pattern *varies in itself*, which is to say in the across-ness of the migratory jumps from instance to instance that only it can accomplish. A pattern or character is *in-variant*, not in the sense of not varying, but in this sense of varying in itself. Reciprocals, by contrast, are *co-variant*. They are bound in relation to a joint destiny that is the playing-out of that relation. A pattern's destiny is to lift itself off from any given playing-out, to come again, elsewhere and otherwise, in-varying. The otherwise is not an alterity, but the pattern's modulation of itself, in itself—in the iterative across-ness that it is in its own movement.

The difference between co-variance and in-variance of patterns can be understood in analogy to the conjugation of a verb. The singularity of a verb is expressed in the infinitive. The conjugated forms immanently populate it, giving it a constitutive multiplicity that does not contradict its singularity. "To do" is still the same verb even when it occurs as "did" (or "done" or "does"). The infinitive envelops the multiplicity of the variations. It names a *singular-collective*. The playing-out of reciprocals is singular in the sense that it constitutes an occasion. An occasion is only itself and no other; and no other is identical to it. An infinitive, on the other hand, is multiply singular, dividing internally into variations on itself, across occasions. It populates itself with differences. It is internally other in itself. Its singularity is a differing difference.

A pattern conjugating itself in different occasions with different content is the same pattern across those occasions, just as "done" is the same verb as "doing." But the meaning of the "same" has palpably changed. It now denotes the continuous variation of a dynamic form in its differing difference, rather than the self-identity of a static form or an unchanging content. If we deploy this logic to class names, we're back at Peirce's suggestion that they can be understood as general ideas that index a singular-collective (or collective singular). "The dog," singularly-collectively, is a population of individual dog-occasions in a continual state of variation, as singular instances of dog are born, age, and die, and the species evolves across their iteration all the while remaining the same, in the infinitive. "The dog" is a fractal population: uncountably many due to the constant turnover, bounded but without the boundaries being exactly placeable (as when they re-breed with wolves), ceaselessly dividing into itself and varying through reproduction. It constitutes a nondenumerable fuzzy set.

The singular-collective is this unbounded multiplicity of instantiations of the same character. It is a species of being in the infinitive: "to dog." What it is not is an abstract general idea subsuming individuals under an abstract general category by a selective judgment of resemblance, construing them as particular cases meeting its standard: the dog, in the conventional logic. Abstract general ideas select and limit. Singular-collectives proliferate and populate, conjugating their class name (which means the name is not really a noun, which declines instead of conjugates, but a verb in noun's clothing). Their proliferation is a self-affirmation, in an evermore of itself, as opposed to a judgment. They form a spreading network of historic routes sharing not only a dynamic form, but a real kinship (filiative, in the sense of sharing genetic elements passed down the historic routes, as touched on in part 2 in the discussion of personhood coming out of Whitehead's definition; and in alliance, through connective forms of sociality). Singular-collectives are collective individuations whose proliferative patterning constitutes a collective personing.

To bring the discussion back closer to the animating concerns of this essay, Nahum Chandler analyzes W. E. B. Du Bois as deconstructing the abstract general category of race by what amounts to infinitivizing it, treating it as what is called here a collective singular. Chandler shows that there is no "finally accomplished existent" corresponding to race, and no invariant properties defining it in abstract general terms.[13] Race is a thing. And it does things. There is a reality to it. But it is not a thing in the sense of having the ontological status of a finally accomplished existent with essential properties. It is, as Chandler and Fred Moten would say, para-ontological—in other words, processual (in differential

---

13 Nahum Dmitri Chandler, "On Paragraph Four of 'The Conservation of Races,'" *New Continental Review* 14, no. 3 (2014): 258.

becoming). The collective singular provides a logical category for the para-ontologically real.

The questions of the abstract general idea are: Does this one qualify? Do its properties match the standard? Is it in or out? If it is in, what is its degree of conformity to the standard, and in what position in the hierarchy of particulars subsumed under the top dog of the category does that place it? Just bend your head down for this overcoding to come down on it, and grin and bear it.

The question of the singular-collective is: What else? How else can a dog be? Raise your head, watch, wait, and wonder. To dog will not disappoint. Rather than judge, the singular-collective evokes belief in the world. Think of this in terms of race, or of gender. What singularly collective becomings does the world have in store?

The differing difference of the singular-collective is a *real distinction*. Modal distinction is also a differing difference, but it pertains to the inseparability of reciprocals toward their joint product. *Real distinctions pertain to the separability of that product across occasions.* A body is composed of modally distinct factors or tendencies that are reciprocally *bound* in relation to each other. A character is composed of in-variations taking off from the body's occasion to claim an *autonomy* of real distinction from them, and amodally across them. The singularity of the playing-out of modally distinct reciprocals varying-with each other *individuates* the body (remembering that bodies are always collective, containing multitudes). The sameness of the real distinction of a character *impersonates* itself across its self-varying, in the across-ness of its in-variance. Its movement is a personing.

The logic of real distinction goes all the way down, which complicates it considerably. Movements have sub-relations of movement and rest, each with its own pattern. Patterns thus have sub-patterns, and persons sub-characters. There are rhythms within rhythms. Modal distinction and real distinction are imbricated at every level. This makes any logic deploying them complex by nature. That is the point. The point of thought is not to simplify reality, but to become equal to its complexity. This is not an easy task, but it is a necessary one if the desire is to embrace potential and foster it, rather than triage and discipline it.

With all of the emphasis on movement in the definitions of both modal and real distinction, it might be asked where objects as such fit in—humble, everyday objects like a stool that just seems to sit there to be sat on and stubbornly is what it is, stolidly fixed and discrete, a stranger to spin. It's a matter of lensing. If you fast-forwarded the entire history of an object from emergence or manufacture to rotting or recycling, it would indeed go for a spin. It would be in movement across qualitative changes, as the reciprocal elements composing it, such as its colors and shape, play their relation out. It would morph to the playing out. An object is a movement, at low speed, approaching the limit of rest, and at a lower degree of intensity, approaching the limit of stolidity. Modal distinction pertains just as much to it. So does real distinction. The coming-together of the contrasts in its coloration and shaping produce a conjunctive unity (which is precisely why we directly perceive an object as a unitary thing) that carries a pattern, but because of its low speed and low intensity, its continuous variation shows as static in the everyday lens.

Umbral Union

Modal distinction concerns the mutuality of reciprocals playing out an intimacy of relation to produce an emergent unity. Real distinction concerns the processual autonomy of the amodal patterns characterizing those emergent unities. Umbral union, which was discussed at some length in part 3, concerns *radicles*. Radicles are minima: pure relations at the limit of existence.

The easiest way to approach the notion of the radicle as minimal relation at the limit of existence is to begin by thinking of it through quantity. Think of a curve approaching another curve at a given angle and speed of approach, heading for an intersection with it at a tangent point. Since extensive space is infinitely divisible, the curve will never arrive at the tangent point. It will approach it infinitely as a limit never reached. If you extrapolate that approach-to-the-limit to the extreme, toward infinity, at a certain point the differential between the two curves will shrink to the point that it becomes a "vanishing quantity."[14] It becomes so small that it doesn't even answer to the concept of quantity anymore.

The quantity will vanish *because* the angle and speed of approach, which is the "shape" of the relation between the curves, doesn't. The vanishing is the product of that relation continuing. In other words, *the relation is preserved* when the quantity vanishes into itself—into an immanence in itself. The "shape" of the relation is its character. The preservation of the relation *preserves character*.[15]

The preserved relation is the radicle: pure relation. Pure relation retains the character of a dynamic (angularity and rate of change) without the stuff of it. Where there is no quantity, there is nothing actually, no content. A radicle is a differential relation—a dynamic in-between of things—distilled down to pure relational character.[16]

Now think of the imbrication of modal and real distinction just mentioned, going all the way down, just like the movement of quantity into its own immanence. Think of every differential, every tendency, every pattern, every contrast, receding step-by-step through embedded variations on itself, into a vanishing of itself, immanent to itself. Extrapolating to the absolute limit, no hint of content or separable form remain, and since there is no quantity, there is no actual spacing. The radicles can be conceived only as being in a state of *superposition*. This is not a layering one atop the other—that would still have thickness, a remnant of spatiality. Rather, it is an immediate in-each-otherness that preserves differential character. This is not an implosion into indifference. It is the most radical distillation *of* difference.[17]

Peirce's choice of the word "umbral" gives an image of this subsistence of differences in the distillation of a coming-together. The umbra is the darkest part of a shadow, at its center. Think of an object

---

14 Simon Duffy, *The Logic of Expression: Quality, Quantity and Intensity in Spinoza, Hegel and Deleuze* (Farnham, UK: Ashgate, 2006), 49.

15 On the preservation of relation at the limit, working through Deleuze's take on infinitesimal calculus in *Difference and Repetition*, see Duffy, *Logic of Expression*, 49–54.

16 On minima of relation, see also Massumi, *99 Theses*, 92–94, 96–97.

17 This corresponds to the virtual in Deleuze and the realm of eternal objects in Whitehead.

in a room. Light rays reflecting off different surfaces and arriving at different angles are differentially occluded by the object. The umbra is formed by a superposition of their occlusions. Their angles of approach leave traces of themselves as a barely perceptible texturing. The umbra comprises a field of subtle textures of darkness. Peirce expressed dissatisfaction with this image, presumably because it is still spatial and object-oriented, as well as the fact that it implies a negativity (light blockage). A reverse prism might be a better image. Think of all the colors of the spectrum reversing their course through a prism and focusing back down into white light as they exit where they came in. The white light is the superposition of their respective wave-lengths, still remaining but no longer showing in their individuality. Think again of Deleuze and Guattari's "white wall." Of course, this example is limited as well: at the limit of immanence, there is no one to see; in spacelessness, there is no place to be. There is no perception at the limit of pure immanence. But then, the white wall only appears as such on the approach to it, shy of the limit. It is the form in which immanence actually appears, at a distance from itself, from an objective perspective in space and time.

In the superposition of radicles, there is only coming-together of differences. Even though the differences subsist, they have no individuality because in their in-each-otherness they are in absolute proximity, without spacing. There is no individuality in absolute proximity. Where differences subsist in absolute proximity, there is a singularity of pure multiplicity (using "singularity" here in a sense in something like its meaning in cosmology). An image Deleuze often invokes to express the dynamism of this is an infinity of movements running into and through each other and back again at infinite speed from all directions at once: absolute speed. This is an image of chaos.[18]

According to Peirce, the one thing that continues to subsist besides character is wanting: conatus, striving, a minima of tendency. The plane of immanence is bare activity at the limit. What is preserved is the tendency of tendency to unfold, and the character of that potential unfolding. There is a tendency toward the expression of tendency. By expression is meant the unfolding of a tendency from plane of imma-

18 Deleuze, *Difference and Repetition*, 201–18.

nence into full body, and through the full body into individuations and personifications. The absolute recessive limit of difference is simultaneously a turnaround point, toward emergence. Emergence is at bottom qualitative: an unfolding of characters, re-spacing themselves, asserting their place in the world, taking on body, pacing their trajectories through historic routes, phasing through qualitative changes, keeping their own time to their rhythms of pacing and phasing, taking place and making time to form their own order out of chaos.[19] Time, here, would emerge from a pacing of absolute speed—its slowing down.[20]

The preservation of difference and character: *memory*. The plane of immanence is the memory of the world. It is the world's memory of its own potential.[21] Reaction holds on to traces, so that the memory cannot be sufficiently purified of form and content. Because of this, subsequent iterations will have a tendency to unfold in like manner to prior unfoldings, finding repetitive form and content, under variation but within the limits of what is recognized as the same. This is the conservative use of the preservation of memory. At its extreme, it is trauma. The radical use is to affirm the distillation into the pure difference of pure relation conserving only character. This is the only way to affirm the spectrum of potential and the change its unfolding brings with it. It is essential to enacting belief in the event. This is Nietzsche's active forgetting, as much a political practice as a metaphysical principle.

Why go through these metaphysical contortions when the problem is to think fascism? For the very good reason that we need a different logic to think fascism, and as we have known ever since Kurt Gödel, no logic is self-grounding. There is always a point beyond which it cannot go where the logic breaks down. The plane of immanence is a way of giving the logic that this account holds is needed for rethinking fascism—it will be called a logic of *mutual inclusion* in the next section—a grounding

---

19 In "Of the Refrain" (*Thousand Plateaus*, 310–50), Deleuze and Guattari show how space-time is emergent through rhythm and tendency.

20 Deleuze, *Difference and Repetition*, 205.

21 This is Bergson's "pure past" as virtual (Deleuze, *Difference and Repetition*, 81–85). In Whiteheadian terms, it is pure potential as realm of eternal objects (with real potential being the taking of space and making of time for individuation in emergence).

in an account of the breakdown of its own powers to make distinctions. It cannot go further than pure multiplicity, and in pure multiplicity it cannot actually discern the differences it postulates, their having been carried to the vanishing point.

It can't go further—but it can turn around and come back, emergent, expressing itself in singularity resurgent, alluviating into individuations. The coming-back-around is possible because at the very limit of what it can do, the logic preserves its own character (in-each-otherness; a logic of relatives). The grounding of a logic in its own breakdown is a kind of logical myth of its (and the world's) reorigination that draws its capacitation from its point of impotence, bootstrapping itself into operation by its own wanting. The relevance for the analysis of fascism is that the plane of immanence—which like all myth has to be posited as real in order to function—gives a limit-account of potential. The concept of potential is necessary to think emergence, change, newness, and event. These in turn require a notion of singularity: the incomparable; that which is such as it is, unique in its emergent manner; like none other, sui generis.[22] Potential and singularity are precisely what the commonsense stupidity of reaction systemically unthinks.

Modal distinction gives tools for thinking singularity without placing it in contradiction with multiplicity, actually making multiplicity native to it (through the figure of reciprocality, as involving at least two but most often more). Real distinction gives tools for thinking singularity without placing it in contradiction with generality, actually making generality's fundamental mode complementary to it (in the figure of the singular-collective). Umbral union enables a thinking of potential in itself, in its pure multiplicity, at its own immanent limit, where it is forever resurgent. Where else would it go when it is not in an unfolding, if not into the plane of immanence? And how, approaching the plane of immanence, could it not re-unfold?[23]

22 Massumi, "Such as It Is: A Short Essay on Extreme Realism," *Body and Society* 22, no. 1 (2016): 115–27.

23 On the paradoxical mode of appearance of qualitative-relational potential, see Massumi, "Virtual Ecology and the Question of Value," in *General Ecology: The New Ecological Paradigm*, ed. Erich Hörl (London: Bloomsbury, 2017), 345–73.

Mutual Inclusion

These three modes of distinction, modal, real, and umbral union, belong to the logic of mutual inclusion. Mutual inclusion is when differences come-together without losing their difference, in disregard of the principle of noncontradiction that enforces mutual exclusion.

In modal distinction, mutual inclusion is *reciprocal* (reciprocals playing out a relation that is made and moved by their difference). In real distinction, mutual inclusion is *contrastive* (the call-and-response of different patches or moments of a pattern echoing each other into the composition of its unity, and of different instances of the same pattern resonating in each other at a distance). In umbral union, mutual inclusion is *superpositional* (a folding over and into each other of differences entering into absolute proximity). All three are *differential*. A differential, as construed here, is a splay of different elements, each of which has its own positivity (a wanting, a tendency, a tone, a manner), and which collectively come-together across their difference without erasing it.[24]

All three modes of distinction concern the differing of difference. They serve logics resisting the subordination of difference to the same, consigning it to the negativity of being a mere contradiction of it or deviation from it as judged by a principle of resemblance.

In modal distinction, the inclusion is in the same concrete *event* (or pulse of process playing out a relation enacting qualitative change). In real distinction, the inclusion is the envelopment of different playings-out in the same dynamic form of *expression* (the serial and distributed exhibiting of a manner or character). In umbral union, it is a receding into a *field of immanence* (a mutual in-each-otherness taken to the limit).

24 This assertion of the positivity of the differential distinguishes this approach from the notions of diacritical difference in structuralism, where differential elements are defined purely negatively as not being each other: *b* as not-*p* and *p* as not-*b*. But what motivates the choice of these two? There is obviously something that recommends them to each other: the fact that they are both plosives. Plosivity is in the genesis of each of them, and its qualitatively differing across them is what governs their contrast.

The logic of mutual inclusion that these distinctions of distinction inform provides an alternative to the mutual exclusion practiced by the logic of the general abstract idea, whose categories conform to the logic of classical sets. The principle of noncontradiction at the basis of this logic is disingenuous. It makes it out as if there can be no alternative logic to it, because any logic not obeying its central precept can, from its point of view, only be contradictory, or lacking in logic. This is a ruse. Mutual inclusion does not obey the law of noncontradiction, but it is not contradictory. Its logic is otherwise capable of making effective distinctions—in fact, finer distinctions that honor singularity.

The logic of mutual inclusion may not be contradictory, but it is paradoxical, because what are normally considered opposites come-together in reciprocity, contrast, or superposition. But again, that is strength, not a lack. We all know, for example, how love and hate are often mutually included in each other. We have also seen how a certain intellectuality and stupidity can go together. We have also seen how a certain masculinity can include what are conventionally considered to be feminine characteristics in its makeup. We have seen how adequate ideas envelop objective illusions in order to "double" them. Races and genders, we all also know, come in many alloys, in-betweens, bridgings, and crossings-over. These are not contradictions. They are positive phenomena of composition, deserving a positive account. Only a logic of mutual inclusion is capable of making the kinds of distinctions that can provide them with that account with a precision respecting their difference and complexity.

Modal Metaphysics

There was a final level of thought that was discussed earlier, following Spinoza. This was the general idea as singular-universal. It was described as involving the body as a nexus, bearing on its powers to think, feel, and act in *any* situation, and how these powers augment and diminish as the body passes from *any* one situation to another. This is a superabstract idea, close to impossibly abstract. To make it even more abstract, the singular-universal can also be thought of in terms of the collective singulars that bodies populate. In any given nexus, the bodies in encounter will present a multiplicity of different collective singulars, and the augmentation and diminishment of their powers coming out of the encounter will depend on how their differences play out in it. The singular-universal bears on the coming-together of sets of collective singulars, in *any* number, factoring in the potential accords, discordances, and settlements between the tendencies the bodies under their cover carry.

It was said, again following Spinoza, that the knowledge of the singular-universal, not being able to be held in reflective thought, was intuitive. Another way of putting it is that the singular-universal lies on the horizon of the explicitly thinkable, beckoning thought. It is a lure for thought, inviting an approach. But given the impossibility of arriving, the invitation to approach is much the same as an exhortation to turn back and return to explore, using the other species of idea and ways of making distinctions. It is an invitation to explore what else might appear to thought, under the renewing power of the lure of the singular-universal; to re-explore thought, and to experiment with the abductive enactments that thinking-feeling might prime for. In the end, the impracticability of the singular-universal is in the service of this *pragmatism* of thinking-feeling in the act.

The lure for the logic of mutual inclusion is an image of thought: the image is of what Tarde called *universal variation*. Universal variation is the changeability of any and all bodies through their encounters with each other.[25] How they modulate each other, coming to be what they are by becoming together. How they are what they are relative to each other and the situations they collectively populate, and how this relativity is their truth: as Deleuze would say, not the relativity of truth, but the truth of relativity. In a word, relation: how the world is made of relation, how there is a primacy of relation. How the character, or manner, of relations qualify all. Universal variation is universal mannerism.

This idea was already suggested in the discussion of modal distinction. But with the singular-universal it is expanded to the horizon, and

25 Gabriel Tarde, "La variation universelle" (1895), in *Essais et mélanges sociologiques* (Paris: A. Maloine, 1895), chap. 11, http://classiques.uqac.ca/classiques/tarde _gabriel/essais_melanges_sociologiques/essais_melanges.html.

to all bodies, populations, situations, events it envelops—not to mention the distinctions of distinction discussed in this postscript. Modal distinction, real distinction, and umbral union are themselves reciprocals. The modal distinction that applied to the bodies expressing the potentials held in umbral union and conjugating their playing out into a dynamic unity effectively counting for one in real distinction also applies to modal distinction itself in its relation to real distinction and umbral union. "Modal" in a wider sense can be used to qualify the overall form of thought that the image of thought of the singular-universal beckons to. In other words, the process-oriented thinking advanced in this essay constitutes a *modal metaphysics*.[26]

The idea of the singular-universal idea is the attractor of process-oriented thinking. It polarizes the field of process thinking in a way that orients it toward certain kinds of result, while orienting it steadfastly away from being content with merely abstract general ideas.

Formal Distinction

Formal distinction, as construed here, is the province of the abstract general idea. It is the principle of separation between particulars. A particular is understood to be discrete: definitely bounded and occupying its own space in a way that enables it to stand over against any other particular. The principle of mutual exclusion is the guarantor of formal distinction. This is another name for the principle of identity: that something can only be itself, and no other. This excludes the constitutive ingress of the other discussed earlier. It excludes the integral witthess of relation as producing the terms in relation. It excludes the in-each-otherness of elements mutually modulating immanently to each other. It excludes resonance, the immediacy of the activity of the one being in the activity of the other in ways that are qualitatively transformative. It excludes everything a processual account needs to think complexity and becoming.

26 Sjoerd Van Tuinen, *The Philosophy of Mannerism: From Aesthetics to Modal Metaphysics* (London: Bloomsbury, 2023). "Modal" is being used here in a broader sense than its traditional use in logic as pertaining to judgments of necessity, contingency, and possibility.

The logic of mutual inclusion is ontogenetic: concerned foremost with becoming. Formal distinction is ontological: concerned foremost with being. It places a discrete, already-constituted being under a general category, identifying it as a particular case of that category. The general category is constructed as a classical set holding a number of members that exclusively belong to it according to a principle of resemblance. The operation of the logic of resemblance, and the way it subordinates difference to the same, was discussed at length above. It is not necessary to rehearse it here, except to say that the application of the general category to particulars covers the differences between them with the overlay of its own self-sameness (overcoding). There is no longer co-variation or in-variance. There is only under-variation: surreptitious variation under abstract cover of the general. The only differences that subsist between members of the category are on the level of negligible details that are too small to overpower their resemblance to the general standard and call in question their subsumption by it. These differences are treated negatively: as simple deviations from the standard category's norm. They are discarded; simply factored out. But don't these *undercover differences* of detail mark a uniqueness of the covered elements that tinges or inflects their particularity, making it singular in spite of it all? Formal distinction factors this singularity out as a matter of principle.

The principle of mutual exclusion operates according to a binary principle: this is not that. It elevates that contrast into an opposition: a standing apart the only alternative to which is a contradiction that would undermine the entire logic. Unless, that is, it is made into a virtue. When it is, it marks a shift into another logic: a dialectic. Dialectical thought begins with mutual exclusion and contradiction, but then tries to overcome them at the higher level of a supervenient synthesis. The synthesis is transcendent, occurring on the highest possible level of generality: totality (the absolutization of the same).

In process philosophical thinking and the logic of mutual inclusion, there is no totality. The world is of emergence, constitutively open. The ultimate is immanent to the self-renewing event of emergence. All wholes are open wholes: open to the ingress of the other, and through it to becoming. No whole is all-encompassing. This makes each whole a part of a larger whole: always more world around; excess of being.

Finally, every unity is composed out of and envelops ineradicable multiplicity. It is not just one world with more world around it, but many worlds in reciprocity, contrast, and superposition. The logic of mutual inclusion is pluriversal.

Duality without Dualism

It might be objected that this account has itself indulged liberally in duality, in spite of its protestations to the contrary. This charge is often leveled against Deleuze and Guattari. It betrays a misunderstanding of the modes of distinction mobilized by the logic of mutual inclusion practiced by process thinking.

Take "up" and "down." Go up far enough and you end up in space, where the difference is extinguished. Go down far enough and you end up in the earth's center of gravity, where again the difference is extinguished. "Up" and "down" are not binaries. They are limit-poles. Between the limits of their contrasting extinguishments, there is a polarized field. Any movement in that field will tend one way or the other. The limit-poles govern tendencies. As we have seen, it is of the nature of tendencies to come-together. The polarity positively produces a field of multiple tendencies. It governs a field of multiplicity, in which tendencies come-together to express their difference.

Not to mention the fact that up–down is nothing without its reciprocal polarity, right–left. The up–down dimension is meaningless without the horizontal dimension of right and left, without which there would be nothing to go up and down across. Up–down can only actually form a field in collaboration with left–right (a field of one axis is not a field, but a line, or at best a vector).

If taken to the limit, right and left are also self-extinguishing. Go right far enough and you circle around the earth and return from the left. Likewise for the cardinal directions. Go to the South Pole, and all directions are north. It is also of the nature of polarities to come-together and relay. Together, they compose fields of greater and greater dimensionality, which is to say, more and more degrees of freedom for tendencies to relay and relationally play themselves out.

The charge of binarism evaporates. Polarity is only apparently du-alist. In practice, it immediately invokes multiplicity. Duality reduces multiplicity to its lowest limit: from n to 2. Polarities produce the con-ditions for tendential complexity, their termini serving as pivot points for any number of movements to and relays through: from 2 to n. Their dualism self-extinguishes in the multiplicity they sustain. Duality, on the other hand, draws down to the minimum, in the face-off between just two, and leaves it there.

A polarity still has two terms, it is true. So it is senseless to deny that duality factors in in some capacity. But it's a processually capacitated duality, one that is in put in place only to cede immediately to multiplic-ity. It is a logical device leveraging multiplicity, for a logic of mutual inclusion. A duality without dualism.

Strategic Abstract Generalism

It is an unfortunate feature of the world that the logic of the abstract general idea is impossible to forgo completely. First, it is baked into common sense and the dominant functioning of the human world, so it is non-optional that all of us partake of it in order to get by. Second, it furnishes a shorthand that streamlines thought in useful ways, and no one can entirely escape the dictates of utility.

The problem arises when it is forgotten that the logic of the abstract general idea does not provide an adequate account of difference. It is constitutionally deficient with respect to difference, and as a conse-quence does not rise to the world's complexity. Its tendency, when put into practice, is toward the misplacing of import and the mis-taking of the relational nature of causality.

The problems become intractable when the overcoded particulars of the abstract general idea are misrecognized as the "concrete." They are in fact a certain kind of abstraction:[27] the product of a reductive appli-cation of a general resemblance that filters out the unique "details" in

---

27 This is Whitehead's fallacy of misplaced concreteness. Whitehead, *Science and the Modern World*, 51–52, 58.

which singularity reside. Their fit is loose.[28] Much escapes their comprehension. And it is onto those escapes that becoming latches. The abstract general idea is the Major, the Standard, disciplining the escape of the minor tendencies. The possibility of change hinges on these tendencies' potential for affirming their own differing difference so that it can play out relationally in its own right, out from under the constricting cover of the category. This is a reminder that the logical is political.

One of the most pressing reasons the logic of the abstract general idea is impossible to forgo completely is that it is politically applied. It is applied to bodies in order to ascribe them a particular social role. This normative application constitutes an oppression under whose weight many bodyings chafe and suffer. But since the power mechanisms instrumentalizing the abstract general idea know no other logic, to get their attention in order to resist them and press for reform, it is necessary to take on their own logic and turn it against their order as currently constituted.

This is the strategy of identity politics. It is practiced as a strategic necessity. But it becomes more than that when the particulars subsumed under the categories mistake that abstract general status for their concrete reality. This results in a form of endocolonization, where the logic of oppression becomes internal to the self-definition of those who resist it. This in turn results, unsurprisingly, in a war of exclusions and disciplining judgments of relative value (now in relation to an alter-standard of resistance) among members of the oppressed group or between groups that would seem to fall more to the "friend" than the "enemy" side of the divide. Cancel culture and trans-phobic feminism are contemporary examples. In terms of the foregoing account of fascisizing tendencies, such phenomena must be recognized as micro-fascisms.

28 Toward the beginning of his essay "The Conservation of Races," W. E. B. Du Bois critiques the concept of race on the basis of this looseness of fit that misses complexity and singularity (51–66). Nahum Chandler works with these passages to generate a powerful deconstruction of the concept of race that could be extrapolated to call into question all general categories of its kind. He takes up Du Bois's call for a logic of the "intermingling" of categories, moving in the direction of what is called "mutual inclusion" here. Chandler, "On Paragraph Four of 'The Conservation of the Races.'"

Even in the best-case scenario, when the strategic nature of the assumption of identity and the taking on board of the logic of the abstract general idea is kept in view, the strategy is still limited. It can serve for reform of the Standard, for example under the banner of human rights and constitutional rights. This kind of reform is a necessary act of self-defense aimed at relieving the violence of the Man-Standard. If practiced as an end in itself, however, it filters out the revolutionary potential of minor tendencies, and curtails the potential for change.

There is a need for a strategic duplicity: engaging as needed in identity-based reform politics as a palliative for the systemic violence affecting the lives of the oppressed, but also, and in the long run more importantly, as a way of carving out a greater margin of maneuver for minor tendencies, toward their revolutionary self-affirmation.

Minor tendencies are not to be confused with "minorities."[29] Minorities are particular sub-categories recognized, or vying for recognition, under the regime of the overarching general idea of the category of the human ("Man"; huMan). As such, they are ready-made constituencies for identity politics. They are vectors of systemic change only when they leak, affirm the escapes, and foster their multiplying and varying across qualitative transformations that potentially amplify and resonate throughout the social field.

It is then that they become harbingers of the anti-fascist life.

---

29   For a non-quantitative concept of minority, see Deleuze and Guattari, *Kafka*, 16–27; and Deleuze and Guattari, *Thousand Plateaus*, 469–73.

BIBLIOGRAPHY

Adorno, Theodor W. "Freudian Theory and the Pattern of Fascist Propaganda."
In *Psychoanalysis and the Social Sciences*, edited by Géza Róheim, vol. 3, 279–300.
Madison, CT: International Universities Press, 1951.

Adorno, Theodor W., Else Frenkel-Brunswik, Daniel J. Levinson, and R. Nevitt
Sanford. *The Authoritarian Personality*. New York: Norton, 1969.

Anti-Defamation League. "QAnon." September 24, 2020. https://www.adl.org
/resources/backgrounder/qanon.

Appelbaum, Yoni. "'I Alone Can Fix It.'" *Atlantic*, July 21, 2016. https://www
.theatlantic.com/politics/archive/2016/07/trump-rnc-speech-alone-fix-it/492557.

Arendt, Hannah. *The Origins of Totalitarianism*. 1951. Reprint, New York: Harcourt
Brace, 1973.

Associated Press. "Trump Baby Balloon Enters Museum of London Collection."
January 18, 2021. https://www.nbcnews.com/news/world/trump-baby-blimp
-enters-museum-london-collection-n1254594.

Bella, Timothy. "Who Is Andrew Tate, 'King of Toxic Masculinity,' Accused of Trafficking?" *Washington Post*, December 30, 2022. https://www.washingtonpost.com
/technology/2022/12/30/andrew-tate-explainer-arrested-greta-misogyny.

Beller, Jonathan. *The World Computer: Derivative Conditions of Racial Capitalism*. Durham,
NC: Duke University Press, 2021.

Bendix, Trish. "Jimmy Kimmel Responds to Reports He Caused a 'Trumper Tantrum.'" *New York Times*, February 28, 2023. https://www.nytimes.com/2023/02/28
/arts/television/jimmy-kimmel-trump.html.

Bennett, Bruce. "Trump's Body." *Sociological Review*, November 18, 2016. https://
thesociologicalreview.org/collections/2016-us-election/trumps-body.

Bennett, Jane. *Influx and Efflux: Writing Up with Walt Whitman*. Durham, NC: Duke
University Press, 2020.

Bergson, Henri. *Creative Evolution*. Translated by Arthur Miller. Mineola, NY: Dover,
1998.

Bergson, Henri. *The Creative Mind: An Introduction to Metaphysics*. Translated by Maybelle L. Andison. Mineola, NY: Dover, 2007.

Bergson, Henri. *The Two Sources of Religion and Morality*. Translated by R. Ashley
Audra, Cloudsley Brereton, and W. Horsefall Carter. London: Macmillan, 1935.

Blake, Aaron. "Study Shows Trump Is a Super-Spreader—of Coronavirus Misinformation." *Washington Post*, October 1, 2020. https://www.washingtonpost

.com/politics/2020/10/01/study-shows-trump-is-super-spreader-coronavirus
-misinformation.

Blanchot, Maurice. *The Infinite Conversation*. Translated by Susan Hanson. Minneapolis: University of Minnesota Press, 1993.

Blanchot, Maurice. *The Space of Literature*. Translated by Ann Smock. Lincoln: University of Nebraska Press, 1989.

Blee, Kathleen M. *Inside Organized Racism: Women in the Organized Hate Movement*. Berkeley: University of California Press, 2002.

Blee, Kathleen M. *Women of the Klan: Gender and Racism in the 1920s*. Berkeley: University of California Press, 2008.

Breslin, Maureen. "84% of Trump Voters Are Worried about Discrimination against Whites: Poll." *Hill*, August 10, 2021. https://thehill.com/homenews/news/575899-84 -percent-of-trump-voters-are-worried-about-discrimination-against-whites-poll.

Bump, Philip. "By a 3-to-1 Margin, Trump Supporters Embrace His Personality over His Policies." *Washington Post*, August 23, 2018. https://www.washingtonpost .com/news/politics/wp/2018/08/23/by-a-3-to-1-margin-trump-supporters -embrace-his-personality-over-his-policies.

Burke, Edmund. "On Taste," "On the Sublime and Beautiful," "Reflections on the French Revolution," "Letter to a Noble Lord." Harvard Classics. Edited by Charles W. Eliot. New York: P. F. Collier and Son, 1909.

Burns, Katelyn. "President Trump Briefly Drove by the 'Million MAGA March' on His Way to the Golf Course." *Vox*, November 14, 2020. https://www.vox.com /policy-and-politics/2020/11/14/21565197/trump-million-maga-march.

Calabresi, Steven G., and Christopher S. Yoo. *The Unitary Executive: Presidential Power from Washington to Bush*. New Haven, CT: Yale University Press, 2008.

Carnes, Nicholas, and Noam Lupu. "It's Time to Bust the Myth: Most Trump Voters Were Not Working Class." *Washington Post*, June 5, 2017. https://www .washingtonpost.com/news/monkey-cage/wp/2017/06/05/its-time-to-bust-the -myth-most-trump-voters-were-not-working-class.

Chandler, Nahum Dmitri. "On Paragraph Four of 'The Conservation of Races.'" *New Continental Review* 14, no. 3 (2014): 255–88.

Choski, Niraj. "Trump Voters Driven by Fear of Losing Status, Not Economic Anxiety, Study Finds." *New York Times*, April 24, 2018. https://www.nytimes.com/2018 /04/24/us/politics/trump-economic-anxiety.html.

Citton, Yves. *The Ecology of Attention*. London: Polity, 2017.

Combes, Muriel. *Gilbert Simondon and the Philosophy of the Transindividual*. Cambridge, MA: MIT Press, 2012.

Connolly, William E. *Aspirational Fascism: The Struggle for Multifaceted Democracy under Trumpism*. Minneapolis: University of Minnesota Press, 2017.

Connolly, William E. "Bodily Stresses, Cultural Drives, Fascist Contagions." *Theory and Event* 25, no. 3 (2022): 689–709.

Conway, Madeline. "Trump: 'Nobody Knew That Health Care Could Be So Complicated.'" *Politico*, February 27, 2017. https://www.politico.com/story/2017/02 /trump-nobody-knew-that-health-care-could-be-so-complicated-235436.

Cooper, Melinda. *Counterrevolution: Extravagance and Austerity in Public Finance.* New York: Zone, 2024.

Cramer, Ruth. "Trump Is 'Fascist to the Core,' Milley Says in Woodward Book." *Washington Post,* October 12, 2024. https://www.washingtonpost.com/nation /2024/10/12/mark-milley-donald-trump-fascist.

Dans, Paul, and Steven Grove, eds. *Mandate for Leadership: The Conservative Promise.* Project 2025. Presidential Transition Project. Washington, DC: Heritage Foundation, 2024. https://static.project2025.org/2025_MandateForLeadership_FULL.pdf.

Daughertym, Owen. "Poll: 62 Percent of Trump Fans Say They Support Him No Matter What." Hill, November 11, 2019. https://thehill.com/homenews/administration /469058-poll-62-of-trump-supporters-say-nothing-the-president-could-do-would.

Dawsey, Jack, and Michael Scherer. "Trump Jumps into a Divisive Battle over the Republican Party—with a Threat to Start a 'MAGA Party.'" *Washington Post,* January 23, 2021. https://www.washingtonpost.com/politics/trump-republican-split /2021/01/23/d7dc253e-5cbc-11eb-8bcf-3877871c819d_story.html.

Dean, Kenneth, and Brian Massumi. *First and Last Emperors: The Body of the Despot and the Absolute State.* New York: Autonomedia, 1992.

Debaise, Didier. "Une métaphysique des possessions: Puissances et sociétés chez G. Tarde." *Revue de métaphysique et de morale* 4 (2008): 447–60.

Deleuze, Gilles. *Cinema 2: The Time-Image.* Translated by Hugh Tomlinson and Robert Galeta. Minneapolis: University of Minnesota Press, 1989.

Deleuze, Gilles. *Difference and Repetition.* Translated by Paul Patton. New York: Columbia University Press, 1994.

Deleuze, Gilles. *Expressionism in Philosophy: Spinoza.* Translated by Martin Joughlin. New York: Zone, 1992.

Deleuze, Gilles. *The Fold: Leibniz and the Baroque.* Translated by Tom Conley. Minneapolis: University of Minnesota Press, 1993.

Deleuze, Gilles. *Foucault.* Translated by Séan Hand. Minneapolis: University of Minnesota Press, 1988.

Deleuze, Gilles. *The Logic of Sense.* Edited by Constantin V. Boundas; translated by Mark Lester with Charles Stivale. New York: Columbia University Press, 1990.

Deleuze, Gilles. *Negotiations.* Translated by Martin Joughin. New York: Columbia University Press, 1995.

Deleuze, Gilles. *Nietzsche and Philosophy.* Translated by Hugh Tomlinson. New York: Columbia University Press, 2006.

Deleuze, Gilles, and Michel Foucault. *Desert Islands and Other Texts, 1953–1974.* Edited by David Lapoujade; translated by Michael Teomina. New York: Semiotext(e), 2004.

Deleuze, Gilles, and Félix Guattari. *Anti-Oedipus: Capitalism and Schizophrenia.* Translated by Robert Hurley, Mark Seem, and Helen R. Lane. Minneapolis: University of Minnesota Press, 1983.

Deleuze, Gilles, and Félix Guattari. "Balance-Sheet Program for Desiring-Machines." Translated by Robert Hurley. In "Anti-Oedipus," special issue, *Semiotext(e)* 2, no. 5 (1977): 117–35. Originally published as an appendix to the second edition of the French original of *Anti-Oedipus.*

Deleuze, Gilles, and Félix Guattari. *Kafka: Toward a Minor Literature*. Translated by Dana Polan. Minneapolis: University of Minnesota Press, 1986.

Deleuze, Gilles, and Félix Guattari. *A Thousand Plateaus*. Translated by Brian Massumi. Minneapolis: University of Minnesota Press, 1987.

Deleuze, Gilles, and Félix Guattari. *What Is Philosophy?* Translated by Hugh Tomlinson and Graham Burchill. New York: Columbia University Press, 1994.

Denby, David. "The Three Faces of Trump." *New Yorker*, August 12, 2015. https://www.newyorker.com/culture/cultural-comment/the-three-faces-of-trump.

Diamond, Jeremy. "Trump's Doctor: Trump 'Will Be Healthiest Individual Ever Elected' President." CNN, December 14, 2015. https://www.cnn.com/2015/12/14/politics/donald-trump-medical-bill-health/index.html.

Diawara, Manthia, and Édouard Glissant. "Conversation with Édouard Glissant Aboard the Queen Mary II." August 2009. https://www.liverpool.ac.uk.

Dolphijn, Rick, and Rosi Braidotti, eds. *Deleuze and Guattari and Fascism*. Edinburgh: Edinburgh University Press, 2022.

Draper, Robert. "A Republican Platform That Could Read Like a Trump Rally." *Washington Post*, July 8, 2024. https://www.nytimes.com/2024/07/08/us/politics/trump-republican-platform.html.

Du Bois, W. E. B. *The Conservation of Races*. In *The Problem of the Color Line at the Turn of the Twentieth Century: The Essential Early Essays*, compiled and edited by Nahum Dimitri Chandler. New York: Fordham University Press, 2015.

Du Bois, W. E. B. *The Souls of Black Folk*. Introduction by Henry Louis Gates Jr. New York: Bantam, 1989.

Duffy, Simon. *The Logic of Expression: Quality, Quantity and Intensity in Spinoza, Hegel and Deleuze*. Farnham, UK: Ashgate, 2006.

Dwoskin, Elisabeth, and Craig Timberg. "The Unseen Machine Pushing Trump's Social Media Megaphone into Overdrive." *Washington Post*, October 30, 2020. https://www.washingtonpost.com/technology/2020/10/30/trump-twitter-domestic-disinformation.

Eco, Umberto. "Ur-Fascism" (1995). In *How to Spot a Fascist*. New York: Vintage, 2020. Ebook.

Economist. "Who Is Andrew Tate, the Misogynist Hero to Millions of Young Men?" *Economist*, December 30, 2022. https://www.economist.com/the-economist-explains/2022/12/30/who-is-andrew-tate-the-misogynist-hero-to-millions-of-young-men.

Esposito, Roberto. *Third Person: Politics of Life and Philosophy of the Impersonal*. Translated by Zakiya Hanafi. Cambridge: Polity, 2012.

Ettinger, Bracha L. *The Matrixial Borderspace*. Edited and with an afterword by Brian Massumi; foreword by Judith Butler; introduction by Griselda Pollack. Minneapolis: University of Minnesota Press, 2006.

Evans, Brad, and Julian Reid, eds. *Deleuze and Fascism: Security, War, Aesthetics*. London: Routledge, 2014.

Fenster, Mark. *Conspiracy Theories: Secrecy and Power in American Culture*. 2nd ed. Minneapolis: University of Minnesota Press, 2008.

Ferreira da Silva, Denise. "Towards a Black Feminist Poethics." *Black Scholar* 44, no. 2 (2015): 81–97.

Foucault, Michel. *The Archaeology of Knowledge.* Translated by A. M. Sheridan Smith. London: Routledge, 1989.

Foucault, Michel. *The Birth of Biopolitics: Lectures at the Collège de France, 1978–1979.* Translated by Graham Burchell. New York: Palgrave Macmillan, 2008.

Foucault, Michel. *Discipline and Punish: The Birth of the Prison.* Translated by Alan Sheridan. New York: Vintage, 1979.

Foucault, Michel. *Security, Territory, Population: Lectures at the Collège de France, 1977–1978.* Edited by Michel Snellart; translated by Graham Burchell. New York: Palgrave Macmillan, 2007.

Frenkel, Sheera, and Alan Feuer. "'A Total Failure': The Proud Boys Now Mock Trump.'" *New York Times*, January 20, 2021. https://www.nytimes.com/2021/01/20/technology/proud-boys-trump.html.

Gabriel, Trip. "Trump Escalates Anti-immigrant Rhetoric with 'Poisoning the Blood' Comment." *New York Times*, October 5, 2023. https://www.nytimes.com/2023/10/05/us/politics/trump-immigration-rhetoric.html.

Gangle, Rocco. *Diagrammatic Immanence: Category Theory and Philosophy.* Edinburgh: Edinburgh University Press, 2016.

Garfinkle, Madeline. "Gen Z's Main Career Aspiration Is to Be an Influencer, according to a New Report." *Entrepreneur*, September 20, 2023.

Gartenstein-Ross, Daveed, and Madeleine Blackman. "Fluidity of the Fringes: Prior Extremist Involvement as a Radicalization Pathway." *Studies in Conflict and Terrorism* 45, no. 7 (2018): 555–78.

Gedeon, Joseph. "'Trump Is a Messianic Figure in the QAnon Calls': Trump's Embrace of the Conspiracy Theory Is Growing Stronger." *Politico*, September 23, 2022. https://www.politico.com/news/magazine/2022/09/23/trump-is-a-messianic-figure-in-the-qanon-calls-00058671.

Genosko, Gary. "Black Holes of Politics: Resonances of Microfascism." *La Deleuziana*, no. 5 (2017). http://www.ladeleuziana.org/wp-content/uploads/2017/12/04-en-Genosko-Resonance_MicroFascism.pdf.

Gerson, Michael. "Trump's Rhetorical Schizophrenia Is Easy to See Through." *Washington Post*, August 24, 2017. https://www.washingtonpost.com/opinions/trumps-rhetorical-schizophrenia-is-easy-to-see-through/2017/08/24/2163ab42-88f3-11e7-a50f-e0d4e6ec070a_story.html.

Gil, José. *Metamorphoses of the Body.* Translated by Stephen Muecke. Minneapolis: University of Minnesota Press, 1998.

Gilmore, Ruth Wilson. *Abolition Geography: Essays toward Liberation.* Edited by Brenna Bandar and Alberto Toscano. London: Verso, 2022.

Ging, Debbie. "Alphas, Betas, and Incels: Theorizing the Masculinities of the Manosphere." *Men and Masculinities* 22, no. 4 (2019): 638–57.

Glissant, Édouard. *Poetics of Relation.* Translated by Betsy Wing. Ann Arbor: University of Minnesota Press, 1997.

Gowen, Annie. "An Ex-Professor Spreads Election Myths across the United States, One Town at a Time." *Washington Post*, September 8, 2022. https://www .washingtonpost.com/elections/2022/09/08/an-ex-professor-spreads-election -myths-across-us-one-town-time.

Guattari, Félix. *Chaosmosis: An Ethico-Aesthetic Paradigm*. Translated by Paul Bains and Julian Pefanis. Bloomington: Indiana University Press, 1995.

Guattari, Félix. "Everybody Wants to Be a Fascist." In *Chaosophy*, edited by Sylvère Lotringer, 225–50. New York: Semiotexte, 1995.

Guattari, Félix. *The Machinic Unconscious: Essays in Schizoanalysis*. Translated by Taylor Adkins. New York: Semiotext(e), 2011.

Guattari, Félix. "The Micro-politics of Fascism." In *Molecular Revolution: Psychiatry and Politics*, translated by Rosemary Sheed. New York: Penguin, 1984.

Guattari, Félix. *Schizoanalytic Cartographies*. Translated by Andrew Goffey. London: Bloomsbury, 2013.

Guattari, Félix, and Antonio Negri. *New Lines of Alliance, New Spaces of Liberty*. Translated by Michael Ryan, Jared Becker, Araine Bove, and Noel LeBlanc. London: Minor Compositions; New York: Autonomedia, 1990. Originally published as *Communists like Us*. Translated by Michael Ryan. New York: Semiotext(e).

Haberman, Maggie, Glenn Thrush, and Peter Baker. "Inside Trump's Hour-by-Hour Battle for Self-Preservation." *New York Times*, December 9, 2017. https://www .nytimes.com/2017/12/09/us/politics/donald-trump-president.html.

Harney, Stefano, and Fred Moten. *The Undercommons: Fugitive Planning and Black Study*. London: Minor Compositions, 2013.

Harwell, Drew. "QAnon Believers Seek to Adapt Their Extremist Ideology for a New Era: 'Things Have Just Started.'" *Washington Post*, January 21, 2021. https://www .washingtonpost.com/technology/2021/01/21/qanon-faithful-biden-trump.

Harwell, Drew, Michelle Boorstein, and Josh Dawsey. "Trump's Close Call in Assassination Attempt Fuels Talk He Was 'Chosen' by God." *Washington Post*, July 16, 2024, https://www.washingtonpost.com/nation/2024/07/16/trump-religion-messiah.

Helderman, Rosalind S., Josh Dawsey, Ashley Parker, and Jacqueline Alemany. "How Trump Jettisoned Restraints at Mar-a-Lago and Prompted Legal Peril." *Washington Post*, December 18, 2022. https://www.washingtonpost.com/national -security/2022/12/18/trump-life-after-presidency.

Hesse, Monica. "Trumpist Masculinity Reaches Its High Water Mark." *Washington Post*, January 12, 2021. https://www.washingtonpost.com/lifestyle/style/capitol -riot-zip-tie-guy-men-trump-masculinity/2021/01/12/486a516e-5447-11eb-a08b -f1381ef3d207_story.html.

Hesse, Monica. "The Weird Masculinity of Donald Trump." *Washington Post*, July 16, 2020. https://www.washingtonpost.com/lifestyle/style/the-weird-masculinity-of -donald-trump/2020/07/15/0dfe3854-c43e-11ea-b037-f9711f89ee46_story.html.

Hobbes, Thomas. *Leviathan*. Rev. student ed. Edited by Richard Tuck. Cambridge: Cambridge University Press, 1996.

Hofstadter, Richard. *The Paranoid Style in American Politics and Other Essays*. 1963. Reprint, Cambridge, MA: Harvard University Press, 1996.

Holmes, Kristen. "Trump Calls for the Termination of the Constitution in Truth Social Post." CNN, December 4, 2022. https://www.cnn.com/2022/12/03/politics /trump-constitution-truth-social/index.html.

Hume, David. A Treatise on Human Nature. Vol. 1, Text. Edited by David Fate Norton and Mary J. Norton. Clarendon Hume ed. Oxford: Oxford University Press, 2011.

Jackson, David. "Donald Trump Defends Speech as 'Totally Appropriate,' Won't Take Responsibility for Deadly Capitol Riot." USA Today, January 12, 2021. https://www.usatoday.com/story/news/politics/2021/01/12/donald-trump -refuses-take-responsibility-attack-u-s-capitol/6636699002.

Jackson, Zakiyyah Iman. Becoming Human:Matter and Meaning in an Antiblack World. New York: New York University Press, 2020.

Jaffe, Alexandra. "Kellyanne Conway WH Spokesman Gave 'Alternative Facts' on Inauguration Crowd." NBC News, January 17, 2017. https://www.nbcnews .com/storyline/meet-the-press-70-years/wh-spokesman-gave-alternative-facts -inauguration-crowd-n710466.

James, William. Essays in Radical Empiricism. Lincoln: University of Nebraska Press, 1996.

James, William. A Pluralistic Universe. Lincoln: University of Nebraska Press, 1996.

James, William. The Principles of Psychology. Vol. 1. Mineola, NY: Dover, 1950.

Jamieson, Amber. "President Trump Parrots Fox News Again with Attack on Chelsea Manning." Guardian, January 26, 2017. https://www.theguardian.com/us -news/2017/jan/26/donald-trump-chelsea-manning-traitor-fox-news.

Kagan, Robert. "A Trump Dictatorship Is Increasingly Inevitable. We Should Stop Pretending." Washington Post, November 30, 2023. https://www.washingtonpost .com/opinions/2023/11/30/trump-dictator-2024-election-robert-kagan.

Kantorowicz, Ernst H. The King's Two Bodies: A Study in Medieval Political Theory. Princeton, NJ: Princeton University Press, 2016.

Keefe, Patrick Radden. "How Mark Burnett Resurrected Trump as an Icon of American Success." New Yorker, January 7, 2019. https://www.newyorker.com /magazine/2019/01/07/how-mark-burnett-resurrected-donald-trump-as-an-icon -of-american-success.

Kennecott, Philip. "Trump NFTs Are Not Art. Unless You Consider Grifting an Art Form. These $99 Trading Cards Are Laughably Bad. That's the Whole Point." Washington Post, December 17, 2022. https://www.washingtonpost.com/arts -entertainment/2022/12/17/trump-trading-card-nft-art.

Kessler, Glenn, Salvador Rizzo, and Meg Kelly. "Trump's False or Misleading Claims Total 30,573 over 4 Years." Washington Post, January 24, 2021. https://www .washingtonpost.com/politics/2021/01/24/trumps-false-or-misleading-claims -total-30573-over-four-years.

Klion, David, and Corey Robin. "Almost the Complete Opposite of Fascism: Interview with Corey Robin." Jewish Currents, December 4, 2020. https:// jewishcurrents.org/almost-the-complete-opposite-of-fascism.

Kornfield, Meryl. "Jewish Florida Lawmaker Breaks from DeSantis and Endorses Trump." Washington Post, October 24, 2023. https://www.washingtonpost.com /politics/2023/10/24/randy-fine-desantis-ally-endorses-trump.

Kuipers, Halbe. "Perspectives and Event: A Study on Modes of Existence and the More-Than-Human; Perspectivism and Process Philosophy." PhD diss., University of Amsterdam, 2022.

Lamarre, Thomas. *The Anime Ecology: A Genealogy of Television, Animation, and Game Media*. Minneapolis: University of Minnesota Press, 2018.

Lamoureux, Mark, and David Gilbert. "QAnon Is Dead. Long Live QAnon." *Vice*, November 15, 2022. https://www.vice.com/en/article/wxnkzq/qanon-q-drop -midterms.

Langer, Susanne. *Feeling and Form: A Theory of Art*. New York: Scribner's, 1953.

Langer, Susanne. *Mind: An Essay on Human Feeling*. Vol. 1. Baltimore: Johns Hopkins University Press, 1967.

Langer, Susanne. *Philosophy in a New Key: A Study in the Symbolism of Reason, Rite, and Art*. New York: New American Library, 1948.

Lapoujade, David. *William James: Empiricism and Subjectivity*. Translated and with an afterword by Thomas Lamarre. Durham, NC: Duke University Press, 2020.

Lazzarato, Maurizio. *Signs and Machines: Capitalism and the Production of Subjectivity*. Translated by Joshua David Jordan. New York: Semiotext(e), 2014.

Lee, Benjamin, and Randy Martin, eds. *Derivatives and the Wealth of Societies*. Chicago: University of Chicago Press, 2016.

Le Guin, Ursula. "Introducing Myself." In *The Wave in the Mind: Talks and Essays on the Writer, the Reader, and the Imagination*, 3–7. Boulder, CO: Shambhala, 2004.

Leibovich, Mark. "When Joe Biden's in Town, but It's Hard to Know." *New York Times*, September 22, 2020. https://www.nytimes.com/2020/09/22/us/politics/joe -biden-campaign.html.

Lepselter, Susan. "The License: Poetics, Power, and the Uncanny." In *E.T. Culture*, edited by Debbora Battaglia, 131–47. Durham, NC: Duke University Press, 2005.

Lepselter, Susan. *The Resonance of Unseen Things: Poetics, Power, Captivity, and UFOs in the American Uncanny*. Ann Arbor: University of Michigan Press, 2016.

LeVine, Marianne. "Trump Calls Political Enemies 'Vermin,' Echoing Dictators Hitler, Mussolini." *Washington Post*, November 13, 2023. https://www.washingtonpost .com/politics/2023/11/12/trump-rally-vermin-political-opponents.

Link, Taylor. "White House Defends Trump's Claim That He Witnessed the Devastation of Hurricane Harvey 'First Hand.'" *Salon*, August 31, 2017. http://www .salon.com/2017/08/31/white-house-defends-trumps-claim-that-he-witnessed -the-devastation-of-hurricane-harvey-first-hand.

Lorde, Audre. "The Master's Tools Will Never Dismantle the Master's House" (1984). In *Sister Outsider: Essays and Speeches*, 110–14. Berkeley, CA: Crossing, 2007.

Manning, Erin. *For a Pragmatics of the Useless*. Durham, NC: Duke University Press, 2020.

Manning, Erin. *The Minor Gesture*. Durham, NC: Duke University Press, 2016.

Manning, Erin. *Politics of Touch: Sense, Movement, Sovereignty*. Minneapolis: University of Minnesota Press, 2007.

Manning, Erin. *Relationscapes: Movement, Art, Philosophy*. Cambridge, MA: MIT Press, 2009.

Manning, Erin, and Brian Massumi. *Thought in the Act: Passages in the Ecology of Experience*. Minneapolis: University of Minnesota Press, 2014.

Manning, Erin, Anna Munster, and Bodil Marie Stavning Thomsen, eds. *Immediation*. 2 vols. London: Open Humanities, 2019.

Marasco, Robyn. "Reconsidering the Sexual Politics of Fascism." *Historical Materialism*, June 25, 2021. https://www.historicalmaterialism.org/blog/reconsidering-sexual-politics-fascism.

Marcuse, Herbert. "State and Individual under National Socialism." In *Technology, War and Fascism: Collected Papers of Herbert Marcuse*, vol. 1, 67–89. New York: Routledge, 1998.

Marcuse, Herbert. "The Struggle against Liberalism in the Totalitarian View of the State." In *Negations: Essays in Critical Theory*, 1–30. London: Mayfly, 2009.

Massumi, Brian. "Aesthetic Frights and the Politics of Unspeakable Thought." In *The Bloomsbury Handbook of Susanne K. Langer*, edited by Lona Gaikis, 285–305. London: Bloomsbury, 2023.

Massumi, Brian. *Architectures of the Unforeseen: Essays in the Occurrent Art*. Minneapolis: University of Minnesota Press, 2019.

Massumi, Brian. *Couplets*. Durham, NC: Duke University Press, 2021.

Massumi, Brian. *99 Theses for the Revaluation of Value: A Postcapitalist Manifesto*. Minneapolis: University of Minnesota Press, 2018.

Massumi, Brian. *Ontopower: War, Powers, and the State of Perception*. Durham, NC: Duke University Press, 2015.

Massumi, Brian. *Parables for the Virtual: Movement, Affect, Sensation*. 20th anniversary ed. Durham, NC: Duke University Press, 2021.

Massumi, Brian. *The Power at the End of the Economy*. Durham, NC: Duke University Press, 2015.

Massumi, Brian. *The Principle of Unrest: Activist Philosophy in the Expanded Field*. London: Open Humanities, 2017.

Massumi, Brian. *Semblance and Event: Activist Philosophy and the Occurrent Arts*. Cambridge, MA: MIT Press, 2011.

Massumi, Brian. "Such as It Is: A Short Essay on Extreme Realism." *Body and Society* 22, no. 1 (2016): 115–27.

Massumi, Brian. *A User's Guide to "Capitalism and Schizophrenia": Deviations from Deleuze and Guattari*. Cambridge, MA: MIT Press, 1992.

Massumi, Brian. "Virtual Ecology and the Question of Value." In *General Ecology: The New Ecological Paradigm*, edited by Erich Hörl, 345–73. London: Bloomsbury, 2017.

Massumi, Brian. *What Animals Teach Us about Politics*. Durham, NC: Duke University Press, 2014.

McCarthy, Tom. "'I Am the Chosen One': With Boasts and Insults, Trump Sets New Benchmark for Incoherence." *Guardian*, August 21, 2018. https://www.theguardian.com/us-news/2019/aug/21/trump-press-conference-greenland-jewish-democrats.

Melamed, Jodi. "Racial Capitalism." *Critical Ethnic Studies* 1, no. 1 (Spring 2015): 76–85.

Menn, Joseph. "Surging Twitter Antisemitism Unites Fringe, Encourages Violence, Officials Say." *Washington Post*, December 3, 2022. https://www.washingtonpost.com/technology/2022/12/03/twitter-antisemitism-violence-jan-6.

Mercia, Dan. "Dr. Ronny Jackson's Glowing Bill of Health for Trump." CNN, January 16, 2018. https://www.cnn.com/2018/01/16/politics/dr-ronny-jackson-donald-trump-clean-bill-of-health/index.html.

Meyers, Ethan. "Trump's Return to Rally Stage Met with Prayers, Excitement and Confusion over JD Vance." *Guardian*, July 20, 2024, https://www.theguardian.com/us-news/article/2024/jul/20/trump-vance-michigan-rally.

Mezzadra, Sandro, and Brett Neilson. *The Politics of Operations: Excavating Contemporary Capitalism*. Durham, NC: Duke University Press, 2019.

Milbank, Dana. "Lincoln Was a Republican, Slavery Is Bad—and More Discoveries by President Obvious." *Washington Post*, March 22, 2017. https://www.washingtonpost.com/opinions/lincoln-was-a-republican-slavery-is-bad—and-more-discoveries-by-president-obvious/2017/03/22/3360c622-0f2c-11e7-9b0d-d27c98455440_story.html.

Miranda, Gabriel. "2 in 5 Americans Believe Ghosts Are Real and 1 in 5 Say They've Seen One, Survey Says." *USA Today*, October 28, 2021. https://www.usatoday.com/story/news/nation/2021/10/28/do-ghosts-exist-41-percent-americans-say-yes/8580577002.

Moten, Fred. *Consent Not to Be a Single Being*. Vol. 1, *Black and Blur*. Durham, NC: Duke University Press, 2017.

Muirhead, Russell, and Nancy L. Rosenblum. *A Lot of People Are Saying: The New Conspiracism and the Assault on Democracy*. Princeton, NJ: Princeton University Press, 2019.

Nayazunissa. "Prices of Donald Trump's NFT Collection Plummet More Than 70%." *TheNewsCrypto*, December 26, 2022. https://thenewscrypto.com/prices-of-donald-trumps-nft-collection-plummet-more-than-70.

Nazaryan, Alexander. "What If the Chaos Is Strategic?" *Atlantic*, June 18, 2019. https://www.theatlantic.com/ideas/archive/2019/06/chaos-works/591688.

Nietzsche, Friedrich. *The Gay Science*. Edited by Bernard Williams; translated by Josefine Nauckhoff and Adrian Del Caro. Cambridge: Cambridge University Press, 2001.

Nietzsche, Friedrich. *Nietzsche: "The Anti-Christ," "Ecce Homo," "Twilight of the Idols," and Other Writings*. Edited by Aaron Ridley; translated by Judith Norman. Cambridge: Cambridge University Press, 2005.

Nietzsche, Friedrich. *Writings from the Late Notebooks*. Edited by Rudiger Bittner; translated by Kate Sturge. Cambridge: Cambridge University Press, 2003.

O'Brien, Timothy L. "How Much Is Trump Worth? Depends on How He Feels." *Newsweek*, October 19, 2015. https://www.newsweek.com/how-much-trump-worth-depends-how-he-feels-384720.

Oprysky, Caitlin. "'I Don't Take Responsibility at All': Trump Deflects Blame for Coronavirus Testing Fumble." *Politico*, March 13, 2020. https://www.politico.com/news/2020/03/13/trump-coronavirus-testing-128971.

Oxenden, McKenna, and Jenny Gross. "Andrew Tate Is Charged with Human Trafficking and Rape in Romania." *New York Times*, December 30, 2022. https://www.nytimes.com/2022/12/30/world/europe/andrew-tate-romania-arrest.html.

Parker, Ashley. "New Book Portrays Trump as Erratic, 'At Times Dangerously Uninformed.'" *Washington Post*, January 15, 2020. https://www.washingtonpost.com/politics/new-book-portrays-trump-as-erratic-at-times-dangerously-uninformed/2020/01/15/4d45bf44-370f-11ea-a01d-b7cc8ec1a85d_story.html.

Peirce, C. S. *The Essential Peirce: Selected Philosophical Writings*. Vol. 1. Bloomington: Indiana University Press, 1992.

Peirce, C. S. *The Essential Peirce: Selected Philosophical Writings*. Vol. 2. Bloomington: University of Indiana Press, 1998.

Peirce, C. S. *Pragmatism as a Principle and Method of Right Thinking: The 1903 Lectures on Pragmatism*. Albany: State University of New York Press, 1997.

Pengelly, Martin. "[Secretary of Energy] Rick Perry Tells Donald Trump: 'You Really Are the Chosen One." *Guardian*, November 25, 2019. https://www.theguardian.com/us-news/2019/nov/25/rick-perry-donald-trump-chosen-one.

Posner, Sarah. "White Evangelicals Think Trump Is Divinely Ordained. He'll Do Almost Anything to Keep It That Way." *Los Angeles Times*, June 14, 2020. https://www.latimes.com/opinion/story/2020-06-14/donald-trump-st-johns-church-white-evangelicals-campaign-2020-pandemic-protest.

Raunig, Gerald. *Dividuum: Machinic Capitalism and Molecular Revolution*. Vol. 1. Translated by Aileen Derieg. New York: Semiotext(e), 2016.

Ravaisson, Félix. *Of Habit*. Translated by Clare Carlisle and Mark Sinclair. Preface by Catherine Malabou. London: Continuum, 2008.

Reagan, Ronald. "How to Stay Fit." *Parade Magazine*, December 4, 1983, 4–6.

Reagan, Ronald, and Richard B. Hubler. *Where Is the Rest of Me?* 1965. Reprint, New York: Karz, 1981.

Rettner, Rachael. "Trump Thinks That Exercising Too Much Uses Up the Body's 'Finite' Energy." *Washington Post*, May 14, 2017. https://www.washingtonpost.com/national/health-science/trump-thinks-that-exercising-too-much-uses-up-the-bodys-finite-energy/2017/05/12/bb0b9bda-365d-11e7-b4ee-434b6d506b37_story.html.

Robin, Corey. *The Reactionary Mind: Conservatism from Edmund Burke to Donald Trump*. 2nd ed. Oxford: Oxford University Press, 2018.

Robinson, Cedric J. *Black Marxism: The Making of the Black Radical Tradition*. 2nd ed. Chapel Hill: University of North Carolina Press, 2000.

Ronayne, Kathleen, and Michael Kunzelman. "Trump to Far-Right Extremists: 'Stand Back and Stand By.'" AP News, September 30, 2020. https://apnews.com/article/election-2020-joe-biden-race-and-ethnicity-donald-trump-chris-wallace-0b32339da25fbc9e8b7c7c7066a1dbof.

Rothschild, Mike. *The Storm Is upon Us: How QAnon Became a Movement, Cult, and Conspiracy Theory of Everything*. New York: Melville House, 2021.

Rucker, Philip. "Trump's Whiplash: Three Personas in Three Speeches, but the Same President." *Washington Post*, August 23, 2017. https://www.washingtonpost

.com/politics/trumps-whiplash-three-roles-in-three-speeches-but-the-same
-president/2017/08/23/bb3c4602-881c-11e7-a94f-3139abce39f5_story.html.

Rucker, Philip, and Robert Costa. "Commander of Confusion: Trump Sows Uncertainty and Seeks to Cast Blame in Coronavirus Crisis." *Washington Post*, April 2, 2020. https://www.washingtonpost.com/politics/commander-of-confusion -trump-sows-uncertainty-and-seeks-to-cast-blame-in-coronavirus-crisis/2020 /04/02/fc2db084-7431-11ea-85cb-8670579b863d_story.html.

Rucker, Philip, and Felicia Sonmez. "Trump Defends Bungled Handling of Coronavirus with Falsehoods and Dubious Claims." *Washington Post*, July 19, 2020. https://www.washingtonpost.com/politics/trump-defends-bungled-handling -of-coronavirus-with-falsehoods-and-dubious-claims/2020/07/19/1b57cb3e-c9e6 -11ea-91f1-28aca4d833a0_story.html.

Ruyer, Raymond. *Neofinalism*. Translated by Alyosha Edlebi. Minneapolis: University of Minnesota Press, 2016.

Saad, Lydia. "Do Americans Believe in UFOs?" Gallup News, August 20, 2002. https://news.gallup.com/poll/350096/americans-believe-ufos.aspx.

Sargent, Greg. "New Revelations Just Wrecked Trump's Last Remaining Defenses." *Washington Post*, November 27, 2019. https://www.washingtonpost .com/opinions/2019/11/27/new-revelations-just-wrecked-trumps-last -remaining-defenses.

Scherer, Michael, and Josh Dawsey. "Books, Speeches, Hats for Sale: Post-presidency, the Trumps Try to Make Money the Pre-presidency Way." *Washington Post*, January 28, 2022. https://www.washingtonpost.com/politics/trump-money -businesses/2022/01/27.

Schmidt, Samantha. "'Make America Big Again'? The Headache of Translating Trump into Foreign Languages." *Washington Post*, January 23, 2017. https://www .washingtonpost.com/news/morning-mix/wp/2017/01/23/make-america-big -again-the-headache-of-translating-trump-into-foreign-languages.

Schmitt, Carl. *The Concept of the Political*. Expanded ed. Translated by George Schwab. Chicago: University of Chicago Press, 2007.

Schmitt, Carl. *Political Theology: Four Chapters on the Concept of Sovereignty*. Edited by George Schwab. Chicago: University of Chicago Press, 2006.

Scott, Eugene, and Josh Dawsey. "Trump Criticized for Dining with Far-Right Activist Nick Fuentes and Rapper Ye." *Washington Post*, November 25, 2022. https:// www.washingtonpost.com/politics/2022/11/25/trump-fuentes-ye.

Sherman, Gabriel. "Ron DeSantis: The Making and Remaking (and Remaking) of a MAGA Heir." *Vanity Fair*, September 27, 2022. https://www.vanityfair.com/news /2022/09/ron-desantis-the-making-and-remaking-of-a-maga-heir.

Simondon, Gilbert. *Individuation in Light of Notions of Form and Information*. Minneapolis: University of Minnesota Press, 2020.

Simondon, Gilbert. *The Mode of Existence of the Technical Object*. Translated by Cécile Malaspina and John Rogove. Minneapolis: Univocal / University of Minnesota Press, 2017.

Singh, Swaran. "Rise and Fall of the PLA's Business Empire: Implications for China's Civil-Military Relations." *Strategic Analysis* 23, no. 2 (1999): 227–39.

Smith, David. "'Executive Time': How, Exactly, Does Trump Spend 60% of His Day?" *Guardian*, February 7, 2019. https://www.theguardian.com/us-news/2019 /feb/07/executive-time-donald-trump-white-house.

Sommerlad, Joe. "Ivana Claims Trump Keeps Hitler Quotes by Bed in Resurfaced Interview." *Independent*, December 19, 2023. https://www.independent.co.uk /news/world/americas/us-politics/trump-hitler-speeches-ivana-poisoning-blood -b2466500.html.

Spinoza, Baruch. *The Ethics*. In *The Complete Works of Spinoza*, edited and translated by Edwin Curley, vol. 1, 408–617. Princeton, NJ: Princeton University Press, 1985.

Stern, Daniel. *The Interpersonal World of the Infant*. New York: Basic Books, 1985.

Strathern, Marilyn. *The Gender of the Gift: Problems with Women and Problems with Society in Melanesia*. Berkeley: University of California Press, 1988.

Struyk, Ryan. "6 in 10 People Who Approve of Trump Say They'll Never, Ever, Ever Stop Approving." CNN, August 17, 2017. https://www.cnn.com/2017/08/17 /politics/trump-approvers-never-stop-approving-poll/index.html.

Suliman, Adela. "Trump Fined Nearly $1M for 'Revenge' Lawsuit against Hillary Clinton, Others." *Washington Post*, January 20, 2023. https://www .washingtonpost.com/politics/2023/01/20/donald-trump-fine-court-clinton.

Swan, Jonathan, and Maggie Haberman. "Why a Second Trump Presidency May Be More Radical Than His First." *New York Times*, December 4, 2023. https://www .nytimes.com/2023/12/04/us/politics/trump-2025-overview.html.

Swan, Jonathan, Charlie Savage, and Maggie Haberman. "Trump and Allies Forge Plans to Increase Presidential Power in 2025." *New York Times*, July 17, 2023. https://www.nytimes.com/2023/07/17/us/politics/trump-plans-2025.html.

Tarde, Gabriel. "La croyance et le désir" (1880). In *Essais et mélanges sociologiques*, chap. 9. Paris: A. Maloine, 1895. http://classiques.uqac.ca/classiques/tarde _gabriel/essais_melanges_sociologiques/essais_melanges.html.

Tarde, Gabriel. *Les lois de l'imitation*. 2nd ed. Paris: Kimé, 1993. http://classiques.uqac .ca/classiques/tarde_gabriel/lois_imitation/lois_imitation.html.

Tarde, Gabriel. *Maine de Biran et l'évolutionnisme*. Paris: Les empêcheurs de penser en rond, 2000.

Tarde, Gabriel. "Monadologie et sociologie" (1893). In *Essais et mélanges sociologiques*, chap. 10. Paris: A. Maloine, 1895. http://classiques.uqac.ca/classiques/tarde _gabriel/essais_melanges_sociologiques/essais_melanges.html.

Tarde, Gabriel. "La variation universelle" (1895). In *Essais et mélanges sociologiques*, chap. 11. Paris: A. Maloine, 1895. http://classiques.uqac.ca/classiques/tarde _gabriel/essais_melanges_sociologiques/essais_melanges.html.

Taussig, Michael. *The Magic of the State*. London: Routledge, 1997.

Taylor, Josh. "Donald Trump's Digital Trading Card Collection Sells Out in Less Than a Day." *Guardian*, December 17, 2022. https://www.theguardian.com/us-news/2022 /dec/17/donald-trumps-digital-trading-card-collection-sells-out-in-less-than-a-day.

Telegraph. "We've Been Too Slow to Fix This Gas Crisis." August 30, 2022. https://www.telegraph.co.uk/opinion/2022/08/30/slow-fix-gas-crisis.

Theweleit, Klaus. *Male Fantasies.* Vol. 1, *Women Floods Bodies History.* Minneapolis: University of Minnesota Press, 1987.

Thompson, Stuart A. "Three Weeks Inside a Pro-Trump QAnon Chat Room." *New York Times,* January 26, 2021. https://www.nytimes.com/interactive/2021/01/26/opinion/trump-qanon-washington-capitol-hill.html.

Toscano, Alberto. "The Nightwatchman's Bludgeon." *New Left Review,* October 29, 2022. https://newleftreview.org/sidecar/posts/the-nightwatchmans-bludgeon.

Trump, Donald J. "Full Text: Trump's Comments on White Supremacists, 'Alt-Left' in Charlottesville." *Politico,* August 15, 2017. https://www.politico.com/story/2017/08/15/full-text-trump-comments-white-supremacists-alt-left-transcript-241662.

Van Tuinen, Sjoerd. *The Dialectics of Ressentiment: Pedagogy of a Concept.* London: Routledge, 2024.

Van Tuinen, Sjoerd. *The Philosophy of Mannerism: From Aesthetics to Modal Metaphysics.* London: Bloomsbury, 2023.

Virilio, Paul. *L'insécurité du territoire.* Paris: Stock, 1975.

Virilio, Paul, and Sylvère Lotringer. *Pure War.* New York: Semiotext(e), 1983.

Viser, Matt. "In Fiery Midterm Speech, Biden Says GOP's Turned toward 'Semi-Fascism.'" *Washington Post,* August 25, 2022. https://www.washingtonpost.com/politics/2022/0 8/25/fiery-midterm-speech-biden-says-gops-turned-toward-semi-fascism.

Viveiros de Castro, Eduardo. *Cannibal Metaphysics.* Translated by Peter Skafish. Minneapolis: Univocal / University of Minnesota Press, 2017.

Weber, Max. *The Theory of Social and Economic Organization.* Translated by A. M. Henderson and Talcott Parsons; edited and with an introduction by Talcott Parsons. 1920. Reprint, Glencoe, IL: Free Press / Falcon's Wing, 1947.

Wemple, Eric. "First Amendment Bails Out Tucker Carlson." *Washington Post,* September 24, 2020. https://www.washingtonpost.com/opinions/2020/09/24/first-amendment-bails-out-tucker-carlson.

Wemple, Eric. "Tucker Carlson Knows Exactly What He's Doing." *Washington Post,* February 6, 2023. https://www.washingtonpost.com/opinions/2023/02/06/hunter-biden-tucker-carlson-threat-letter.

Whitehead, Alfred North. *Adventures of Ideas.* New York: Free Press, 1967.

Whitehead, Alfred North. *Concept of Nature.* Cambridge: Cambridge University Press, 1920.

Whitehead, Alfred North. *Modes of Thought.* New York: Free Press, 1968.

Whitehead, Alfred North. *Process and Reality.* New York: Free Press, 1978.

Whitehead, Alfred North. *Science and the Modern World.* New York: Free Press, 1967.

Whitehead, Alfred North. *Symbolism: Its Meaning and Effect.* New York: Fordham University Press, 1985.

Wolffe, Richard. "Don't Call It a Comeback: Trump's Tulsa Rally Was Just Another Sad Farce." *Guardian*, June 21, 2020. https://www.theguardian.com/commentisfree/2020/jun/20/donald-trump-tulsa-rally-crowd-empty-seats.

Woodward, Bob. "The Trump Tapes: Twenty Interviews That Show He Is an Unparalleled Danger." *Washington Post*, October 23, 2022. https://www.washingtonpost.com/opinions/interactive/2022/trump-tapes-bob-woodward-interviews-audiobook.

Wynter, Sylvia. *Sylvia Wynter: On Being Human as Praxis*. Edited by Katherine McKittrick. Durham, NC: Duke University Press, 2015.

Yergeau, Melanie (Remi). *Authoring Autism: On Rhetoric and Neurological Queerness*. Durham, NC: Duke University Press, 2018.

Zak, Dan. "Fear and Gloating in Cincinnati." *Washington Post*, August 2, 2019. https://www.washingtonpost.com/lifestyle/style/fear-and-gloating-in-cincinnati/2019/08/02/a6055256-b51f-11e9-8949-5f36ff92706e_story.html.

www.ingramcontent.com/pod-product-compliance
Lightning Source LLC
Chambersburg PA
CBHW020822270326
41928CB00006B/411